WESTMAR COLLEGE L

W9-BPS-294

WESTMAR COLLEGE
Title III
LeMars, Iowa 51031

The Development of
European Society
1770-1870

THE DEVELOPMENT OF EUROPEAN SOCIETY, 1770-1870

John R. Gillis
Rutgers University

UNIVERSITY *105090*
PRESS OF
AMERICA

LANHAM • NEW YORK • LONDON

Copyright © 1977 by Houghton Mifflin Company

Copyright © 1983 by

University Press of America,™ Inc.

4720 Boston Way
Lanham, MD 20706

3 Henrietta Street
London WC2E 8LU England

All rights reserved
Printed in the United States of America

Library of Congress Cataloging in Publication Data

Gillis, John R.
  The development of European society, 1770-1870.

  Reprint. Originally published: Boston: Houghton
Mifflin, c1977.
  Bibliography: p.
  Includes index.
  1. Europe—Social conditions—1789-1900. 2. Europe—
Economic conditions—1789-1900. 3. Europe—History—
1789-1900. Title.
HN373.G54   1983   940.2'7   82-20234
ISBN 0-8191-2898-8 (pbk.)

Maps by Richard Sanderson

The chart on page 216 is reprinted with the permission of The Past and Present
Society and L. Stone from "Literacy and Education in England, 1640–1900,"
Past and Present. A journal of historical studies, no. 42 (February 1969), p. 121.
World Copyright: The Past and Present Society, Corpus Christi College, Oxford,
England.

The eleven lines of poetry on page 226 are from "New Year Letter," in *Collected
Longer Poems,* by W. H. Auden, © 1940, Random House, Inc., New York.

"A great man and a saint, for his own sake." by Charles Baudelaire, on page 230,
is translated by César Graña, from *Bohemian Versus Bourgeois: French Society
and the French Man of Letters in the Nineteenth Century,* by César Graña, © 1964
by Basic Books, Inc., Publishers, New York.

For Christopher and Benjamin

Contents

Charts and Maps

Charts

Maps

Preface

The comparative perspective

For the past thirty years the world's attention has been riveted on the Asian, African, and Latin American countries' struggles to become modern nations. An earlier preoccupation with European and American history has given way to a more global perspective that promises to enlarge our understanding of not only today's new nations but the Western historical experience itself. Just as the lessons of European history were once used to illustrate to colonized peoples the path to modernity, the present problems of modernization may be able to shed some light on the period of European history from roughly 1770 to 1870, which corresponds to the stage of history through which much of the world is presently passing.

Modernization is a general term covering such a variety of patterns of change that some have rejected it as unworkable. Yet in all societies that move from what is loosely described as tradition to modernity certain tendencies are evident. Most observers would agree that modernization involves the centralization and integration of the political, cultural, and economic levels of societies that have previously been highly fragmented and decentralized. The so-called social mobilization of peoples who were previously attached to specific localities or particularistic social groups (families, clans, tribes, estates) is a further dimension of modernization—namely, the process of making social and cultural norms universal. In the process of modernizing, new systems of symbols that transcend the old cultural divisions are created in order to induce mass participation in a more centralized social, economic, and political order. These symbols encourage individuals to detach themselves from narrower traditional roles that they have been assigned by birth or place of origin so that they can participate in institutions where individual achievement rather than family name or local recognition is the key to success. Modernization also implies a greater degree of equality in opportunity, though this does not always bring with it greater equality in status or power.

A third major characteristic of modernization is specialization of function (for example, division of labor, professionalization, bureaucratization), which often brings with it new social divisions. With specialization comes the separation of an individual's social, economic, and political roles. Almost universally, modernization involves some degree of separation of politics and economics from the function of the family, thereby producing larger social identities (classes, parties, and so on) that coexist with the narrower realm of family life. The relationship of the private and public spheres of life is altered, resulting in reorientation of child rearing and education, changes in male-female roles, and personality changes that contribute to a world view consistent with what has been called the modern mentality. What this term usually means is the acceptance of change as something to be valued rather than feared. This is precisely the cultural aspect of modernization that transcends individual differences in the mode and direction of change. An emphasis on progress, whether personal or societal, is everywhere the hallmark of modernizing societies.

So far I have been talking about modernization as though it were a unified, simultaneous process. It is important to make distinctions among the various sectors of modernization, however, for in some cases political modernization may proceed at a faster rate than economic change, or vice versa. For example, in many of today's new states the degree of political integration, a heritage of the previous colonial regime, may be significantly higher than the integrative power of the economy. So the state is likely to take a much greater part in economic modernization than did the governments in Europe, where the state was less centralized than the economy. These discrepancies in various developmental sectors are not without significance, for they account for many of the problems that are apparent in the first stages of modernization. We must keep in mind that political modernization can proceed in the absence of significant economic development and that cultural change (mass literacy, for example) is not a necessary precondition for economic modernization.

As we shall see, individual European countries started from very different points in 1770. Some countries, notably England, were economically advanced but lacked an efficient, modern bureaucracy. Prussia, on the other hand, possessed an efficient state, but had made little economic headway. France lay somewhere between these two extremes. These same three states reached relatively similar levels of modernization by the 1870s, but they arrived there by different routes. The point at which they had begun, together with the variations in the sequence by which political, economic, and social modernization occurred, had much to do with the differences in their political and social systems. Where political modernization preceded and thereby determined the course of economic change, as in Prussia, authoritarianism resulted. England, which negotiated the transition from tradition to modernity without a highly developed bureaucratic state, managed to retain a greater degree of individual liberty.

The term "transition" best describes the period from 1770 to 1870, when Europe was fumbling toward modernity without wholly abandoning many of its traditional characteristics. The Third World is still in such a transitional period, distinct from both traditional and modern society. Europeans were not unaware of the unique characteristics of transition. John Stuart Mill described the early nineteenth century as an "Age of Transition," when "mankind have outgrown old institutions and old doctrines and have not yet acquired new ones," a description applicable to all societies caught between the eclipse of traditional symbols and allegiances and the point where modern institutions such as the factory system, the political party, and universal schooling are sufficiently developed to take over and regulate the course of further change.

Everywhere the transitional period has been characterized by social and political disorder. For both Europe and the Third World the most comprehensive type of upheaval, namely revolution, has been most likely to occur at this time. This is the period of the most severe political dislocation, when governments must exchange one type of legitimacy for another. It is also a period of structural economic crisis when elements of the old economy work at cross-purposes with the new. With economic change comes population growth, which often strains the still weak productive capacity of the economy. Transitional stages are often marked by massive population movements and rapid urbanization, as a result of overpopulation in the countryside.

Transitional societies find it difficult to contain social discontent or resolve major civil conflicts. In this period class divisions are pronounced and mass movements contend ideologically over the ends as well as the means of achieving the new society. The intensity of conflict is partly attributable to the inability of cultural institutions, themselves in flux, to legitimize either the old or new orders. The role of the intellectual then becomes crucial—another of the unique dimensions of the transitional phase of modernization.

The achievement of modernity does not eliminate individual or collective discontents, but it does isolate and contain different types of conflict (economic, political, social) so that upheavals on the scale of revolution become a thing of the past. Europe reached this point at mid-nineteenth century when institutions such as collective bargaining and the political party began to acquire sufficient power and legitimacy to contain economic and political conflict. At about the same time the reorganization of family life reached the point where generational tensions, so typical of the period of transition, ceased to be disruptive. And at this point the volcanic millennial movements that had sprung up in the late eighteenth century began to disappear, marking the incorporation of popular spiritual strivings within the new cultural institutions. This by no means brought an end to religion per se, but rather signaled its adjustment to a cultural system more in tune with the goals of modern society.

It is important to remember that Europe's new nations were the first, together with those of North America, to cross the frontier between tradition and modernity. It was an expedition of trial and error through uncertain terrain. The inventors of new industrial machines were not the only ones who had to experiment with new ideas. Statesmen, artists, heads of families, women—indeed, nearly everyone who was confronted with rapid rates of change—were also placed in that position. Even the concept of nation had to be invented, for this central legitimizing concept of the modern state had only been vaguely developed before 1789. Today, new states begin with the concept of the nation and can choose from a variety of established political and economic systems. To be sure, the forerunner countries of the nineteenth century—France and England—provided models for their less developed neighbors, but not to the extent of today's consciously planned imitation.

Now political and economic development in new nations is much more likely to take place under central direction. These nations are not likely to permit the kind of leeway that European governments allowed free enterprise, for the urgency of development under the pressure of rapid population growth is too great. Furthermore, many of the new regimes have come to power through armed overthrow of the previous colonial power and are much stronger to begin with. Revolutions in the Third World are usually seizures of power by highly organized movements, unlike the series of European revolutions in 1789, 1830, and 1848 that came about less by the action of organized insurgents than by the collapse of the old elites. As we shall see, even revolution tended to be experimental in Europe, and organized revolutionary movements emerged very late, as much a result as a cause of successive societal upheavals. Europeans lacked the capacity to "finish" their revolutions, leaving many questions to be resolved. While Europe's period of revolution tended to be more prolonged, it was less destructive than many of the militarized conflicts of the Third World.

The high degree of militarization among insurgent movements in Asia, Africa, and Latin America is caused in part by the intervention of outside powers. With the exception of France's domination of Europe during the Napoleonic period, this element was absent in Europe. For the most part, external imposition of techniques or ideologies was rare. Each country experimented on its own, a process that was terribly inefficient but at the same time abundantly productive of new ideas and institutions. Until the 1850s most governments repeated one another's mistakes, unable or unwilling to learn from the experience of other countries. But they could not have done otherwise, since they tended to be at such different stages of development. The result was an unparalleled flowering of national cultures, each strikingly diverse and dynamic within itself.

The late eighteenth and early nineteenth centuries were rich in ideas, social experiments, and artistic endeavors of all sorts precisely because there were so few central institutions that could claim universal allegiance. It was a rich and stimulating period, but one that left Europe deeply divided socially and culturally. In new states today uniformity is likely to be dominant. Modernization means the early introduction of uniform standards, reinforced by powerful, centralized communications media; the standards are instilled through a national educational system. However, Europe had to fabricate standards through trial and error, a process that created as many forms of culture as there were social classes.

In culture, as in almost every other area, the European experience was a good deal more anarchic. As a result, the burdens of modernization were distributed very unevenly, with both native and foreign labor (including the slave labor of the New World) bearing a great share of the social costs. The socialist and democratic ideologies of many Third World nations would seem to exclude similar exploitation, though practice often differs from the ideal. However, it is not my purpose in this book to weight the moral balance. Nor do I attempt a rigorous comparison of Europe and the Third World. Instead, my more limited objective is to place this formative epoch of European history—the period from 1770 to 1870—in a broader world perspective. Using the present to illuminate the past is always a risky business; but if the process can reveal aspects of the universality of the human experience without obscuring what is indigenous to Europe itself, then I will have achieved the purpose of this book.

A brief note on the concept of modernization

Modernization is used here to describe a *tendency* or set of *tendencies,* not a fixed course of events with a prescribed outcome. Both modernity and tradition are notoriously difficult to define. Furthermore, students of modernization should be aware that tradition and modernity are not two completely different conditions. Elements of modernity—for example, the recognition of merit over birth—existed to some degree in preindustrial society. By the same token, the traditional factor of advantage from birth is still powerful in most modern societies, despite every effort to give all children equal opportunity. Yet few would deny that over the past two hundred years merit has become more important and birth less so in determining the many important functions in a society. It is therefore the tendency toward equal opportunity rather than the realization of total equality that we describe as modernization.

It will also become apparent to the reader that in my view modernization as it took place in Europe is not the one true path to human progress. Modernization is not a uniform process; nor does the form it takes at one point in history predetermine its direction in subsequent eras. While modernization in the nineteenth century developed a capitalist economy in the context of the nation-state, this does not mean that modernization will always be contained within that particular political and economic structure, even in the Western world. In reviewing both European history from 1770 to 1870 and Third World history to date, we discover alternative processes, paths not taken, that could conceivably provide other, perhaps more attractive, scenarios for modernity in the future.

This book is the product of dialogue carried on with students and colleagues over more than ten years. I am particularly grateful to Ted Rabb and John H. Wilson, who read the final result with such care and sympathy.

John R. Gillis

PART ONE

THE CHALLENGE

It is easy enough from hindsight to call the period 1770-1870 an "Age of Reform" or "Age of Improvement," but knowledge of Europe's successful modernization tends to obscure the real character of an age that was by no means one of consistent optimism or uniform progress. Indeed, until the 1850s self-perpetuating modernization was as uncertain in western Europe as it is in many parts of Asia and Africa today. Massive population growth constantly threatened to overtake and overwhelm gains made in the economic sphere. Not only did population growth disrupt such basic societal institutions as the family but it also called into question the capacity of existing political systems to deliver services such as protection of property and social security, and to provide cultural continuity. Crime, disease, and social protest—indicators of social disruption—all increased dramatically in the late eighteenth century and produced a challenge to political stability that did not diminish until the middle of the next century. But while population explosion, social unrest, and political collapse represented the end of the old Europe, they also provided the necessary stimulus to the new.

Chapter 1 examines the world as it was in 1770. Chapter 2 departs from strict chronological sequence to explore the economic and demographic causes of the general crisis period 1770–1850. This period requires special attention for it is the backdrop against which all subsequent developments are to be understood. Chapter 3 returns to the decades just prior to the French Revolution of 1789 to deal with those conditions that brought on the collapse of the old regimes.

1

—

Population, Economy, and Society in 1770

Each new generation seems fated to discover for itself the limits of human possibility, ignoring and often rejecting the experience of its elders. The same holds true for nations. Today's newly developing countries are caught up with population and economic problems whose consequences, if not immediate causes, would be all too familiar to Europeans of the 1770s. The Europe of 1770 is as foreign to modern Europeans as life in contemporary Africa and Asia is to them, and perhaps even more so. Therefore, it requires as great an effort of understanding to grasp the institutions and mentalities peculiar to preindustrial Europe* as it does to fathom the ways of today's developing countries.

Because this book is a study not just of political institutions but of entire societies as well, I begin with what was most central to everyday life in the 1770s—namely, the constant struggle against the limits nature imposed, including human biology itself. The legacy of thousands of years of preindustrial existence was an abiding sense of human impotence. Promising periods of population growth, accompanied by rising prosperity, has always been reversed by famine, plague, or devastating wars (most recently in the seventeenth century), thus reinforcing folk fatalism about the possibilities of change. Both urban and rural poor were extremely sensitive to signs of overpopulation and to the first hint of epidemic or indication of a food shortage. A significant number of educated people shared this popular pessimism, viewing population pressure with trepidation. Although subsistence crises were less frequent by the

*The use of the words "Europe" or "European" is meant to include the British Isles.

early eighteenth century, even then a series of bad harvests, with accompanying malnutrition and susceptibility to disease, was sufficient to create panic. When the plague visited Marseilles in 1720, an eyewitness named Dr. Bertrand wrote:

> I have seen the latest epoch of misery; I have seen hunger transformed into passion, the inhabitants of a region without a harvest wander, led astray by suffering and deprived of everything, envy the fate of domestic animals, lie down in a meadow to eat grass, and share the food of wild beasts.

Behind this terror of deprivation and suffering lay the long history of European population growth, with its rising slopes of prosperity and valleys of despair. The late seventeenth and early eighteenth centuries had been a period of relative stability. As moderate population growth expanded into boom around 1750, many Europeans became uneasy. The acceleration appeared enormous, particularly to those who perceived the environment as inherently threatening, although the rate of growth at its peak rarely exceeded 1.5 percent per annum—a seemingly small figure when compared to the more than 3 percent per annum in many developing countries today.

According to folk wisdom, economic resources were so limited that even a mild rise in numbers would bring disaster. In times of dearth, infanticide became an accepted practice. The weak and dependent were the first to be sacrificed, the old as well as the newborn being "helped to die" so that others might live. Old women were particularly victimized in times of scarcity; in seventeenth century England they were stigmatized as witches and thereby cut off from communal resources. As late as the 1850s, French peasants practiced what amounted to parricide. An old man, noted the historian Joseph Bonnemère, "carries the wretchedness of his last days with him from cottage to cottage, unwelcome, ill received, a stranger in his children's house. At last he dies . . . but it is well for him to make haste, for greed is there, and greed nerves the arm of hidden parricide."

The Facts of Life and Death

We must try to understand practices that seem to us so inhuman in the context of historical biological experience and be prepared to delve beneath the surface of conventional history to those social and even psychological depths that will permit proper understanding of the preindustrial mentality. To grasp that society's concept of individual and collective destiny as a wheel of fortune beyond human control, we must begin with the experience of life and death itself. On one level of popular meaning, the wheel of fortune represented the unbroken, timeless character of historical experience; on another level, it symbolized the speed with which death overtook life. While societal patterns remained unchanged, the human life cycle moved with greater rapidity than it does today. Birth and death intruded more frequently then, and so the overlap of generations was significantly less than it is today. It was rare for a grandfather to know his grandchildren, because both young and old were so much more vulnerable to death. Marriage was short-lived, not because of divorce (which was virtually unknown), but for natural reasons. In compensation for the terrors of a life that was, as Thomas Hobbes described it, "nasty, brutish and short," the popular notion of history held that human institutions, being divinely ordained, remained substantially unchanged..

We must keep in mind that the average life expectancy of males prior to the mid-eighteenth century rarely exceeded forty years. It was not the fact that longevity was rare among adults, but rather that child mortality was enormously greater, that reduced the *overall average* life span. In preindustrial Europe between 40 and 50 percent of children born alive did not survive to their twenty-first birthday. Because of inadequate germ theory and the absence of sterilization technique, many infants died in the critical first weeks of life; others succumbed in childhood to diseases like smallpox and diphtheria that we no longer regard as killers, because of modern immunization and advanced medical technology. In preindustrial Europe, mothers, too, were much more vulnerable to diseases that often made childbirth a double tragedy.

In this context, the consequence of high mortality levels was high fertility. Reproduction was absolutely essential for social and economic security. Family interests not only required that a male heir survive to inherit and thus preserve family property, but also that, even where parents were without property, children should serve as a kind of old age support. Under conditions where life expectancy averaged as low as forty years, at least four children had to be born if there was to be even a 60 percent chance of one male heir surviving to the age of inheritance. As there was no way to be sure which children would survive, family strategy dictated a relatively rapid succession of at least four births, at a terrible price to the health of both mother and infants. Childless marriage was one of the few situations that could legitimize divorce. Adoption was resorted to, not in the interests of the child, but for the benefit of adults.

Accustomed as we are today to both low mortality and low fertility rates, it is shocking to think that childbearing and rearing took up at least twice as much of a married woman's life in preindustrial Europe as it does now. Today the average European and American mother has completed childbearing by her mid-twenties. The risk of childbirth to her is minimal, and the assurance that her first-born will survive to maturity relieves her of the necessity of multiple pregnancies. The effect of high mortality and high fertility upon preindustrial populations was obvious. It reinforced the prevalent idea of biological determinism, restricted most married women's roles to that of maternity, and had the further effect of making the male/female distinction seem unalterable. A fatalistic attitude penetrated every aspect of life and death. When death intruded it was resented, but procreation continued once the victims had been mourned.

The churches taught that there was something both natural and divine about maternity and tried to prevent the spread of contraceptive devices like the condom. Until well into the nineteenth century, mechanical means of birth control remained exceptional, used by prostitutes and their clients but restricted primarily to the city. However, the country folk had their own means of family limitation. Coitus interruptus, abortion, infanticide, and, perhaps most effective, delay of marriage—all were practiced before 1770. Except among a very few wealthy people, however, these means were not used in the modern, premeditated way of family planning. Older parents, already burdened with large numbers of children, might try to prevent further births, but young couples did not begin marriage with an ideal number of children in mind. Instead, they submitted to a biological fate that was beyond their control. As late as the 1870s, marriage rates faithfully followed economic fluctuations, decreasing sharply in hard times, and rising with prosperity. Once marriage had been consummated, the cruel facts of life and death took control.

In most parts of western Europe, marriage was directly linked to the establishment of a new household and family. Young marrieds today may postpone and even omit childbearing, but in 1770 wedding and pregnancy were still closely associated, with conception occurring either shortly before or immediately after the ceremony. In peasant society intercourse between betrothed partners seemed to be quite common and was acceptable to the community as long as a "cover-up" marriage was reasonably certain. Small village communities could force men to become responsible for their sexual conduct, and in most places pregnant women could make valid their paternity claims. Sexual relationships were closely controlled through traditional courtship rituals. Virginity was not a fetish on any level of society, but although premarital intercourse was common, illegitimacy rates were relatively modest in the early eighteenth century.

Marriage, procreation, and the establishment of a new household were economic and social arrangements controlled to some degree by individual choice, but hedged by social and biological necessity. Where property was involved, marriage was as much an arrangement between two families as between two individuals. Peasant fathers bargained their daughters' dowries; sons often had to wait for their fathers' death or retirement, with the average age of peasant marriage thus delayed to the late twenties or early thirties. Where resources were scarce, permanent spinster- or bachelorhood was the accepted fate of younger sons and daughters. In Europe the confirmed celibates, voluntary and involuntary, comprised as much as 10 percent of the population, a proportion higher than in most non-Western preindustrial societies. But then the western European age of marriage also was much higher than in other parts of the world.

Late marriage was the most effective check on population growth; men married in their late twenties, women two or three years earlier. The fact that women could not be expected to bear children beyond their mid-forties constituted an effective check on fertility, though it also meant that, during their prime, women were enslaved to childbearing and rearing. Just as maternity seemed beyond their control, so, too, did the methods by which they brought up their children. In a period before pasteurization of milk, there was no healthy alternative to breast feeding. Sick or malnourished mothers often found their own milk supply inadequate. The rich overcame this difficulty by using wet nurses. Those employed in this capacity were poor women, especially unwed mothers. In preserving the children of the rich, they put their own children at risk, abandoning them to the dangerous practice of dry feeding. Illegitimate children were particularly vulnerable and, as late as 1870, 80 percent of those children born in London died within their first year.

With the most arduous part of child rearing taken care of for them, wealthy women could afford to take a benign view of their offspring. But, for the poor, as long as feeding remained a struggle between mother and child for a limited supply of resources, the mass of the population adhered to an older view of infancy. Among the vast majority of Europeans exhausted mothers regarded their hungry infants as little beasts, insatiably aggressive and destructive. "All children are naturally greedy and gluttonous," one seventeenth-century doctor concluded, thereby justifying what seems to us the unusually harsh, insensitive treatment children received at the hands of adults prior to the end of the eighteenth century.

The contented child was probably unusual; the practice of tight swaddling, together with frequent use of opiates, was further evidence of the constant battle between parents and infants, in which the weapons became more severe as the child grew older. Strong disciplinary measures were deemed necessary to break willfulness of children. On every side "beating, whipping, abusing and scolding children and holding them in great fear and subjection" was common. Future kings were strapped as regularly as stable boys; Louis XIII of France received a beating every morning of his young life, administered not out of cruelty but because of the universal belief that a child, "hardened" in such a manner, had better chances for survival.

Child Rearing and Personality

"Childhood is a brutish life," Jacques Bossuet commented. The severity and limitations of the environment impressed themselves on consciousness from birth. Everything—food, freedom of movement, even love—were demonstrated to be in short supply. Thus, from infancy the concept of the *limited good,* a view of the world and its resources as inelastic, became part of the individual's operating principles. Early childhood experience also taught that the basic structure of life was hierarchical and relations between persons unequal. Father was superior to mother, males superior to females, older children superior to young, a rank order of precedence within the family itself that became the operational model for the equally restrictive and hierarchical world outside. Under conditions of high fertility, limited resources, and crowded houses, children had to grow up quickly and get out on their own. As early as seven or eight years of age they left their parents' homes to join other households as helpers or servants. Later, they would begin apprenticeships in the same manner. For the poor this was the means by which parents were relieved of the costs of feeding and housing surplus children. But even among those who could afford to keep their children at home, the custom was to send them out at early ages to do "service" in the homes of others. The rich feared they might spoil their children through unguarded tenderness, preferring the preparation for life that other households provided to that offered in their own. In turn, they took in the offspring of others, thus accounting for the high rate of circulation of children in 1770.

Far from being a reflection of parental indifference, this system of exchange of dependents was the only possible solution for the predicament of the vast majority of families that even in times of population stability were producing a larger number of children (not all of whom would survive) than their own resources would allow. The households of the quarter or so of the population who lived securely above the margin of subsistence therefore received and supported the older children of the rest of the population in return for their cheap, live-in labor. The receiving households provided for the children's and youths' spiritual as well as material well-being, subjecting them to the same strict rules of subordination that they applied to their own children. Even sons and daughters of the aristocracy were sent to households of their peers to wait on table and receive instruction in the social amenities. Together with the children of the poor, they remained there as live-in servants until the time (ages fourteen or fifteen) when they were expected to begin a more formal apprenticeship in a trade or profession, ordinarily lasting another seven years. For the children of poverty, service continued much longer, often until marriage or, for those who never married, until death.

What must seem to us an unusually long period of subordination was often spent away from the natural family. For the young artisans who had completed their apprenticeship, the journeyman's years (from age 21 on) followed, a time of travel and training, before marriage and mastership. Surplus youth of the Swiss cantons served their time abroad as mercenaries in foreign armies, while in England youths commonly sought their fortune in London or some larger town, returning later to their birthplace to claim inheritance and marriage. In a period of overseas expansion, the journey could be much longer, often without return. Preindustrial youth enjoyed a great deal of geographical mobility and were, by the standards of modern adolescence, quite free from direct parental control. Yet because marriage and inheritance of property were the key to full adult status, the position of the young, like that of the very old, was still a subordinate one. Separate institutions—the patriarchal household, the apprenticeship, and, for the privileged few, the school, academy, or convent—provided for the well-being of youth, but also underlined their lack of standing in an economy in which a minority of property-owning males held nearly complete authority.

In 1770 Europe wealth was primarily real property (land, tools, furniture, jewelry, and so on) rather than liquid capital (paper money, shares, coin). This wealth could not easily be shared or coadministered, and thus it was rare that sons came into any economic power before the death or retirement of their fathers. It was natural that the young should view the old as obstacles, and generational harmony was maintained only by constantly rehearsing the ancient rituals of deference that marked all religious and secular ceremony and procession. As the arrangement of the church pews by social rank reinforced a sense of hierarchical social order, so the seating of children by age around the dinner table reinforced the patriarchical household structure. In the eighteenth-century view, as the Father in Heaven ruled over His flock, so the head of each household ruled those entrusted to his authority. Fatherhood, broadly interpreted to include not only natural parents but also employers, teachers, clergy and, of course, secular rulers, was the central legitimizing symbol of religious and secular authority. The Biblical Fifth Commandment simultaneously instilled popular political and social obedience. When seventeenth-century Calvinists asked the meaning of the Fifth Commandment, they expected the following reply:

> Answer: Though no mention be made expressingly but of the father and mother, yet we must understand in them all masters and magistrates: for so much as there is one manner of consideration of them all.
> Question: What is that?
> Answer: Because God hath given them preeminence: for there is no authority of Parents, of Princes, or Magistrates, Masters, neither any office or title of preeminence, but such as God hath ordained.

Even so, youth often repaid the cruelty suffered while growing up, when the father, too feeble to carry on farm work, turned over control. Yet many younger persons never attained the full adult status that came through property inheritance. Where primogeniture reigned, younger children were simply conditioned to accept a fate of lifelong subordination to family interests. Even among the aristocracy, younger sons ordinarily had to seek their fortunes in less prestigious occupations, while younger daughters traditionally married beneath themselves. As for those wholly without prospects, some found their way in Catholic countries to the monastery or nunnery, which latter place Milton rightly called parents' "convenient stowage for their withered daughters."

To preindustrial society tight restrictions on the young seemed all the more necessary, because their numbers were so great compared to the number of adults. Through a combination of high fertility and high child mortality, the age group 0–19 comprised 49 percent of the population (as compared with 29 percent in Europe today). In keeping with this age distribution, the young had to bear a greater share of the work of the *labor-intensive* economy. In 1770 only a little over one-third of the English population was over thirty years of age. Since men did not marry until their late twenties and about 10 percent of men and women never married, less than 15 percent of the entire population fell in the patriarchal category of married males. This was indeed a small elite, compared to the some 25 percent that married men constitute in English society today.

Conditioned from birth to view resources as limited, most Europeans accepted the patriarchal order. The authoritarian ideology of Christianity reinforced the generational equilibrium observable in preindustrial society, and the masters of households, guilds, schools, and other dominant patriarchal institutions maintained it. In addition, the fraternal traditions of various craft and village youth groups helped to regulate aspirations and prevent conflict among peers over scarce resources. Articles of apprenticeship usually stated that youths were to be kept under tight control, and were not allowed to gamble, drink excessively, or court women prematurely. The celibate traditions of various craft, school, and fraternal orders to which youth belonged reinforced a ban on young marriage. In the towns, bachelor artisans, students, law clerks, and other young professionals formed their own fraternities, paralleled in the villages by youth groups called Abbeys of Misrule in France and Brotherhoods in Germany. These organized groups maintained strict control over bachelors, regulating the marriage market and contesting the right of both younger males and older men to interfere with the pool of eligible females. The smooth succession of older youths to inheritance and marriage was thus maintained and generational harmony guaranteed.

Sometimes the prerogatives of fraternity clashed with the authority of paternity, but prior to the middle of the eighteenth century these two most important sources of authority remained in mutually supporting equilibrium. Fraternity also served to transmit economic skills and social values from generation to generation: it respected the precedence of heads of families and subordinated the individual to a collective interest which— whether it was that of the family, peer group, or community—always had precedence over personal interest or ambition. The degree of subordination and self-sacrifice that a society of limited resources required would inevitably produce tensions, but these were expressed through rituals of protest carefully orchestrated and generally well understood by those

involved. In France, for example, frictions between young and old were
the occasion for mocking processions, profane songs, and threatening
gestures on the part of the Abbeys of Misrule. An old man marrying a
young girl would be visited at night, his fences torn up, and windows
shattered; the girl's doors would be decorated with the symbols of her
shame. Where economic issues were at stake, journeymen had their way
of redressing grievances, including the traditional charivari (public mock-
ery) and boycotts of offending masters. Students, too, had their rites of
misrule, the most colorful of which was the secular version of the medieval Feast of Fools, in which novices dressed themselves in bishop's
garb and for a brief moment each year inverted the established order,
parodying the foibles of their superiors in a raucous manner. Women could
also invert the social order on occasion by wearing the pants, thereby
reversing male dominance in a moment of catharsis.

Not all outbursts of feeling were so controlled, however. Preindustrial
society was much more accustomed to accept violence and cruelty, because these actions were internalized in early childhood and therefore
beyond the power of individual conscience to constantly control. Whether
it was dueling nobles or brawling apprentices, the mentality was the same:
the acceptance of cruelty as the natural condition of humanity. Periodic
acting out of conflicts served to redress injustices as well as to relieve
pent-up frustrations; because the purpose of violence was to restore the
commonweal rather than to transform society, disruption was usually
short-lived. Tensions between fathers and sons, mothers and daughters-in-
law, husbands and wives—themes that permeated folk art and song—were
accepted as irremediable facts of life. The tendency to see events as part of
a fixed, repetitive natural order was reinforced by stylized treatment of
important events such as birth, betrothal, marriage, and death. Every event
was attended to in time-honored ritual, reflecting the acceptance of the
basic continuity of life as it was reinforced by the fixed seasonal aspects
of most craft and agricultural endeavors. Joy, grief, anguish, and exalta-
tion were not individualized emotions but shared sentiments that had a
communal rather than private expression. A host of female relatives
normally attended childbirth; marriage feasts ended with a merry throng
escorting the bride and groom to their bed; the funeral was also a communal event, bringing together persons who had not seen one another for
long periods of time. If the deceased seemed to be forgotten during the
funeral festivities and emotional loss emphasized little, it must be remembered that at the traditional wake emotions were focused on the eternal
and collective rather than on the temporal and individual.

From cradle to grave, the priority of the collective interests over individual feelings was emphasized. In representations of the cycle of life
popular in the eighteenth century, life was envisioned as a series of steps
ascending to young adulthood, with its paternal and maternal duties,
then descending again through years of feebleness and retirement to death.

This was an idealized picture of life that less than half those born would ever live to experience, but its symbolism revealed much about the preindustrial mentality, in its tendency to emphasize the general rather than the particular, and the collective rather than the individual. A social-psychological development that encouraged strong identification with group and community interests at the expense of individual identity produced such a world view. For the young there was no such thing as an adolescent identity crisis, not only because the choice of careers was more restricted, but also because individualized feelings were subordinated to collective necessity. The world was supposed to contain only a finite body of natural and social resources, the *limited good,* which could not be expanded. Despite considerable mobility between households and regions, the socialization of the young took place within strong institutions that reinforced the consciousness of a fixed and unalterable world.

At the same time, a strong sense of place accounted for the uninhibited sociability of the preindustrial age. At feasts, fairs, and within the patriarchical household, all ranks of society rubbed shoulders freely without fear of the erosion of status differences that otherwise were so strongly marked. Until demographic and economic change began to undermine this pattern of social and psychological conditioning later in the eighteenth century, prince and pauper viewed one another as compatible parts of the same natural order, a hierarchy characterized by a limited good, whose maintenance depended on the submission of child to parent, female to male, poor to rich. From such a perspective, anything that upset this equilibrium was feared, because always before the result had been to spread resources dangerously thin. Leveling equality was perceived as the common enemy of the poor as well as of the rich, of woman as well as man, of young as well as old.

The Preindustrial Economy

The sense of social and biological limitations was powerfully reinforced by ever present economic pressures. In 1770, Europe was predominantly agrarian in its population's residence and occupation. The proportion of the population engaged directly in agriculture varied, from a high of nearly 90 percent in most parts of eastern Europe to a low of about 60 percent in England. But even where village crafts and urban employment offered alternatives, their real importance was small in comparison to food production. Despite certain technical improvements such as the yoke and the scythe, agriculture remained much the same as it had been since the Neolithic Revolution five thousand years before the time of Christ. In 1770 agriculture was still heavily labor intensive, using not only large amounts of human energy but also the strength of animals, a power source that had to be maintained out of the annual supply of grain. While it is true that some gains in the yield per acre had been achieved in previous centuries, a plateau in productivity had been reached.

The traditional method of fertilization was to allow the land to lie fallow, and to bring it into cultivation after it had regained its nitrogen content. Thus, at any given time between one-half and one-third of European farm land was out of production. Animals were permitted to graze on fallow land, but in the process their manure was lost; modern fertilizers were not yet available. Furthermore, there was strong resistance to new crops that might use the land more efficiently. The potato, an import from the New World, was gaining popularity only slowly, and most Europeans still considered the tomato inedible. The expansion of production that did take place usually resulted from the expansion of acreage rather than the application of new methods; during the early eighteenth century, when population was stable, demand inelastic, and grain prices low, there was little incentive for expansion either among the larger estate holders or the lesser peasantry.

Agriculture remained tradition bound and thus unattractive to those entrepreneurial spirits who had ready money to invest and a willingness to experiment. Other sectors of the economy, such as cloth manufacture, the various crafts, and the building industry, had been more dynamic in the sixteenth and seventeenth centuries but were now also relatively stagnant. By world standards, Europe's productive capacity in 1770 was by no means overwhelmingly superior. For centuries Asia had been far more technologically inventive than Europe. Indian cotton products (calicoes) were so superior to what the British wool industry was producing in 1770 that wool interests tried to prohibit their import into the English domestic market, and porcelain from the Far East was sufficiently superior to European china that manufacturers copied it slavishly. Previous periods of European economic growth, beginning in the twelfth century, had been notable for the expansion of the commercial sector, but these earlier periods had not left a system of textile production, apart from wool, that could match the great domestic spinning and weaving areas of India and Bengal. Thus, in the early eighteenth century European manufacturing seemed to have settled into a period of inflexibility. The dynamic growth that domestic demand provided was declining, slowed by low levels of population growth. There was a distinct tendency to turn outward in search of new markets and profits, to reap gain through commercial exploitation rather than increased internal productivity.

Trade expansion was the one dynamic sector; it appeared to be moving into a new phase in the late seventeenth and early eighteenth centuries. The dominance of the Dutch was being broken by both the French and the English, whose increasingly aggressive mercantilist policies were based on the concept of creating an excess of exports over imports as a basis for national prosperity. High tariffs, combined with subsidies to export industries, were used in conjunction with aggressive naval and colonial policies to obtain trade advantages. In balance, the English were more successful than the French, even though French foreign trade quadrupled in the eighteenth century. Tonnage at British ports increased six times during the period 1660–1760, the English gaining benefit not only from the re-export trade in colonial tobacco and sugar, but also from commerce in its own metal and woolens to all parts of the world.

Earlier, Europeans interested in plunder from Africa, Asia, and the Americas had sought quick return in gold from military conquest. This had quickly given way to another kind of exploitation based on the control of colonial markets and plantations. Sugar produced in the West Indies was a source of enormous profit, as were tobacco and cotton. Except for the northern colonies of America, the new colonists were either unwilling or unable to rely on their own free labor. Thus the traffic in slaves increased enormously, raising the number of Africans imported into the Americas from approximately three million in the seventeenth century to an estimated seven million in the eighteenth. In the Caribbean area, high death rates combined with the low reproductivity of the slave populations to increase this traffic enormously.

The influence of slavery on eighteenth-century human relations cannot be overestimated. The English were perhaps the most deeply affected, for even when the human cargoes were not directed to British colonies, British ships carried the largest share of slaves to the New World. The English bought humans by selling British-made goods to native African slave traders, and their ships then reaped the profit of carrying charges. Cheap sugar, tobacco, and (ultimately) cotton, products of slave labor in the West Indies and the Americas, benefited the market place. By keeping the English cost of living low, British exports became even more competitive, not only in Africa but also in the rest of Europe and the Levant. It is not a little ironic that, on the eve of the revolutionary industrial utilization of inanimate sources of power, European prosperity was becoming dependent on the intensified use of the most debased form of human energy. Wrote the commentator Joshua Gee in 1729: "All this great increase in our treasure proceeds chiefly from the labour of negroes in the plantations."

Furthermore, not only the colonies showed the regressive effects of commercial capitalism. Something very similar to the human exploitation of slavery had begun to occur in eastern Europe in the sixteenth and seventeenth centuries, also in response to the growth of world trade. Commercial capitalism produced a demand for grain and forest products from the large estates of eastern and central Europe. Instead of enriching the native peasantry, this trade led to their further servitude. Because town life was weakly developed in Prussia, Bohemia, Poland, and Hungary, the rural population there had no alternative but to submit to the landowning nobility's effort to bind them to the soil. These states, dependent on their nobility for military and civil service, offered no resistance, and this once relatively free frontier region of Europe plunged into a new feudalism much worse than what western Europe was divesting itself of at approximately the same time. Prussian peasants found themselves liable to extensive services, while in Bohemia and Hungary, forced labor took up three or four days of every week.

In Russia the effects of economic exploitation were even worse. There the landlords had won the right to recover runaways. In 1646 free peasants were bound permanently to the land. Peasant hatred of the new decrees in 1667 gave rise to the massive revolt led by Stephan Razin, but when the revolt was crushed, the nobility demanded an even more complete form of human bondage. In 1675 serfdom was transformed into virtual slavery when it became legal to sell and transfer peasants from estate to estate. Serfs could henceforth be used in any capacity, including mining and industry, for they had become articles of private property without recourse to the protection of law.

Central and eastern Europe became increasingly dependent on western Europe, in what amounted to a neocolonial position. Trade bound their elites to France and England, developing among them a taste for Western luxury goods and culture, imports separating them still further from the peasant population. Repeated attempts at westernization met with popular resistance, reinforcing caste differences in taste and expectation. Instead of becoming an agent of further economic growth, serfdom reduced the purchasing power of the general population and decreased incentive for native industry. Western commercial capitalism supplied such luxuries as silks from India, spices from the East Indies, and sugar from the West Indies for the upper classes but failed to stimulate a mass market for manufactured goods in either eastern Europe or, much closer to home, in the neocolonial areas of the Scottish Highlands or Ireland. In countries like Russia and Hungary, the regressive impact of trade with western Europe lasted well into the nineteenth century. In the 1840s Magyar landowners were still using feudal dues to squeeze more labor out of the peasants in order to fill profitable orders for grain and wood from the expanding cities to the west. Real income in Russia had made no significant increase despite rising food prices, because there, too, production continued to be labor intensive, causing population increases that ate up economic growth.

Commercial capitalism inhibited the growth of domestic manufacturing capacity because its greatest profits came from trade in imported goods. Attempts by English manufacturers to exclude competitive foreign products were opposed by commercial interests like the East India Company. Not until the 1730s did English wool manufacturers manage finally to exclude the import of Indian calicoes by the East India Company. The company itself was not abolished until 1815, and it was only then that domestic manufacturing interests could proceed to destroy the Indian and Bengal weaving communities that caused them so much competition. In Holland commercial interests insisted on low tariffs to maintain their favorable trade position. The low tariffs hurt infant industry and domestic manufacturing failed to develop in Holland. French domestic production was similarly inhibited by trade companies that were able to import many items at prices cheaper than native industry could produce them.

Commercial capitalism was the area in which the quickest profits could be made, and it was in foreign markets that opportunities seemed most inviting. One reason for this was the backwardness of Europe's internal markets. Makers sold direct to the customer or took goods on the road to visit the various fairs and market days that were still the main focus of European buying and selling. In this period before the growth of fixed shopkeeping, the itinerant peddler brought the shop to the customer. Many markets were controlled by local authorities who had the right to regulate both supply and price. Economists still viewed increased consumption by the lower classes as a dangerous luxury rather than as a spur to production, fearing as they did that domestic consumption might drive up the price of goods and thus inhibit the export trade, which they viewed as the key to national prosperity. As late as 1800, William Green was still warning of the threat to England of domestic consumption:

> The rapid increase of vanity and extravagance in this island is a subject pregnant with mischief and alarm. Commercial monopoly and Eastern opulance . . . have already fostered dissipation and immorality into monsters of colossal magnitude, that every moment threatens the humbler classes of independence, with ruin. That frugality which once characterized the middling and lower classes of society amongst us is no more. . . .

Well into the nineteenth century, many states retained sumptuary laws that prohibited the common people from clothing themselves like their betters. Prohibitions on early marriage were also an attempt to keep down consumption, and in many professions and trades, marriage before the age of thirty was frowned upon as extravagant. Not until the Industrial Revolution was already established in the nineteenth century did the notion of consumer demand as a stimulant to production really take root. Up to that time low wages and restricted consumption were assumed to be necessary to an economic prosperity that was still measured in terms of the excess of exports over imports and the volume of trade in luxury goods.

Privileged companies trading in oriental silks or handmade Swedish steel had no wish to see domestic industries compete with their imports. Furthermore, much of the investment in trade was speculative, with money remaining liquid rather than being applied to fixed plant or large inventories. Commercial investors were not interested in fixed plant because they could still find enough cheap cotton cloth and pottery from small, mainly rural domestic producers to supply markets in Africa, the Americas, and parts of eastern Europe. In fact, the trend was away from concentrations of mechanized production in facory-type units. At the beginning of the eighteenth century, commercial capitalism found it in its interest to encourage the dispersal of production processes like spinning, weaving, nail, and pottery making throughout rural areas such as the West Riding of England, the Zurich Highlands of Switzerland, and German Silesia. Craft monopolies that the cities once enjoyed were challenged when many producers moved to the suburbs or even further into the hinterlands to escape traditional restrictions on production.

There were many reasons for this ruralization of manufacturing, but a prime cause was the guild structure of the cities, which prevented the kind of expansion of production that trade now encouraged. Craft regulations emphasized quality of production, not quantity, and guilds were hostile to innovations that might lower the "honor" of their trade or challenge their monopoly over production or sale of their craft. Economic recession in the late seventeenth century had made artisans even more intractable. For much of the eighteenth century, many trades became almost castelike, recruiting only from the ranks of the guild members and their relatives, sacrificing economic growth to social exclusivity, and strongly, even at times violently, opposing all outside influences. Economic self-interest rationalized itself as moral and social preservation. In eighteenth-century Germany, for example, restrictions against the admission into trades of the illegitimate, the lowborn, or persons associated with nonconformist religions multiplied to the point that a kind of urban aristocracy of labor dominated most small towns. Even in places such as England, where guild tradition was relatively weak, there were similar trends. The London Stationers' Company had become increasingly restrictive in its intake of apprentices, and the same held true for several of the city's other craft guilds.

Attempts to reduce the power of the guilds met with strong resistance; it was not by accident that merchants wishing to increase production for the export trade turned to the countryside as the source of both labor and initiative. There they found ample opportunities for what was called the putting-out system of manufacture, in which entrepreneurs supplied cottage workers with raw materials and bought back the finished product, which was then retailed on the domestic or foreign market. No investment in plant was required of the merchants, because the worker carried on the actual production at home or, where a somewhat greater space was needed, in small barns or sheds. In the eighteenth century most so-called domestic workers were either small peasants or landless wage earners, for whom the additional earnings from a spinning wheel, loom, or small anvil were a virtual godsend. Many urban dwellers also entered domestic production. Despite complaints by the guilds, the number of Londoners and Parisians who survived by working on materials at home or in temporary sweatshops multiplied enormously, particularly in the suburban fringes of those cities. In the eighteenth century manufacturing in this small-scale, labor-intensive manner far overshadowed larger, factory-type operations. In fact, the few factories that did exist in eighteenth-century Paris disappeared in the early nineteenth century, because employers found it cheaper to employ people in their homes at no overhead costs to themselves.

The advantages of domestic industry to the commercial capitalist were enormous, for the relatively cheap labor he was dealing with was unorganized, unlike the guild artisans, and therefore less able to make demands in return. In slack time, the entrepreneur simply cut back on production, and the weaver, straw plater, or nailmaker absorbed the cost of idle equipment and unsold inventory.

Exploitative as some aspects of the putting-out system were, in good times, when demand for finished goods outran supply, the domestic workers were in a relatively strong position. Subject to no direct discipline, they could work as much as they deemed necessary to maintain the accepted traditional standard of living. Domestic labor was highly attractive with the margin permitted by a bit of yarn saved or materials embezzled. Whole families worked together, children preparing the yarn, mothers spinning, and fathers weaving it. Straw plating and nail making were similarly organized. For many of those who began domestic work in the off seasons of agriculture, farming often ceased to be their main occupation, though many managed to keep a çow, a pig, or a small garden plot. Children brought up in these circumstances lost direct contact with the soil, whole villages devoted themselves to particular trades, and a type of manufacturing developed that was neither typically rural nor completely urban in its characteristics. Nevertheless, much of the traditional life-style was retained. Where the family worked as a unit, with women and children sharing in the work, traditional divisions of labor, old sex roles, and customary collective observances tended to be perpetuated.

Yet domestic manufacturing imposed limits on productivity by the nature of its social and technical organization. It was extremely labor intensive and thereby subject to the limitations of human endurance. Water power was sometimes applied to some of the simpler processes, but this increased productivity only marginally. The productive unit was small and inefficient for complicated tasks. Even more important, however, was the fact that the social character of the production unit could not easily expand. Usually the unit consisted of families working to sustain themselves at a traditional standard of living. Additional workers were not particularly welcome, and when the family had earned enough to meet its own needs, it was difficult to get the members to do more. Discipline was entirely internal and the merchants constantly voiced their disgust at the unresponsiveness of workers to the external incentives of supply and demand, as these were generated by distant national and international markets.

Old Regime Government

Today, countries faced with similar problems of low productivity attempt various combinations of incentives and coercive measures to increase output. The governments of the eighteenth century (referred to here as the old regimes) were accustomed to regulating the traditional agrarian and craft economies, creating trading opportunities, and even subsidizing certain prize export industries, but they were structurally as well as intellectually incapable of envisioning the kind of massive planning required to bring about large-scale economic growth. Indeed, most eighteenth-century European states had lost the dynamism that had characterized their seventeenth-century predecessors. They had become peculiarly stalemated, incapable of responding to the requirements of populations that, for the most part, still had only the most minimal contact with central government as such.

Unlike today's new nations, many of which derived from their colonial past relatively centralized governmental structures, the state in Europe had a very different origin. The term "state" derived from the word "estate," reflecting the fact that monarchical institutions had themselves originated from private domains that had only gradually established themselves as public authorities superior to other private properties. Although the limits of state power had long since exceeded the boundaries of the king's private territory, the concept of proprietorship was still embodied in the notion of state itself. Not only did the state "belong" to the monarch, but many of its institutions were still the property of private persons. Army commissions and civil service posts were bought and sold, even bequeathed, as private holdings. Military and civilian functions were performed by private individuals in a way that blurred the distinction between public and private, between state and society. On the local level, social and political power were virtually indistinguishable, with large landowners exercising judicial and administrative powers that, in a modern polity, are the sole monopoly of the state. The public and private functions of guilds and town councils were similarly intertwined.

Terms like "public" and "private" are not easily applied to the eighteenth-century state. The civil service had only recently been separated from the monarch's household retinue; thus the distinction between service to the state and personal loyalty to the crown was just coming into focus. Those bureaucrats and military officers who owed their place solely to patronage could be dismissed as easily as servants; those who owned their office were well protected, however, because the laws of private property applied to offices as well as to real estate. The notion of an autonomous civil service, with clearly defined rights and duties, could only come into being once the public sphere was clearly distinguished from the private, and this did not begin to occur until the end of the eighteenth century.

The rights of the ordinary person were defined in much the same way as those of state officials. Rights were privileged possessions—bought, inherited, or earned—of the individual or his family, not inherent rights accompanying birth or residence within the boundaries of the state. The concept of citizenship in its modern form was unknown, with its implications of horizontal relations among a population who share equally and inherently in a body of rights and duties. In eighteenth-century European states, the primary relationships were vertical rather than horizontal, allowing for no common political identity as citizens.

This is not to say, however, that individuals and groups did not enjoy a great deal of liberty, as this was defined under the old regimes. Rights, defined as immunity from such things as taxation and conscription, were recognized, but were distributed in such a way as to emphasize the differences rather than the similarities among individuals and groups. If freedom is defined as autonomy from central control, then eighteenth-century populations were undoubtedly freer than citizens in modern democracies. Layers of feudal privilege, royal indulgence, and local custom protected many German towns so completely that they were virtually states within the state. In France, provincial legislative bodies called Estates could successfully defy royal edict. When students wished to protest onerous regulations, they simply marched out of town and beyond the territorial jurisdiction of university officials, thereby establishing de facto immunity from prosecution. Where civil and political rights were vertically organized and geographically fragmented, there were many sanctuaries from royal law. Even after Church property ceased to offer immunity, persons wishing to avoid prosecution would simply do so by keeping on the move. At the same time, local authorities found it advantageous to keep all "foreigners" (defined as anyone not of the locality) from settling there. Therefore, large numbers of the poor, having no settlement rights in any particular community, were kept constantly on the move.

The absence of universal rights and duties was also reflected in the institutions of the state itself. Before 1789 the definition of "office" was a highly personal matter, adjusted to the qualities of the individual official rather than to an abstract definition of the job itself. The kind of specification of function and specialized training that we expect of modern bureaucracy was largely absent. In France, where purchase of office was encouraged, an individual was free to accumulate as many positions as he could afford, regardless of his capacity to fulfill their duties. Not until 1808, when departmentalization was finally introduced, did Prussia accomplish the kind of differentiation of ministries that we associate with modern government. Until that time only the military and foreign offices had been subject to the modern division of labor. The absence of rationalized systems of procedure accompanied the lack of clearly defined requirements and training. Prussian military commissions were reserved for the aristocracy, regardless of aptitude. The situation in most European countries in 1770 was not much different, with purchase, patronage, or inheritance determining access to office.

Of course, wealth and noble birth did not exclude real talent, and in France the sale of offices was a way of increasing royal revenues while encouraging successful persons to enter state service. Performance was not necessarily worse than that of modern civil service, but the goals pursued and the methods employed were certainly different. The era of red tape and routinization still lay in the future. However, in attracting to government the rich and the titled, the monarchy had to accept a leisured, aristocratic way of doing things, and officials conducted the business of state in ways we would find most irregular. Prussian officials were paid in part by housing subsidies, because they were expected to conduct much of their work at home. Likewise, university professors were expected to provide classrooms in their homes. Social and political affairs were so inseparable that the highest officials normally received very large sums so that they could maintain the style of life expected of members of the court.

It was not uncommon for monarchs to ennoble their highest civil officials. This was not only a means of ensuring the prestige and power of government by associating it with the status of aristocracy, but also a way of economizing by paying officials in symbols of rank rather than in regular salary. Associating social with bureaucratic rank allowed the state to borrow social prestige, a quality more important to most eighteenth-century monarchs than efficiency as such. Thus it was social custom rather than standards of utility that set the pace for eighteenth-century bureaucracy. Not until the mid-nineteenth century did English officials keep regular office hours, and even then the highest officers were exempted from the discipline of the clock, an instrument considered appropriate to those of low rank but demeaning to those of gentle birth. Lack of uniform standards of recruitment and performance made coordination of state functions exceedingly difficult. Transfer of officials from one part of the state to another was nearly impossible because of the difficulty of differences in provincial law, even regional languages.

As one might expect, the level of integration of most European states was extremely low, in comparison to that of today's developing nations. Attempts by central governments to universalize tax and conscription procedures were often met with local insurrections that could develop into separatist movements. Europe's feudal heritage of extreme dispersion of power among local authorities made the balance between the center and the periphery a very tenuous one, rendering states vulnerable to civil war. Instead of attempting to centralize the functions of government, most monarchs were content to rely on the fiction of absolutism, allowing provincial assemblies, local corporations, and private groups or individuals to handle many of the functions, including police, schooling, and many welfare measures, that the central state today performs. With the exception of foreign affairs and the military, the real power of the central monarchy was severely limited.

Lacking autonomous executive institutions capable of overcoming the forces of regional and corporate particularism, it was not surprising that eighteenth-century monarchs feared popular participation. Today the level of contact between people and their central government is infinitely greater, because the organs of central authority are recognized as legitimate in almost all spheres. This is not to say that people were not active at the local level in the eighteenth century, but rather that their contact with the central state was marginal. Peasant villages often elected their own leadership, who were responsible for tax collection and other local duties. In the towns, guilds and other corporate bodies kept alive a tradition of self-government that stretched back to the Middle Ages. But in every case the sense of participation was circumscribed socially as well as geographically, with various estates—nobles, clergy, burghers, peasants— electing representatives from within their own number rather than from the total body of citizens. The technique of monarchical rule involved keeping these estates apart and maintaining political relationships that were primarily vertical rather than horizontal. The same tactics meant that mass political mobilization was kept to a minimum, with the crown maintaining the illusion of patriarchal authority over a largely passive, divided population.

In comparison to modern states, the size of central government and its power to affect people in an immediate way was remarkably slight. The French monarchy at Versailles consisted of but a few thousand persons, many of whom were courtiers with no defined duties. As late as 1830, the English higher civil service comprised only thirty-five hundred employees, while the university educated segment of Prussian administration numbered about eleven hundred. This was government by omission, dependent for its legitimacy as much on what it avoided as on what it did. Until the nineteenth century, the vast majority of a ruler's time was devoted to social display, public ceremonies, and processions rather than to the less visible office work. Yet it must not be imagined that the time devoted to receptions and feasts constituted decadent luxury. On the contrary, in a political system where social prestige and political power were so interdependent, where politics and social life were so intertwined, the government that preferred the privacy of paperwork to the publicity of pomp and glory was endangering its own existence.

This very limited authority of central government contrasted strongly, however, with the broad powers that most European monarchs claimed for themselves. They claimed to rule by divine right. In most Protestant countries, the king claimed to share with the Church certain religious functions. Although the state still delegated broad areas of government to local authorities, it was theoretically involved in the control of prices and wages as well as the regulation of the labor supply, functions believed necessary to the well-being of the general population. In the case of England, government services remained relatively decentralized. The same local elites administered them, who earlier had been responsible for the needs of the peasantry and the lower orders of the towns. Extension of authority along the lines of traditional social hierarchy worked reasonably well in England, and also proved transferable to the colonies in America, where local government handled welfare with tolerable efficiency.

The expansion of the government's role proceeded in a different manner in most Continental states, however. In Prussia, for example, the monarchical welfare state tried to emancipate itself from its traditional rivals, the landed aristocracy and the Church, by establishing a bureaucracy to handle the task of governing. Originally part of the king's retinue of personal servants, civil servants gradually established themselves both ideologically and institutionally until they reached the point of viewing themselves as serving not only the king, but also a concept of the state that transcended even the royal personage. At the same time the bureaucracy was becoming gradually professionalized by substituting merit qualifications for patronage as the standard of entry and establishing its own ethical standards of public service. By 1770 there was a nearly complete set of welfare measures on the books, laws covering Prussian subjects from cradle to grave, guaranteeing them adequate food supply, sanitation, police protection—indeed, most of the services we expect of a modern state, with the exception of compulsory schooling. Despite the expanding claims of monarchy, these laws were never translated into full reality, however. Aristocrats, whose qualifications for office varied enormously, still staffed the higher bureaucracy. Long a rival of monarchy, this aristocracy was bound to use its official position to protect its vested interests. Thus, from within the very group that was supposed to implement the concept of monarchical absolutism came resistance to extension of state power.

Prussia went as far with centralization as was possible in any eighteenth-century state. Voltaire and other political theorists adopted it as their model of enlightened absolutism; other monarchs tried to copy its institutions. Under Maria Theresa and Joseph II, the Austrian monarchy moved rapidly in the direction of centralization, a course that meant trimming not only feudal but also ecclesiastical powers. The development of absolutist government in the mid-eighteenth century stirred opposition from the Catholic church and also from the various provinces of the Austrian empire, where local elites resisted the shift of power to Vienna with the vigor of the revolt of the Belgium and Hungarian provinces in the 1780s. The Spanish monarchy encountered similar resistance when, under the pressure of international competition, it began to try to strengthen itself through bureaucratic rationalization. And French monarchy, which had been moving toward centralization since the seventeenth century, began to encounter serious resisfance among provincial and corporate vested interests when it attempted to translate the illusion of absolutism into the reality of effective power. Even England, which had been reasonably successful in accomplishing reform within its relatively decentralized system, found the American Colonies a stumbling block when it tried to rationalize their taxation system. The objections by the colonists to centralized (and equalized) taxation raised more pointedly than had either the Dutch or Belgian revolts the question of whether the expansion of government could be accomplished without more fundamental changes in the relationship of the individual subject to the state.

This question did not agitate the mind of Europe in 1770, however. We must not conclude from what we know of the violent history of the last third of the eighteenth century that monarchy was somehow discredited. The attractiveness of the idea of absolutism had never been greater, particularly among the enlightened intellectuals. However, discontent with any particular form of government is determined by two conditions: first, the expectations that the general population places on its operations and second, the capacity of those institutions to fulfill popular demand. As long as population expansion did not press too strongly upon economic resources, the state was able to meet traditional political expectations. Just how serious the stalemate of government really was, was to become clear in the 1770s and 1780s, when social and economic crisis would reveal its gravest weaknesses.

2

Population Explosion and Economic Crisis, 1770–1850

The eighteenth century had begun on a note of optimism; yet it closed with the prophecy of despair. The Reverend Thomas Malthus, in *Essay on the Principle of Population* published in 1798, proposed that economic growth could not keep up with the rate of population increase:

> The power of population is infinitely greater than the power of the earth to produce subsistence for man. Population, when unchecked, increases in a geometrical ratio. Subsistence increases only at an arithmetical ratio. A slight acquaintance with numbers will show the enormity of the first power in comparison with the second.

By the beginning of the nineteenth century, the European population was increasing at an annual growth rate of as much as 1.5 percent. (See Chart 1.) Although this increase seems small compared with the more than 3 percent per annum population expansion that Asian and South American countries often attain today, it was enough to activate the deepest fears of the populace and reactivate archaic survival instincts. The population crisis that commenced in the 1770s did not end until after the Irish famine of 1845–1847, about which the 1851 Census Report noted that "starving people lived upon the carcasses of diseased cattle, upon dogs, and dead horses, but principally upon the herbs of the field, nettle tops, wild mustard, and water cresses. In some places dead bodies were found with grass in their mouths." Although the Irish famine was exceptional in its severity and came at a time when the real threat of subsistence crises was actually receding, there were several other periods in the years 1770–1850 when the reality of starvation—or, what is equally important, the fear of starvation—prevailed. There were times when Malthusian arithmetic applied to Europe and when that area seemed headed for disasters similar to those evident today in parts of the developing world.

Now the memory of plague and famine is remote to Europeans. The fears that moved Malthus and his contemporaries gave way by the end of the nineteenth century to a concern about underpopulation; until quite recently historians paid little attention to the subsistence crises that occurred so regularly in the past. They assumed that these crises had little relevance to the larger historical process or were so dependent on other factors as to be of little interest in and of themselves.

The current crisis of world population has changed all that, however. We can explain renewed interest in the history of European population during the period 1770–1850 by the fact that, during this period, European countries were passing through a stage of development similar to that which is happening in other parts of the world today. Then, as now, the changes were more than numerical. But as we shall see, quantitative change reflected more fundamental transformations in the character of those institutions that regulate population size, including the family itself. In the case of Europe, the demographic crisis of the late eighteenth and early nineteenth centuries encompassed epochal alterations in patterns of marriage, procreation, and child rearing, changes that had an effect not only on social structure but also on individual and group psychology.

Perhaps the most important effect of the late eighteenth-century population boom was that it shattered the previous ecological relationship between numbers and resources, a relationship reflected in the traditional concept of the "limited good." For out of the profound shock and suffering of this era came the realization that numbers could expand, apparently almost indefinitely, without precipitating the ultimate catastrophe of plague or starvation. Of course, this conclusion was possible only because a remarkable economic development was occurring simultaneously: the process of industrialization that by 1850 had increased income per capita beyond the limits set by a purely agrarian economy and that thus permanently altered the relationship between population and economic resources in western Europe. Unfortunately, the ability of the economy to cope with steadily expanding needs was by no means obvious to those who lived through the late eighteenth and early nineteenth centuries. Whether Reverend Malthus or Swabian peasant, contemporaries lived with a sense of impending ecological disaster, a disaster that repeatedly threatened to strike but that, with the sad exception of Ireland, never did. Only after 1850 did the optimistic notion of infinitely expanding resources begin to replace the concept of permanent scarcity.

Chart 1 Growth of Population in Various European Countries, 1700–1900.
(Figures from Herbert Moller, *Population Movements in Modern European History,*
Macmillan, New York, 1964, p. 5.)

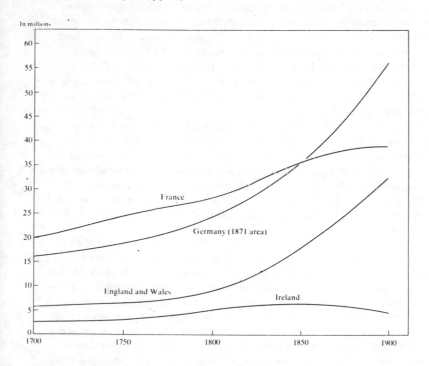

Changing Rates of Mortality and Fertility

At odds over the causes of the rapid population growth that began in the
last third of the eighteenth century, historians are divided between those
who ascribe the increase to declining mortality and those who ascribe it
to rising fertility. The former point to the decline of famine and epidemic
after the terrible Marseilles plague of 1720 as proof of greater food supply
and improved health conditions. The introduction of the potato has been
adduced as a cause of better nutrition, itself a factor in reducing the incidence of infant mortality. In addition, some argue that smallpox immunization, begun in the 1760s, may have had a similar effect. Indeed, fatal
epidemics did seem to have been decreasing.

   On the other hand, the defenders of the fertility thesis point out that
the real breakthroughs in medicine, sanitation, and sterilization occurred
much too late to contribute to population increase. Louis Pasteur made his
discoveries in the 1860s, with modern germ theory coming even later. The
cholera epidemics of 1831–1832 and 1849 had already carried off tens of
thousands, and various child killers remained prevalent until the very end

of the nineteenth century. These historians are therefore skeptical about the claims of falling mortality as the cause of population increase, pointing out that the effect of nineteenth-century city growth was to raise the incidence of infant death rather than lower it. Historians who see a decline in living standards beginning in the late eighteenth century, and reversed only in 1850 when the real incomes of workers began a steady rise, have also called into question improved nutrition as a factor in declining mortality. The looming example of the Irish famine of 1845–1847 refutes the thesis that the potato had the universal effect of reducing mortality, though, among favored groups like the aristocracy and upper-middle class, mortality did appear to be decreasing.

Those who argue for rising fertility as a major cause of population growth base their case on considerable evidence from registers of births and baptisms showing that reproduction rates of young wed and unwed mothers increased from about the 1760s onward. The cause of this change is not yet clear, though it seems that, in many places, inducements to early and more frequent marriage, together with favorable prospects for child labor, may have had much to do with it. Also, improved nutrition may have increased the average woman's fertility.

We know that the age of menarche (female puberty) fell rapidly once better nutrition became available, though this was probably not a factor in the increased fertility of this period. It would appear, instead, that in many parts of Europe, particularly where new forms of employment were being added to the traditional peasant economy, the nexus between marriage and inheritance was breaking down. In the Swiss cantons near Zurich, for example, cottage spinning and weaving allowed the children of peasants to circumvent the traditional wait for parents' death or retirement to set up their own households. Not having to wait until their late twenties, male domestic workers were marrying earlier than their peasant cousins. A Swiss pastor, Saloman Schinz, described Swiss girls as:

> raised at the wheel or the loom, without knowledge of other housework or field work, daily almost in bad company until late into the night, and when the work is over, spending the daily pay or part of it for sweets or drink, indulging every lust and not scorning for the purpose any means, however shameful, even embezzlement of the materials to be worked or theft of wares from the house of her parents, and then entering into marriage, when compelled by necessity, often with a youngster equally light-minded and poor, owning between them neither bed nor household utensils . . . .

The possibility of early marriage, combined with the fact that children were an employable resource within the domestic system of manufacturing, meant that population tended to grow at a faster rate in areas dominated by domestic industry than in either peasant areas or the larger cities. In the more traditional farm or craft settings, young workers lived in the households of their employers and exchanged their labor for board and room, subject to patriarchal discipline and unable to marry. In Germany the craft guilds controlled marriage, permitting it only to those who had attained mastership, thus keeping a check on population growth. But where patriarchal and fraternal institutions were absent, the marriage market was free to find a new level. Parents could no longer control courtship, and a new standard of personal choice, associated with notions of romantic love, filled the vacuum left by the disappearance of arranged marriage. "The so-called practice of bundling [courting in the bedroom] comes to be looked upon as a right and a freedom, and to be considered as nothing sinful. Marriage is always the sequel to pregnancy," it was reported. Rates of both legitimate and illegitimate births tended to rise much faster in areas of domestic industry, for as one unsympathetic Swiss pastor noted, "The cotton industry, like a foul pile of dung, has produced and given birth to all this vermin, the crawling and proud beggar pack." Complaints we associate with the growth of cities in the nineteenth century actually began in the hinterlands considerably earlier.

Where peasants had become landless wage earners, the age of marriage also tended to fall. The heavy demand for agricultural labor at the end of the eighteenth century may have encouraged larger numbers of children. In England poor relief favored men with dependent families; in Ireland early marriage became the norm for a different reason. There the introduction of the potato meant that an adequate supply of food could be produced on a small amount of land. This fact encouraged the practice of partible inheritance, by which the father divided his land more or less equally among his children even before his death or retirement, allowing them to establish a household on what before would have been a grossly inadequate holding.

The argument that increased fertility caused population growth does not rule out the possibility that mortality may have been falling at the same time. Indeed, it seems very probable that both factors were operating as causes of population growth during the period 1770–1850—fertility as a cause in the early phases when mortality rates were still high and parental strategy still dictated large numbers of births in order to guarantee social and economic security, and falling mortality as a cause later on, when fertility was still high, with the result that more children survived into adulthood.

The Effects of Population Explosion

Whichever the cause, the effects of population boom were reasonably clear; first among these was increasing numbers of children, resulting in an increased proportion of young persons in the age bracket 15–29 as compared with the total population of adults 30 years and over. The ratio of youth to adults reached nearly the levels (75–80 percent) common in

Asian and South American countries today. Not until 1870 did levels begin to drop toward the 35 percent now common in European societies.

During the late eighteenth and early nineteenth centuries, each group of individuals born on the same date was larger than the next, creating a situation that seriously strained all the institutions, including the family, that were involved in the rearing and control of the young. Also threatened were those educational and professional institutions whose old rates of intake were insufficient to absorb the growing numbers of youth wishing to enter them. The German university population, for example, expanded from five thousand in 1800 to three times that number in 1830, a rate of growth that was well in excess of the overall rate of population increase in that country. By contrast, English universities lagged behind; Oxford increased from two hundred students in 1800 to four hundred in 1820, but still constituted only a minute portion of the young population. French educational opportunity expanded enormously under Napoleon, but there was no corresponding expansion of professional places. University youth in post-Napoleonic France found places occupied by older professionals who saw no reason to expand the number of positions which had been adequate for their own much smaller generation but which were now inadequate for the expanded flow of graduates. In the 1820s the French author James Fazy denounced this attitude as the tyranny of what he called a "gerontocracy" and he spoke bitterly of "asthmatic, gouty, paralytic beings with weakened powers who have no wish for anything but peace and quiet." Similar expressions of generational conflict were heard in every western European country.

Among the laboring population, apprentices and journeymen, who found masters unwilling to expand opportunities commensurate with the new demographic proportions, encountered parallel difficulties. In the eighteenth century, journeymen silk weavers in London struck against the restrictive practices of their masters. During the 1840s in Prussia, the number of apprentices increased much more rapidly than did masterships, with the result that young workers became extremely discontented with the whole concept of patriarchy. They demanded entry to master status for all those qualified in their craft, plus the shortening or abolition of apprenticeship, which they perceived as a weapon of the old against the young. Masters resisted because it was not easy for the older persons to compete with the younger, particularly in those labor-intensive jobs that relied on human endurance. Said one of Victor Hugo's characters in *Les Misérables:*

> One gets old when one's still quite young in that job [wheelwright] —
> A man's done for at forty—I was fifty-three, that was hard—And the
> young workmen are so nasty. When you're not so young as you were,
> they jeer at you as a stupid old gaffer!

Population increases were so vast that people had difficulty adjusting to the scale of changes necessary in schools, trades, and professions to accommodate each expanded generation. As long as they continued to think in the old terms of the limited good, expansion seemed to threaten the very nature of things. Indeed, changes in size did have the effect of transforming the very character of traditional insitutions. For example, when the Prussian army numbered about eighty thousand in the 1770s, the Hohenzollern monarch, Frederick the Great, had known every officer (most of them nobles) by name. In 1850 this was no longer possible and the monarch was resigned to approving commissions for those about whom he knew nothing, except that they had passed the required tests. As for the officer corps itself, it had experienced profound social change as the result of its expansion during the nineteenth century. Unable to supply enough candidates out of its own ranks, the landed aristocracy was forced to give up its earlier monopoly over officer positions. Nonnoble officers poured in and by the 1860s the army was of such a size that the aristocratic predominance was permanently broken. While the social hegemony of the nobility continued, it never re-established its numerical superiority.

The experience of other trades and professions was similar. There were tensions between younger and older members of the guilds. The professions of law and medicine, which had previously relied on patronage and birth for standards of selection, were forced to create standards appropriate to the vastly enlarged numbers of candidates. Everywhere the rapid growth of population was challenging old procedures that, by their very nature, tended toward restriction rather than expansion. Even within the family itself, larger numbers of siblings meant adjustment of family priorities. This was slow to occur, however, and many families reacted in the traditional manner. Surplus children were forced to take to the road in even greater numbers. Foundling homes were overwhelmed with children that desperate parents, particularly unwed mothers, had dropped at their doors. In both England and France, abandonment became epidemic, accounting for the swarms of young migrants that Victor Hugo observed in Paris during the 1840s:

> . . . wandering children abounded in Paris. Statistics give us an average of 260 shelterless children picked up yearly by the police patrols on unfenced lots, in houses under construction and beneath the arches of the bridges. One of the nests, which has remained famous, produced the "Swallows of the Arcole Bridge." This, incidentally, is the most disastrous of social symptoms, for all the crimes of man begin in the vagrancy of the child. . . .

Separation of children from their parents was not an unusual occurrence in preindustrial society. The tradition of boarding out, the *Wanderjahre* (travel for the purpose of training) of the itinerant crafts, and the practice of poor children "claiming kin" among relatives in distant towns— all these were established forms of relief for overburdened parents. The difference between the new migration and the old lay in the fact that, while before most young people had expected to be cycled back to their place of birth to settle down, now an ever larger portion would never return. *Robinson Crusoe* became youth's most popular reading in the late eighteenth century because so many felt kinship with the position of Daniel Defoe's famous castaway. When their destination was not North or South America, Asiatic Russia, or Australia (the four largest reception areas for European migrants), it was the great cities, whose environment often seemed as alien and forbidding as any of the extra-European frontiers. The largest group of newcomers to the cities in the nineteenth century was in the 20–40 age group, mostly single men and women whose predicament was already the cause of concern in the late eighteenth century.

The patriarchal institutions that had once accommodated the migrant young were breaking down under the strain. The old practice of boarding with the master was in decline, for humanitarian Jonas Hanway noted even in 1780 that in London "there is scarce an apprentice boy turned fifteen years of age who, contrary to the practice of our forefathers, is not suffered to go abroad [out of the house] as soon as the shop is shut." By 1800 the well-to-do in many parts of Europe would no longer board strangers in their households. Growing awareness of social differences between rich and poor caused the propertied classes to make a distinction between their own children and servants or apprentices, assigning the latter to a position "below the stairs" and a life quite apart from the immediate family. Employers now treated employees as strangers, the responsibility for whom ended with the payment of a wage. Employees were free to find their own lodging and meals elsewhere. The shift from payment in room and board to cash was all the more significant because now many servants and apprentices were allowed to establish an independent life-style, even to marry if they wished. Women in servant positions still tended to be protected by live-in arrangements, but those in other types of urban employment—seamstresses and home-workers—gained a new freedom. Munich's police chief noted in 1815:

> Many young girls leave service when they grow tired of waiting on people and under one pretext or another take a room somewhere, living from their own industry. But they do little real work and let themselves be supported by boyfriends; they become pregnant and then are abandoned.

Paris was full of young persons desperate for fame and fortune in the 1770s and 1780s. Late eighteenth-century literature is full of outcasts and outlaws like Robinson Crusoe, Moll Flanders, and Jonathan Wild, who were the objects of romanticization by German as well as French and English writers. In the public mind, however, servants without masters and runaway apprentices inhabited the same world as the destitute and the criminal. John Howard and Jonas Hanway's reports of rising juvenile delinquency began to enter public consciousness in the late eighteenth century. Fear of youthful depravity reached a peak again in the 1830s and 1840s, partly from novels like Charles Dickens's *Oliver Twist* and Hugo's *Les Misérables*. Also, widespread fear of sexual delinquency existed, triggered by the rising illegitimacy rates recorded in most parts of western Europe from the 1760s onward. In Paris in the early nineteenth century, more than one-third of those born were illegitimate. In parts of Germany as many as 40 percent of the total births were illegitimate, before dropping to 20 percent after 1870.

A typical predicament of young persons in the late eighteenth century is shown in a case from the records of the London Foundling Hospital. Susan Thomas, an English domestic servant, was courted by William Miller, a drover, for almost a year. With marriage promised, intercourse took place just before William had to tramp in search of work. They lost contact and Susan, pregnant, came to London to look for William. Not finding him, she had to abandon her illegitimate infant at the Foundling Hospital. In many cases like this, it was the woman's traditional expectation of marriage following pregnancy that proved her downfall. Worsening economic conditions and high rates of geographical mobility produced additional thousands of Susans, victims of conditions beyond their comprehension.

Later in the nineteenth century, when young men and women became more accustomed to the circumstances of modern urban life, they took greater care to control conception, and illegitimacy rates began to fall; but in this period of transition, old moralities resulted in new evils when applied in the wrong situations. Frightened by rising birth rates, German authorities in the 1820s passed laws setting minimum requirements of age and wealth for wedlock. So strong was the desire for marriage, however, that couples continued to form unions, and the recorded rate of illegitimacy shot up drastically. Under conditions where two (or more) could live cheaper than one, this was bound to be the consequence.

Desperate to halt population growth, some states tried to reassert traditional communal restrictions on marriage. As in the German case just mentioned, these efforts were generally ineffective. Communal and patriarchal authority were so disrupted by social and economic change that any restoration of external restraints was bound to fail. To the Reverend Malthus and other liberals, the remnants of the old social order only seemed to stand in the way of a solution through individual self-control. They argued that old forms of charity and paternalistic benevolence were themselves positive incentives to high fertility and should be abolished so that the poor would then be forced, out of self-preservation, to control their birth rate. While the individual would ultimately assume the responsibility of birth control, this did not begin in most places, with the exception of France, until the 1860s and 1870s, largely because the material incentive to birth control—namely, a rise in living standards large enough to reduce mortality and compensate families for the loss of the earning power of extra children—did not take place until after 1850.

Unlike today's newly developing countries, Europe had no recourse to scientific solutions to its population problem. Cheap mechanical or chemical contraceptive devices were not available, and even if they had been, there was no guarantee that they would have been accepted. Even in the eighteenth century, a crude type of condom was used by city people and coitus interruptus was common everywhere. Incentive to use these birth control techniques was lacking, however; as long as economic and health standards were not such that large numbers of children were a burden rather than an asset, the poor would continue to multiply. There is evidence that the very rich were beginning to prefer fewer children, beginning to think of the individual child as an expensive investment in care and education, and therefore wanting fewer. However, for the 80 percent of the population that was still caught in conditions of high mortality, producing fewer children was beyond the realm of possibility. Child fatality might be declir·.ig among the favored few, but among the mass of Europeans it was still appallingly high, perhaps even rising, and was thus an incentive to increase rather than reduce the birth rate.

Failing to check its own population growth, Europe did have one option not usually open to developing countries today; its world military and political hegemony allowed for migration, sometimes subsidized by private or governmental funds. Together with a still high death rate, migration helped keep the pace of population growth at less than half that experienced in many developing countries in this century, which, in turn, restrained population from consuming all the gains in economic growth that were occurring in the late eighteenth and early nineteenth centuries, preventing, except in Ireland, the ultimate catastrophe of famine. Comparing the European experience of population expansion to that of much of the Third World, today, we can see that Europe's expansion from 1770 to 1870 was neither so fast as to cause ecological disaster nor so slow as to produce economic stagnation. Instead, it provided economic stimulus by increasing demand without overburdening the capacity for supply.

Agricultural Revolution

Once again, however, it is only by hindsight that we know that Europe managed to avoid the disaster of overpopulation. Those who suffered through the periodic crop failures and deep economic recessions from 1770 to 1850 had no way of knowing that agricultural production was actually keeping pace (if barely) with population growth. Even the most heavily industrialized nation, England, remained 90 percent self-sufficient for most of the period 1770–1870. Since England's population more than tripled during that period, we may assume that its food production capacity also increased by the same amount. Productivity in Germany, Italy, and France also responded sufficiently to consumer demand so that those countries were able to feed their people, though at a somewhat lower than normal standard. Although the threat of famine did not absolutely disappear until after improved transportation made available the yields of the midwestern American grain fields in the 1870s, much of Europe did undergo what historians now call an "agricultural revolution."

The agricultural improvement that took place from the mid-eighteenth century on was scarcely conceivable in the early eighteenth century when agricultural prices were low and there was little incentive for investment. But from the midcentury onward, population provided growing demand and prices rose, reaching a peak during the period of the Napoleonic Wars. Money flowed to where profits could be made, and food production began to climb. Heavy investment of capital in agriculture began in the Netherlands, where farmers were able in the early eighteenth century to increase the fertility of the soil. The traditional method had been to let the land lie fallow and to bring it into cultivation only after it had regained its chemical content. The Dutch devised a method of crop rotation that allowed certain nitrogen-producing crops, such as clover, to substitute for grain. Charles Townsend, an Englishman who introduced turnips into the rotation to break up as well as replenish the ground, perfected the method. Another Englishman, Thomas William Coke of Holkam, developed the process still further, utilizing four crops to increase his annual yield as much as ten times. Thus the new technique drastically reduced the number of fallow fields. Growing fodder crops allowed progressive farmers to keep larger numbers of cattle and to slaughter animals after stall feeding them. Previously, farmers had to pasture animals on extensive lands, thereby losing their manure. Stall feeding encouraged the efficient use of manure, Europe's primary fertilizer until the introduction of chemical substitutes in the later nineteenth century.

Improvements in breeding and the introduction of new crops, such as the sugar beet, the tomato, and the potato, also helped to increase productivity. Easy to cultivate and rich in calories, the potato had been introduced to Europe from the Americas two hundred years earlier. However, its acceptance awaited the rise of grain prices in the eighteenth century, for only then did the poor begin to turn to it as a substitute. Louis XV of France was so eager for its acceptance that he wore a potato flower in his lapel to show that the vegetable was not poisonous. The sugar beet came into use around 1750 as a replacement for cane sugar imports. Like other new foods, particularly vegetables, its use owed much to journals such as Arthur Young's *Annals for Agriculture* (1784), which spread the latest techniques throughout the Western world.

Improvements in farm implements also contributed to efficiency on progressive farms. The scythe gradually displaced the sickle, and in 1771 an all-iron plow was invented. An Englishman, Jethro Tull, introduced the harrow and seed drill into use, ending the ancient wasteful practice of scattering seeds by hand. Other mechanical improvements arrived more slowly. Primitive reapers and threshers became available by the early nineteenth century, but the great combine harvesters were not invented until the 1880s, when the American plains began to deliver their unprecedented yields. It is important to keep in mind that real mechanization did not proceed rapidly or uniformly in Europe until well into the twentieth century.

The agricultural revolution of the eighteenth and early nineteenth century was labor intensive, using human and animal energy to implement improvements in growing and breeding; it actually delayed the application of inanimate sources of power until the later nineteenth century at a time when labor became scarce. This was true not only of those areas where small farms predominated—namely, the Low Countries, France, and western Germany, which used crop rotation and improved husbandry to develop higher yields of meat, poultry, and vegetables—but also of those regions, primarily England, eastern Germany, and the Po Valley of Italy, where estates were large enough for grain production. Not only did the abundance of cheap labor make it unnecessary for employers to introduce labor-saving machinery, but where employers did so field workers reacted to innovation with violent hostility. From 1815 through 1830, English rural laborers organized a series of partially successful revolts against the introduction of threshing equipment that threatened to deprive them of winter employment. Similar protests inhibited mechanization in France and Germany as well.

Gains in productivity were due not only to increased yield per acre but also to the extension and consolidation of land put into production. The disruptive effects of economic change were most evident here. In England some two million additional waste acres were brought into cultivation between 1700 and 1850, mostly achieved through enclosure, a legal process that involved the consolidation of smaller, scattered parcels of land into larger, more productive units. Not only private property but ancient common lands as well were reorganized, with each owner receiving a consolidated package of ground commensurate with his rights. Deeds were updated and those without legal claim to the land (squatters and cotters) were simply pushed off.

Enclosure was a parliamentary act supervised by official commission, but its results, however legal they might be, benefited the larger landowner more than the small freeholder, and the freeholder more than the cotter or squatter. Between 1700 and 1845, one-quarter of England's arable land was reorganized in this way, with the result that from the 1770s onward something like large-scale capitalist agriculture came into being. The English peasantry, small holders of twenty-five acres or less, were driven out of business, with more efficient enterprises being organized for profit in a national market. "The small farmers were generally reduced in every county, and almost annihilated in some," noted one contemporary. The old rural hierarchy, with its infinite gradation of rich and poor, was replaced by a simpler social order: a few very rich larger landowners at the top, some tenant farmers in the middle, and a great mass of landless wage earners at the bottom.

The procedure followed in Prussia's 1807 land reform was similar to enclosure, and there, too, the lesser peasantry was destroyed. Only the well-to-do peasants could afford the investment needed to improve production in grain and cattle raising. The improvements introduced—cutting forests, draining marshes, building new farm houses and barns, rotating crops, breeding animals—provided increased employment sufficient to hold most Prussian families to the land but payed so little that it confirmed them in the permanent status of wage labor. The desire to capitalize agriculture contributed strongly to the emancipation of serfdom in central Europe (Austria in 1781, Denmark in 1788, Prussia in 1807, Hungary in 1848), but where large estates predominated, emancipation was achieved in such a way that it created more wage laborers than independent peasants. In Prussia, emancipation benefited the larger landowners and the wealthier peasantry, who together accumulated almost half the cultivated land by 1850. In England, where the concentration of landholding went the furthest, half the country's farmland was held by a mere 2,250 persons in 1873.

Even if the distribution of land had been more equitable, the effect of enclosure and land reform would have been revolutionary as far as rural society was concerned. The consolidation of fields meant that old rituals of cooperation fell into disuse. When holdings were still scattered and it was difficult for one owner to use his land without access through the property of others, cooperation was absolutely necessary at times of sowing and harvesting. In many European villages, a council decided the date of the harvest, allotted the use of common land, and arranged for annual feasts of thanksgiving. Tradition effectively limited the rights of even the largest property owners, who through the practice of boarding laborers and exercising other paternalistic functions in village life remained in close contact with the common people. Land reform introduced the absolute sovereignty of private property, shattering communal rhythms and intersecting the old relations between rich and poor. Among the first customs to be abandoned by capitalist landowners was that of live-in help. When William Cobbett asked why farmers no longer fed or lodged their workers, he answered himself by saying, "They cannot keep them upon so little as they give them in wages. This is the real cause of the change."

Wealthy farmers were eager to hire young, cheap hands, but they did not want them to associate with their own children. They felt contact with field hands was demeaning and, therefore, they were happy to have social responsibility stop with the payment of the wage. At the same time, they made sure that they retained administrative and judicial power over the lives of the poor. In England the new capitalist landlords were no less vigorous than their predecessors in using their position as local magistrates to enforce game laws and put down rural rebellion. The Prussian landed aristocrats, the Junkers, retained their judicial powers until 1848 and continued to control the rural administrative structure into the 1880s. As the social cohesion of villages decayed, so, too, did the inhabitants' ability to resist exploitation. The poor were being deprived of control over their own destiny, particularly in those areas of large estates. A traveller named Moore found in England's County Norfolk:

> the houses tumbling into ruins and the common fields all enclosed; upon enquiring into the cause of this melancholy alteration, I was informed that a gentleman of Lynn had bought that township and the next adjoining it . . . and upon my further enquiring what was becoming of the farmers who were turned out, the answer was that some of them were dead and the rest had become labourers.

Rising farm prices did not operate everywhere to the advantage of capitalist agriculture, however. In France, the Netherlands, and western Germany, the incentive to put more land into production came not from the larger landlords but from the peasantry. Small holding was already well advanced in these areas and the large landlords there had traditionally seen the feudal dues extracted from peasants as their main source of income rather than profits taken from market sales. Thus, as the eighteenth century advanced, absentee noble and bourgeois estate owners sought to keep abreast of their own rising costs of living by extracting greater dues and services from the peasantry. Ancient feudal rights were invoked and transformed into cash payments, much to the exasperation of the peasantry, who were forced to put more land into cultivation just to meet their own costs.

Although French peasants owned about 30 percent of the land outright, this amount became increasingly inadequate to their needs. The kinds of improvements that were occurring in England were impossible on small peasant plots and even if they had had the opportunity to farm larger acreage, it is doubtful that the bulk of French peasants would have increased productivity voluntarily. They distrusted the new market economy almost as much as they hated feudal taxation. Theirs was a self-contained economy based on small local markets, whose autonomy peasants and their neighbors vigorously defended. Their land hunger was, therefore, not of the same kind as that of the capitalist enclosers, for it was stoked primarily by a fervid desire to maintain a certain customary standard of living, not to make profits by sales of surplus on a wider national or international market.

The French Revolution might have been expected to bring French agriculture into the age of the expanding market economy, but it did not. The events of 1789 onward swept away feudal taxation and placed Church lands, amounting to 15 percent of rural France, up for sale. Small holders undoubtedly gained substantially from these changes, but not so as to break their attachment to the traditions of a peasant economy inherited from the eighteenth century. There were pockets of agricultural progress in France, just as there were in the Netherlands and western Germany, where the French Revolution also had its impact. But, socially as well as economically, the peasantry remained attached to the past. The custom of cooperation continued in French villages well into the nineteenth century, and production continued to be for local rather than for national consumption. The encroachment of capitalist agriculture on common lands and forests continued to be so bitterly resented that in 1848 French peasants used the occasion of the breakdown of political authority to recapture communal lands from bourgeois landowners.

The peasantry of France and western Germany managed to survive in the period 1770-1850 not by vastly increasing productivity (though there was some gain), but by reducing personal consumption. In France in the 1860s, one-half of the rural population owned some land, but only one-quarter had sufficient land on which to make an independent living. By that time many had become tenants, sharecroppers, or field hands, supplementing their earnings by additional work in domestic industry, mining, or building. Yet despite this rural poverty, depopulation of the French countryside did not begin until 1850. Agriculture remained labor intensive, and although wages were meager, attachment to soil and village was so strong that French peasants preferred to limit their birth rate rather than send surplus sons and daughters to the city or, as the German peasantry was already doing, encourage their migration to America.

A lowering of the birth rate was noticeable in the poorest rural regions of France as early as the 1790s, a unique response to overpopulation and pauperization and one not duplicated by the lower classes in any other part of Europe at the time. In France the Napoleonic Code of 1804, a law that dictated equal inheritance for each child, may have encouraged family limitation among peasants unwilling to see their lands further subdivided. Yet the same rule of inheritance in Ireland did not result in similar family planning. On the contrary, because the potato could be cultivated on very small parcels of land, population growth continued until the disasters of the 1840s. France's early acceptance of family limitation was an exception to the general European rule.

The leveling off of the birth rate did not prevent France from experiencing severe rural overpopulation from the 1770s through the 1850s, however. Limitation of fertility is an effective remedy to poverty only when it is accompanied by the kind of increase in expectations that results in a rise in consumer demand and, in turn, increases in productivity. The French peasantry did not reduce fertility in order to increase consumption but rather to maintain a standard of living inherited from the eighteenth century. Therefore, there was no increase in consumer demand that might have stimulated either the kind of agricultural revolution that was taking place in England in the eighteenth century or the industrial revolution that would take place there in the nineteenth century. In France, western Germany, and the other places where the traditional peasant economy continued to prevail, rising population continued to eat up income that might have been spent on consumer goods or invested in agricultural or industrial improvement. In these areas, the rural economy was treading water, keeping just ahead of the population growth but providing no great surpluses.

Beginnings of Economic Growth

Agricultural improvement and land reform created more problems than they alone were capable of resolving. The introduction of chemical fertilizers and labor-saving machinery would have sufficed to push food production far enough ahead of population to allow a dramatic increase in per capita wealth, but these were not improvements that an agrarian society could generate by itself. They arrived in the second half of the nineteenth century after a second economic and social revolution—the Industrial Revolution—was well under way. Without the technical resources that this revolution provided, the sixfold increase in grain production achieved in America in the 1880s would never have been possible. Furthermore, by creating new forms of urban employment and draining population from the countryside, industrialization provided an incentive for the introduction of machinery and the ultimate abandonment of labor-intensive methods by which the first stages of the agricultural revolution had been attained.

Some application of industrial technology to agricultural productivity is the obvious goal of today's developing countries, but for Europe, with no model to guide it in the nineteenth century, the initial trial-and-error period of industrialization was exceptionally painful. That Europe, or more specifically England, should be the first to industrialize was by no means foreordained. As late as the sixteenth century, Europe was still relatively backward; until about 1500, the wealth of western Europe was hardly comparable to that of Islam and its technological capacity lagged behind that of China. We have seen how, after the economic boom of the sixteenth and seventeenth centuries, the internal economies of Europe stagnated despite overseas expansion. Cities lost manufacturing to the countryside and merchants found it difficult to extract greater productivity from the domestic work force. Nevertheless, the expansion of the putting-out system, together with agricultural gains, was responsible for the growth of rural population in the eighteenth century. The excess of villagers flowed to the cities, where they became a new force in the national market for consumer goods. Together with foreign trade, this expanded domestic demand had the effect of raising incentives for merchants to squeeze still further the productive capacity of their domestic suppliers.

We have already discussed the reasons that domestic industry was not infinitely expandable. By 1770 the elasticity of the putting-out system was showing strains, particularly in England. The obscure valleys of the West Riding, the Black Country, and Lancashire could simply not supply merchants with the finished products expanding markets required. Between 1700 and 1750, production for the home market had risen 7 percent; exports had increased 67 percent. Labor found itself in a relatively favorable position. Wages were rising as commercial capitalists bid against one another, and workers found themselves having to take on less work for the same wages, thus spending more time at leisure without endangering their traditional standard of living. The mid-eighteenth-century worker was still free to regulate work time and still subject largely to the rural calendar with its seasonal rhythms of work and innumerable holidays. Defoe, author of "Giving Alms No Charity," cynically described this worker:

> There is nothing more frequent than for an Englishman to work till he has got his pockets full of money, and then go and be idle or perhaps drunk till this is all gone. . . . Ask him in his cups what he intends, he'll tell you honestly, he'll drink as long as it lasts and then go to work for more.

What workers regarded as rightful freedoms, eighteenth-century employers saw as shirking laziness. The conflict of interests was the same in the early nineteenth century, wherever entrepreneurs continued to rely on the putting-out system. The struggle was more intense, however, because the number of people involved was so much greater by that time. Even in England, where a revolutionary new centralized *factory* system of production in spinning cotton was in place by 1820, its initial effect was to increase the number of domestic or cottage weavers to handle the expanded production in yarn. Although the number of factory workers in textiles rose from ninety thousand in 1806 to one hundred eighty-five thousand in 1830, the number of domestic weavers increased to almost two hundred forty thousand in the same period. Until the power loom took over completely in the 1840s, employers still repeated Defoe's criticism of traditional worker freedoms:

> The employer of domestic weavers can never tell within a fortnight or three weeks when every web sent out to the neighborhood will be returned . . . embezzlement of yarn . . . the risk of being taken out of

the loom to be sold or pawned by a dishonest weaver . . . wrangling
and disputes between the foreman and the men. . . .

The history of textiles was not exceptional in this respect, for the number of domestic workers grew in every trade during the late eighteenth and early nineteenth centuries. As later chapters will show, the first stages of what we now call the Industrial Revolution, namely, factory production, first promoted and then destroyed domestic manufacturing. Yet it is only by hindsight that we can designate the spread of factory forms of industry as the key to material progress. Contemporaries did not see it that way, for they often attempted to smash the new machines, assaulting the factories in an attempt to maintain the older, independent traditions of manufacture. This struggle lasted right up through the 1840s and 1850s in some parts of Europe, often with the tacit approval of those parts of the bourgeoisie who still relied on labor-intensive methods. Only then did it become clear that factory organized mechanization, the essence of the Industrial Revolution, had come to stay.

For most of the period 1770 through 1850, the intensification of human and animal labor, the same means that had accounted for every major period of growth since the twelfth century, brought about expansion of production. This was as true of manufacturing as it was of agriculture, at least until the 1830s and 1840s. The distinction between *economic growth* and *economic development* is of critical importance here. Economic growth refers only to the increase in real income per capita, and growth in this sense was not new. Similar periods of expansion had occurred in the sixteenth and seventeenth centuries, but no industrial revolution had taken place. Economic development, on the other hand, means fundamental change in the character of economic institutions, change in both production and consumption. Prior to the eighteenth century, economic growth had time and again pushed labor-intensive methods to their limit without resulting in any decisive economic development. Each time this had happened, as in the fourteenth and seventeeth centuries, another human "energy crisis" had occurred, with the result that supply failed to meet demand, economic stagnation set in, and, worse still, there was actually reversal of income growth.

Beginning in the 1770s, Europe seemed to be entering into another of its periodic energy crises. Population growth, itself a stimulus to increased production, constantly threatened to consume a greater share of per capita income and thus repeat the old pattern of regression. This population threat came from two sources. On the consumption side there was the fact that most of the additional persons needing to be fed, housed, and clothed were unproductive children. Money and other resources that might have gone into investment were being consumed in ways that did not contribute to increases in productivity. On the supply side of this still labor-intensive economy, there was, despite population boom, a shortage of skilled labor relative to demand. The cost of skilled labor was rising, making production less profitable, and capitalists were more wary about investing in expansion. In the past, the reaction to such conditions had been to cut back. Many entrepreneurs did just that, but there were a daring few who attempted to cut costs of human labor by introducing labor-saving devices powered by inanimate sources of energy. From their experiments grew the Industrial Revolution, an economic development so significant that it overshadows all other changes since the domesticization of agriculture in 5000 B.C.

Crisis of Productivity

Because we know the outcome of the industrialization process, it is easy to assume that the solution to the eighteenth-century energy crisis was quick and simple. On the contrary, the steps that led to the Industrial Revolution were fraught with controversy. The epic struggle between population and resources hung in the balance for most of the period 1770–1850. Even in England, the country that led the world in the use of steam power, it was not until the 1820s that anything like a steam powered factory system existed and then only in the area of cotton manufacturing. At issue was not just the entrepreneurs' reluctance to change their form of investment from the relatively light demands of the putting-out system to the capital-intensive factory plant, but also the reluctance of domestic and craft workers to accept the discipline of factory employment. Most of the population was still rural, and as long as agriculture was competing with manufacturing for labor, it was very difficult to attract people to the industrial cities.

In France, rural overpopulation inhibited urban growth and industrialization well into the nineteenth century; German peasants preferred to emigrate to America rather than seek employment in native towns; and even in England, where the mobility of population was probably greatest, the movement of people from the low-wage southern agricultural counties to the high-wage northern manufacturing and mining areas was very slow, despite the obvious economic advantage. As we have seen, French peasants were willing to reduce consumption rather than change their place or way of life. The rural Irish were the most tenacious in trying to eke out an existence on tiny plots of land, constantly subdivided each generation. Welfare measures kept the English rural poor barely above the minimum of subsistence from the 1790s onward. Local authorities made up the difference between farm wages and the cost of living, and no less than one-tenth of the English population was permanently on the dole, with whole villages being subsidized. Until almost 1850 it seemed that the mass of the European population preferred the poverty, even starvation, of the countryside to life within the factory system in the towns.

Welfare measures like the English Poor Law subsidized the laboring

poor and thus provided an excuse for employers to keep wages low. The
dole also kept birth rates artificially high, thus diverting savings to the
feeding and care of children rather than to investment in economic innovation. Added to the obstacle of labor immobility was the problem of
uncertain consumer demand and the lack of a highly developed domestic
retail market. Despite the entrepreneurs' desire to take advantage of the
inflationary situation that had prevailed for much of the eighteenth
century and into the early nineteenth century, the fact that prices stayed
ahead of wages and thus produced handsome profits did not guarantee
economic development as such. Indeed, these good times encouraged
reliance on old, proven methods and therefore helped perpetuate domestic
as opposed to factory manufacturing. When the long rise of prices and
profits suddenly came to an end about 1810, the European economy found
itself in a situation similar to that faced by today's developing countries,
where population growth consumes too large a share of capital investment.
Prices dropped at the end of the Napoleonic Wars; profits and investment
faltered as costs moved ahead of prices; wages were cut and employment
fell; the level of consumption declined and the cost of poor relief mounted
everywhere. It seemed a downward spiral had begun, to result in conditions
paralleling those found in parts of the non-Western world today. As one
contemporary described it:

> Men of all trades wander for employment. Failures of manufacturers,
> destruction of machinery, combinations, etc., send thousands on the
> tramp. . . . Wives are hunting for runaway husbands (seldom the re-
> verse); children for runaway parents. . . . The excitement produced
> by the acts of political agitators has, no doubt, produced a general
> spirit of restlessness, which makes many leave the homes of their
> youth with diminished anxiety, makes them reckless of shame among
> strangers, and easily led away to vice and crime.

The economy recovered in the early 1820s, but it had lost the buoyancy
that had been provided by rising prices in the preceding seventy years.
Even in England, where the factory system had made greatest headway
(there were eighty-five thousand power looms in England in 1833, while in
France the number did not reach ten thousand until the 1860s), it was
increasingly difficult to get the kind of investment needed to finance
further industrial capacity. As the opportunity for quick profits declined,
the rich looked elsewhere to invest. French industrial pioneers were forced
to finance most expansion directly out of their own profits, and this
tended to inhibit growth, making for conservative family firms. In England,
where the first cotton mills had been financed on loans and mortgages as
low as £100, struggle over investment resources was particularly sharp.
Entrepreneurs complained as bitterly about the unproductive wealth of
landed interests, the Church, and unreformed government as they did

about the "irregular" habits of the workers. As the profit squeeze intensified in the 1820s and 1830s, entrepreneurs turned to wage cutting as a way of reducing costs.

Declining demand inhibited the incentive to invest. Even England, which had captured most of the world's colonial markets during the Napoleonic Wars, had expanded its exports to the limit. The domestic market did not look healthy either. By the 1830s England appeared to have reached the point faced by many developing countries in the twentieth century, where population growth consumed the surpluses that might otherwise have stimulated further economic development. The income of agricultural labor had stagnated and perhaps declined since the 1790s. Now higher paid factory and domestic workers were beginning to see their wages reduced. Real income actually dropped in the 1830s for the first time since 1700, a sign that the long period of economic growth might be ending. This was precisely what did happen during the next few years, when Europe was struck by a series of economic depressions, in the periods 1829–1835, 1838–1842, and 1846–1848. During what was called the Hungry Forties, particularly during the disastrous slump of 1841–1842, the English cotton industry suffered a series of almost catastrophic shocks. German and French observers were grateful that their countries were not so heavily dependent on industry. In England itself economic crisis provoked a general reaction against industrialism. There was a strong back to the land movement, promoted partly by conservative interests but also encouraged by radicals such as Feargus O'Connor who saw no future in industry.

As it turned out, these same crises were crucial in consolidating the position of the factory system. Once again, necessity proved the mother of invention. We will have a chance to examine this process in detail in Chapter 7, but for the moment it is important to keep in mind that the crucible of this extraordinary industrial change was social and economic chaos. Unlike later depressions that have plagued developed capitalist countries, this one took place within a society that was seesawing between tradition and modernity, without a clear sense of direction or of its political capacity to control change. No wonder, then, the common people were so stirred by apocalyptic faiths that swung wildly between predictions of doom and fervent expressions of hope. The 1830s and 1840s in particular produced a flock of prophets and a series of social experiments that looked both forward and backward for sources of salvation.

Population pressures, declining real income, and unemployment all contributed to a contemporary fascination with disaster and disease. The cholera epidemic of 1832, which took 18,402 lives in Paris alone, was received with the darkest premonitions as evidence of a fatally sick society. Disease, violence, and political upheaval seemed closely related contagions. Paris experienced a worker revolt immediately after cholera assailed the city. The poor turned not only against the rich but also against one another; there were rumors of poisonings and murders, and the slums became jungles in which residents preyed upon one another. To the Parisian banker, Casimir Perier, moral foundations appeared to have been undermined: "This is not the thinking of civilized people. It is a race of savages." Another Frenchman, Alexis de Tocqueville, voiced the same conclusion after visiting Europe's premier industrial city, Manchester: "Civilization works its miracles and civilized man is turned back almost into a savage."

Tocqueville was better able than most to grasp the contradictory character of this period. It was one in which some could proclaim the dawn of unprecedented material expansion while their neighbors lived in daily terror of starvation and disease. Yet to understand economic development and the capitalist form it took, we must understand the context of crisis in which it occurred. It is well to keep in mind that as late as the 1840s industrialization was still viewed by most contemporaries as problematical rather than inevitable. The term "industrial," meaning a mechanical process, was just beginning to be understood as different from the older word "industrious," referring to the application of human energy. During the recurring economic crises of the late eighteenth and early nineteenth centuries, the problem was conceived to be one of finding ways of making people more productive. This was the challenge, given urgency by massive population growth, that dominated from 1770 to 1870, just as it dominates developing countries today. What makes Europe unique is that it had no blueprint to follow. Even if it had, it is doubtful that its political structures would have been able to impose a five-year plan, or similar solution. Europe's response had no precedent and thus was fraught with many pitfalls that latecomers, with benefit of hindsight, may try to avoid. Europe's response involved the creation of a fundamentally new system of production that would not only change the course of European economic and social history but that would shape the future of the world as well.

3

Collapse of the Old Regime: State, Society, and Culture in the 1770s and 1780s

The eighteenth century began with one of the longest periods of domestic peace in European history. No significant social upheaval disturbed western Europe from 1700 to the 1770s. However, a series of disturbances began then that did not abate until some seventy years later. The first signs of unrest came in 1773, when British colonists in Boston attacked tea ships to protest rising taxation. At Lexington, two years later, sporadic rioting gave way to armed revolt that did not end until British rule was destroyed in 1783. The American War of Independence had repercussions in both Britain and continental Europe; it was one of the causes of the Gordon Riots, a week of insurrection in 1780 that saw the British monarchy lose control of London.

In 1782 uprisings in Geneva, Switzerland, and Holland paralleled the American revolt. In Geneva, mainly the shopkeepers and artisans attempted to overthrow the rule of the wealthy oligarchs of that city. The Dutch revolt aimed at reducing the power of the *Stadthouder*, William V of Orange. It was more complicated than the Genevan revolt in origin, but drew support from similar strata of society. Further riots took place in Utrecht in 1785 and in Amsterdam in 1786.

Somewhat earlier France experienced another kind of upheaval, the so-called Flour War of 1775, which fears of dearth had provoked among a swollen population reacting to the high price of grain. Again it was the *menu peuple*, the "little people," those small-property holders, artisans, and shopkeepers who were not rich but at the same time were not part of the wage-earning poor, who participated in scenes such as the following. A bookseller named Hardy is describing Paris in May 1775:

> Unrest spread quickly through the city centre and the suburbs; most tradesmen closed their shops, warned by people who were rushing about the streets urging citizens to take this precaution. The mob attempted to ransack the Corn Market and tear open all the sacks of flour; but fortunately they were unable to achieve their object; they made up for it by visiting all the markets and forcing bakers to hand over their bread, as well as private individuals who happened to have some in store. . . .

Rumors of hoarding or, worse, profiteering produced in many countries, including both France and England, a rash of bread riots in the 1770s and 1780s. In turn, civil disorder agitated the imagination of the populace, for whom all disturbances, foreign or domestic, had prophetic meaning. William Blake expressed a popular expectation of apocalypse in the poem "America a Prophecy," writing of the spirit of rebellion that seemed to be spreading from America through all parts of Europe:

> Stiff shudderings shook the heav'nly thrones! France, Spain, & Italy
> In terror view'd the bands of Albion, and the ancient Guardians,
> Fainting upon the elements, smitten with their own plagues.
> They slow advance to shut the five gates of their law-built heaven,
> Filled with blasting fancies and with mildrews of despair,
> With fierce disease and lust, unable to stem the fires of Orc
> But the five gates were consum'd, & their bolts and hinges melted;
> And the fierce flames burnt round the heavens, & round the abodes
> of men.

Europe was a society accustomed to thinking of war, famine, and civil strife in metaphorical terms of contagion. Therefore, to many the events of the last quarter of the eighteenth century seemed to signify not just the upset of particular regimes, but also symptoms of the agonizing death of an entire civilization. However, Blake and other prophets worked within a Christian apocalyptic tradition in which death was not the end but the beginning. Hellfire imagery blended with symbols of rebirth and regeneration. Blake's close friend, Richard Price, wrote: "May we not see there the dawning of right on earth, and a new creation rising?"

The excited climate that existed from the 1770s onward explains why each successive upheaval, beginning in France in 1789 and ending with the Revolutions of 1848–1849, was greeted with such cosmic hopes and fears. Yet probably no European who lived through the period, including the poet-prophets themselves, had any real premonition of the nature of the changes that lay ahead. In the eighteenth century, the word "revolution" still meant simply a return to some previous condition. Europeans using the word before 1789 meant the restoration of some golden age, not the shattering break with the past that revolution became associated with once the cataclysmic events of 1789–1848 began to unfold.

Growing Popular Unrest

Nothing in the upheavals of 1770–1789 would have foretold the future, for the dimensions of domestic and international conflict still corresponded to the traditional definition of revolution. Yet, with the benefit of hindsight, it is possible to detect substantial change taking place in parts of the Western world. From the eastern seaboard of the American Colonies to the faltering Kingdom of Poland, a process was under way that, whether it ultimately took the path of peaceful reform or turned toward violent upheaval, would transform the body politic beyond recognition. Everywhere demands were being placed on governments to which they would be unable to respond, because of their lack of specialized, autonomous central institutions. As a result of their former colonial status, many of today's new states begin with relatively centralized modern political institutions. These possess an autonomy and strength that allow them to impose solutions on the much more archaic societies over which they preside. But Europe's old regimes, where political institutions still were tied to localized, particularistic social norms, had difficulty in mobilizing strength for true national purposes.

We have seen how the old regimes relied on the exclusion of popular participation. In a society where people felt strongly attached to their local clan or community and resented intrusions from the outside, whether by foreign invaders or state officials, this exclusion worked reasonably well. But society was rapidly changing at the end of the eighteenth century; as the emergence of nationwide economic markets and the growth of communication networks altered the needs of the population, they made new demands on the central state. Mobilization of the greater numbers of persons demanding a say in public affairs came from two sources: (1) new groups, such as the commercial and bureaucratic bourgeoisie, who had no place in the old local and corporate hierarchies and who, therefore, sought new means of affecting state policy; and (2) older groups, such as the peasants and artisans, who, upon finding their old position undermined, also mobilized to exert pressure on the centers of power.

With few exceptions, the old regimes were ill equipped to deal with these new demands, not because monarchs initially lacked the will to meet the needs of their people, but rather because the level of institutional development that characterized most of the eighteenth-century states was inadequate to sustain new functions and higher levels of popular involvement. The close connection between state and society and the lack of distinction between public and private functions made it difficult for monarchs to divorce themselves from the old social order in order to meet the needs of the new.

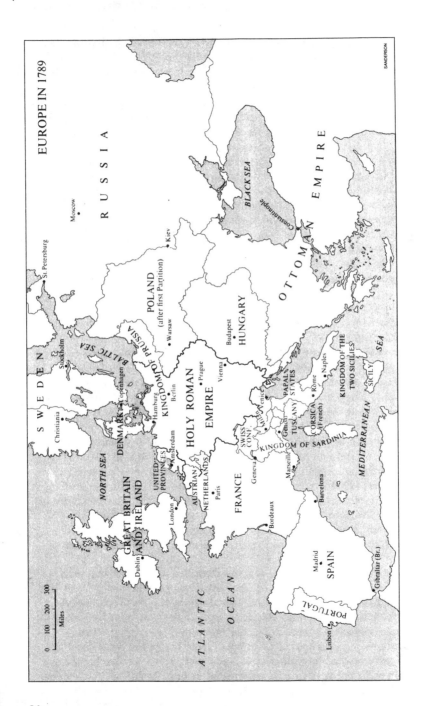

EUROPE IN 1789

SANDERSON

RUSSIA

Moscow

St. Petersburg

POLAND
(after first Partition)

Kiev

BLACK SEA

Constantinople

OTTOMAN EMPIRE

SWEDEN

Stockholm

Christiania

BALTIC SEA

Warsaw

KINGDOM OF PRUSSIA

Budapest

HUNGARY

NORTH SEA

Copenhagen

DENMARK

Hamburg

Berlin

HOLY ROMAN
EMPIRE

Prague

Vienna

SEA

KINGDOM OF THE
TWO SICILIES

SICILY

Naples

PAPAL
STATES

Rome

GREAT BRITAIN
AND IRELAND

UNITED
PROVINCES

Amsterdam

AUSTRIAN
NETHERLANDS

London

Paris

FRANCE

Dublin

Bordeaux

Geneva

SWISS
CONF.

KINGDOM OF SARDINIA

Marseille

Genoa

TUSCANY

CORSICA
(French)

Venice

MEDITERRANEAN

Barcelona

ATLANTIC

OCEAN

Madrid

SPAIN

PORTUGAL

Lisbon

Gibraltar (Br.)

Miles
0 100 200 300

50

The civil and military elites also lacked the kind of flexibility and autonomy that would have allowed smooth adjustment to the needs of a new society, and thus their legitimacy tended to be called into question, along with that of the states they served.

A crisis of political stability ensued in the 1770s that did not end until the 1850s, when a new set of national institutions capable of meeting new needs and sustaining new levels of mass participation came into being. Jean-Jacques Rousseau, one of the few eighteenth-century thinkers to understand the real dimensions of the problem, saw that the remedy lay not simply in reform but in the creation of an entirely new relationship between state and society as well. According to his *Social Contract*, the state would have to sever its old vertical ties with the privileged orders and create a body of equal citizens, "a form of association which will defend and protect with the whole common force the person and goods of each associate, and in which each, while uniting himself with all, may still obey himself alone and remain free as before."

Ironically, rising popular expectations concerning governmental capacity resulted largely from the old regimes' own efforts to extend and strengthen their traditional form of legitimacy. Perhaps the most serious contradiction in the development of monarchy was its encouragement of demographic and economic growth, a process whose ultimate implications were largely unforeseen by those who directed policy. Traditional political doctrine held that the strength of a state depended on its wealth and population; as population seemed to be stagnating in some states in the early eighteenth century, monarchs in some central European countries launched campaigns to encourage immigration. Other states, afraid of losing population, liberalized their marriage laws to promote fertility.

Official policy also supported economic growth through state subsidies to industry and the encouragement of commercial enterprise. State policy had contributed as much as other factors to the long period of mild inflation that had begun in the early eighteenth century. Liberal fiscal policy had increased the money supply, a process that helped keep prices running ahead of wages and thus brought profits to those who had money to invest in the agricultural sector, in trade, or in the various infant manufacturing processes. The chief beneficiaries were, of course, the well-to-do, but the prosperity had been sufficiently distributed as to encourage initial optimism among a large part of the population.

Based on past experience, economic growth was supposed to benefit monarchy. In theory at least, government was equipped with sufficient instruments of economic control, including the ability to set maximum prices on staple foods such as meat and grain, to regulate local markets, and to control employment and settlement, thus protecting the common good against exploitation for personal profit. However, rural and urban entrepreneurs were finding ways to escape regulations on excessive profit by circumventing the controlled markets where prices were fixed by magistrates. Prior to the eighteenth century the sale of grain was strictly localized. Market regulations permitted the poorer inhabitants to buy their share of grain or other necessities before it was offered up for sale to outsiders. The mechanism of the fair price was now breaking down because nonlocal merchants, concerned with national and even international markets, had learned how to corner the supply of food even before it reached the local marketplace. Large-scale jobbers bought up crops before the harvest, and the price of grain was left to find a level subject to the processes of supply and demand that were beyond the locality's ability to control.

The beneficiaries of the new market mechanisms defended them as both more efficient and more equitable than the old locally controlled economies, but this hardly pacified the poor who could no longer purchase their food in the familiar way and were forced to turn to retailers, whose prices fluctuated in a manner that was as mysterious as it was unpredictable. The response of both the poor and those local officials whose vision of paternalistic government also opposed the free market mechanism was to demand tighter state controls over the economy. Their protestations increased after 1770, when poor harvests, combined with even poorer transportation, caused sudden, periodic rises in the cost of flour and bread. It was not uncommon for the price to increase 300 percent in the short term, a rise that drove the poor, for whom the cost of bread normally amounted to as much as one-half their income, to desperation.

In a society where one-third to one-half of the entire population lived constantly at the margin of subsistence, without any possibility of savings and often in debt, it is easy to see why rising prices led directly to popular demands for government intervention. So reported one royal official from Chartres in July of 1788, just before the harvest, at a time when supply was short and prices highest:

> The general temper of the populace at the moment is so highly charged that considering its present pressing needs it may well feel itself authorized to ease its poverty as soon as the harvest begins. They may seek more than the gleanings, their usual part—driven to the last extremity by high prices and shortages, they may well say: Make amends for our past misery; let us share and share alike when things are short; fill our bellies. . . . An eruption from the people could be as bad as a hail storm. Dire necessity considers neither what is right nor what is reasonable.

Reports of beggars or brigands in a neighborhood were often enough to arouse panic. During the summer of 1788, the situation was so bad that an official report stated that "requests for troops to guard the harvest are coming from all parts of Picardy." Similar extraordinary demands were heard throughout Europe in the 1780s, wherever population pressed severely on food supply. Fear of famine stalked the general population. Merchants and officials did their best to reassure the people, but tales of earlier disasters remained vivid in the popular imagination. There was a strong tendency, consonant with the concept of the limited good, to withdraw into extreme localism in times of crisis. The circumstances in France turned village against village and town against countryside, as had happened previously in the so-called Flour War of 1775. During this most serious outburst of violence in France before 1789, the poor and their allies among the local officials and gentry had turned their wrath on the urban merchant manipulators of the new market economy, hijacking grain wagons, threatening bakers, and breaking milling machines. "Down with Prices, Long Live the King!" shouted the peasant foot soldiers of the Flour War, a cry of desperate expectation that was echoed in every part of Europe. In England, eighteenth-century bread rioters used the traditions of popular justice to gain what they believed was due them under the ancient law of the fair price. The Sheriff of Gloucestershire wrote to his superiors in 1766:

> They visited Farmers, Millers, Bakers and Hucksters shops, selling corn, flour, bread, cheese, butter and bacon, at their own prices. They returned in general the produce [i.e. the money from the sale] to the proprietors or in their absence left the money for them; and behaved with great regularity and decency where they were not opposed, with outrage and violence where they were; they pilfered very little, which to prevent, they will not now suffer Women and boys to go with them.

Such crowds felt they were enforcing rather than violating the law. They often enlisted the help of local authorities in setting a fair price, shouting "God Save the King" when the job was properly done. Clearly, these Europeans had little faith in Adam Smith's assertion that in a free-market economy supply and demand, if left to themselves, would produce an abundance unimaginable under the old, controlled economy. Of course, they had good reason to distrust those merchants who, behind the façade of free-market mechanisms, were able to reap quick profits by manipulating supply. These jobbers had the best of two worlds—access to control where this was profitable, and freedom from control where this suited their purpose. In their infancy the new national markets offered considerable opportunity for the most obvious kinds of exploitation, thereby justifying the flood of consumer protests and insurrections that occurred during the last third of the eighteenth century.

Reform before 1789

Under the old regimes, paternalistic monarchy, buttressed by the theory of the divine character of kingship, had propagated the fiction of power to provide for general welfare. Now it was failing to deliver on that promise. The poor were encouraged to look to the monarchy for redress of grievances in the same way children are taught to rely on their fathers. The poor expected much from royal administration but governmental services, instead of improving, stalemated and even declined. This was most evident in times of war—1740-1748, 1756-1763, 1776-1783—when the state was put to the ultimate test both externally and internally. Standing armies had been kept at levels equal to 1 percent of the population. Now it cost governments much more to maintain this. Only England, whose defense required a navy but no army, escaped this dilemma.

France, by contrast, found its capacity constantly strained by military expenditure, a cycle of war, financial crisis, and social conflict that escalated over the course of the eighteenth century. France had an inadequate financial system based on a discriminatory land tax, the *taille,* that fell mainly on the peasantry because it allowed extensive exemptions to the nobility and the propertied bourgeoisie. The Catholic Church, which had traditionally made a voluntary contribution to the state, was not paying its fair share of revenue.

In 1748 the monarchy attempted to equalize the burden by introducing an income tax for all persons, but strong resistance by the provincial *parlements* (courts dominated by nobles) and the provincial Estates (assemblies made up of the three caste orders—clergy, nobility, and everyone else) caused Louis XV to rescind his efforts. The Seven Years' War, 1756-1763, renewed the financial crisis, and on this occasion the king moved decisively to replace the recalcitrant *parlements* and to make his peace with the Estates. This act of reconciliation with the privileged interests solidified his regime temporarily but failed to solve the budget deficit. The monarch embarked on a new approach, appointing as his chief minister Turgot, a popular progressive thinker whose solution to France's problem was to increase its agrarian and commercial capacity, thus producing more taxable income and softening the blow of future financial reform.

Prosperity was to be won, however, by the introduction of freedom of trade, both in commodities and in occupations. Guild privileges were abolished and a national free market in grain was allowed to operate. These measures were bound to produce popular discontent, which privileged interests emphasized when in 1776 Turgot proposed an equalization of taxation. Another rebellion in the *parlements* and the provincial Estates took place, and Turgot was forced to leave office, reforms unfinished.

France's contribution to the American War of Independence worsened the crisis of the budget; by 1786 France's financial situation was so desperate that Calonne, the new prime minister, drew up plans for the abolition of tax exemptions and even the confiscation of Church lands. Going still further, he proposed new representative institutions that would substitute for the old Estates a broader representation of propertied interests. He tried to legitimize his reforms by calling a special Assembly of Notables in 1788. The assembly failed to reach a compromise between the interests of the king and the privileged Estates, and Calonne was replaced by Lomenie de Brienne, who tried the earlier tactic of breaking aristocratic opposition by abolishing the *parlements*. Rioting broke out with the announcement of abolition; all over France the nobles organized popular defense of their privileges and roused the lower orders of village and town with a campaign of antimonarchical propaganda that at times seemed to take on the attributes of radical republicanism, which favored the elimination of monarchy.

Faced with the almost total breakdown of governmental services, the monarchy moved to compromise, and on June 5, 1788, it agreed to call into session the long-discontinued national assembly of Estates, the so-called Estates General, to discuss tax reform. Every rank of the French people greeted the announcement with almost universal enthusiasm. The three Estates—the clergy, nobles, and Third Estate (all the rest of the population)—would elect their representatives by May 1789, sending them together with petitions of grievance (*cahiers de doléances*) to Versailles to discuss reform. What appeared a great triumph for the aristocracy and their allies among the clergy struck observers, not as the beginning, but as the end of a revolution—the reassertion of ancient privileges, a step back from the previous thrust of centralization, and thus a triumph for localism, even feudalism.

Similar confrontations between the centralizing and universalizing powers of the state and the entrenched particularistic interests of society were developing in almost every European country by the end of the eighteenth century. The Hapsburg Emperor Joseph II had attempted thoroughgoing reform that included the abolition of the legal privileges of the nobility, the reduction of the Church to dependence on the state, and the abolition of serfdom. While certain of these changes remained in effect after his death in 1790, they provoked a storm of protest, culminating in revolt against reform in both the Hungarian and Belgian provinces of the Empire. Resistance by Magyar landowners and Netherland burghers proved too much for the instrument of central power, the bureaucracy, and by 1792 the Hapsburg monarchs were turning their backs on reform, the state becoming one of the most reactionary in central Europe.

Frederick the Great encountered no similar rebellion in his efforts to build the strength of the Prussian state, but the limits of his achievements also were apparent at the end of his forty-six-year reign in 1786. He had continued to build upon the Hohenzollern tradition of a strong army and bureaucracy; he had abolished serfdom on royal domains and had laid the groundwork for the rationalization of Prussian law. But after his death the pace of centralization faltered, for his successors were unequal to the task of further reform, and the bureaucracy lacked the momentum to carry through change against royal apathy. A decade later, the Prussian state, former model of enlightened absolutism, was ruled by a stifling, obscurantist regime, whose foreign and domestic policies showed little of the thrust of Frederick the Great's reforms.

In Russia, too, absolutism had reached its limits. The reign of Catherine the Great had begun in 1762 with the promise of matching the greatest achievements of Western enlightened monarchs. She seemed determined to subordinate the aristocracy to the state, harnessing this group as civil and military officials to progressive reforms. But the vast Pugachev uprising of 1773–1774 demonstrated the difficulty of dispensing with the traditional alliance of throne and nobility. Pugachev, himself a peasant, recruited enslaved workers of the Ural mines, as well as serfs from the Volga region, to mount a powerful threat to the regime. He proclaimed himself the "true Czar" and in his cause activated native peasant millennialism, which expected rapid and total change. Only with great difficulty was the rebellion defeated. Famine decimated his armies and Pugachev was brought to the capital in an iron cage for trial and execution. So ended one of the most extensive social movements of the eighteenth century, with the aristocracy being rewarded draconian powers that made Russian serfdom even more like chattel slavery than it had been earlier in the century. Instead of becoming a new aristocracy of service dependent on the state, the Russian provincial nobility became more powerful and more independent than before, effectively terminating the progress of centralization in Russia after the reign of Catherine the Great.

Even England was not an exception to this pattern of reaction, although there the limitations of the absolutism of parliament rather than of the king were demonstrated in the late eighteenth century. The American rebellion was a response to the extension of parliamentary power. The American cause raised the cry of liberty in England itself, and when the Gordon Riots broke out in London in 1780, popular resentment against central power reached its height. The rioters attacked the Bank of England and abused royalty. But they also demanded the repeal of Catholic toleration legislation and showed the less attractive side of opposition to the universalizing and equalizing tendencies of the state through their fierce bigotry. Similar resistance effectively forced George III to grant an Irish Parliament in 1782, a further setback for centralization in Britain.

The Failure of Enlightened Absolutism

Absolutism, whether monarchical or parliamentary, had produced contradictions that checked, or even reversed, the thrust of centralization. The old regimes attempted to fulfill the goals of a modern nation-state without providing the instruments required of such a political system. In particular, they lacked the separation of social and political functions necessary for effective central rule. Had absolute monarchy been able to develop an autonomous professional bureaucracy, it might have freed itself from reliance on localized, reactionary social interests. However, officialdom attempted to enhance its power through reliance on these same privileged social orders, a policy that was bound to be contradictory. In France, England, Austria, and to a lesser extent Prussia, monarchy had relied on the status and influence of the aristocracy, only to find that this ultimately worked to its disadvantage.

Even in Prussia, where the Hohenzollerns had attempted to create an independent civil service that could serve only royal interest, this elite tended to emulate the old nobility and view itself as an aristocracy of service, thus making it, too, an unreliable instrument of further onslaught against privilege. In France the sale of offices, an arrangement designed originally to overcome the tyranny of birth and to open up the bureaucracy to the talents of rich nonnobles, also created a new kind of aristocracy the so-called nobles of the robe. Although the notion of merit examinations had been introduced in some places, the growth of university education was not sufficiently great to promote the kind of competition that would have freed service from birth and privilege. Even where there was a surplus of educated persons, as in Prussia, the resistance of older officials to the new concept of merit sufficed to prevent further professionalization.

In the absence of an independent bureaucracy, monarchs had no alternative source of authority to which they could appeal above the heads of entrenched interest groups. No developed political parties, no organized mass movements existed to break the deadlock between state and society, and social and economic changes were moving too slowly to offset the power of traditional elites. The press was in its infancy and the reading public was small. Instead of creating independent pressure groups that might have challenged old interests, most persons of talent, including many of real vision, tended to enter state employment, thereby becoming entangled in its elaborate inertia. On the eve of 1789, the successful member of the French bourgeoisie was more likely to invest money in a state office than to reinvest it in business. In Prussia the frock coat of the civil servant was to the ordinary burgher what the officer's uniform was to the nobility. Even in England, it was rare for merchant families to remain in trade for more than two generations. The attractions of country living and gentry status were too strong for all except those religious dissenters, like the Quakers, whose religious scruples kept them from emulating the old nobility.

The peasantry and lower orders of the towns possessed no mass organizations that the state might have appealed to above the heads of vested interest. The peasantry remained indifferent to the central state except when its interventions disrupted their traditional way of life, their faith in royal authority more like religious belief than active political creed. In the decade before 1789, popular sentiment in most European towns and cities was more likely to be on the side of the aristocracy than of centralization. This was not so much because the urban *menu peuple* rejected state action, but rather that they feared the economic accompaniment of centralization, namely, freedom of trade. Artisans and shopkeepers were no less committed to localism than were the peasantry.

The new states in Africa and Asia in the twentieth century often experience a similar gap between central and local interests, but their executive and legislative institutions, inherited from previous colonial regimes, have usually acquired a degree of autonomy and strength that allows them to dominate particularistic regional and social interests. Furthermore, these governments are able to use modern means of communication, such as radio and television, to appeal directly to the population at large, whatever their degree of literacy. European governments in the eighteenth century lacked not only the instruments but the concept of popular propaganda. European rulers had to rely on the written word for a population that was less than half literate (literacy may have been as high as 50 percent in England, as low as 15 percent in parts of central Europe).

The literate elites placed themselves between the state and the people, making direct appeal nearly impossible. The very notion of appeal to the people was impossible in any case, because the concept of "the people" was unheard of. The ancient legend of the "good king" could sometimes mobilize the peasants, as in the case of the Pugachev rebellion, but the urbane monarchs of the 1780s were not comfortable with this usage. They, like the aristocracy, continued to regard the general population as docile subjects rather than as active citizens, a position consistent with the heritage of European monarchy but inimical to the solution of the crown's most pressing problems. As post-1789 political development would demonstrate, the notion of "the people" was essential to the creation of strong nation-states, whether authoritarian or democratic.

The Intellectual Opposition

The concept of public opinion as an independent source of authority as yet had no place. Classical political theory, a legacy of the ancient world that had been revived in the Renaissance and modified by Christian tradition, made no provision for any court of appeal apart from the monarch. Despite some modern features, classical theory made no distinction between the individual and the state, nor, for that matter, between the state and society. Rights were, therefore, derived directly from the state itself, and in theory there was no other source of authority. This, however, did not mean that the rights of individuals in the old regimes were immaterial or that persons were directly subject to the arbitrary power of the state. On the contrary, the definition of freedoms was often much more inclusive, and the personal autonomy from central state control much greater than now. For example, the merchant who possessed the Freedom of London was accorded a range of rights that included not only a voice in city government, but also special settlement and trade privileges. An Austrian noble's rights often included wide immunity from common law, including the right to hunt over peasant land without fear of damage suits, the right to avoid certain taxes, and the right to be exempt from ordinary conscription.

What traditional Europeans meant by "rights," we would call "special privilege." These were particular to the person or group and could be bought or inherited, but they were in no way inherent universal human rights as we know them. Rights were derived from and attached to particular status and function. In theory at least, for each right there was a duty. Nobles were to fight, clergy to pray, peasants to work the fields—legal fictions that in the eighteenth century were becoming more difficult to justify because political and economic changes were displacing some old status groups and introducing new ones. The Prussian General Code of 1794 attempted to balance the old Estates (aristocracy, clergy, burghers, and peasantry) with the new professional orders (bureaucracy and military) to produce a more up-to-date constitution of privilege. The English managed to keep their rather simple distinction between Lords and Commons, but not because the latter was actually representative of all non-nobles. In reality, Commons was almost as subject to aristocratic influence as was Lords. The fiction that bodies such as the English Houses of Parliament or the French Estates General were representative of the interests of the commonwealth was increasingly difficult to maintain. Before being called into session in 1788, the Estates General had not met since 1648, and during the intervening period new groups had emerged that made the old division into three Estates (clergy, nobility, and everyone else) quite archaic.

Nevertheless, disputes over rights and representation did not really threaten the legitimacy of the political system until 1789. Montesquieu in France and Justus Möser in Germany might speak out for the rights of individuals against the growing power of the monarchy and argue for a balance of powers between legislature and executive, but they were conservatives defending the traditional constitution against what they regarded as inroads by the absolute state. When the "liberals" of the day, like Voltaire and Diderot, entered the fray, they did so mainly in support of what they felt to be the progressive tendencies of enlightened absolutism. Their enemies were the entrenched local interests, particularly the Church, which censored their books and thus inhibited their wish to earn their living as "men of letters."

As a youth, Voltaire had spent eleven months in the Paris prison, the Bastille, because he had dared to argue with a noble. Yet we must not imagine that he or any of his literary circle wished to overthrow the nobility. Though his career had begun poorly, Voltaire had done very well for himself. As royal historian, he wrote in praise of absolutism in the monumental *Age of Louis XIV.* He was also a confidant of Frederick the Great of Prussia, with whom he lived in Potsdam for two years. Likewise, Diderot, Claude Helvétius and Jean D'Alembert were lionized in the salon world of eighteenth-century Paris. There they had access to men and women of enormous wealth and influence and, with an abundance of patronage, grew wealthy. Although these older *philosophes* continued to fight for religious tolerance and to protest against royal censorship, they became a kind of "priesthood of high culture," absolute arbiters of taste in the last years of the Old Regime.

This senior generation of the period known as the Enlightenment established its position within society, not in opposition to it. Their great achievement, the *Encyclopedia*, published in installments from 1751 to 1772, was a work of great practical didactic value. It carried within it articles that urged reform but that did not take an openly oppositional stance. The sociology of the eighteenth-century men of letters precluded their becoming an independent source of public opinion, speaking for society against the state. They were not journalists. Writing for a living was demeaning to the genteel status to which the *philosophes* aspired.

In both France and England there was a body of popular writers, called by Alexander Pope "scribblers," who can be regarded as the forerunners of the alienated intellectuals of the nineteenth century. However, these writers had no professional identity comparable to that of modern intellectuals and certainly no status equal to that of the established men of letters. Magazines and reviews (Joseph Addison's pioneering *Spectator* began in 1711) were still in their infancy; even where newspapers were tolerated, primarily in England, average circulation was not more than five thousand copies per issue. Edmund Burke estimated the active English reading public to be no more than eighty thousand persons, and this was large by European standards. Living by one's wits, writing tracts for anyone willing to pay the price, as young Jacques-Pierre Brissot and Jean Paul Marat did in Paris during the 1770s, was not conducive to the formation of an articulate, independent critique of society.

What intellectual opposition existed in the eighteenth century centered on the eccentric figure of Jean-Jacques Rousseau (1712–1778). He was perhaps the only one among the older *philosophes* who broke the mold of the traditional man of letters and, with it, the limits of traditional social and political thought. Rousseau, whose pedagogical writings in *Emile* and *La Nouvelle Héloïse* were to lay the foundations of modern child care and pedagogy, was the product of an unhappy childhood, a runaway at the age of sixteen, who during his entire life was never able to adjust to the demands of social convention.

Yet in many ways Rousseau was quite conservative. While he exposed the injustice of inequality among human beings, he defended the patriarchal family and defined the woman's role as strictly that of wife and mother, thus creating a cult of domesticity that was to have enormous influence in the nineteenth century. He was able to convince future generations that both women and children were closer to nature, that they were more moral and spiritual than men, but also less intelligent and capable. The woman's place was in the home as conservator of moral values. "The appeal of the domestic life is the best counter-poison to bad morals," he wrote. "When the family is lively and animated, the domestic cares are the dearest occupation of the wife, and the most delightful entertainment of the husband."

A consistent theme in all of Rousseau's work was the distrust of the demands civilization made on the individual human being, who, in his view, possessed inherent qualities of goodness and moral self-direction. In the *Origins of Inequality among Men* published in 1753, Rousseau argued, contrary to the whole canon of classical liberal and conservative political theory, that man had been a better being before the imposition of civilization. Although Rousseau wished no return to the precivilized state of nature per se, he insisted that the qualities with which the individual was born should be nurtured rather than repressed. The task of both parents and society was, therefore, to construct institutions that would encourage the growth of moral character, for it was through spiritual regeneration that political and social reconstruction was to be achieved.

Although his central political work, the *Social Contract,* published in 1762, was virtually ignored in his own lifetime, in it Rousseau had come to terms with the central problem emerging from political development in the eighteenth century. Europe had reached the point where the traditional fiction of legitimacy, namely, that at some previous time the people had sworn obedience to their rulers in exchange for security and protection of property, could no longer be maintained. Property owners could still identify their interests with those of the state, but the growing body of persons without property could no longer feel the same. In order that their interests be served, a new social contract was necessary, which this time would not be a contract drawn between the people and their rulers, but among the people themselves. The result would be what Rousseau called the General Will, a consensus that would provide a new basis for legitimacy for the state and a new definition of rights for society.

Here, for the first time, was a revolutionary notion of equal citizenship and the concept of a public opinion that would be a court of appeal against the unjust actions of the state. It also made possible the emancipation of the state from the hereditary and localized interests of society by introducing the notion of separation of social and political functions. Society, through the social contract, granted the state its autonomy in return for the state's recognition of the innate natural rights of the individual. In short, Rousseau offered a way to break the stalemated relationship between state and society, a relationship that was becoming critical in the 1770s and 1780s.

Millenarian Undercurrents

Rousseau was bold enough to suggest that men (if not women) were their own source of authority. Before this, the source of legitimization had been located either in a religious conception of divine will or in the classical notion of natural law. On this point liberal Voltaire and his conservative enemies among the clergy were in agreement: models of perfection existed on some higher plane than humanity itself. Rousseau's belief in the inner sources of goodness, which he identified as much with emotion as with reason because feelings were closer to the core of personality, represented a more unqualified acceptance of the self than anything that had gone before. Not surprisingly, the implications of Rousseau's social and political beliefs were scarcely explored in public when he died in 1778.

Romanticism, the movement of ideas most closely associated with his name in his own day, was largely concerned with Rousseau's cultural and psychological observations and not with the more revolutionary implications of his politics. Rousseau's censure of the restraints imposed by civilization inspired a pastoral revival in France and the cult of the natural and the primitive in Germany. Goethe, Schiller, and other young leaders of the early romantic movement made the exploration of the feelings their central mission. Because youth was identified with deep, strong emotions, romanticism made of it a kind of cult. Goethe's *Young Werther* exalted adolescent passions and inspired youth to adopt a natural, unconventional style of dress and manners, which we identify with romantic rebelliousness. But while cultural revolt became fashionable in the 1780s, the deeper political implications of the shift from external to internal sources of authority did not become apparent until 1789.

Rousseau's emphasis on the inner sources of illumination also reinforced the tide of mystical religiosity that was flowing swiftly in Europe from the mid-eighteenth century onward, apparent not only in sectarian Christianity such as English Methodism and German Pietism but also in the occult practices carried within the influential Freemasonry movement. After 1770 Freemasonry took a distinctly spiritualist direction under the influence of Adam Weishaupt's *illuminati* movement, which blended rationalism with occult rituals. In Protestant countries the new mysticism, with its emphasis on the personal sources of divine inspiration, usually retained a Christian orientation, but in Catholic areas, where any kind of sectarian deviation was persecuted by the regular church, it was often forced to take an anticlerical, even anti-Christian orientation. The Catholic Church was attacked not for its spiritual qualities, but for its lack of them. Those seeking a more personalized, less ritualistic faith turned away from the established religions in both Catholic and Protestant countries. Voltaire's offensive against superstition and bigotry had succeeded all too well.

In an effort to divest itself of survivals of folk religion, the urbane Church hierarchy had virtually emptied religion of its spiritual content. In some places the campaign of "enlightened" clergy seemed intent on dismantling the apparatus of established religion itself. Hostility to the Jesuit Order resulted in the expulsion of that group from most countries, and in 1773 the pope himself declared the Jesuits disbanded. But while purging archaic elements, the clergy had put nothing in their place. The void was most strongly felt by the parish clergy, who in trying to find ways to deal with the needs of the faithful had become deeply resentful of the cynical ways of the high-living bishops and abbots, some of whom were declared atheists.

Given the spiritual deficiencies of Enlightenment religion, it is easy to understand why popular religiosity increasingly broke the bounds of the established churches from the 1770s onward, often becoming indistinguishable from the powerful undertow of occult, pagan, and spiritualist subcultures that were appearing at the end of the eighteenth century. Among the educated classes, newly discovered sources of primitive and Eastern religions caused almost as much interest as did the ancient Greeks and Romans, who inspired the eighteenth-century neoclassical revival. French and English men of letters, fascinated by accounts of North American Indians, Druidic rites, and Hindu practices, pressed their search in the historical sources for faiths untainted by the corrupting influence of civilization. Methodists thought of themselves as inspired by the practice of the early Christians, and Freemasonry traced its origins to the ancient Hebrews, while William Blake found in the records of the early Britons refreshing alternatives to a civilization that he believed had grown old and corrupted. In art, pagan heroes replaced Christian saints as the subjects of popular painting.

This search for roots—a sign of Europe's growing instability—stimulated much legitimate historical scholarship but it also produced more than its share of hoaxes and forgeries. The credulous temper of the times was reflected in the audiences that innumerable prophets and seers gathered in the 1780s. In the years immediately preceding the French Revolution of 1789, the central topic of conversation in Paris was not the momentous struggle between the king and nobility, but the miracle cures of the German Mesmer and the first balloon flight in 1785. In England, too, Blake and others, calling themselves Antiquarians, were recovering the prophetic traditions of earlier centuries. The cult of the supernatural went even further in Germany. There, Goethe and his Pietist patroness, Susanne Katharine von Klettenberg, set the fashion of dabbling in alchemy, a form of spiritualism that became a passion among young Germans from the 1770s onward.

The search for purer, more personal sources of spiritual experience typified a generation of educated persons who came of age in the last quarter of the eighteenth century, who had perhaps read Rousseau or, by circumstance, identified their frustrations with the civilization that he condemned. However, few wanted to overthrow the social and cultural traditions of the older generation of rationalistic *philosophes.* Indeed, those like Goethe and Blake were passionately interested in putting their beliefs on a sound basis of reason and science. But at a time when canons of scholarship and research were not yet firmly established, the distinction between the quack and the scientist was not always clear. Medicine was particularly victimized by this confusion, but so, too, was historical scholarship. Myth blended freely with truth about the past.

In looking for past examples of the general crisis in which they now found themselves, Europeans were bound to revive the particular cyclical interpretation of history that was associated with the Judeo-Christian tradition and that contained within it the apocalyptic interpretation of natural and human events. The coming of famine or disorder was certain to be interpreted as the prelude to a broader kind of upheaval. The first indication of how strongly this view of history was establishing itself in the eighteenth century was the response to the Lisbon earthquake disaster of 1755 in which thousands perished. This event caused Voltaire's fictional Dr. Pangloss to abandon his belief in progress and withdraw from the world to cultivate his garden. On the more popular level, the disaster had produced any number of prophets of doom, who interpreted wars, bad harvests, fluctuations in prices, and government crises as a prelude to the Biblical millennium.

The Collapse of Authority

The older generation of *philosophes* might calmly tend their intellectual acres, but many, on all levels of society, were profoundly disturbed by the portents of the 1780s. In many places government was bankrupt, both fiscally and politically. In a period when state and society were still so closely interwoven, political crisis was bound to have momentous consequences. The response of many Europeans was consistent with the tradition of individual privilege and corporate immunity; they simply turned their backs on the central government as crisis deepened. As for the common people, they had no haven. With no models of political organization apart from traditional religious movements to draw on, they naturally reverted to old communal and religious forms of solidarity and self-preservation.

In the final decades of the century, the forces of privilege and localism were intensifying, even as the demands on government were increasing. This was an era of religious millennialism on a scale not seen for over a century. Men and women turned to prophets of personal spiritual salvation because there were no social movements yet able to offer an alternative. The new sectarianism of Methodism and Pietism, like the more secular variations of Freemasonry, tended not only to divert people's attention from worldly things, but also to reinforce the social and geographical boundaries characteristic of traditional Europe. Each step in this direction made it more difficult for the central states to rescue Europe from the impending crisis.

Contributing further to the internal division and loss of political will was the widespread tendency to look to the past as the source of authority. Instead of looking forward, the mood of Europe in the 1770s and 1780s was distinctly nostalgic. However, because so many of the links with the past had already been severed by economic and social change, the kind of conservatism this nostalgia represented tended to be strongly idealistic rather than practical in its orientation. The golden age of the past sought by so many Europeans contained strong elements of fantasy and wish fulfillment, elements that could easily be oriented in the direction of the future as well. Many spoke of the need for revolution, thinking only of a return of the good old days, but their words took on new meaning when the path of retreat into the golden past became blocked by contemporary crisis.

The crisis of the 1780s was a crisis of will as well as of institutions. There were no groups, bureaucracy and military included, that could provide effective leadership. All the elites lacked the level of organization and the autonomy necessary to deal with the worsening financial condition of the state. Lack of money meant still higher levels of disaffection within the ranks of government. The Gordon Riots had shown the weakness of the English State; the Hapsburg monarchy had been similarly challenged; now it was the helplessness of France, the eighteenth century's governmental giant, that fascinated observers. Revolution did not have to overthrow the Old Regime; undermined by combined demographic, social, and cultural crisis, it collapsed of its own accord.

PART TWO

TOWARD THE MODERN NATION-STATE

Today we are accustomed to thinking of revolutions as organized seizures of power, motivated by a clearly defined program of social and political transformation. Regardless of their ideological persuasion, contemporary revolutionaries usually have a clear blueprint for the industrial and political development they wish to implement. By contrast, the major European revolutions of 1789, 1830, and 1848 seem almost accidental, resulting, as they did, from the collapse of old regimes rather than from the premeditated actions of organized oppositions.

In Europe revolution erupted at the very beginning of the process of societal modernization. Therefore, revolutionaries had no very clear idea of the future society they wished to create. For them, as well as for their opponents, revolution was a learning process, out of which the outlines of the modern nation-state finally crystallized. It took European revolutionaries until 1848 to achieve a level of national organization approaching that of their Third World counterparts today. Ironically, by that time, revolution itself was no longer attractive as a vehicle for social and political change. The emergent modern nation-state, itself a product of sixty years of struggle, marked the end of Europe's age of revolution.

Chapters 4, 5, and 6 deal with the period 1789–1848 as a unified process of political development in which revolutions were the major guideposts. Chapter 4 deals with the origins of upheaval in the French Revolution; Chapter 5 assesses the effect of revolution and war on the rest of Europe. The subject of Chapter 6 is the gradual establishment of national political stability, the product of the ongoing dialectic of revolution and reaction.

4

Revolution in France, 1789–1804

Revolution is a unique historical phenomenon, relatively rare in the sweep of world history and peculiar to periods when societies are passing through the first difficult stages of modernization. It is at a time when old ideas and institutions are called into question and new ones are not yet firmly in place that this type of sudden and total societal upheaval happens with any frequency. Other, more limited, types of rebellion and coup d'état take place in almost all historical circumstances; revolution is unique in being confined to periods of epochal transition from traditional to modern society, such as had begun in Europe in the 1770s.

The political centralization that disrupted the functioning of traditional political authority did not replace it with a workable nation-state. Economic and demographic change discredited old social and economic institutions without clearly establishing the superiority of industrial production, and cultural institutions were in a similar state of turmoil, contributing to the mixed mood of hope and fear that Charles Dickens was later to describe so accurately in *Tale of Two Cities:*

> it was the best of times, it was the worst of times, it was the age of wisdom, it was the age of foolishness, it was the epoch of belief, it was the epoch of incredulity, it was the season of Light, it was the season of Darkness, it was the spring of hope, it was the winter of despair, we had everything before us, we were all going direct to Heaven, we were going direct the other way.

Of course, revolution of the type France experienced was not inevitable, nor was it the only avenue to modernization; England did not experience the revolutionary upheavals that swept through its Continental neighbor in 1789 and again in 1830 and 1848, nor was the history of revolution in Germany and Italy quite the same as in France. Despite the fact that France was in many ways exceptional, its size and influence meant that its experience would have far-reaching consequences, not only for Europe but for the entire world as well. The French Revolution's universal appeal also can be explained in the same way as the attraction of the Russian and Chinese revolutions in the twentieth century, however. As an example of one developing country's attempt to deal with societal as well as political modernization, France was bound to become a model for other developing areas in and outside Europe.

The relationship of revolution to modernization explains some of the similarities between Europe in the period 1789–1848 and the Third World today. It also accounts for the differences between Europe's sixty-year cycle of revolution and the relative brevity of revolutions today, where even the longest upheaval, the struggle for Vietnamese independence, lasted only twenty-five years. The fact that Europe's transition to modernity was so much more gradual can account for this difference. As the first of the world's regions to develop socially as well as politically, Europe inevitably proceeded more hesitantly, with a greater number of starts and stops. The alternation of revolution and reaction from 1789 to 1848 accurately reflects this overall pattern. Not until the 1840s and 1850s were the main characteristics of political and societal modernization institutionalized and it was then that Europe's long revolutionary cycle ended.

The revolutions in the Third World take place in societies that are at least partially modernized by prior contact with more developed nations. Revolutionary movements, therefore, partake of modernity and are highly organized, even militarized. Only forces equally well equipped politically and militarily can overthrow colonial or postcolonial regimes, themselves relatively highly developed. In sharp contrast, the European revolutions from 1789 to 1848 were triggered by the breakdown of the old regimes rather than their overthrow by organized insurgency. It cannot be said that the Bourbons were deliberately overthrown in 1789, for no organized political parties or revolutionary movements existed in France or anywhere else at that time. Even as late as 1848, professional revolutionaries numbered in the mere hundreds and commanded no organizational strength remotely comparable to that of the movements headed by Mao, Castro, or Kenyatta in the twentieth century. Whereas modern political organization is the precondition of successful revolution in the Third World, in Europe political development was the result of revolution rather than an initial cause. In France in 1789, aristocratic reaction brought on upheaval.

Although the European revolutions from 1789 to 1848 were to speed the pace of modernization, the revolutionaries themselves were often ambivalent toward those things, including economic and political centralization,

that we associate with a modern state and society. This first generation of revolutionaries was intensely concerned with personal and societal
revitalization; they demanded a return to a golden age or, rather, to a new
age in which the desirable elements of the old could be revived. They, no
less than their conservative opponents, were likely to be attracted to
charismatic messiahs rather than practical organizers, one of the major reasons that neither the revolutionaries nor the reactionaries of the period
1789–1848 were able to maintain themselves in power for very long. The
level of organizational strength of both revolutionary and reactionary
movements was low compared with that of modern political movements.
Their struggles were eventually to give birth to modern political institutions, but at the beginning both movements tended to revive archaic forms
of action which actually frustrated rather than fostered their own attempts
to take and hold power, a prime reason that the European cycle of revolution was so prolonged.

Coinciding with the initial stages of social and economic development,
the politics of the years 1789–1848 had its own unique character, different
not only from the politics of the old regimes but also from that of the
modern nation-state. At the same time, the decades of alternating revolution and reaction revealed a dialectic of change leading toward a highly
centralized society in which revolution would disappear. By 1848, with
the last of Europe's great revolutions, the outlines of the stable nation-
state were clearly visible. In this and the next two chapters, we examine
how revolution, as a force in Europe's political development, led to its own
extinction.

From the Estates General to the Fall of the Bastille

In 1788 the French monarchy's financial plight brought it to the point of
conceding to the demands of its most formidable enemy, the aristocracy.
The decision, in that year, to call the Estates General confirmed the triumph of privileged and provincial interests against the centralizing thrust
of monarchy. It threatened, too, to turn back the clock on more than a
century of political development that had failed to make real headway in
France's intolerable political situation. Yet the long series of disputes that
led to the 1788 decision had unforeseen repercussions by encouraging
expectations on the part of other groups frustrated by the lack of strong
effective government. The months that preceded the opening of the
Estates General in May 1789 were filled with wrangling over procedural
points and disputes over representation and voting that gradually became
issues of principle rather than of detail.

At the center of dispute was whether the three Estates (clergy, nobility,
and the Third Estate, that is, all the rest) should vote by Estate or by
individual deputy. The clergy and nobility wished to reconfirm the ancient

notion of society divided into castelike units and therefore favored vote by order rather than by head. The Third Estate strongly supported the alternative, for their numbers (doubled by royal order in January 1789) could achieve parity with the first two Estates only if the vote were by head. Pamphleteers debated this issue with increasing violence during the winter and spring of 1789, each side claiming to represent the best interests of the "nation," an assertion first injected in politics during the long struggle of the aristocratic *parlements* against the central state in the previous decades. Neither side—neither the clergy and nobility nor the Third Estate—proposed to overthrow the old order but rather to revitalize those elements of national unity whose absence was seen as the root cause of France's pitiful condition. Radical notions of liberty and equality were not yet a part of the essentially fraternal appeal that Abbé Sieyès made in behalf of the Third Estate:

> What is the Third Estate? Everything. What has it been until now? Nothing. What does it ask? To be something.
>
> Who would dare to deny that the Third Estate has within itself all that is necessary to constitute a nation? . . . Take away the privileged orders, and the nation is not smaller, but greater. What would the Third Estate be without the privileged order? A whole by itself, and a prosperous whole. Nothing can go on without it, and everything would go on far better without the others. . . . This privilege class (nobility and clergy) is assuredly foreign to the nation by its do-nothing uselessness.

The issue of the Third Estate was unresolved when the Estates General convened at Versailles on May 4, 1789, in ceremonies that invoked, in the strongest symbolic terms, the traditional social and political order. The elected deputies marched by Estate, in inverse order of rank and prestige, behind a processional cross to the Church of Saint Louis. First came the Third Estate, dressed in austere black, the ancient costume of French burghers. The nobles followed, resplendent in black and white satin robes trimmed in gold lace, and topped by plumed hats. Next came the clergy, the bishops distinguished from the lesser clergy by their elaborate purple gowns. Following them was the Blessed Sacrament, carried by the Archbishop of Paris, and finally the king, wearing the magnificent Bourbon coronation cloak.

Not until the next day, when the deputies settled themselves by Estate into their meeting hall, did the tensions produced by the ceremonial humiliation of the Third Estate begin to show. The king seated himself and put on his hat, the privileged orders doing likewise. When the Third Estate attempted to follow suit, Louis XVI quickly bared his head, thus avoiding another dispute over precedence. Frustrated in their attempt to acquire recognition symbolically, the deputies of the Third Estate, most of whom were well-to-do lawyers, proceeded to try to force substantial concessions from the king. When further procedural wrangling over voting confirmed the impression that the monarch intended to side with the nobility and clergy, the Third Estate took the dramatic step of constituting itself as a National Assembly, asking individuals from the other two orders to join it on the basis of "one man, one vote." A few clergy, mainly parish priests who were at odds with the Church hierarchy, came over, with the result that the National Assembly suddenly gained sufficient legitimacy to frighten both the king and the privileged orders. The monarch showed his displeasure by locking the Assembly out of its meeting hall, a step that produced even stronger solidarity, however. On June 20 the recalcitrant deputies met in the royal indoor tennis court to pledge "not to separate, but to meet together whatever circumstances may require, until such time as the constitution of the kingdom shall be firmly established on solid foundations. . . ."

Still, the famous Tennis Court Oath was in no way an act of rebellion. It spoke of the National Assembly's mission "to settle the constitution of the kingdom, to bring about the regeneration of public order and maintain the true principles of the monarchy. . . ." The deputies meant to win Louis XVI to their vision of a revitalized France, not to overthrow his regime. If they seemed to be demanding a new order of things, it was only because the monarchy's strength could best be revived within the context of moderate change.

As members of the educated property-owning elite, these deputies feared social upheaval as much as anyone. Even during the elections of the previous spring, their claim to represent the nation had encountered serious challenge among the less privileged people of Paris and other places. Unlike the closed, orderly proceedings of the first two Estates, elections to the Third Estate had been the occasion for public dissension. The well-to-do had been jostled as they went to the polls by those who, because they paid no tax, were not allowed to vote. According to a pamphlet by Dufourny de Villiers, there were some who were already calling themselves the "Fourth Estate," who were asking why they had been "cast out of the bosom of the nation? Why is it [the Fourth Estate] the only order which, in accordance with the old tyrannical customs of bygone barbarous and ignorant days, is not summoned to the national assembly; and is treated with as much scorn as injustice?"

The Third Estate was, indeed, as one observer put it, "afraid of what is called *the populace*." But they were willing to use the crowd for their own purposes when the moment seemed right. As June stretched into July the National Assembly remained isolated. The privileged orders began to talk of pre-emptive counter measures, and France was filled with rumors of movements of soldiers and aristocratic plots—stories often encouraged by the leaders of the Third Estate to rally popular support to their shaky position.

Three months of intensive politics had produced none of the expected reforms and had left the government even more paralyzed than before in the face of mounting food prices (caused by poor harvests) and widespread unemployment aggravated by free-trade policies that allowed cheap English goods to flood the domestic market. Popular hopes generated in the spring turned to deep foreboding in those early summer days when the crops were in the ground but the fate of the new harvest could not yet be determined. Many peasants had been forced to consume their seed grain during the previous winter, planting had been curtailed, and fear of famine rose during June and July. Panic expressed itself in the increasing incidence of bread riots, peasant revolt, and urban strike activity, movements that at first had little connection with political events at Versailles but that gradually took on political implications as the governmental crisis deepened.

The first sign that popular unrest was not going to follow a traditional pattern came in early summer when rumors of famine began to be associated with the notion of an aristocratic plot to starve the people into submission to the privileged orders. Nobles were said to be employing brigands to destroy crops—an unsubstantiated claim, but one which had agitated the peasant imagination for centuries. Rumor infected the towns as well and in both town and country there were marches demanding reduction in the price of bread. Grain riots multiplied in May, becoming in June a full-scale countermovement against the alleged treachery of the privileged orders. Provincial officials reported to Versailles:

> There is daily talk of attacking the nobility, of setting fire to their chateau in order to burn all their title-deeds. . . . In those cantons where unrest has been less sensational, the inhabitants meet daily to pass resolutions that they will pay no more rent or other seignorial dues, but fix a moderate price for the redemption of these . . . ; and endless hostile projects of this sort spring from that spirit of equality and independence that prevails in men's minds today.

Just as popular memory of past disasters generated fears of famine and brigandage, so, too, did it generate the solutions that the peasants favored. Despite a growing "spirit of equality and independence," there was no hint of rebellion against the monarchy. The social order which the peasantry wished to revive was based on traditional concepts of justice and communal harmony and incorporated a strong emotional attachment to the patriarchal authority of the crown. Royal authority was frequently invoked to legitimate bread riots and peasant jacqueries, crowds chanting "Long live Louis" as they set about fixing the price of bread or rents.

Yet, little that Louis XVI did reinforced the immense popular devotion to monarchy evident at the beginning of 1789. On July 12, 1789, when it became known that Louis had dismissed his popular minister Necker, panic gripped the country. The notion spread of:

> the princes, associated in their own interests with the nobility, the clergy, and the *parlements*, . . . having hoarded all the corn in the

kingdom. . . . Their abominable intentions are to prevent the meeting
of the Estates General, and to make part of the people die of hunger
and the rest rise against their King.

In Paris people rushed to the Palais-Royal, the city's rumor center, to hear
speakers like journalist Camille Desmoulins denounce the treachery of
those close to the throne:

> Citizens, you know that the Nation had asked for Necker to be
> retained, and he has been driven out! Could you be more insolently
> flouted? After such an act they will dare anything, and they be plan-
> ning and preparing a Saint-Bartholomew massacre of patriots for this
> very night! . . . To arms! To arms! Let us wear green cockades, the
> color of hope. . . . The famous police are here; well, let them look at
> me, observe me carefully! Yes, I call on my brothers to seek liberty!

The popular response was instinctive, dictated by traditions of local self-
defense characteristic of the Old Regime. On the night of July 12, towns-
people invaded Parisian arsenals and armed themselves against what they
believed to be an aristocratic coup. The next day civic militia patrolled the
streets, disarming vagrants and suspicious "foreigners." In the tradition of
the charivari, rough justice was meted out to those who showed aristocratic
sympathies. Restif de la Bretonne was grabbed by the collar. "'Here's an
abbé!' the guard shouted. 'No, no, my friends, I have children and grandchildren.' 'He's too old!' said someone else." Restif was pushed into the
mud but escaped unharmed.

At the same time, the crowds expressed a traditional sense of justice by
hanging thieves on the spot. Custom, reinforced by the belief that royal
authority sanctioned self-defense, led on the morning of July 14 to an
expedition to the ancient royal bastion, the Bastille, located near Saint
Antoine, one of the most agitated artisan suburbs. The expedition intended
to persuade the Bastille's governor, a man named de Launey, to stop what
appeared to be military preparations on the turrets overlooking the suburb
and the narrow streets below. De Launey appeared conciliatory to the
delegation that met with him inside the Bastille, but outside, the crowd of
militia, reinforced by troops who had fraternized with the population in
the previous few days, became impatient. Pleas were made to the pension-
ers who made up the bastion's garrison to surrender. Some of the crowd
invaded the Bastille's courtyard, and in the confusion, shots were fired.
People raced back to the streets crying "Treachery!" and according to
one eyewitness:

> The fighting became more and more violent; the citizens had become
> inured to fire; on all sides they were climbing up on the roofs, into
> rooms, and as soon as a pensioner appeared between the battlements
> of the tower he became a target for a hundred marksmen . . . women
> did their utmost to back us up; even children, after every volley from

the fortress, ran here and there picking up bullets and shot, then dodged back joyfully to take shelter and give these missiles to our soldiers. . . .

The battle lasted just three or four hours, and the death toll was only eighty-three when de Launey signaled surrender. Yet, the struggle had transformed a peaceful though disorganized crowd into a formidable force, penetrated emotionally if not intellectually with the desire to destroy what now seemed a monster within the heart of Paris. The very language in which eyewitnesses described the crowd's subsequent actions reflects the apocalyptic mentality of that moment, when light and darkness, liberty and despotism were crystallized in the images of the Bastille and its besiegers. The newspaper *Les Revolutions de Paris* reported on the events:

> Holy, august Liberty, for the first time was introduced into that region of horror, that fearful abode of despotism, of monsters and of crimes . . . cries of vengeance and delight sounded on all sides; the rioters, triumphant and loaded with honors, bearing the arms and trophies of the vanquished, the banners of victory, the militia mingling with the soldiers of the fatherland, the tributes offered them on every side, all formed a terrible and splendid spectacle. When they reached the Place de Greve, the populace, impatient for revenge, did not allow de Launey nor the other officers to face the city's tribunal; wresting them from the hands of their captors, it crushed them underfoot, one after the other; de Launey was stabbed a thousand times, his head was cut off and carried, streaming with blood, on the end of a spear.

The fall of the Bastille produced an effect out of proportion to its strategic importance. The defeat of a poorly supported bastion of no major military significance did not threaten the ability of the monarchy to act decisively. Yet its psychological impact was enormous, not only on the people, who immediately perceived it as a prophetic sign, but also on the king and those close to him. Upon hearing the news of the fall, the king is supposed to have exclaimed to his aide, the Duke de Laincourt, "Why, it's a revolt," to which the Duke made this reply: "No, Sire, it is a revolution."

From that point, things moved swiftly. Necker was recalled as chief minister, and strong pressure was exerted on the monarch to come to Paris to reassure the people of his loyalty to their cause and that of the National Assembly. On July 17 the king entered the gates of Paris, where he was met by Mayor Jean-Sylvain Bailly, who declared, "Henri IV had won back his people, whereas now the people had won back their King." In contrast to the ceremony two months earlier at Versailles, the symbolic arrangements placed the ordinary people closest to the king, with the privileged orders occupying an inconspicuous place on the periphery. Mayor Bailly reported that as Louis made his way to the center of the city

"the way was lined by national guards armed with guns, swords, pikes, lances, scythes, sticks, etc. There were women, monks, friars all carrying guns! The utmost order was maintained everywhere, nobody broke ranks or stepped out of line, although an immense crowd of spectators was standing behind. The air rang with continuous shouts of *Vive la Nation! Vive le Roi! Vive Messieurs Bailly, La Fayette, les députés, les électeurs!"*

Pageantry expressed a concept of solidarity—images of fraternity combined with symbols of patriarchalism—that stood in striking contrast to the castelike division by Estates in May, two months previous. On the steps of the city hall, the king accepted another symbol of the reconciliation with his subjects, a red, white, and blue cockade. Lafayette, the head of the National Guard, had thought to add to the red and blue of Paris the white of the Bourbon monarchy, thus creating a symbol that would stand for revolution for the next sixty years. "In all the world's annals there is no mention of a revolution like this one," reported the Portuguese ambassador. "A King of France in an army coach, surrounded by bayonets and muskets of a huge crowd, finally forced to display in his hat the cockade of liberty."

It was a magic moment that released in the credulous traditional mentality the deep longing for a lost social order. For those who crowded close to the king's carriage, this was a moment of personal salvation and societal regeneration, much like a religious revival. To a culture well versed in prophetic signs, it seemed to promise a new beginning. The *Morning Post* of London welcomed the conquest of the Bastille as "one of the most IMPORTANT REVOLUTIONS the world has ever seen"; and another witness, the German Heinrich Steffans wrote, "It is not merely a French but a European Revolution." Blake's friend, Richard Price, preached a sermon interpreting the events as the fulfillment of Biblical prophecy: "I am thankful that I have lived to [see] it: and I could almost say, Lord, now lettest thou thy servant depart in peace, for mine eyes have seen thy salvation."

On learning of Price's ecstatic vision, a compatriot, Edmund Burke, set to work to prove the revolution the work of the devil, publishing the famous *Reflections on the French Revolution* as reply. This passionate attack was no less in tune with the excited atmosphere of the time than were the writings of Blake, Wordsworth, Southey, Schiller, Goethe, or any of the visionary poets who welcomed the happenings in France with apocalyptic joy and imagery. Southey later wrote: "Few persons but those who have lived in it can conceive or comprehend what the memory of the French Revolution was, nor what a visionary world seemed to open upon those who were just entering it. Old things seemed passing away, and nothing was dreamt of but the regeneration of the human race."

The rapidity with which the events of July entered popular consciousness reflected the desperate anxiety of the months just preceding. A revolution had taken place, almost by accident. There had been very little premeditation (beyond self-defense) in the capture of the Bastille. To many, the swift events of July 14 seemed nothing short of miraculous, requiring an explanation that bordered on legend. Almost immediately, the myth of the Bastille as a chamber of horrors gripped popular imagination. In song and street play, heroes of that day were transformed into a revolutionary sainthood.

A contractor named Palloy was commissioned to dismantle the symbol of tyranny, and pieces of the Bastille were sold in every part of France, where they came to serve as relics in a new kind of civic religion. July 14 became an instant national holiday, rivaling Christian celebrations in its solemnity and ritual. Places where the insurgents fell became places of worship, and the Place de la Bastille, now empty, became a pilgrimage point in the massive processions that were organized each July 14th.

Palloy managed to combine profit with patriotism, making chains found in the cellars of the Bastille into medals, paperweights, keys, and even dice boxes. Paper salvaged from its cellars was used to manufacture playing cards and fans on which were painted commemorative scenes. Red, white, and blue cups, plates, and chamber pots sold well, as did clothing in the national colors. Street vendors did a lively business in the national cockade, which became compulsory dress for all who wished to avoid popular displeasure. But despite this readiness to commercialize the revolution, there was no question that the popular yearning for a new faith, one that contained the promise of new beginnings, was chiefly responsible for the enthusiasm with which the events of July were received and interpreted.

Popular Revolution in City and Country

Occurring as it did prior to the general modernization of French society, the Parisian upheaval was not only unpremeditated, but also quite unexpected. In contrast to twentieth century insurrections, it seemed almost accidental. Even the Third Estate was unprepared to take the lead. The National Assembly, now comprising representatives of all three Estates, had scarcely begun its deliberations when events were again taken out of its hands by a second great unanticipated upheaval, this time in the countryside. Grain riots had been endemic in rural areas since the beginning of 1789, but it was not until July and August that these were transformed into a full-scale onslaught on the social system of feudalism. Popular belief that the nobility meant to starve France into submission produced panic; whole villages were mobilized to defend the crops against brigands, who in most cases never appeared.

In an atmosphere that historians have come to call The Great Fear, peasants engaged in pre-emptive attacks on the sanctuaries of privilege— nobles' chateaux and Church properties—demanding the renunciation of tithes and feudal dues. Very often a whole village—men, women, and children—would march behind a drum to the manor house. The village head would ask for bread and wine and then sit down with the owner to present demands. Everything was done in an orderly way, and when faced with the obvious determination of the peasants, most owners complied, tearing up feudal titles. Sometimes, however, an owner was absent and the crowd would descend on his cellars or pigeon house, making itself merry in the absence of real business. Some chateaux were burned and churches ransacked, but there was remarkably little violence to persons. Like the grain rioters before them, these people saw themselves as upholding the law, rather than breaking it. Near Beuce, according to an official report, "when the inhabitants heard that everything was going to be different they began to refuse to pay both tithes and *champart* [feudal dues], considering themselves so permitted, they said, by the new law to come."

That new law was enacted by the National Assembly on the night of August 4, 1789, when several nobles and clergy rose to voluntarily renounce feudal privileges. In abolishing feudalism, the deputies merely ratified the results of The Great Fear that had already swept away most of the remnants of rural servility. Serfdom, which applied to only a very small number of peasants, was ended and feudal dues and Church tithes terminated. However, the legislation of August 4 did not violate the sacred right of property, as dear to the peasantry as to the larger landowners.

Throughout the summer of 1789, the general population set the pace for the deputies. On August 26 the National Assembly enacted the Declaration of the Rights of Man and Citizen, whose first article established that "men are born and remain free and equal in rights." The document stated that civil liberties would be protected by law and that law would be legislated by "the people" who, in the manner of Rousseau's general will, were now declared "sovereign." The exact nature of the relations among the king, legislature, and people was left to later meetings of the Assembly to work out, but with the Declaration, the parameters of future debate were established.

A new concept, the modern notion of "citizen," had been introduced, wiping away the legal distinctions of the estates system and ratifying the remarkable set of social and psychological changes that had taken place since July. The Assembly was simply ratifying a new civic identity that was already institutionalized in language, dress, and manner. The ancient hierarchy of status, codified by modes of address like Monsieur and Madame, was being leveled by the plain language of Citizen and Citizeness. A national debate developed over the replacement of the formal *vous* with the more familiar fraternal *tu*. It was argued that "if *vous* is suitable to the gentleman, *tu* is suitable for a citizen"; and by 1792 *tu* had become obligatory for official correspondence: "Henceforth the only language suitable to French Republicans would be the language of fraternity."

In the first moments of revolutionary enthusiasm, sartorial distinctions were also cast aside as men and women of all ranks donned the equalitarian costume of the revolution. The plain jacket replaced the ruffled coat, long trousers the fancy knee breeches (*culottes*), and natural hair the wigs and elaborate hairdos of the Old Regime. In the same manner that seventeenth-century English religious dissenters had abandoned fancy dress for austere, uniform clothing, the revolutionaries manifested their dedication through equally simple, sober attire. In 1792 all ranks of the army were ordered to wear wooden epaulets, but this was not enough to satisfy the advocates of equality. Wrote one republican:

> Tell me why generals and their aides-de-camp don't wear the national uniform. Why are they covered with gold braid? Perhaps you will reply that there must be differences between ranks, so that we can recognize our leaders; but should republicans be distinguishable by their fine clothes? . . . if we are all equal . . . we must put a stop to the snob value of clothes and particularly in the Army.

But nowhere was the revolution more evident than in hair style, now cut and groomed in a more natural, uniform manner. The wig-making trade went into deep depression in 1789, recovering only when the reaction brought the trade back into fashion six years later.

With the exception of the English Puritan movement of the preceding century, political change never had been so closely associated with so great an upheaval in everyday life. The symbols of revolution were everywhere, stitched into clothing, painted on women's fans, baked on plates. Children's toys, playing cards, items of both work and leisure carried the message of "Liberté, Égalité, Fraternité," thus breaking down divisions between the private and public compartments of life to make revolution the same kind of consuming everyday activity to the revolutionaries that religion is to the true believer.

Nowhere was this more evident than in Paris itself, where the mass of the *menu peuple*—artisans, shopkeepers, petty officials, journalists, students, all groups that stood between the rich and the very poor—were swept up in what John Stuart Mill later called the "revolution of the mind." They were indeed the "saints" of the revolution, the same sort of men and women who had stormed the Bastille, who now bore witness to their intense belief in liberty, equality, and fraternity through the newly established daily rituals of revolution. The well-to-do, who secretly despised the leveling impact of this civic puritanism, contemptuously labeled them *"sans-culottes"* (those without knee breeches), a term they readily adopted because it fit so well their equation of austerity with morality and patriotism.

The *sans-culottes* were intolerant of any indulgence or pleasure seeking that diverted energy from the goals of revolution. Still representative of the traditional mentality that regarded resources as severely restricted, they felt an instinctive hatred of those who claimed more than their fair share.

They were particularly harsh on prostitutes and gamblers, for as one *sans-culotte* put it: "The foundations of a republic lay in its morality. Without morality, there will be no government; without government there would be no safety; without safety there could be no freedom." Their ideal of citizenship was scarcely distinguishable from the traditional view of good family government, patriarchal and at the same time fraternal: "A decent man was a good son, a good husband and good father; to combine, in one word, every public and personal virtue. Herein lies the real definition of patriotism." In short, collective need must prevail over individual desire.

The premodern character of large segments of French society was also reflected in the concrete, moral definition the *menu peuple* gave to "Liberty, Equality, and Fraternity." Revolutionary slogans aroused among them a deep, emotional desire to embody the virtues of the old communal way of life in the emerging institutions of the new nation-state. The contradictions built into this process were not always apparent, particularly in the early stages of the revolution. Its symbols attracted both rich and poor elements. The less fortunate turned to the refurbished language of fraternity in the hope that in brotherhood they would find material and spiritual security. The fraternal idea could equally well serve those somewhat higher up the urban social scale who, with the collapse of the old order, were looking for ways to justify re-establishment of social control. Both agreed that idle, criminal, or dissident behavior should be repressed on the pretext that it was antisocial and unpatriotic.

The *sans-culottes* generally combined fraternity with patriarchalism—initially in their support of constitutional monarchy, and later in devotion to La Patrie (fatherland) once monarchy was overthrown. In line with this tradition, the sense of brotherhood was strictly male, with women occupying a subordinate place in the economic and political order. Although women had been very active in the disturbances (particularly the bread riots) of 1789, from that point onward their place was in the home. Much to the dismay of those women (mainly educated women like Mary Wollstonecraft) who saw 1789 as a new beginning for both sexes, the role of motherhood was the only one expected of women in this revolution. The virtues ascribed to the proper citizeness included "simple manners, a frugal board, a mother who nurses her own child. . . ." Most of the leading male revolutionaries followed the teachings of Rousseau in glorifying the authority of the family, an attitude that precluded all attempts to gain equality for women and children. As one feminist petition in 1789 put it, "You have destroyed all the prejudices of the past, but you allow the oldest and more pervasive to remain, which excludes from office, position and honour, and above all from the right of sitting amongst you, half the inhabitants of the kingdom."

Similar subordination was demanded of the young, whose emancipation the *sans-culottes* viewed with considerable anxiety. Given the rising generational tensions of the eighteenth century, it is easy enough to see why harmony was stressed. "Education will be based on explaining to children their duties and obligations toward their country and their parents; . . . we will nurture their natural goodness, teach them pity, respect for the aged." "Goodness" meant return to the old virtue of filial obedience that the Church had preached for centuries and that was now revived in street corner sermonizing, a favorite propaganda instrument of the revolution. "No one can be a good citizen who is not a good son, a good father, a good brother, a good husband."

In a still preindustrial France, revival of old virtues appeared in no way inconsistent with the almost ecstatic expectation of the emergence of the new revolutionary citizen. Popular culture was just emerging from the domination of the Church, and having no other large-scale organizations which might serve as models, it was inevitable that the early revolutionary movements should take on many of the forms previously associated with Christianity. The civic pageantry that began in 1789 and rose to a crescendo in 1793-1794 was adapted from traditional religious processions. In some cases, the revolutionaries simply co-opted religious holidays for their secular purposes. As the revolution intensified, churches were taken over as temples of honor to revolutionary martyrs. The civic sainthood conferred on Marat in August 1793 was but one example of this transfer of popular devotion. Jacques Louis David's remarkable painting of the murdered man captured in its reverent simplicity the essence of martyrdom. Marat's effigy immediately appeared on the altar of the Bonne-Mouvelle church next to the female statue of liberty, thereby creating a new holy family. The church itself was draped in national colors and above the great doors were placed the words: "Entrance of the Temple of Liberty."

The halls where the Parisian *sans-culottes* held almost nightly meetings during the years 1793-1794 were similarly decorated. Busts of classical and modern heroes lined the walls, and the Tricolor, the flag, together with the symbols of republican virtue, the red cap and the pike, dominated the scene. As in traditional churches, men and women sat on benches opposite one another. Meetings opened with a pledge of allegiance and closed with the singing of the revolutionary hymn, the "Marseillaise." Frequently the oratory generated emotions similar to those of a religious revival. Women wept and men embraced as brothers with tears streaming down their faces. Enthusiasm proved contagious in an atmosphere that was already penetrated by fear and hope.

The strength of the popular revolutionary movement had depended from the very start more on belief than on organization; the typical *sans-culotte* was hostile to bureaucracy in the same way that sectarian religious groups reject the hierarchy of the established church. Bureaucracy and hierarchy seemed unnecessary, even immoral, in a society emerging from extreme localism where most things could be settled face to face, without reference to the authority of the central state. This emphasis on direct control was both the strength and weakness of the grassroots revolutionary movement that depended so heavily on the active participation of true believers rather than permanent organization.

Any separation of functions, even between elected representatives and the people, was unacceptable. The most radical revolutionaries called for popular participation by which local assemblies had the right to veto all decisions from above. Officials and judges were to be elected, with instant recall in cases of popular displeasure. In the manner of the religious sectarians of the seventeenth century, the *sans-culottes* would tolerate no centralization or specialization that would remove from the community of activists its right to determine the future.

The ideal revolutionary was, then, like the ideal believer, a person totally consumed by what amounted to a full-time activity. In his job, during his free time, on every holiday, the *sans-culotte* was involved in meetings, ceremony, or drill. Every moment of time had its sacred revolutionary purpose; every diversion was a threat to purity of purpose. Of course, millions of the French, probably the majority, were only marginally involved in this intense revolutionary experience. The *sans-culottes* were more prevalent in the cities than in the countryside, and were more likely to be drawn from the rooted, moderate- and small-property owners than from either the rich or, on the other end of the scale, the wage earners without property. Migrants, beggars, prostitutes—groups that did not owe allegiance to a particular community—were least likely to be involved. They, like the aristocracy and the well-to-do bourgeoisie, were too detached from the traditional sense of solidarity to accept the kinds of restrictions on personal freedom that the *sans-culottes* demanded. Together they shared a contempt for the austerity and puritanism of the revolutionary sainthood. Yet scorn only reinforced the *sans-culottes'* sense of mission, embodied in the ideal of the new revolutionary as described in a contemporary radical pamphlet:

He's a man who goes everywhere on his own two feet, who has none of the millions you're all after, no mansions, no lackeys to wait on him and who lives quite simply with his wife and children, if he has any, on the fourth or fifth floor. He is useful, because he knows how to plough a field, handle a forge, a saw, a file, to cover a roof, how to make shoes and to shed his blood to the last drop to save the Republic. And since he is a working man, you'll never find him in the café de Chartes or the places where they plot and gamble or at the théâtre la Nation where they show *L'Ami des Louis* or the *Vaudeville for La Chaste Susanne.* . . . In the evening, he's at his Section, not powdered and perfumed and all dolled up to catch the eye of the *citoyennes* in the galleries, but to support sound resolutions with all his power and to pulverize the vile faction of *hommes d'état.* For the rest a *Sans-Culotte* always keeps his sword with an edge, to clip the ears of the malevolent. Sometimes he carries his pike and at the first roll of the drum, off he goes to the Vendée, to the *armée des Alpes* or the *armée du Nord*.

Experiment in Constitutional Monarchy

To the average *sans-culotte* activist, the meaning of "revolution" was profoundly moral and emotional. It represented a kind of personal and communal salvation from the hell of hunger and unemployment that plagued France and the rest of Europe during the 1780s and 1790s. The great outbursts of popular participation—the fall of the Bastille, The Great Fear, and the numerous *journées* (great days of demonstrations and violence) between 1789 and 1795—all combined traditional kinds of protest, including bread riot, charivari, and jacquerie, with an apocalyptic vision of a revitalized society. It was this vision that momentarily gave the revolution its breadth of appeal, linking local groups into a national mass movement. At the same time, we must remember that the longing for revitalization could work for conservative purposes as well. In those areas of France where the previous century of change had not penetrated as deeply, the peasantry could envision the revival of the golden age without a new framework of liberty, equality, and fraternity and thus support efforts to turn back the clock. In places like the Vendée, two visions of revitalization contended in vicious civil war from 1793 onward.

Not only overt reaction was at odds with the *sans-culottes* movement; even among those who declared themselves pleased with 1789, there were profound differences on what it meant and how it was to be implemented. The peasantry, once it had won the abolition of feudalism, returned to relative passivity, watching the politics of Paris suspiciously and jealously guarding their stocks of grain against urban merchants as well as royalist brigands. No peasants or artisans were among the members of the National Assembly who, in the autumn of 1789, settled down to the long process of creating a working constitution. The deputies were differently situated, with an entirely different, less traditional perspective. They were persons of education and property who were accustomed to thinking in terms of universal ideas and large-scale institutions that transcended local interests. The business people among them were already interested in a national market economy; the lawyers already thought in terms of abstract principles rather than concrete customs.

When they talked of liberty, they meant something quite different from what either the peasant or the urban *sans-culotte* did. People of their position had already abandoned the traditional view of the world as one of limited good; to them the greatest good could be accomplished by granting the greatest degree of freedom to individual enterprise, regardless of the claims of collective interest. They therefore set about creating the conditions under which business and commerce could flourish. They abolished feudal restrictions on trade and disestablished guilds; after 1791 it was illegal for either employers or employees to form associations in restraint of trade. The internal toll barriers of France were ended and every effort was made to facilitate the national exchange of goods and services on a cash basis. The revolution, which had been provoked in part by protests against just such a free-market economy, saw its rapid development from 1791 onward.

It was also consonant with the modernizing thrust of these elites to legislate an end to the traditional system of patronage. Among the first acts of the National Assembly was the overhaul of the entire bureaucratic and military system of the Old Regime, prohibition of the sale of offices, and opening of all offices and commissions to talent. The incredible tangle of local jurisdictions inherited from the Old Regime was simplified into eighty-three departments. At first, considerable local self-government was provided, but as it was feared that aristocratic enemies of the revolution would use their traditional local powers for subversion, the trend toward centralization was inevitable.

Not surprisingly, the Assembly's definition of equality as guaranteed in the Declaration of the Rights of Man and Citizen stopped short of political equality. The male citizens of France were divided into "active" and "passive" categories along lines dictated by property holding, a provision that gave about half the adult males the right to vote. The active electorate was further restricted by a system of indirect elections in which about fifty thousand electors, selected in the first round of voting, had the final voice in choosing deputies. While the notion of civil equality (equality of the citizen before the law) was affirmed, the National Assembly had no intention of extending it to the political and social spheres as well. "Citizenship" meant making each individual available to the state for the purpose of public education or military service. It did not imply, as the *sans-culottes* would have it, making the state available to the citizens by dismantling the specialized functions of the bureaucracy or the legislature.

The National Assembly had no desire to eliminate monarchy, so long as the crown remained subject to the constitution and had only suspensive veto power over legislation. The crown seemed perfectly compatible with the concept of the nation-state to which the Assembly was devoted, and the deputies saw the king as a useful symbol of unity in the process of centralization. Nor did the deputies wish to destroy the Church. They confiscated the Church's lands, amounting to about 10 percent of the country, with the intention of placing the priesthood on a new financial basis as elected and paid officials of the state. The moderate bourgeoisie were too fearful of anarchy to dispense with religion as the moral cement of society. The Civil Constitution of the Clergy, enacted in 1790, foresaw the revitalization of the Church within the framework of the nation-state as a kind of department of health, education, and welfare, salaried and

This dilemma became even more desperate in the spring when the French armies began to retreat in the face of Austrian and Prussian invasion. In May 1793, the situation had become so desperate that the Hébertists and their *sans-culotte* allies invaded the Convention and expelled all but the most radical republicans, leaving the government in the hands of the faction known as the Jacobins, led by Robespierre, Danton, Marat, Saint-Just, and Carnot.

The war that moderates had begun in order to shore up the constitutional monarchy had destroyed that regime and now threatened the existence of its republican replacement. Ironically, war required centralization of government; not only did those provincial interests in Lyon, Marseille, and the Vendée who revolted against the revolutionary government in Paris resent this, but also the grassroots democratic movement itself, whose concern with revitalizing the spirit of community on the local level was contradicted by the massive war preparations. The war required the kind of bureaucratic and economic development that ran counter to the interests of the *menu peuple* who, however patriotic they might be, were threatened by the growth of the modern war machine. The Jacobins were forced by the logic of political and economic necessity to favor the kind of free-market economy that could supply the government with needed revenues and material. The *sans-culottes,* on the other hand, insisted on the fair price and the fair wage, practices of the small-scale, community-oriented economy they sought to revitalize. They succeeded in getting the Jacobin government to enact a general maximum limit on consumer prices. The cancellation of all peasant indemnities for feudal dues in 1793 was a similar gesture of reconciliation.

In the summer of 1793 the Jacobins felt compelled to promise social as well as political equality. Robespierre began to talk about property as a social institution to which every Frenchman had a right. Saint-Just argued that the goal of government was "to give every Frenchman the means of getting the necessities of life, without his being dependent on anything except the law and without mutual dependence within the civil state. . . . Man must be independent . . . there should be neither rich nor poor." For a moment in time, the *sans-culottes'* ideal seemed realized. Their hatred was directed not against the industrious person who had built up a small business to respectable proportions, but was reserved for "those big men who continue to swallow up little men." During the desperate times of shortages and rising prices in 1793–1794, Parisian radicals were reported saying "the streets should be carpeted with the heads of merchants. . . . Blasted merchants! Blackguards! . . . I'll eat 'em up, every bit of 'em." Most resented were those middle men, one remove from the actual producer, who could gain profit not from their own labor but by speculating on the market. To the *menu peuple,* they were no better than the aristocrats who lived off rents; they were in the same class as criminals who stole from the worker. The *sans-culotte* was just as resentful of the idle poor as the idle rich, for they both threatened the ideal of a stable, orderly community.

Intense conflict between large- and small-property holders reflected France's relatively low level of economic development. In the country and even in cities like Paris, the small-scale moral economy of local markets and face to face relations between producer and consumer continued. Alongside it, however, was growing an economy of larger scale, operating in an impersonal way according to laws of supply and demand. The *sans-culottes* were still a part of the former, the merchants representative of the latter. There were no modern industrialists to speak of, and the fact that France's economy was still mainly labor intensive made the *sans-culottes'* emphasis on the dignity of labor and the just reward for individual effort all the more appealing. "All men have an equal right to a minimum standard of living and to all agricultural products indispensible for his (sic) survival," declared the radical *Ami du Peuple* in August 1793. The ideal—the small-property owner earning enough to maintain himself and his family—was clearly drawn from the essentially agrarian and artisan economy of the past. Ironically, the new framework of freedom, the liberal nation-state, encouraged precisely the kind of enterprise that threatened to destroy this traditional economy.

The *sans-culotte* faced backward and forward at the same time. He was conservative in his economic and social views, radical in his politics. The "big men," including the educated and propertied bourgeoisie from whom the Jacobin leadership was drawn, were the opposite. They favored economic and social modernization but tended to be suspicious of direct democracy, because this smacked of local autonomy and economic controls which they sought to avoid. Given these basic divisions, it is little wonder that the Jacobin alliance with the *sans-culottes* flourished only in the superheated atmosphere of 1793–1794, under conditions known as The Terror. The campaign of trials and executions against enemies of the regime diverted popular attention from social and economic tensions within the republican ranks. Some forty thousand persons died in these years, mainly in military campaigns against internal centers of rebellion like Lyon and the Vendée and as a result of treason trials. Not all those killed were monarchists; moderate republicans were consumed as well. But The Terror did cement the alliance between the Jacobin elite and the *sans-culottes* for almost two years.

During this time republicanism moved to create its own symbols of legitimacy soon after the execution of the king. Any attempt to use established religion as a basis for loyalty was out of the question since the priesthood was the enemy. Radical Hébertists had launched a campaign of de-Christianization, closing churches (after looting and defacing them), terrorizing priests, and replacing old rituals with what they called the Cult of Reason. When the Cathedral of Notre Dame was taken over in November 1793, a prostitute was installed as high priestess. Yet, outright atheism could never have appealed to the general population. They developed their own cults along more traditional lines, substituting popular heroes for old saints. When it came to setting up an official cult in 1794, Robespierre wisely chose to fashion his Cult of the Supreme Being from elements of Catholic ceremony combined with democratic symbolism. This version of eighteenth-century deism was decked out in colorful ritual so as to appeal to popular tastes, but it emphasized civic virtue along with personal salvation as the basis of what Robespierre called the Republic of Virtue.

The notion of the strength of the Republic being dependent on the disciplined morality of the people drew on both classical neo-Stoic political theory and popular millennial vision. Aware that material interests divided Jacobin from *sans-culotte,* Robespierre stressed their shared spiritual vision of republican virtue. A common sense of new beginnings was heightened by altering the calendar. September 22, 1792 began Year One, and the weeks were organized in units of ten days that allowed the substitution of new revolutionary holidays for the old royal and Church festivals. The grand processions and festivals of the years 1793-1794, emphasizing the theme of social harmony, rivaled in pomp and splendor anything the Old Regime had offered. Themes of fraternity and patriarchy were combined in the Festival of Youth, when youths took their oath to the Republic before the eyes of their elders. On the floats that were a part of the revolutionary processions, themes of youth, motherhood, and aging all had their appropriate place, recalling peasant tradition.

The design of these dramatic ceremonies was the work of Jacques Louis David, the famous painter, whose didactic masterpieces, *Oath of the Horatii* and *Brutus,* had forged the link between the arts and civic education even before the revolution. David and his coworkers at the *Club revolutionaire des arts* adhered to the principle that all art must have a "utilitarian aim; not the particular utility of the highest caste, but the general utility of the nation, of the masses." By 1793 it was no longer necessary for them to clothe their political statements in historical garb. David's famous *Death of Marat,* painted soon after the assassination of the revolutionary leader, set a precedent for artistic realism. It exemplified the universal feeling of new beginnings, the break with the past symbolized in the great processions on July 14 and August 10 that touched base with the places of revolutionary devotion, including the Bastille, but carefully avoided those spots that evoked popular memory of monarchy.

The substitution of civil for religious holidays served the same purpose. The new calendar eliminated sixteen Sundays and innumerable saints' days in what amounted to an onslaught on the traditional patterns of work and leisure. Every tenth day was a day of rest, when the militant *sans-culotte* would attend republican mass at the Temple of Reason and then stroll the streets to hear people singing patriotic songs and watch civic dancing. "Such poorly dressed people, who would formerly have never dared show themselves in areas frequented by people of fashion, were walking among the rich, their heads as high as theirs. . . ." noted one observer.

Reaction and the Rise of Napoleon

Faith can mask reality for just so long, however. Occurring as it did on the eve of full-scale social and economic modernization, the revolution could not call upon the powerful organizational and technological forces that characterize contemporary insurrectionary movements. The *levée en masse* (general call-up for the army) relied on the millennialistic enthusiasm of the general population, who had fought with admirable zeal and formidable courage, but the forced requisitions and prolonged draft also angered many of the French, particularly the provincials. As soon as foreign danger abated, their hatred erupted in counterterroristic assassination of officials and ordinary republicans. By 1794 Robespierre had to admit that "the people are getting tired." When the French armies beat back the invaders and began to achieve victories in Belgium in June 1794, the urgency of national mobilization slackened. One immediate result was the fall of Robespierre himself, who was condemned to death by the National Convention in July 1794. There was no popular resistance and the Thermidorian reaction, so named for the month in the new republican calendar when Robespierre fell, moved ahead to abolish those social measures, including the general maximum, that had cemented the Jacobin–*sans-culottes'* alliance in the previous two years. The final break came with the enactment of the Constitution of 1795, which placed twenty thousand propertied electors in the position of choosing the new bicameral legislature, which in turn was subordinated to the five-member Directory.

It would be wrong to view the Directory as an aristocratic or monarchical revival. It was, instead, the triumph of the "big men" over the *menu peuple,* the culmination of five years of confused struggle that had gradually clarified divisions scarcely visible when the revolution began. Now the liberal bourgeoisie moved ruthlessly against its enemies. The Directory imprisoned the leaders of the Jacobins and *sans-culottes,* the latter taken with surprisingly little resistance. True to its origins and nature, the popular revolutionary movement had failed to build resistant organizations.

During the very severe economic crisis of 1796, militants would again take to the streets, but only to lower the price of bread rather than to save the democratic republic. There were some radicals, led by Gracchus Babeuf, who rallied what was called the Conspiracy of Equals. But this, too, was easily infiltrated and the leaders were arrested in the same year. Like a religious revival whose members expect salvation momentarily, the *sans-culottes* had built no permanent organization. Therefore, when prophecy failed they lacked the strength to survive a period of repression and disappointment.

Indicative of the shift in public mood was the social reaction to The Terror's reign of civic puritanism. The moral purity and material austerity of the *sans-culottes* were mocked by men and women of the upper classes, who adopted thè most frivolous and daring styles in dress, language, and manners. Bands of bourgeois youth, known as the Jeunesse dorée, flaunted their idleness in a grotesque parody of republican virtue. Eyewitnesses reported so-called victims dances held on the sites of churches desecrated during The Terror. The dancers wore red ribbons around their necks in memory of those guillotined. The rich quickly abandoned the language of fraternity and insisted on the formal *vous,* while older men revived the powdered wig and women went back to the high hairdos of the Old Regime. Fashionable circles revived the low-cut gown, whose nudity mocked the republican ideal of chaste motherhood.

The Directory turned away from the domestic policies of The Terror but did not abandon its foreign and military objectives. For the next four years, the fate of the regime would hinge as much on conditions abroad as on those at home. France had claimed Austrian lands in Belgium as part of its own territory and the republican armies in Italy, led by a brilliant young general named Napoleon Bonaparte, continued to make gains there as well. The momentum of bureaucratic and military development could not be reversed, and the beneficiaries of the abolition of privilege, the young civil and military officials, made certain that their status was secure. Bonaparte operated in Italy almost as an independent force, dictating foreign policy to the civilians back home. The threat that monarchical restoration posed to the Directory strengthened his position. There was a yearning for the Bourbons among some circles, but the pretender to the throne, Louis XVIII, made the mistake of demanding that France be returned to its pre-1789 position, something neither the civil service nor the army would stand for. The threat of restoration caused the Directory to become more dictatorial in 1797, a move that played into the hands of the generals.

Republican members of the Directory plotted with the thirty-year-old Bonaparte to establish a consular regime in which Napoleon would be First Consul. On November 9, 1799, this coup was achieved with almost no opposition. The First Consul declared that he had saved France from the dual threat of monarchical restoration and permanent anarchy. To prove his point, he authorized a plebiscite on the question of the consulate. The results were overwhelmingly favorable to the government and, subsequently, a new constitution was dictated. It retained the symbols of 1789 but reinterpreted the principle of popular sovereignty to justify a dictatorial rather than legislative form of government. Universal suffrage was maintained, but elections were indirect and the candidates for office were restricted to a select body of notables chosen by the consuls. There was no longer any pretense of legislative powers.

The growing power of Napoleon was due not only to his military genius, which he continued to demonstrate in a series of victories that pushed the

French boundaries to the banks of the Rhine, but also to his grasp of internal affairs. He was an enormously energetic person whose mind was capable of dealing with all the functions of government both simultaneously and well. Unsentimental, even cynical in his attitude toward people, he was wholly convinced of his own destiny, which he had come to associate not only with that of France but also with that of all Europe.

Napoleon combined bureaucratic acumen with prophetic charisma; intellectuals, including Goethe, Beethoven, and Hegel, could initially admire him as the epitome of the heroic genius, whose insight and intelligence transcended all laws, natural and moral. He also had a mass appeal, being portrayed as a savior figure in street ballads and cartoons. It seemed to the credulous that he had superhuman powers, an impression that he did not fail to perpetuate in the pomp and ceremony of which he was so fond. Yet Napoleon himself was largely devoid of the emotionalism that surrounded him. His mind had been shaped by the Enlightenment, which was organized, pragmatic, and essentially utilitarian in its approach to politics. Above all else, his military training caused him to place high value on the orderly, disciplined, and rational adjustment of means to ends.

These qualities were exemplified in the Consulate from 1799 to 1804, when the foundations of modern French military and civil administration were permanently laid. The Napoleonic heritage might be viewed as an extension of monarchical absolutism if it were not for the fact that its legitimating principle was sovereignty of the people and, therefore, its form that of the modern nation-state. A revolutionary principle of civil equality was incorporated into a governmental structure that was far more centralized than the Old Regime. All corporate and local privilege was dissolved, and some three hundred different law codes inherited from previous regimes were reduced to a single uniform code for all of France.

In some respects the law was a step back from the democratic principles of 1793–1794. Women's civil rights were diminished and employees were placed at a disadvantage to employers in new master-servant codes. Civil equality did not imply political equality, and social rights, as these had been defined earlier, were neglected. Yet the framework of universal laws, centrally administered, was maintained. The question was no longer (as it had been in 1789) whether France should be a state with one order of citizens or a series of Estates, but rather how the principle of citizenship should be articulated. Furthermore, however cynically Napoleonic government might abuse the concept of popular sovereignty, there could no longer be any appeal to legitimacy other than the will of the people. When the Bourbons were restored to power in 1815, they found themselves using the modern language of popular sovereignty to legitimize their regime.

The thrust of bureaucratic development and military conquest carried forward equality and fraternity. Bureaucrats and generals found that for efficiency's sake everyone had to be treated equally, making distinctions among persons only according to their function, not according to their birth. Equally necessary to a strong regime was the concept of brotherhood expanded to the national level. Napoleon's regime was the first in living memory to collect taxes regularly, maintain financial stability, and guarantee the integrity of state contracts. In perhaps his greatest diplomatic move, Napoleon also solved the festering question of church and state by concluding with the Pope a concordat in 1801. It restored papal discipline over the French bishops and gave to the bishops control of the parish clergy. The split within the Church that had resulted from the Civil Constitution of the Clergy in 1790 was resolved by dismissal of both contending parties. The Pope renounced claims to Church property confiscated since 1789, and the clergy became state salaried, swearing an oath to uphold its authority. Catholicism was once again the official "religion of the great majority of French citizens," though no longer the state within the state that it had been when it owned its own lands. A modern separation of functions was achieved, with the state exercising public authority and the Church administering to people in the private sphere, with details to be worked out in the future.

Whereas the American Constitution had opted for strict separation of church and state, France still seemed to require religion as the moral cement of its political fabric. The so-called Imperial Catechism of 1807 required that children be taught this dictum: "Christians owe to the princes who govern them, and we owe in particular to Napoleon I, our Emperor, love, respect, obedience, fidelity, military service, and the tributes laid for the preservation and defense of the Empire." Napoleon, like all modern dictators who followed him, preferred to obtain the divine blessing through the voice of the people rather than have it delivered by the benediction of bishops. A year after the concordat he arranged a second major plebiscite which made him Consul for life, and two years later crowned himself Napoleon I, Emperor of the French.

David, the artist who had placed his skills at the service of almost every regime since 1789, was there to help arrange the pomp and ceremony, as well as paint a picture of the great event. At the center was the emperor, surrounded by monarchical trappings—the crown, mitre, and sword. Powerful secular and religious figures were in attendance too, but their role was different from that in coronation ceremonies under the Old Regime. They were grouped around Napoleon, not as privileged orders, but as representatives of a larger nation. Soldiers and officials attended as symbols of achievement rather than birth, and the subordination of religion to public interest was symbolized by Napoleon's act of taking the crown from the Pope and placing it on his own head. This was the gesture of a self-made person, a self-conscious rejection of the ritual and magic with which the monarchs of the Old Regime had legitimated themselves. Here Napoleon is making his own history, for he thought of immortality in a thoroughly modern way, not as salvation, but as fame.

The Fruits of Revolution

The French must have asked themselves in 1804 just how much fifteen years of revolutionary upheaval really had accomplished. With an emperor on the throne, the Church restored, and a new Napoleonic "aristocracy" of military and civil service in place, it seemed to many that the revolution had been a mere interlude, even an aberration, in the history of hierarchical and authoritarian France. Certainly the average person had not gained much in the area of political liberty, having no voting rights in 1804 and being subject to several new obligations, including conscription. The Napoleonic codes imposed an unaccustomed discipline on manual workers, at the same time prohibiting them from organizing themselves. The equality that had been achieved was certainly not that envisioned by the *sans-culottes* in 1793–1794. It is true that all French men (not women and children) were equal before the law, that feudal jurisdictions had been abolished and Church courts eliminated, but civil equality did not pretend to be political or social equality. There was certainly no equality of condition, only equality of opportunity. Careers were now open to talent regardless of birth, yet few peasant or artisan sons could afford to acquire the education or had the patronage necessary to obtain one of the higher offices of state.

The distance between the rich and the poor may or may not have been greater in 1804 than in 1789, but there is no doubt who had benefited from the long period of inflation that accompanied the revolution. Wages lagged behind prices and war profiteering benefited the merchants at the expense of lesser property holders. Peasants gained from the sale of Church lands, but not nearly as much as the bourgeoisie who had the capital to buy up ecclesiastical estates and lands left by émigré nobles. The urban and rural wage-earning class without property had probably grown, even though France still had many more small landholders and independent artisans than did England. Yet the peasantry was managing to maintain itself only by limiting the size of its families and by reducing levels of consumption. Peasants held tenaciously to the land, yet did little to improve agricultural production.

Ironically, one of the chief effects of the French Revolution was to make the peasants even more conservative than before. Now that they had cast off their feudal burdens, they saw little reason for further change. Their reluctance to leave the land inhibited the growth of cities and limited the supply of labor for industrial development. In France, low consumer demand reduced incentive for increased production, one of the reasons that France lagged behind England in the development of modern industry.

The revolution did heighten the sense of fraternity, but not in the way the *sans-culottes* had envisioned. "Fraternité" became something quite different when it was transformed by successive wartime appeals into an abstraction that united the French as a nation but left them socially divided by class and locality. Brotherhood was too easily detached from both liberty and equality; by the time of the Empire it had begun to lose that redemptive dimension that had made it so appealing not only to the French but also to Europeans generally. In the first years of the revolution, France had become the fatherland of all those, including English, Germans, and Italians, who shared an enthusiasm for new beginnings. By the time of the Empire, however, many had abandoned the New Jerusalem. Some, like William Wordsworth, had turned away from politics to seek a more personal kind of salvation. Blake continued to write against war and imperialism; Beethoven broke with Napoleon; Fichte turned away from France to seek redemption in the German *Volk*. Instead of uniting humanity, fraternity transformed into nationalism ultimately shattered it, though elements of the original messianic idealism remained a part of European nationalism through the middle of the nineteenth century.

The limits of the French Revolution are understandable, however, when we consider the fact that France was still in the very first stages of social and economic modernization. Uneven economic growth, the dislocation of major social groups, and cultural disorientation—all facets of transition from traditional to modern society—contributed to the onset of upheaval. At the same time, the incomplete nature of modernization in 1789 was reflected in the numerous contradictions within the popular revolutionary movement and in its ultimate failure to accomplish its original objectives. On the other hand, the course of events pushed forward modernization, particularly that of the state. During these years the French nation-state freed itself from entanglements with society, gaining a measure of autonomy that made it much more powerful than its predecessors. The immediate beneficiaries of the French Revolution were the military and civil services, whose members found themselves in the position of being thrust into leadership roles. Napoleon was only the first of a number of "men on horseback" who would be called on to exercise power, a result not only of his extraordinary abilities but also of the fact that, as in developing countries today, the military was one of the few able, forward-looking groups in France.

In the first stages of political modernization, the separation of state and society was extraordinarily sharp; society seemed backward compared with the state; political parties and agencies of public opinion were very slow to develop. This was the case not only because they were repeatedly repressed, but also because, even at the high tide of revolution in 1793–1794, they took such an intensely localized form that the development of broader organizations was actually inhibited. For both the peasantry and the *sans-culottes,* revolution offered the opportunity to revitalize archaic social and cultural values that, while expressed in the new symbols of liberty, equality, and fraternity, actually came into conflict with the development of permanent and effective political movements on the national level.

It must be said, therefore, that revolution came too early, before French society had developed the level of integration and communication necessary to transform the desire for revitalization into effective political consciousness. The great mass of the people remained excluded from active participation in nation building for another half century or more. Alexis de Tocqueville warned his compatriots as late as the 1850s that the French Revolution had strengthened the state at the expense of society: "This new power was created by the Revolution or, rather, grew up almost automatically out of the havoc wrought by it." Revolution had created a body of citizens equal among themselves, but incapable of combining to oppose state power.

In the discrepancy between the modernization of the state and the relative backwardness of French society lay the dynamic of the next sixty years as well. Until French society reached a parallel level of modernization, sporadic upheaval would continue. Tensions between the center and the periphery, between tax collectors and peasants, between the market economy of the nation-state and the communal traditions of the *sans-culottes*—these were not resolved until the 1850s.

The fact that Europe, as the first area to modernize, had to work out simultaneously both political and societal modernization accounts for the protracted period of instability from 1789 to 1848. In today's developing areas, similar problems are much more likely to be solved quickly and definitively, though with greater violence and loss of life. This is, of course, a reflection of the higher levels of organization and technology currently available to all sides in civil conflicts. Because Europe was the first to develop, its agony was of a different dimension, perhaps no less cruel but certainly less bloody.

5

War and Peace in the Napoleonic Era, 1804–1815

In 1804 empire replaced republic and Europe's revolutionary era seemed at an end. William Blake's gloomy prophecy that "humanity shall be no more: but war & princedom & victory!" was directed as much against those who girded to fight Napoleon as against the emperor himself. Yet, while individual freedoms undoubtedly suffered, there were many areas in which conflict accelerated the pace of change. It can be reasonably argued that war has been one of the most powerful agents of social change over the past two hundred years; while this observation applies more to the twentieth century than to the late eighteenth or early nineteenth, war was certainly a catalyst in the first stages of modernization.

When we call the modern era the age of total war we not only are referring to the duration and extent of military operations, but also to the degree of involvement of society at large. With respect to duration, the wars in the period 1792–1815 are quite different from those of the twentieth century, which, with the exception of guerilla wars, have been relatively short and intense in character. Because of organizational and technological capacity, clashes between highly developed countries have become increasingly brief, though ever more costly. However, countries at the beginning of the nineteenth century were only starting to achieve these levels of production and social mobilization, and thus their struggles tended to be drawn out affairs, often with a confused mixture of civilian and professional involvement.

But wars, whether they took the form of guerrilla conflict or massive engagements, were coming to involve more of the population in the nineteenth century than in previous centuries. Whereas in the seventeenth century an estimated .13 percent of the population was actively engaged in fighting, by 1800 it was .52 percent. The percentage of the population killed in war was a reflection of larger armies and more intensive conflict. In the seventeenth century those killed averaged .32 percent, during the Napoleonic era increasing to 1.54 percent—less than one-third of the human cost of World War I, but a very large increase all the same. Material costs are more difficult to measure, but these, too, were most certainly increasing, though expanding national wealth may have kept pace with some of them. Some states like Prussia by the eighteenth century already had military budgets that consumed a considerable share of the state's resources. France, it will be remembered, broke down under the burden of its intervention in the American War of Independence. But the old regimes' way of supplying and paying standing armies relied heavily on the private initiative of the soldiers themselves, so much of the expense is not included in the state budgets.

With the coming of the revolution, France was equipped with a tax base that made possible military operations undreamed of earlier. Even more important, it tapped the real resource of the new warfare: the citizen soldier. The citizen army, whether volunteer or conscript, was generally larger, cheaper, and unfortunately for its members, more expendable than the mercenary or draft troops of the past. Because desertion was less of a problem, armies could move faster and farther, making possible the Napoleonic strategy of direct attacks on the enemy's main force. Earlier, the object had been to outmaneuver the enemy, saving valuable troops; now the goal was to destroy the adversary at all costs, a lesson reflected in Karl von Clausewitz's famous observation: "War is an act of violence pushed to its utmost bounds." Eighteenth-century armies had relied on advanced bases for supply; their successors tended to live off the land. Finally, in this new era armies could be used for the purpose of occupation of other countries, something unheard of in the eighteenth century when officers had enough trouble disciplining their own troops, much less controlling a civilian population as well. In short, the history of war is inseparable from the general history of societal modernization in the late eighteenth and early nineteenth centuries.

The Modernization of War

Before 1789 war was between princes, not peoples. The idea of an armed citizenry was abhorrent to absolute monarchy not only because it threatened their power politically, but also because they wished to reduce the level of domestic violence, including banditry and dueling. As late as 1745 Jacobite rebels had come within a few miles of London before being turned back. And if the great Pugachev rebellion was not enough, plenty of local brigandage still was occurring in France, Italy, and Spain, as well as Russia. Pirates dominated parts of the Mediterranean, and Londoners found it dangerous to travel in that city's suburbs, which were inhabited by daredevil thieves. Along the Rhine, criminal bands, sometimes numbering in the hundreds, constituted a state within the state until well into the nineteenth century; in France murder gangs, sometimes hired by political factions to settle scores, remained unchecked up to the Napoleonic period. Depriving the private citizen of dangerous weapons was perhaps the only way, prior to the creation of efficient police forces, that violence could be reduced. In Germany, in an attempt to reduce the incidence of fatal duels, particularly among students, all but the nobles were forbidden to wear swords.

The sword was the symbol of the nobility's original function as society's fighting elite. Throughout the late eighteenth and early nineteenth centuries, gentlemen clung to the cruel custom of the duel as much to save their collective status as to preserve individual honor. Yet, it became increasingly clear that they held this privilege only at the behest of the state, which sought to turn the military talents of the nobility to its own advantage. In his last testament, Prussia's Frederick William I laid down the strategy for his monarchy:

> . . . my successor must try to work towards this goal: that counts and other noblemen from all his provinces . . . shall be employed in the army and that their children be taken on as cadets. It will be a great advantage to you to have the whole nobility reared in your service from youth onwards and knowing no other lord but God and the King of Prussia.

Reserving the officer corps for the nobility worked reasonably well in the eighteenth century; it made war more genteel and perhaps less cruel, though it opened a great gap between the officer and the soldier, who was usually a mercenary or unfortunate conscript. Countries that maintained large standing armies by the draft did so by dragging peasants off to service or impressing vagrants from the towns. Sons of the well-to-do who enjoyed student exemptions were safe from this fate. So many youths were being sent to school for this purpose that, in Prussia, authorities had to introduce examinations to weed out the student population. The British had no conscription but allowed impressment gangs to prowl the streets of seaports, picking up the drunk and idle, sending them in chains as crews for the ships of the royal navy. It was even rumored that London masters sold their apprentices into service.

The least disturbing way of raising an army was to buy soldiers. Many of the German and Swiss youth who were not needed on the overcrowded land hired themselves to any side that could afford them. Armies learned to use mercenaries sparingly since they were expensive, and battles in the eighteenth century were usually like a game of hide-and-seek, with each side avoiding battle in order to win through financial exhaustion. It was rare for an army to attack directly or to try to ruin the enemy's civilian war-making capacity. With rare exceptions, like the Battle of Culloden in 1745 when British soldiers brutally hunted down and slaughtered men, women, and children of Scottish highland clans supporting the Jacobite rebels, there was only limited danger to civilians in time of war. Civilians seemed willing enough to leave warfare to the soldiers, and except in frontier areas like colonial America, the notion of a local militia was almost forgotten.

The American and French Revolutions did much to revive the ideal of the citizen-in-arms. The minuteman's rifle and the *sans-culotte's* pike were symbols of a new era of civilian-military relations that broke sharply with the monarchical tradition. The concept of the nation-in-arms first sprang into being in the name of France, then in the Spanish and German Wars of Liberation against the French. Although the new model armies were often commanded by kings and emperors, they no longer thought of themselves as fighting for princes. Rather, they were fighting for peoples.

"War is the sole art of him who rules," Machiavelli wrote in the sixteenth century. Dynastic politics determined the uses of violence until the end of the eighteenth century, but by that time some princes were already talking as if their personal or family interests were subordinate to those of the state. Frederick the Great, who regarded himself as "the first servant of the state," rode at the head of his armies and was contemptuous of those "kings in Europe, who believe that they are lowering themselves if they assume command of their armies." Napoleon could not afford to state that the French armies served any purpose other than the nation itself, whatever his personal ambitions might be. Moreover, the identification of the army with the nation was more than just a convenient fiction by 1800, for it shaped the sociology of the military, its relationship to society, and even its internal politics. Most importantly, this identification totally redefined war itself, relating it in new ways to social, economic, and political conditions. This was the revolution of which the Prussian military reformer Clausewitz spoke in the famous book *On War*, written during the Napoleonic period:

> War of a community—of whole nations—always arises from a political condition and is called for by a political motive. . . . War is therefore a continuation of policy by other means . . . we see first, therefore, that we must in all circumstances think of war not as an independent thing, but as a political instrument. . . . This alone opens the great book to intelligent appreciation.

In suggesting a close relationship between war and society, Clausewitz was not advocating militarism but pointing out the new, tightly woven order of civil-military relations that had been apparent from the first

French *levée en masse* in August 1793. The old French military elite, the aristocracy, had proven untrustworthy, and so the Republic had to restructure military service on a new principle of merit rather than birth. Egalitarian principles permeated the new citizen army. Because the common soldier could no longer be expected to obey the command of officers on the basis of traditional deference, it was necessary to find a new principle of authority.

At first the notion of elected officers supplied this, but after 1795 it gave way to a less radical but equally new idea: the professional officer corps in which achievement legitimized rank and authority. A clear line was drawn between the social origin of a soldier and his professional abilities. Napoleon, who made his own meteoric rise to commander something of a national myth of "careers open to talent," proclaimed that every recruit carried in his knapsack the potential of a marshal's baton. Commissions ceased to be the personal property of the officer, and salaries and pensions were regularized so as to reduce corruption and tighten the chain of command.

Soldiers had once served out of fear or the desire for profit. Now a new basis for morale was found in the concept of service to the nation. In the critical years 1793-1794 it drew on the intense spirit of self-sacrifice of the *sans-culottes,* who saw the army as the vanguard of democracy. Later, national service lost some of its social content, but nevertheless, the army remained associated with the republican tradition. Even under Napoleon it remained the "school of the nation," one of the few institutions to bring the French of all social and geographical origins to a sense of common identity.

As in developing countries today, the army was a popular career. Population growth and unstable economic conditions insured its attractions. The fact that it was one of the few institutions that recognized talent and fostered rapid mobility, provided honor as well as security, made it very appealing. Furthermore, as a form of fraternity, the army offered an alternative to an increasingly fragmented society. Its brilliant uniforms, abundant ceremonies, and regimental traditions were one of the vital links to the archaic symbols of moral and social resurrection that moved people so strongly at the beginning of the nineteenth century. Particularly under Napoleon, the army became a kind of secular religion, complete with veneration of campaign relics, a hagiography of heroes, and a crusading tradition that recalled the revitalization movements of 1793-1794. Until well into the nineteenth century the army remained more closely associated with left wing than with right wing traditions.

The crusading ethos of the French army had been strongest during the campaigns waged on the frontiers of France against the First Coalition (principally Austria, Prussia, and England) in the years 1792-1797. These campaigns resulted in the annexation of Belgium in 1795 and the declaration of the Netherlands as the Free Batavian Republic in the same year.

Subsequent French victories brought domination of the left bank of the Rhine, the creation of a series of satellite republics in Italy in 1796, and the transformation of parts of Switzerland into the Helvetian Republic in 1798. The invading French army brought revolutionary change, including the abolition of feudalism, establishment of civil equality, and the separation of church and state.

Because it was identified with new beginnings, the French army was greeted with enthusiasm, particularly by the educated middle classes whose political ideals and economic interests benefited from the military collapse of the old regimes in their respective countries. The Low Countries, northern Italy, and the western parts of Germany were the only areas of Europe outside England whose economic and social development was comparable to that of France, however. Parts of these regions had already rebelled against aristocratic rule; because the ideals of liberty, equality, and fraternity had not yet fostered intense nationalism, native radicals could cooperate with the invading French forces without being discredited by this alien intrusion.

French ideas were not welcome in every nation that was at a similar stage of development, however. The case of England during the 1790s illustrates how the crusading spirit of the French armies could be counterproductive in countries with an already established sense of national identity. The French Revolution had been greeted favorably by many English, particularly those associated with the native tradition of religious dissent. Something very much like the *sans-culottes* movement appeared soon after 1789, taking the form of radical Corresponding Societies in the 1790s. English radicals saw the parallels between themselves and the Jacobin–*sans-culottes* movement and tended to draw on the same social constituency—radical intellectuals and independent artisans—for support. Much of the same desire for moral and communal revitalization infused English politics, except that the English rural population, already largely reduced to the condition of wage earners without property, remained passive. Radicalism tended to be urban, capitalizing on the apocalytic mood recorded in John Stedman's diary of 1794:

June 5   London disloyal, superstitious, villainous, and infamous. An earthquake is prophesied by (Richard) Brothers. Many leave town.

June 9   . . . 75 guillotined at Lyons. Insurrection quell'd at Toulon. At Salisbury, Irishmen flogg'd—a dozen. . . . Dined with Palmer, Blake, Johnson, Rigaud, and Bartolozzi. La Vendée and Brittany in arms.

June cont. All infantry ordered home. . . . A riot at Birmingham. Saw Deslomes, who was robbed of about 5,000 pounds sterling.

August . . . The King's coach insulted. . . . Met 300 whores in the Strand. French prisoners come home. . . .Saw a mermaid. Meat

and bread abused. Russian fleet down. Two days at Blake's.
Quiberon expedition failed, 188 emigrants executed.

But despite conscription riots, rising prices, and severe food shortages
that brought on a series of bread riots, the English government remained in
control. Efforts to pacify the countryside by increased poor relief were
successful, and forceful action against urban radical groups, including sus-
pension of civil rights and the imposition of censorship, proved effective.
There was genuine revulsion in England against the excesses of The Terror,
and some, like Wordsworth and Southey, abandoned politics for quieter
pursuits. Thomas Paine continued to be read; Blake continued to write,
though not in an overtly political manner. All radical activity was labeled
pro-French and therefore unpatriotic.

Prime Minister Pitt's well-organized propaganda machine activated the
established tradition of English nationalism. Even popular custom came to
serve the patriotic cause when, for the traditional November 5 burning of
the effigy of the seventeenth-century Catholic regicide Guy Fawkes, a like-
ness of Napoleon was substituted. British industry came to the aid of the
war effort by producing thousands of chamber pots with Bonaparte's face
staring upward. The arts as well as religion were summoned to the defense
of the status quo. Painters were commissioned to glorify national heroes,
the first of these Nelson, whose death at Trafalgar in 1805 inspired plans
for a monument to match Napoleon's Arc de Triomphe in Paris. Later, the
hero of Waterloo, the Duke of Wellington, was transformed through popular ballad and cartoon into the English counterpart of France's imperial
savior. Resentful of living on what portrait painter John Opie called the
"mere scraps, offals, and the dog's meat of patronage," most English artists
were ready to paint, sculpt, and sing the praises of British liberty.

The long years of war, marked by peace only in 1802–1803, introduced
a period of political reaction in English politics at a time when the country's economic development was flourishing. Here again we see the increasingly tight linkage between war and society. The discipline of war gave
business people the opportunity to deal with their labor problems in a
decisive way. It provided the occasion for the Combination Acts of 1800,
which forbade trade union organization, and for the creation of strict
master-servant laws that suited a political as well as economic purpose. To
Blake, war was making "all the arts of life . . . into the arts of death." In
The Four Zoas, Blake's images of internal repression and external aggression
came together:

> And in their stead intricate wheels invented Wheel without wheel
> To perplex youth in their outgoings & to bind to labours
> Of day & night the myriads of Eternity that they might file
> And polish brass & iron hour after hour laborious workmanship
> Kept ignorant of the use that they might spend the days of wisdom
> In sorrowful drudgery to obtain a scanty pittance of bread

War worked on England differently than it did on France, partially because the former already had a head start in economic development. War's high prices may have made the French peasantry and artisan groups politically volatile but they also reinforced their traditional economic cautiousness, probably inhibiting industrialization. On the other hand, English entrepreneurs were inclined to be politically conservative but economically innovative, taking advantage of rising prices to expand production at the economic expense of the independent artisan and the social expense of the land-owning aristocracy. By 1815 the English middle class had become aware of its strength as an independent force, whose contribution to the successful war against the French entitled it to a share in power and glory. Thus, despite its reactionary political elements, war had accelerated the pace of social change in an England that now completely dominated world commerce.

Impact of the Napoleonic Wars on Europe

A third pattern of relationships between war and society emerged in those more backward eastern and southern areas of Europe where struggles against imperial France strengthened the forces of reaction rather than progress. There war seemed to energize aristocratic and clerical forces, who were able to seize the leadership of popular uprisings against the French. Peasant rebellion was not entirely backward looking, however, and here and there rural insurrection took up the symbols of liberty, equality, and fraternity, interpreting them in anti-French fashion as freedom from imperial taxation and conscription or as the right to local autonomy.

Often, members of the aristocracy and clergy seized upon peasant discontent for their own purposes, but the leadership of anti-French movements varied from place to place. In Italy, for example, local bandits inspired opposition to French invasion in 1798-1799, enhancing and exploiting the popular image of the bandit as a Robin Hood, robbing from the rich to give to the poor. In Austria the respectable tavern owner Andreas Hofer led the Tyrolean peasants in a futile revolt in 1809. In Spain, the clergy became identified as leaders of resistance to France from 1808 onward. And during the Napoleonic invasion of Russia in 1812-1813, local nobility led peasants in guerilla action.

Invading armies had long been the traditional nemesis of the peasantry, for they lived off the land, disrupted local markets, and carried off youth as conscripts or forced labor. The French army was less likely to conscript locals, but it did live off the land—campaigns were planned to take advantage of local resources because in most parts of Europe transport was still too primitive for modern supply methods. Thus the increased size and longer thrust of the army added to the negative impact of imperial policy; the result was that peasant populations in central and southern Europe were driven to resistance that, beginning as simply anti-French, often ended up as antirevolutionary as well. This was the case in Spain, where the long and brutal guerilla war cemented the alliance between clergy and peasantry. In similar manner, liberalism became associated with foreign influence, and conservatism with patriotism in parts of Germany and Italy.

But even where warfare produced strong anti-French and antiliberal reactions, it did not necessarily set back the thrust of modernization. To cope with the challenge of a dynamic France, conservatives were forced to abandon old methods and to adopt new ones. The most dramatic examples of conservative adaptation of revolutionary principles occurred in Germany. The French gained relatively easy hegemony in western Germany, but both Austria and Prussia resisted change. It was not until 1803 that Napoleon began a thorough reorganization of Germany that ended with the abolition of the ancient Holy Roman Empire in 1806. A myriad of tiny princedoms, city-states, and ecclesiastical holdings that had cluttered the map of central Europe for centuries were consolidated. Consistent with the revolutionary principle of separation of secular and religious power, the bishoprics of Cologne, Mainz, and Salzburg were abolished. The ancient free city-states were reduced to 4 and the number of sovereign territorial units diminished from 234 to 40. Countless overlapping jurisdictions were eliminated and the reorganized states became sovereign units, free of the Hapsburg-dominated Holy Roman Empire. Chief beneficiaries in this process of centralization were the larger states of Prussia, Württemberg, Baden, and Bavaria, which were encouraged to free themselves of Hapsburg influence.

The interests of France dictated the changes in Germany. France's old rival, Hapsburg Austria, was seriously weakened and none of the other German states was made strong enough to take its place. Furthermore, in their scramble for territorial gains the remaining German princes had undercut the traditional legitimating principle of the divine right of kings. They had not only acquiesced in the abolition of the ecclesiastical territories, but also had stood by while other princes were deprived of their lands. As a result, they were forced, whether they liked it or not, to find new sources of legitimacy to substitute for that which they helped destroy.

Napoleon encouraged the adoption of French law codes and administrative procedures, hoping that this would bind the German states even closer to French interests. In the case of the southern and western German states this ambition was fulfilled and the stamp of French culture remained throughout the nineteenth century. But in the larger states, Austria and Prussia, anti-French sentiment was too strong. The Hapsburgs continued to be organizers of hostile coalitions. Napoleon could not afford to see Austria disappear completely, for it was a required piece on the international chessboard, needed as balance against Prussia and Russia. So it was allowed to go its own way, retaining much of the flavor of the Old Regime.

Prussia managed to remain out of a total war with France until 1806, when, in its first confrontation with the French armies at Jena, the proud

Prussian military suffered a complete and humiliating defeat. The armies that Prussia had thrown at Napoleon were a perfect reflection of Old Regime society, with aristocrats as officers and peasants conscripted in the traditional manner. The defeat was all the more shattering because the home front also disintegrated. Some towns opened their gates to the French, the peasantry remained passive, and the Prussian state simply collapsed. Fortunately for the Hohenzollern monarchy, however, there existed a remarkable group of civil and military servants, who even before 1806 had voiced concern over Prussia's unreconstructed condition. The defeat at Jena proved to be Prussia's July 14, for it catalyzed a movement for reform and revitalization that, while it did not reach far down into the population at large, constituted what one of the reformers rightly called Prussia's "revolution from above."

The association of the aristocracy with military service was shattered. The superiority of the French system of "careers open to talent" was demonstrated, with the result that all Prussians were forced to ask the question posed by one of the reformers:

> Why did the courts not grasp the simple and sure means to open a career to genius whenever it shows itself, to encourage talents and virtue from whichever class or rank they may spring? Why did they not choose this way to raise their strength a thousand times and open to the bourgeoisie the *porta triumphalis* by which only the nobleman is allowed to enter?

The answer was to open the officer corps to nonnobles. Prussia's army was to be transformed from an elite of birth to one of professional competence. The Prussian reformers Gerhard von Scharnhorst, Count August Gneisenau, and Karl von Clausewitz were themselves mainly nobles and, therefore, in no way democratically inclined, but they saw the need for the mobilization of talent if the army was to be truly competitive. They also recognized the need for change in the recruitment of the common soldier, who for too long had been subject to arbitrary and humiliating circumstances. To accomplish a nation-in-arms required the creation of a body of citizens, and thus military reform also involved civil transformation. The Prussian military reformer Gneisenau expressed well what the year 1789 meant to those who wished to have the benefits of revolution without revolution itself:

> The Revolution has set in action the national energy of the entire French people, putting the different classes on an equal social and fiscal basis. . . . If the other states wish to establish the former balance of power, they must open up and use the same resources. They must take over the results of the Revolution, and so gain the double advantage of being able to place their entire national energies in opposition to the enemy and of escaping the dangers of a revolution.

The reformers' enemies called them "Jacobins" when they proclaimed the need to overthrow the old caste system that restricted nonnobles from owning land, nobles from entering urban occupations, and tied down the peasantry with forms of serfdom. Beginning in 1807, serfdom was abolished and land reform was introduced. Peasants were allowed to pay off their feudal obligations and gain free title to their land. Although only the better off peasants were able to take full advantage, this reform represented a step toward civil equality. Simultaneously, all restrictions on landowning and trade were abolished. Every effort was made to transform corporate and local identity into the sense of individual citizenship. Political equality was not contemplated and all implications of social leveling were avoided, but in terms of duties to the state (taxes and conscription) everything was a good deal more evenly distributed.

Other important changes flowed from these reforms. The structure of government was centralized and a substantial specialization of functions achieved. Both the bureaucracy and military gained a good deal of autonomy, and their elites saw themselves as an aristocracy of service, superior even to the old landowning nobility. Another achievement was the reform of the Prussian university system, involving the elimination of church controls, the substitution of examinations for patronage, and the creation of methods of original research to replace rote learning. To the patrons of university reform, education was the cornerstone of political as well as cultural revitalization. It was the primary means of mobilizing talent for service to the state in a country that by English and French standards was still economically and socially backward, as well as a means of instilling a spirit of nationalism among the student elites.

Measured by their essentially conservative objectives, the achievements of the Prussian modernizers were an outstanding success. Faith in the state was restored, its army and bureaucracy were strengthened. A strong sense of fraternity arose among the educated elites (if not among the still passive general population) that was translated into an enthusiastic student volunteer movement in 1813-1814. Professor Jakob Fries told the students: "Let your community of youthful fellowship, your federation of youth, be a model for the nation state." They responded by reforming the student fraternities, dedicating them to the revitalization of moral and communal values. Friedrich Jahn's gymnastic clubs were used as cover for patriotic revival and the reformed fraternities (*Burschenschaften*), whose slogan was "Honor, Liberty, and Fatherland," became the core of the anti-French nationalist movement.

Nationalism was a construct of intellectuals rather than a popular response of the general population, however. The idea of nationalism—the desirability of peoples of similar cultural and linguistic character uniting— was first broached in the eighteenth century but was taken up with crusading vigor only after 1789, when it was first used in defense of the French

Republic and then against the Napoleonic Empire in various conquered territories. The concept of national resistance served as a rallying cry for those groups that were trying simultaneously to throw off foreign rule and reform their states internally. Its strongest articulation in Germany and Italy came from groups of intellectuals, including those bureaucratic and military reformers who were attempting to dislodge old corporate and provincial privileges in order to mobilize popular support for the state. In Prussia, Fichte's *Addresses to the German Nation* of 1808 set a standard for direct appeal to the "people" over the head of the old feudal order:

> . . . it must be love of fatherland that governs the state by placing before it a higher object than the usual one of maintaining internal peace, property, personal freedom, and the life and well-being of all. For this higher object alone, and with no other intention, does the state assemble an armed force.

The "people" was a mystical abstraction, invoked as a way of legitimizing reform but rarely meant to legitimize democracy. The service elites who used the concept of nationalism envisioned a "revolution from above," with no thought of popular participation. Theirs was a nondemocratic kind of populism, designed to subvert the traditional social and local hierarchies without diluting the power of the state. The peasantry, though the object of much nationalist oratory, retained its strongly local loyalties.

Popular nationalism did not emerge until the second half of the nineteenth century in Germany and Italy. The landowning aristocracy and urban patriciate, much closer to the "people" geographically and culturally than were the intellectuals, were naturally opposed to any kind of nationalism, for it legitimized the kind of state power that undermined their position. So, too, were the peasants and small-town dwellers opposed, for they loathed the taxation, conscription, and free-market forces centralization represented. Therefore, in most parts of Europe nationalism remained the monopoly of the intellectuals, despised by the aristocracy and distrusted by the population at large.

Despite the nationalist rhetoric, Prussia's conservative approach to modernization precluded social mobilization beyond conscription. There was vague talk of constitutions and national assemblies, but nothing ever came of that once victory had been achieved in 1815. When the student fraternities began to take their own slogans too seriously they were easily repressed, for political consciousness had never been allowed to penetrate too deeply into civilian society. The spirit of fraternity that had been used to reinforce corporate loyalty within the army was not permitted to launch an independent democratic movement. Taking advantage of the lessons of the French Revolution, the conservative elites had managed to co-opt the desire for revitalization and turn it to their own purposes.

The Defeat of Napoleon

Like all imperial systems, Napoleonic France had forced change on its conquered territories, only to see the resulting modernization undermine its
own power. By 1810 the Empire had reached the pinnacle of its success.
The defeat of Prussia in 1806 opened the way for understanding between
Napoleon and Russia's Czar Alexander I, culminating with the agreements
reached at Tilsit in 1807. Like Napoleon, Alexander was a visionary,
although mystical Christianity more strongly influenced him and shaped
his sense of history in an apocalyptic mold. True to the traditions of
enlightened absolutism, he believed himself to be a humanitarian ruler,
obligated to give the people of Russia and Europe the peace and prosperity of which they had been so long deprived. Napoleon impressed him at
first as a man of similar principle with whom he could share the awesome
responsibility of initiating a new millennium. At their Tilsit meeting they
tentatively recognized one another as emperors of the East and West
respectively, creating a loose alliance that was to last for the next five years.
 It is doubtful that two individuals whose common trait was imperial
vision could have maintained this equilibrium for much longer. Napoleon had to deal with his traditional enemy, England, which after the
defeat of the French fleet at Trafalgar in 1805 seemed completely safe
from military conquest. Economically, England was still vulnerable and in
1806 Napoleon took steps to exclude British goods from European markets, a move he hoped would bring the "nation of shopkeepers" to its
knees. However, economic war proved a greater challenge than military
battle. The English threatened to blockade those countries that complied
with the French boycott, smuggling in and out of Europe increased enormously, and no amount of French persuasion could halt it. Finally, Napoleon was forced to seal the borders of the Continent. He invaded Denmark
and placed it under French control, thus completing the northern boycott.
In 1808 he took over Portugal, similarly halting its trade with Britain, a
move that required French entry into Spanish politics as well. This aroused
resistance among the Spanish population that was to involve the French in
endless guerilla war.
 Meanwhile, England was having its own troubles, particularly with the
United States. Finding its trading ships stopped by English vessels, the
Americans used the opportunity to declare war and invade Canada in
1812. The Americans had already gained one windfall from the European
conflicts with the purchase from France of the Louisiana Territory in 1803
and now hoped to extend their borders northward. The effort failed and
England was able to hold onto Canada. Britain was also able to maintain
valuable markets in Latin and South America that more than made up for
its European losses. Its economy expanding, it was able to finance further
anti-French coalitions when the opportunity presented itself.
 Such a possibility occurred in 1812 when the understanding between

Alexander and Napoleon broke down and the latter launched his fateful invasion of Russia. The background to this disastrous adventure was the Napoleonic creation of the Grand Duchy of Warsaw against the wishes of the Russian czar. No longer satisfied with his previous federated system of satellites, Napoleon was moving to create a more autocratically controlled system of kingdoms in orbit around France. He replaced the republics of Holland and Rome with crowned heads of state chosen from among his own relatives; when the Pope resisted he found himself a prisoner in France. Czar Alexander might have been wise to placate the man whom he once recognized as the "Emperor of the West," but frictions over the Continental boycott became insurmountable. At the end of 1810, Russia declared that it would no longer exclude English goods.

The French invasion of Russia was carefully planned with the support of Austria and Prussia. When Napoleon marched in June 1812, his army was an international one, consisting more of Poles and Germans than of French. It had always been the emperor's strategy to seek total victory; thus, when the Russians chose to withdraw without committing their armies to a pitched battle, he simply followed them. By the end of summer Napoleon had reached Moscow, a city deserted and gutted by fires set by the retreating Russians. Not only had he failed to destroy the main enemy force, but his strategy of living off the land also had failed. Winter was approaching and the scorched earth of Russia offered little sustenance to the six hundred thousand invaders. Five weeks of fruitless negotiations with Alexander left no alternative but retreat, a saga of misery and horror unprecedented in military history to that time.

Only about one-sixth of the ranks who had entered Russia managed to leave it in the winter and spring of 1812–1813. Four hundred thousand men died of various causes and another hundred thousand became captives of the Russian troops who, with the help of peasant bands, successfully harassed Napoleon all the way across the plains of Poland and eastern Prussia. There they were reinforced by fresh Prussian and Austrian troops, whose governments had turned against the emperor as he retreated and were now in alliance with the English and the Russians in an all-out effort against the French. German students streamed to the front as volunteers, giving this last coalition something of a popular nationalist flavor that had not been characteristic of previous dynastic coalitions against France.

Napoleon miraculously managed to regroup the French armies in the spring of 1813, but his effort was in vain. In October they were badly beaten at the Battle of Nations near Leipzig and then pushed back into France. Diplomatic negotiations were initiated and for the next few months the members of the coalition argued over the terms to be offered to France. The Russians wished to see Napoleon removed, but the Austrians, represented by Prince Metternich, did not. They feared Russian power and were afraid, too, that the removal of French influence in Germany would encourage their Prussian rivals. Metternich proposed that Napoleon remain on the throne if he would agree to recognize the Rhine as the natural frontier of France. The emperor would have none of this, however, and by his resistance almost managed to split the coalition. Only the work of the English minister Castlereagh kept the allies together long enough to sign a Quadruple Alliance in March 1814, in which they pledged to support one another until a final settlement could be arrived at. With unity restored, the allied armies marched on Paris; in April Napoleon was forced to abdicate, leaving the way open for the only solution Russia, Austria, Prussia, and England could agree on, namely, the restoration of the Bourbon pretender, Louis XVIII.

The decision to restore the pretender was arrived at, not out of royalist fanaticism, but in the knowledge that this was the regime least likely to factionalize a France exhausted after more than twenty years of almost continuous warfare. Alexander demanded that the restoration have a constitutional basis and Louis XVIII agreed. The so-called Charter of 1814 recognized the legal and administrative transformation brought about by the revolutionary and imperial regimes, adopted the Napoleonic Code in its entirety, recognized the Concordat of 1801, and accepted as final the transfers of property that had occurred during the previous twenty-five years.

Though the king was to have the trappings of absolute power, there was to be a legislature elected by a limited number of propertied citizens. This was certainly not a democratic constitution, but then political equality had been a dead letter since at least 1799. To many of the French the restoration appeared considerably more liberal than the Napoleonic regime and, for a population seeking stability and peace, this was sufficient to produce acceptance, if not actual enthusiasm. If it was a restoration, it was a restoration of the monarchy of 1791, not of 1789. The peacemakers had no wish to set off new upheavals by turning back the clock. Indeed, there could be no reversal of the social and political development that, even if it had been tenuous in 1804, had been strongly institutionalized through years of war. The social mobilization that war required had confirmed a modern consciousness of citizenship. There could be no reversion to a decentralized system of Estates once this new identity had been baptized by years of sacrifice and struggle.

Peacemaking, 1814-1815

The political leaders of Europe were wise to see that almost twenty years of war fought on new principles required a peace that was equally revolutionary. Peacemaking began in Vienna in September 1814. Prince Metternich wished the conference to be a social as well as diplomatic success and for several months the Austrian capital did its best to revive the sociability of the Old Regime in an endless round of balls and entertainments. If, however, the princes and bishops deposed by twenty-five years of revolution and war expected restoration of their territories, they were sadly mistaken.

Peace rather than legitimacy was uppermost in the minds of Alexander of Russia, Hardenberg of Prussia, Talleyrand of France, and Metternich himself. The diplomats of 1814–1815 spoke of their work as the restoration of the European balance of power, the creation of a system of states in which no one power could dominate the others. Such a notion had been operative for centuries, with states forming and reforming alliances so as to block the ambitions of single aggressive powers. What was new was the Congress of Vienna's attempt to place the balance on a firm territorial basis, an effort that, however fragile, marked a turning point in modern peacemaking. Despite their reputation for callous diplomacy, the five powers were moved (to various degrees) by a kind of forward-looking idealism that envisioned the possiblility of an era of peace based on the natural laws of statecraft. This idealism looked back to the theories of Grotius in the sixteenth century and forward to the Wilsonian diplomacy of the twentieth. In this respect, the congress can be viewed as the first step toward the creation of modern permanent international peace-keeping institutions such as the United Nations.

The territorial balance was not a restoration of pre-1789 international relations. The internal transformation of monarchy into modern nation-state, however incomplete in 1815, precluded this. Austria, England, Russia, and Prussia were all reasonably united in wishing to establish a ring of strong powers around France. This was accomplished by creating to France's north a Kingdom of the Netherlands, that encompassed the territories we now know as Holland and Belgium. To the southeast, French ambition was countered by the creation of the independent Kingdom of Sardinia and the annexation of the lands of Tuscany, Milan, and Venice to an expanded Austrian Empire. France's borders on the east were trimmed back to the limits of 1792, leaving most of the left bank of the Rhine in the hands of the Prussians, who formed from it two large provinces, Rhineland and Westphalia. The Kingdoms of Baden, Württemberg, and Bavaria were recognized by the major powers, thus providing a further buffer against France.

If the deposed bishops and princelings thought they were going to get back their lands they were badly disappointed. Napoleon's reduction of the number of German states to forty set a precedent for further paring down to thirty-four, which were joined with Austria and Prussia into a loosely constituted German Confederation. The creation of anything like a unified German nation was studiously avoided, however, because this would have provoked the traditional Prussian-Austrian struggle for hegemony. Furthermore, German nationalism, like all other early nationalism, was still associated with liberal and democratic sympathies and was therefore suspect to the great powers.

The modern notion of the nation-state was therefore compromised in

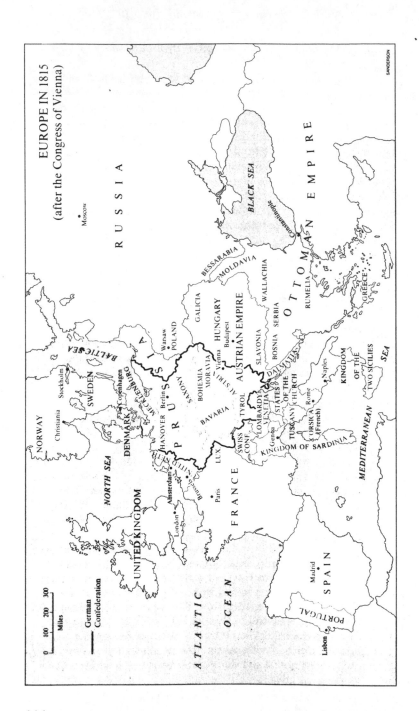

EUROPE IN 1815
(after the Congress of Vienna)

SANDERSON

the case of Italy and Germany, and the notion of a community of nations had as its only supporter Czar Alexander, who envisioned peoples living together in a new moral order. He was strongly moved by his religious views, which, like the millennialism of the early nationalists, envisioned a revitalization of the moral order leading to a golden age of peace and harmony. "If men were vital Christians there would be no wars," he wrote. 'I am sure that the spirit of Christianity is decisive against war."

In the end, however, it was not the charismatic Alexander but the pragmatic Metternich who carried the day. He had little trouble convincing his counterparts, including the French representative Talleyrand, that an order based on idealism was no order at all. Only a territorial arrangement, based on the real interests of governments, not peoples, would restore the balance of power. Given the progress of societal modernization in most parts of Europe at the time, the congress probably went about as far as conservative diplomats could be expected to go in recognizing the integrity of existing nation-states and in furthering the tendency toward centralization in those parts of central and southern Europe less advanced in economic and political development. To have pretended that German or Italian nationalism existed outside the narrow circle of a few intellectual elites would have invited a further round of international anarchy.

The Congress of Vienna could not confine itself to Europe alone because the Napoleonic Wars had been the first true world war of the modern era, affecting not only the Americas, but the Middle East and Asia as well. One major side effect of the conflict was to be the emancipation of the Spanish colonies in the Western Hemisphere. The French invasion of Egypt in 1797 had opened a new era in that part of the world, too, and British rule in India was greatly expanded. The British had managed to cling to Canada, but the French had lost their major stake in the Americas; the English were left in a commanding position on the high seas at a time when imperialism was coming to be based less on colonization than on commercial hegemony.

The full impact of this new imperialism would await the full industrialization of Europe later in the nineteenth century, but one sure sign that old forms of imperial exploitation were giving way to new was the congress's declaration of the abolition of the overseas slave trade. This was backed by no effective policing method, however, and therefore the trade in human cargoes continued well into the nineteenth century. Yet, the formal abolition was significant in so far as it reflected the fact that European countries were becoming less dependent on direct exploitation of foreign black labor as their own agricultural and industrial capacity increased. A strong humanitarian thrust contributed to the abolitionist movement, but just as important was the fact that it was now more economical for Europeans to import American cotton (an indirect use of slave labor) than to grow it on their own plantations. In England, the growth of opposition to the slave trade was directly related to the increasing unprofitability of the plantation economy and the growing profitability of industry at home.

Postwar Unrest

Internal squabbles plagued the congress through early 1815, but the allies were jolted into unity once again when in March Napoleon returned to France from exile on the Mediterranean island of Elba. For one hundred days the former emperor harassed his enemies until finally he was beaten at Waterloo. This time the congress was not so mild in its punishment and exiled Napoleon to the South Atlantic island of St. Helena, where he died in 1821. For France, too, the penalty was severe; there were reparations to pay and an army of occupation. Furthermore, the art that Napoleon had looted from the rest of Europe was ordered returned to its former owners, a kind of deconsecration of Paris as the temple of European arts and science. Although these measures seem relatively mild by twentieth century standards, there was now a precedent for punishing a country as well as its ruler, a distinctly modern, if mistaken, approach to peacemaking.

The final treaties were signed in November 1815. The major powers (this time excluding France) reconfirmed their alliance and agreed never again to allow a Bonaparte to rule France. They reconfirmed the previous provisions of the peace and agreed to a system of periodic conferences (the Concert System). This innovation was to prove less effective than its proponents hoped, but it did establish a precedent for permanent international institutions. Finally, all but England signed a document prepared by Czar Alexander that committed them, as Christian states, to a reign of peace and charity true to the principle of their religion. Although condemned by the liberal nationalists as a "Holy Alliance" of kings to repress their peoples, this declaration was perhaps the most idealistic product of the almost two years of peacemaking, a reflection of the millennial spirit that had been present from 1789 onward.

The diplomats and their retinues had scarcely packed up and left Vienna in early autumn of 1815 when their solution came under attack. There were discontented elements in France, Italy, Germany and Poland. The French felt the reparations unjust; Poles, Germans, and Italians felt themselves cheated of national self-determination. This discontent was confined mainly to the educated elites, however, and the post-1815 nationalism scarcely touched the peasant or urban working classes. It was the German students who had volunteered to fight Napoleon who found it difficult to return to their studies. They regarded university life as juvenile, morally self-indulgent, and politically unregenerate. The patriotic fraternities (*Burschenschaften*) absorbed their energies and in 1817 these held a reunion at Wartburg Castle, a Reformation landmark, to celebrate the three hundredth anniversary of Luther's revolt against Rome, with speakers voicing a hope for national revitalization. Most thought in terms only of a revolution of the spirit, but a few were bent on tyrannicide. When in 1819 a misguided student assassinated a leading conservative playwright, the governments of Germany came down hard on the entire student movement.

Democrats and nationalists were forced to go underground, just as they had done during the Napoleonic period, and conspiratorial movements multiplied in the immediate postwar period. Thousands of youths were being released from service into civilian life, often with disastrous results for themselves and society. Pensions were irregular and the veterans, bored by peace after the glories of twenty years of war, were desperate for a fulfilling purpose. Demobilized officers were prime recruits for the various secret societies, such as the Italian Carbonari and the German Unconditionals. The Italian revolutionary Filippo Buonarroti organized the Sublime Perfect Masters in 1809 in opposition to Napoleonic dictatorship, perpetuating this secret society in various forms for the next twenty years against the restoration regimes. This and similar secret societies attracted a number of young intellectuals and many military officers, but few members of the lower classes. Even in Russia, officers organized the so-called Decembrist conspiracy, which attempted to overthrow the czar in 1825.

In order to explain the nature of postwar radicalism, we must take into account the stage of development in which Europe found itself at the time. Twenty years of war had pushed the military's level of knowledge and organization well ahead of that of civilian society. As in today's developing countries, the army became the repository of the symbols of progress. In France it was a chief carrier of the republican as well as of the Bonapartist tradition; in Germany it was a force for reform; in Spain it was one of the few bulwarks of liberalism. Viewing themselves as an enlightened, forward-looking minority, army officers found it natural to intervene in political affairs. Military involvement was particularly strong in the early nineteenth century, especially in those countries where civilian groups remained unorganized or backward. Only in England had societal modernization kept abreast of political development, and only there did popular movements develop in the immediate postwar period.

Although the conspirators were forward looking, they tended to borrow their symbols and modes of organization from earlier religious and fraternal traditions. Their secret codes, initiation rites, and elaborate cult-like ceremonies were particularly dependent of the Freemason movement of the eighteenth century. Brotherhoods such as the German *Burschenschaften* or Guiseppe Mazzini's Young Italy movement represented something of a transition between the purely moral movements of the Englightenment and the mass political movements of the later nineteenth century. As such they were elite groups, cut off from the general population both by their obsession with secrecy and by their intellectual constituency. Only in the 1830s and 1840s did these revolutionary cadres evolve a more public, popular character and begin to take on the characteristics of a modern, mass-based political movement. By then, however, modernization had made considerable progress among all orders of society.

The Restoration of Order

Modern war had mobilized society; modern peace required demobilization. Governments were only beginning to realize the complexities of modern peacemaking, however, and chaos was the immediate consequence of peace. There was little employment for the returning heroes, because one effect of peace was a catastrophic drop in the demand for manufactured goods and foodstuffs. In England the price of grain dropped to almost one-half its 1813 levels and there were serious depressions in the urban trades. Low grain prices hurt the rural poor without really helping their urban counterparts, for they forced people off the land without necessarily creating jobs in the cities. Poor harvests in 1816-1817 turned prices sharply upward, but only to the benefit of the larger landowners.

For almost five years after the end of hostilities, the condition of the poor remained near the point of desperation in many countries. In England, for example, unemployment combined with overpopulation made this one of the most violent periods in that nation's history. There had been machine breaking as early as 1811, and rural unrest increased by 1819 to the point that England seemed on the verge of upheaval. When crowds estimated at eighty thousand gathered on St. Peter's Field outside Manchester in August 1819 to hear speeches against the ruling landowning class and demands for a reformed parliament with universal suffrage, nervous authorities attacked with cavalry. The ruling class hailed the bloody action as a victory, saving England from revolution, but the radicals called it "Peterloo," a bitter reference to another, more popular English victory five years earlier.

The year 1819 marked the onset of repression all over Europe; it was, for example, the year of the Carlsbad Decrees imposing censorship in Germany. When in early 1820 the Spanish and Neapolitan regimes collapsed after popular demonstrations, the major powers (with the exception of England and France) were ready to take action. Russia and Prussia supported Austria in its invasion of Naples. The reactionary Ferdinand I was restored to the Spanish throne, a sign to the radicals that revolution would not be tolerated. Of the revolutionary wave of 1820-1822, only revolts on the periphery, namely, in Greece and the South American republics, were wholly successful.

Nevertheless, in peace as in war, Europe had begun a pattern of events that was identifiably modern. Wars between peoples meant that peace would be no less disruptive than war, as far as society was concerned. It becomes increasingly difficult to divide history from 1792 onward according to dates of battles and treaties; these become less important than the social, economic, and political processes that were set in motion by the mobilization and demobilization of nation-in-arms. International war had been triggered in 1792 by domestic events, and throughout the next twenty-three years external and internal forces interacted in a way that was only partially subject to the control of generals and diplomats. The relations between war and society had become immensely more complicated than they had been in the eighteenth century, when warfare had been a dynastic decision. Peace, too, was now subject to considerations of internal policy in a way that it had not been before. To paraphrase Clausewitz's observation on war, we might say that peace had also become a continuation of policy by other means because peace settlements, beginning with the Congress of Vienna, henceforth had to take into account the social and political balance of powers within states as well as the external balance among them.

6

The Search for Stability, 1815–1848

At times during the period 1789–1848 it seemed that political stability might be unobtainable. Three decades of intermittent insurrection followed the havoc of the Napoleonic Wars. The major revolutions of 1820, 1830, and 1848 were interspersed with lesser revolts and putsches in 1819, 1822, 1834, 1839, and 1844, to mention just a few of the most violent years. Alexis de Tocqueville, whose lifetime spanned these years, concluded, "If men are to remain civilized or become so, the art of associating together must grow and improve in the same ratio in which equality of conditions is increased." Tocqueville understood the problem to be one of both state and society or, rather, one of establishing new relationships between the two. As he saw it, the state had successfully emancipated itself from its earlier entanglements with the old hierarchical society but had failed to build bridges to the new industrial social order. This lack of balance was the major cause of the dramatic oscillations between revolution and reaction that plagued continental Europe for almost sixty years. There was no question that the state was now stronger but, because it had not yet re-established contact at the grassroots, it was also more vulnerable.

Tocqueville had the genius to see that reaction and revolution were two sides of the same coin. In *The Old Regime and the French Revolution* he wrote in 1858:

> . . . beneath the seemingly chaotic surface there was developing a vast, highly centralized power which attracted to itself and welded into an organic whole all the elements of authority and influence that hitherto had been dispersed among a crowd of lesser, uncoordinated

powers: the three Orders of the State, professional bodies, families, and individuals. Never since the fall of the Roman Empire had the world seen a government so highly centralized. This new power was created by the Revolution or, rather, grew up almost automatically out of the havoc wrought by it. True, the governments it set up were less stable than any of those it overthrew; yet, paradoxically, they were infinitely more powerful. Indeed, their power and their fragility were due to the same causes. . . .

If upheaval from below was frequent, so too were the so-called revolutions from above—military coups, bureaucratic interventions, and intrigues of all kinds. In all respects, Europe in the period 1789–1848 reminds one of many parts of the Third World today where elite groups are as active as the general population in overturning governments and where, in the absence of strong parliamentary institutions and—equally important—strong political parties, the officer corps and civil service press political changes on the faltering regimes. During the first half of the nineteenth century, most European countries, with the exception of England, lacked the kind of intermediary organizations (parties, trade unions, professional bodies) that could channel and resolve conflict between state and society. After the Parisian *sans-culottes* were crushed in 1794, there was no sustained grassroots political movement until the Anti-Corn Law League and Chartism emerged in England in the late 1830s and early 1840s. The Jacobin experiment with clubs as the basis for political association was not repeated until 1848, though there were a myriad of short-lived conspiratorial movements from the 1820s onward.

The history of trade unions and other semipublic associations until the second half of the nineteenth century is also faltering and uncertain. Just as in developing nations today, the organizational power of the executive branch tended to outstrip that of society. The state was suspicious of parties, trade unions, and the popular press not only because these seemed threats to its power, but also because popular action, when it did occur, often tended to be backward looking and in conflict with the concept of centralized government as such. Popular movements were too often concerned with repelling rather than controlling the central political process; not until midcentury did mass movements in continental Europe begin to organize to compete *for* rather than *against* centralized power. In the absence of permanent nationwide parties and self-sustaining voluntary organizations, it was natural for officers and bureaucrats to feel themselves the beleaguered guardians of political modernization. Their fear of popular movements was matched only by their contempt for what they saw as the backwardness of their opponents.

As we have already seen, revolution is peculiar to periods in which traditional institutions have broken down and societies are searching for their replacement. With no previous modernization to guide it, Europe's search was necessarily prolonged and painful. At the same time, the experience of revolution did further developments that would ultimately produce stability; each revolution encouraged centralization and promoted organization at the national level, thus gradually bringing into being those institutions we associate with the modern nation-state. By the 1840s, political movements were beginning to compete for rather than against central power, a change that made the Revolutions of 1848 different in form and consequence from previous upheavals. This chapter explores the dialectic of revolution and reaction out of which emerged the stable modern nation-state.

Popular Unrest in the 1820s and 1830s

The uneven pace of economic development during the first stages of modernization exacerbated political instability. We have seen how the postwar depression caused popular upheaval and contributed to the rash of revolts in the period 1820–1822; agricultural prosperity was not completely restored in the 1820s and there continued to be serious unemployment in rural areas where machines were beginning to intrude. In 1830 England experienced a rural uprising which in scale very nearly matched The Great Fear of 1789.

The so-called Swing Rebellion of that year involved a last ditch effort by a swollen rural proletariat to improve its deteriorating economic situation by restoring something of the ideal of social justice that had been so savagely disrupted by fifty years of enclosure and capitalist agriculture. It was a rebellion of desperation—one that combined a glowing desire for communal revitalization with more practical demands for increased wages and employment. The rural poor paraded their requests in traditional deferential fashion. When refused, they seized the traditional weapons of the weak, the pike and the torch. Believing themselves authorized by tradition to claim a fair wage, they penned scarcely literate threats in the name of their legendary (and nonexistent) leader, Captain Swing:

> This is to inform you what you have to undergo Gentlemen if providing you don't pull down your meshenes and rise poor mens wages, the married men give tow and six pence a day . . . the singel tow shillings, or we will burn down your barns and you in them. This is the last notis.

Barns were burned and the machines that were used to deprive people of work were destroyed. However, the upheaval burned itself out within a few months despite its massive nature, and a quiet spread over the English countryside that was never to be broken again. In subsequent decades England's rural poor abandoned the notion of revitalizing the communal past and began to leave the land for the industrial cities. Swing was England's last rural rebellion, a sign that the long transition from agrarian to industrial forms of protest were nearly over.

On the Continent, however, economic change proceeded more slowly. The revolutionary wave of 1830 involved both town and countryside and was not so easily extinguished. The Belgians rose to separate themselves from Holland; there was massive rebellion in Poland, lesser upheavals in Italy and the western German states, and in July Paris raised the barricades to overthrow a reactionary king, Charles X. As the most practiced revolutionaries in Europe, the French rose mainly in response to the threat of royal coup against the Charter of 1814. It was a grand, almost theatrical revival of the *grand journée* of 1789, with the bourgeoisie and the *menu peuple* joining together in fraternal celebration of the slogans of liberty and, in a much less unanimous way, equality. The barricades were built by crowds that in their goals and composition were scarcely different from those that overthrew the Bastille. The actual insurgents were for the most part artisans, shopkeepers, and resident small-property holders, joined by students and radical intellectuals.

Once Charles had fled, the liberal commercial and banking bourgeoisie fraternized with these *sans-culotte* elements in much the same manner as had the Jacobins of 1792–1794. The rhetoric of liberalism was one of political reconciliation calling for the formation of a common front against absolutism. Even the symbols were those of 1789—the Tricolor, the march on the city hall, civic singing and dancing. And once again the arts were called to the defense of the revolution; the sense of societal renewal was captured by Eugène Delacroix in his famous painting *Liberty Leading the People*, with its mythic female figure uniting workers and students in a fraternal assault on despotism.

Both the intellectuals and *sans-culottes* knew their parts well, but so, too, did the forces of reaction, which gathered much more quickly than in 1789. It was as if the revolutionary drama had been speeded up by the actors themselves, for it was only a matter of days before order was restored and only a matter of weeks before another king, Louis Philippe, was properly installed. The more moderate liberal bourgeoisie elements, who saw in monarchy the only guarantor of social and political stability, had quickly outmaneuvered the republicans and were quicker, also, to reach for the weapons of repression that were much more readily available in 1830 than in 1789. A professional police and loyal army was now available and these were used to put down resistance to the new July Monarchy.

Yet, the bourgeoisie remained sufficiently faithful to the ideal of liberty not to turn back the clock entirely. A constitution was guaranteed and civil rights restored, but the distribution of political rights remained much as it had before 1830. The only significant change was that the franchise, previously limited to wealthy landowners, was now expanded to include commercial and industrial wealth as well. The *sans-culottes* were left outside the "active" nation and so, too, were many students, intellectuals, and less prosperous professionals.

One part of the revolutionary ritual that France had no intention of repeating was the military interventions from 1792 onward. In 1830, refusal of French armies to support revolutions in other parts of Europe doomed those to defeat. The Polish revolution proved difficult to repress, but by 1831 radical elements had been driven into exile. In England agitation, partly inspired by events on the Continent, resulted in the passage of the 1832 reform of Parliament, but this, too, amounted to little more than an extension of the franchise to a larger number of the rich. It left most of the lesser-property holders and the entire body of the poor—that is, 95 percent of the country—without democratic representation.

The Revolutions of 1830 demonstrated that the strength of the revolutionary movement was also its weakness. The *sans-culotte* support of every urban upheaval from 1789 through 1848 was composed of precisely those social groups—artisans, shopkeepers, small-property holders generally—who were being squeezed out by two classes that, by 1830, represented the mainstream of economic development—namely, the industrial bourgeoisie and the wage-earning proletariat. The nature of the *sans-culotte* movement (direct, spontaneous, and localized) could trigger upheaval, but these same qualities prevented the establishment of permanent political organization. Therefore, ongoing organization for revolution was left to the radical intellectuals who originated the conspiratorial movements of the early nineteenth century.

All the major figures of the clandestine movements of the 1820s and 1830s, those like Filippo Buonarroti, Auguste Blanqui and Guiseppi Mazzini, regarded themselves as a prophetic vanguard for the still backward population at large. As educated individuals of bourgeois and even aristocratic origin, they were for, rather than of, the people. Their secret organizations—the Sublime Perfect Masters, League of Outlaws, Young Italy—resembled salvationist cults rather than modern political organizations. They capitalized on the idealism of their mainly middle-class followers through a colorful fraternal mystique, but this was of limited appeal to the general population. Separated from artisan and peasants by birth and culture, this first generation of professional revolutionaries had little real understanding of popular longings; their social program, for example, went no further than vague promises of social justice. They relied more on enthusiasm than analysis, had little interest in the industrial process that was overtaking Europe, and placed all their faith in the sudden, apocalyptic overthrow of power.

While cultural ferment was one of the major causes of instability during the period 1789–1848, the kind of emotional millennialism it produced could hardly be expected to sustain hardheaded political action. Many of this first generation of radical intellectuals were largely apolitical; others, when they did venture into politics, proved inept, even comical. The Revolution of 1830 caught French intellectuals by surprise, and their subsequent attempts to seize power in 1834 and 1839 failed miserably, for they remained largely cut off from those they sought to lead to the barricades. The same ideas, carried into Germany, seemed even more out of touch with popular aspirations and led the next generation of radicals, including Karl Marx, to characterize their ideas, in Marx's words, as "speculative cobwebs, embroidered with flowers of rhetoric, steeped in the dew of sickly sentiment. . . ." When charisma failed, radicals turned to more practical means. Nowhere was this learning process better demonstrated than in England, where during the 1830s emerged the first mass political movement of a modern type, namely, the Chartist movement.

Reform in England

If England escaped full-scale revolution during this period, it was not because its population was passive. In several respects, English society was far more agitated by change, and yet the English state managed to contain most of the forces unleashed by the agricultural and industrial revolutions; it could be argued that the island nation was less vulnerable to the impact of the French Revolution. Militarily this was so, but England, like every other Western country, was easily invaded by radical ideas. A brief period of English Jacobinism in the 1790s was effectively repressed, and during the more than two decades that the country was at war with France, talk of reform remained treasonous.

Even when radicalism re-emerged after 1815, it was hounded until the latter part of the 1820s; then the suppressed pressure for reform of Parliament mounted, until an act was passed in 1832 that cleared away the worst abuses of the old franchise system and provided representation to industrial areas that previously had no members of Parliament. The passage of what was to become known as the First Reform Act had been preceded by a considerable period of agitation by middle-class radicals and liberals and by sporadic popular rioting by crowds who viewed reform as carrying with it economic and social relief as well as political change. However, the reform itself was the work of the old parliamentary elites, heavily dominated by aristocratic landowners, and it was scarcely the revolution that its supporters had been waiting for. The actual extension of the franchise was very slight, increasing the number of voters from four hundred thirty-five thousand to six hundred fifty-two thousand; it did little in subsequent years to change the social composition of the House of Commons.

All in all, the measure probably strengthened the landowning elites, who continued to dominate parliamentary politics for several more decades. The new industrial middle class did not pour into Parliament as expected but rather voted for the aristocratic members of the old Whig and Tory factions, thus wielding their new found power indirectly. Liberal legislation was gradually introduced, but nothing like a modern party system emerged from the 1832 reform. Parties remained loosely organized factions within Parliament rather than mass organizations outside it. Permanent organizations of voters, with paid party organizers and professional politicians, were unheard of in Britain until the 1860s.

The mass of the population found reform extremely disappointing. Not only were they excluded from the franchise, but the poor were immediately subjected to new legislation, including a reform of the Poor Laws that was against their interests. The most revolutionary result of the First Reform Act was the reaction to it by middle and working-class radicals, who revived the notion of parliaments elected by universal manhood suffrage. In 1838 they began a campaign to petition for a charter of reforms that was headed by the demand for universal male suffrage. For the next ten years Chartism braved repression and frustration; in that time it successfully gathered more than three million signatures for one of its three major petitions. It developed a series of working-class newspapers and elected one parliamentary candidate, Feargus O'Connor. This first continuous mass extraparliamentary political organization in history persisted until 1848, when its final petition was rejected. Chartism had failed in its immediate political goals, but its impact on mass political organization was permanent. Ultimately, the parliamentary factions would have to act within a similar organizational framework to reach their constituents, although that did not occur until two decades later, when the Second Reform Act of 1867 broadened the franchise significantly and made modern party organization both desirable and inevitable.

Chartism was unique among European radical movements in its sustained pursuit of *national* objectives. At a time when social protest in France, Germany, and Italy was still directed partly against the power of the central state, English working people were already acting to conquer its power. In England there was no dispute concerning the boundaries of the nation-state and, therefore, nationalism was not a disruptive factor. English national identity was established at least as early as the sixteenth century, in sharp contrast to Germany, Italy, and even France, where provincial loyalties remained stronger for a longer time. In addition, stability was encouraged by the fact that the issue of the distribution of power between the legislative and executive branches had been settled in the seventeenth century. Also, the tradition that the king's ministers were responsible to Parliament already precluded monarchal absolutism. Equally important, the English civil service and military were forbidden to bypass the ministers and Parliament by going directly to the king.

In other states, officialdom retained a special relationship to the monarch and was thus able to subvert the regular cabinet ministers, but England was backward in the development of a civil service, relying on unpaid honorific local officialdom to carry out much of the work of the state. Britain's armed forces were also small, thus inhibiting the interference of the military in civilian affairs. By Continental standards Britain's administrative machinery was diminutive and inefficient, the civil service relying on patronage until the 1850s, the military maintaining purchase of commission into the 1870s. At the same time, this "backwardness" ensured that the state cooperated with society in its quest for political modernization. Nothing like the destabilizing split between state and society that Tocqueville condemned in France occurred in England.

England's traditions of local government remained exceptionally strong, with judicial and administrative power remaining largely in the hands of large landowners in the rural areas and in a series of corporate bodies in the towns. Only during the 1830s and 1840s was this form of government strongly challenged from below, and then the combined powers of the police and military managed to contain rural and urban insurrection. Although the Swing riots of 1830 and the various protests associated with Chartism constituted, in terms of numbers and organization, a much greater force than anything that occurred on the Continent, England's political institutions survived intact. Much of this was due to an extraordinary combination of ruthless repression and sophisticated manipulation employed by English cabinets from the 1790s through 1848, but we must also take into account the fact that England was never in any sense a new nation during this period. It was the only country that escaped foreign invasion or territorial dismemberment, and thus the government did not have to cope with the problem of national integration, except in the case of Irish demands for independence.

Furthermore, by destroying the traditional peasantry and severely undermining the urban artisan groups, England's very rapid economic transformation had dislodged those groups that in other countries were the support for popular revolution. This is not to say that England did not experience its own provincial revolts, such as the Welsh Rebecca Riots of the 1840s, or generate its own urban *sans-culottes*. However, these were more quickly overtaken by strongly integrative national movements like Chartism, which relied on steady organization of the general population rather than on short, violent outbursts of protest to achieve their goals. In short, the relatively highly developed nature of its social movements helps account for political stability in Britain.

Political Instability on the Continent

Equally important, England's parliamentary institutions did not stand in the way of nation building; once the instrument of extension of royal authority, they now could be used to serve a more democratic purpose. By contrast, continental representative institutions had often been bastions of resistance to central government. Prior to the nineteenth century many of these institutions had been abolished by absolutism and those that survived were distrusted both by those who sought repression from above and those who sought revolution from below. As a result, most Continental representative bodies in the early nineteenth century were fragile institutions at a disadvantage with respect to the executive, because the regional and corporate interests that they had previously represented were in decline and there were as yet no modern national-based parties to fill the vacuum. Not really representative of either the old social hierarchies or the new social classes, parliaments in the period 1815-1848 were despised by conservatives and distrusted even by liberals and radicals, who found them vulnerable to reactionary influences. As late as 1848, the revolutionary Auguste Blanqui denounced the idea of an assembly elected by universal suffrage:

> For thirty years the counterrevolution alone has spoken to France. . . . The notables of vanquished factions, principally in the country, alone catch the attention of the people; those devoted to the democratic cause are almost unknown to them.

Nowhere was the lack of prestige of parliamentary institutions more evident than in France, where the concept of legislature had been in eclipse from 1795 through the Napoleonic Empire. In restoring the Bourbon monarchy in 1814, the victorious powers dictated to France a charter that required a bicameral legislature. It excluded the revolutionary concept of the sovereignty of the people, and Louis XVIII ruled what amounted to a constitutional monarchy.

In effect, this was the modernized Napoleonic state under new management, a solution carefully calculated to bring stability to France and peace to the rest of Europe. It pleased almost everyone except the émigrés who upon their return to France in 1814 instituted two years of White Terror directed against not only Jacobins but Bonapartists as well. In an attempt to regain their lost lands and offices they agitated for a return to pre-1789 conditions. Forming the most powerful faction in the French parliament, the Chamber, these ultraconservatives were a constant embarrassment to Louis XVIII and a threat to servants of the state appointed by earlier regimes.

Officers of the Napoleonic army placed on half-pay in 1815 were drawn to subversive conspiracies, resulting in a series of abortive coups against the monarchy in 1821 and 1822. Their intention was not to destroy the state but rather to save it from reactionary forces that appeared intent on using the legislature to dismantle the executive. The Bourbon regime managed to walk the tightrope between contending forces until 1824 when Louis XVIII died and was replaced by the deeply reactionary Charles X.

With the ultraconservatives in the executive saddle, the Chamber became a focus of liberal opposition, led by bankers and industrialists who had managed to qualify by owning land.

The reactionaries had acquired executive power, but in capturing control of a modern state they became captives of those groups—the bureaucracy and the army—who felt threatened by the ultraconservatives' avowed intention to dismantle modern institutions. Steps to restore Church privileges threatened the secular bureaucracy, and by 1830 opposition to the regime was strong within the administration as well as in the legislature. Not sensing their predicament, reactionaries around Charles X organized a coup against the Charter of 1814. In July 1830 the Chamber was dissolved to be re-elected on an even more restrictive basis. The press was censored and the army was ordered to repress opposition. As expected, the liberal opposition raised a hue and cry; they were joined by radical elements, including students and elements of the Parisian *sans-culottes*, who erected barricades in defiance of the government.

Previous regimes had dealt with insurrection with a "whiff of grapeshot," but Charles X had so alienated both the army and the civil service that he found himself standing alone against the Parisian insurrectionaries. The army refused to fire on the barricades; after two days, Charles X abdicated and fled to England. This time there was no emigration. Some two thousand army officers resigned their commissions rather than break their oath to the king, but this was a personal gesture of honor rather than a political act of counterrevolution. For the most part, the propertied bourgeoisie and the service elites stood neutral, desiring only a quick restoration of order. Although radical elements advocated a republic, they had no time to organize themselves before the elites stepped in with a new candidate for monarchy, the Duke of Orleans, Louis Philippe, a person of progressive reputation who was acceptable to almost all factions. He accepted the throne and so began the so-called July Monarchy that lasted until 1848. Again, the Napoleonic state had survived a change of regimes.

The French Revolution of 1830 was more a change of government than a total societal upheaval. The widespread insurrections of 1789 were lacking; in particular, there was no surge of activity in the countryside. The peasantry, who had gained what they wanted forty years before, were passive observers. The revolt was largely a Parisian affair, reflecting the political hegemony of the capital over the rest of France. Popular participation had been evident in July, but the economic and social discontents that drew workers and shopkeepers to the barricades did not spontaneously create an autonomous popular movement. The price of bread, conditions of work, and wages were all at issue, but the revolution was too brief to produce a *sans-culottes* movement of the kind of 1792–1794 and there was as yet no permanent working-class organization capable of sustaining politically what popular protest did then develop. Discontents lingered on through the 1830s, bursting forth in the Lyon insurrection of 1834 and

in the Parisian revolts of 1834 and 1839 but without immediately producing any mass movement like English Chartism.

In other ways, however, France showed signs of moving toward stability. The events of 1830 produced no complete collapse of the state as
had occurred in 1789. The civil and military elites continued to function
effectively throughout July and August, showing the degree of modern
professionalism (measured in terms of efficient neutrality) that demonstrated just how far the modernization of the French state had proceeded
since 1789. In effect, the civil and military personnel had shown that
they would abandon any government that threatened to turn back the
clock. The quick installation of Louis Philippe was, to a large degree, a
coup by the state-building elites against what was perceived as a threat
to the established political order from both above and below.

The July Monarchy was institutionally a virtual carbon copy of the
previous regime, except that the franchise for the Chamber was made
available to another one hundred thousand voters (a total of .6 percent
of the population). This time the government made sure that the high
property qualification included industrial and commercial capital, so that
the wealthy industrialists and bankers who had formed the opposition to
the previous regime were satisfied. This left out the mass of the population
as well as most of the salaried professionals, however, but as long as Louis
Philippe did not toy with ideas of feudal or clerical restoration, the state-
building elites remained satisfied.

During the 1830s and early 1840s, there was still little enthusiasm for
a strong legislature, in any case. The Chamber attracted to it individuals
who were noted for their oratory, but who were so personally ambitious
as to preclude their effective organization of disciplined parties. There
was no provision for the payment of deputies and, therefore, these were
by necessity either people of independent means or individuals susceptible
to corruption. As in all early nineteenth-century Continental parliaments,
deputies were more likely to be elected on the basis of charismatic personality than on party platform. Nowhere were there organized parties at the
local level; thus, the assembly itself was characterized by fluid alliances of
individuals, without discipline or permanence. The Chamber was poorly
organized, without standing committees or permanent staff, and the
executive made sure that debates were either secret or heavily censored,
so that public interest was minimal. The view of the legislature most
widely held was that of the cartoonist Honoré Daumier: a collection
of pompous, ineffective windbags, representing little else than their
own ambition.

But weakness of parliamentary institutions was also due to the lack
of differentiation between legislative and administrative functions, apparent in so many new states. Often personnel overlapped. In France and
England, state officials were forbidden to hold elected office, but in

most other states officials were allowed, even encouraged, to stand for election. The Prussian government found it useful to have its "aristocracy of capacity" (as Hegel termed it) involved in the provincial assemblies as a counterweight to centrifugal forces; almost everywhere, the legal education and social prestige of officials made them attractive candidates. As long as they were not subject to party discipline, there seemed to be no contradiction between their role as legislators and their duty to the state. Indeed, for most of the early nineteenth century, monarchies relied on councils of bureaucrats (the French *Conseil d'état*) as substitutes for elected legislative bodies. As long as the function of the legislature was inferior to that of the executive, there seemed to be no compelling reason to exclude officials from parliaments.

The fastest growing sector of peacetime government was the bureaucracy itself. After the period of uncertainty immediately following 1815, when many governments cut back services for financial reasons, public employment grew steadily, much ahead of the general population rate. Prussia's higher bureaucracy tripled in size between 1821 and 1901, and its lower echelons grew even faster. By the end of the century, there were 272,000 employees on the state payroll. France's officialdom is reported to have increased six times in this same period; counting officials on all levels, there were over a half million persons by 1900. It was calculated in 1910 that there was 1 official for every 57 inhabitants in France. The ratio of officials per 10,000 population was even higher in Belgium, which had 200 to France's 176; the ratio was 126 in Germany and 73 in England.

These figures reflect the wide range of developmental patterns in Europe, from the English model of decentralized government in which local elites continued to carry out much of the administrative and judicial work, to the much more centralized French and Belgian states that had very unified services. The size of the bureaucracies had less to do with the stage of industrialization or urbanization than with the degree of compatibility between the structure of society and the unifying thrust of the state. England, which was most advanced economically, had by far the smallest bureaucracy. Its local elites, including the landed aristocracy, had shown themselves flexible in adapting to the need of the nation-state. England suffered from little of the national disunity that in other countries required the extension of bureaucratic control, and significantly, England's most developed bureaucracy was its colonial service.

By contrast, France had experienced a long history of conflict between the state and the particular interests of society. The Revolution of 1789 precluded the use of the aristocracy or any other intermediary group for modern state building. It was Tocqueville who pointed out in the 1850s, in *The Old Régime and the French Revolution*, that those states that had the most radical break with the old social hierarchies by democratic revolution were the ones most likely to find themselves in greatest need of massive state bureaucracies:

> The first thing that strikes the observer is an innumerable multitude of men, all equal and alike, incessantly endeavoring to procure the petty and paltry pleasures with which they glut their lives. Each of them, a living part, is a stranger to the fate of the rest. Above this race of men stands an immense and tutelary power, which takes upon itself alone to secure their gratifications and watch over their fate. For their happiness such a government willingly labors, but it chooses to be the sole agent and the only arbiter of that happiness.

There is no question that the manner of France's break with feudalism caused the extension of bureaucracy in that state. Although in states like England and Prussia local elites continued to exercise administrative and judicial powers even after the abolition of feudalism, in most places paid officials took up the task of collecting taxes, administering military conscription, and providing basic local services. As populations grew so, too, did the need for more officials. In addition, as modernization progressed there were new services to be provided, such as schools, sanitation, and public utilities (water, gas, and, ultimately, electricity).

Economic development certainly contributed to the growth of bureaucracy, especially where the state was deeply involved in industry and transportation. This was particularly true in Belgium, France, and Prussia, where by the end of the nineteenth century railway officials made up a large proportion of the total civil service. Then, too, there were political reasons for the expansion of bureaucracy. In France, Italy, and Spain, where many civil service positions were filled by patronage, it was to the political advantage of each successive government to expand the bureaucracy in order to find places for its friends without alienating the incumbent officials. Finally, there was the internal dynamic of the bureaucracy itself, which in becoming more professionalized also became more specialized, thus dividing previously unified functions into two or more jobs. In the eighteenth century, "police" encompassed everything from law enforcement to sewer inspection, whereas by 1850 it meant only the former, reflecting the growing differentiation of administrative functions.

Growth in size did not by itself account for the political importance of bureaucracy in the early nineteenth century. In all but Spain and parts of Italy, the quality of bureaucratic training had improved because of the introduction of entrance examinations and the reform of university training. In Prussia and France, the higher bureaucrats were being educated in law, a background that suited them for an extraordinarily broad range of capacities. They were "intellectuals" in the early nineteenth-century sense of that term, inheritors of the eighteenth-century's emphasis on general education. Civil servants and military officers constituted an even higher proportion of the educated elites than they do today, if only because many of the modern professions, such as science and engineering, had hardly come into being at this time. As in today's new states, they therefore constituted *the* enlightened elite, especially in those countries where less than half the population was literate. In addition to this intellectual reputation, the bureaucracy benefited from the social prestige derived from their successful monopolization of education.

The first generation of Europe's reformed bureaucracies was ordinarily led by those from prestigious families, who brought both wealth and status to the office. During the first half of the nineteenth century, salaries of higher ranking officials were pegged to the noble standard of living expected of the highest servants of the crown. The pay of French ministers was one hundred and fifty times that of the lowest ranking officials, competitive with the highest incomes offered by commerce or industry. With such advantages, families of civil servants were able to perpetuate themselves by creating the bureaucratic dynasties that were the mark of almost every early nineteenth-century state.

Particularly in those states where political development tended to outstrip economic growth, the bureaucracy was the recipient of more than its share of the country's talents in the period 1815–1850, leading to the condition that the German radical Georg Herwegh sarcastically observed in the 1840s: "It is the pleasant privilege of our century that it has to recognize a truth as a truth only if it proceeds from the mouth of a bureaucrat." Social rank and general learning propelled bureaucrats to an unprecedented position of leadership not only in society but also in politics. The very fragility of most states forced these officials to take an active political role just to maintain their rank and position. In France, each turnover of government (in the years 1814, 1824, 1830, and 1848) meant the replacement of hundreds of officials and in order to maintain their positions they had to be adept at cultivating political patronage. Some found it useful to gain seats in the Chamber and trade votes for appointments, while others proved adept at mastering the internal politics of the government. Until the civil service became more fully professionalized and tenure in office became more secure, political activism was a way of survival among most European bureaucracies.

Ironically, the popularity of the bureaucratic career was also a cause of the profession's instability. By the 1840s it was attracting more talent than it could support, youths of inadequate means who were clogging the channels of promotion and causing corruption of standards. As early as the 1830s, German parents were advised that "the number of young people who have completed their studies is already more than sufficient to occupy all the positions." Their children were told to turn elsewhere for careers and many did, thus causing the quality of the bureaucracy to decline. But before the pressure was relieved, many were trapped within unrewarding bureaucratic careers.

In Prussia and elsewhere, younger, lower-ranking officials were agitating

for increased salaries and expanded opportunities. The political involvement of the bureaucracy, previously of benefit to the state, was now
turned against it as younger officials used their positions in state and
provincial assemblies to agitate for reform. During the Revolution of
1848, the participation of officials in legislative assemblies reached its
high point and so, too, did bureaucratic radicalism. State officials made
up a sizable proportion of the members of the German national assemblies
and not a few voiced liberal or nationalist sentiments much at odds with
the official government position. In Prussia, some officials took part in
radical democratic movements and supported a tax strike designed to foil
the restoration of absolute monarchy. Until economic development began
to provide more opportunities in the private sector—something that was
dependent on the overall development of society—the bureaucracy would
remain an excessively powerful, if somewhat divisive, factor in European
politics.

The Problem of Nationalism

Counterbalancing the disturbing effects of bureaucracy were the states'
own centralizing integrative tendencies; this struggle between the center
and the periphery is a major cause of disturbance in all new states. In
Europe, centrifugal forces remained powerful through the 1840s, particularly in Italy, Germany, and large parts of central Europe, where the
actual territorial definition of the nation was as yet unsettled. Today, new
states just emerging from colonial domination can usually appeal to
national unity to overcome internal conflict; even where tribal, religious,
or linguistic differences inhibit unity, the contending parties usually claim
to represent the one predetermined national entity and are thus not a
threat to national integrity itself. However, in Europe prior to 1870, the
very notion of the nation-state was the center of debate. There were many
who rejected it outright, and even the so-called nationalists disagreed on
its form. For many in their ranks, nationalism was a means to other social
and political ends. Here again was a source of division and instability.

Nationalism in its modern form was a product of the era of the French
Revolution, though the word "nationalism" entered the popular vocabu-
lary only in the 1830s and 1840s. Like other characteristic aspects of
modernization, nationalism developed fitfully, becoming respectable only
very gradually. One reason for this was the fact that it meant so many
different things to different people. It began not as a self-evident goal, but
as a means of accomplishing other ends. As a political economist, Friedrich
List was attracted to the idea of a German nation-state because he saw it
as a means of economic development and was convinced that a divided
Germany could not survive competition with larger economic units like
England and France. In order to develop an economy of sufficient scale,
List wanted to include Holland and Denmark within his new Germany, a

plan that brought his nationalism into conflict not only with Dutch and Danish patriots but also with the ideas of his fellow Germans. Giuseppe Mazzini was repelled by any kind of imperialism, but he, too, viewed nationalism as a means to an end—namely, the betterment of all humanity. His nationalism had a pronounced social—if not socialist—component.

Unity of man was to overcome the dispersion of modern man in an industrialized mass civilization. . . . Unity of nation was to bind all the free individuals of democracy into a community of liberty and equality. . . . Unity of mankind was to assure the peace and collaboration of all nations. . . .

In addition, there were those who wanted to use nationalism for a specific political purpose. The Girondins of 1792–1793 were perhaps the first practitioners of this art when they rallied national spirit to offset reactionary threats to their revolution. For most of the pre-1848 period, nationalism remained the monopoly of the left; liberals, radicals, and socialists viewed it as a progressive force because it helped accomplish the breakdown of old, particularistic elements associated with aristocracy. Not only did John Stuart Mill call large nation-states "a necessary condition of free institutions," but Karl Marx also supported German national unity as a step toward proletarian emancipation. In the eyes of German and Italian conservatives, there was little difference between nationalists and revolutionaries. With the exception of England, where a clear definition of "nationality" already existed, conservatives initially avoided nationalist appeals because they smacked of democracy.

Pierre Buchez was right when he observed of early nineteenth-century nationalism that "each theorist, each party, each country was able to read into it what it wished, what justified its own aspirations." Although its advocates might talk as if a German, Greek, or Croatian national spirit had always existed, in fact early nationalism did not derive from the grassroots but from the formulations of small groups of middle-class intellectuals. Before 1789, "patriotism" meant something quite local. When peasants talked of their compatriots, they meant people of the same province (*pays*). In England, "going abroad" meant leaving town as well as leaving the country. In its origins, the new, broader definition of nationalism was a strictly elite conception, alien to the mentality of the mass of the population. Where state boundaries already coincided with linguistic or cultural units, as in England or France, a certain sense of identity was already present, but it lacked the emotional intensity of modern nationalism and was by no means the operating principle of traditional politics. All the old regimes, including France and England, had no qualms about incorporating people of different tongues and culture, despite difficulties in integrating them. During the French Revolution, patriotism—interpreted in the sense of local loyalty—had promoted both revolution and counterrevolution and for most of the early nineteenth century continued to divide people of different social and regional backgrounds, political and religious persuasions. When the Catholic cantons of Switzerland formed a federation (*Sonderbund*) in 1844 to defend their decision to introduce Jesuit control of education within their localities, the Protestant cantons invoked Swiss nationalism in order to defeat the move. The civil war that resulted in 1847 led to the complete defeat of the *Sonderbund* and the imposition of the Protestant definition of the nation-state. Similarly, disputes between French and Flemish speakers in Belgium were a continual cause of political instability, and differing interpretations of "patriotism" were to lead to deep schisms during the German Revolution of 1848. Contending Prussian and Austrian (not to mention Bavarian, Hessian, Saxon) patriotisms were a major cause of the defeat of the revolution.

Whether the forces of economic modernization favored one type of nation-state is debatable. Although Friedrich List could argue that economies had to be of the scale of England in order to compete, tiny Belgium did well for most of the century. The well-being of the human race did not, as Mazzini imagined, correlate with national self-determination. Foreign threat was a more compelling force for national unification; however, the absence of European war after 1815 allowed experimentation with more relaxed political associations such as the German Confederation.

Some historians have argued that nationalism is peculiar to periods of early modernization because it provides a substitute faith to replace lost religious sentiments; it also may be that it offers a sense of belonging for those recently emancipated from the narrow confines of family, clan, or ghetto. Ludwig Börne, one of the first generation of emancipated German Jews, became a strong advocate of German nationalism because, as he said:

> I was born without a fatherland . . . and because my birthplace was not bigger than the *Judengasse* [ghetto] and everything behind the locked gates was a foreign country to me, therefore for me now the fatherland is more than the city, more than a territory, more than a province. For me only the very great fatherland as far as its language extends, is enough.

Börne was in the minority, however, as, for most Europeans, patriotism was more localized. Had the national identity of various states been more clearly defined and allegiance to central authority been more universal, political stability would certainly have been achieved much earlier than it was. Before 1848 nationalism appealed more as the embodiment of other social and political ideas than as an end in itself. It was as volatile as its advocates, a free-floating idea that had only a very weak appeal outside the educated elites. At no time, even during the accomplishment of German and Italian unity in the 1860s, did it constitute a mass movement. For Europe, nationalism was more the result of general modernization than an independent factor in and of itself. Before 1848 it was still an idea in search of a reality, a symptom as well as a cause of the unsteady relations between state and society. A sense of national integration was gradually emerging, but not quite fast enough to eliminate entirely those internal tensions that were the cause of upheaval.

The French Revolution of 1848

The weakness of popular nationalism was partially attributable to the fact that so many of its leaders were in exile in the years before 1848. Living abroad in Paris, London, or Zurich, Polish, German, and Italian nationalists tended to fraternize, thus tempering their chauvinism with a certain cosmopolitanism. Later, when national unity became an accomplished fact, this spirit of cooperation would disappear, but up to 1848 nationalists looked to one another for inspiration. In 1847, when the Russian Alexander Herzen made his political pilgrimage to Paris, he approached it as a revolutionaries' mecca. For him, as for thousands of others, the city was "the brain of history, the international bazaar on the Champ-de-Mars, the beginning of the brotherhood of peoples and universal peace."

Two years later, following the experiences of the Revolution of 1848, Herzen despaired of fundamental change in the human condition. He had seem the haves pitted against the have-nots, "on one side avarice, on the other envy." For Herzen the year had been a turning point. "A curse upon you, year of blood and madness, year of triumph of meanness, beastliness, stupidity! A curse upon you!" Herzen's words were prophetic; 1848 marked a major turning point in the history of Western politics, for henceforth domestic revolution would shift eastward. Subsequent internal upheavals, such as the Paris Commune of 1871 and the German Revolution of 1918, were triggered by defeat in war, the only force powerful enough to bring about the total collapse of government in the highly developed western European countries.

The Revolution of 1848 revealed other changes no less disturbing to Herzen and those who shared his millennialistic expectations. The Jacobin concept of a revolutionary popular front was shattered by the appearance of deep class divisions that pitted former allies, the middle class and the *menu peuple*, against one another. The vision of international revolution was also disappointed when the forces of nationalism and radicalism, once partners in the struggle against the old regime, parted company. In 1848 nationalism showed unmistakable signs of shedding its social content and becoming a conservative element. National and class interests surfaced boldly, displacing the more universalist thrust of the early revolutions, and leadership was passing from prophets to those of a more pragmatic nature, for whom politics was not a quest for personal or societal regeneration but the adjustment of concrete interests within a given institutional system of the nation-state.

When it began, the Revolution of 1848 appeared to repeat the pattern established in 1789; by the time it had ended, though, it was clear that Europe's long era of revolution was drawing to a close. The conditions of instability—uneven economic development, cultural conflict, tensions between the center and the periphery—were being overcome by the 1840s. The sixty-year dialectic of revolution and reaction had pushed forward economic development and political centralization to the point where groups were beginning to compete for, rather than against, the institutions of the nation-state. When this situation was reached, insurrection would not only be more difficult but also less desirable. As the events of 1848–1849 were to show, by midcentury Europe was reaching the point where revolution was to become obsolete.

The Revolution of 1848 began, as all previous revolutions had, with a series of demographic and economic crises. Economic development was just beginning to relieve population pressure, when a series of disastrous harvests in the years 1845–1847 caused food prices to double and the condition of the poor to worsen considerably. In the autumn of 1845, the potato crop in various parts of Europe turned black and inedible, and a blight, starting in eastern Europe and working its way west to Ireland, spread further havoc in 1846 when the crop was an almost complete failure. Harvests improved somewhat in 1847, but not sufficiently to reduce the price of food. There were grain riots in France and Italy, while in the spring of 1847 Berlin was troubled by what was called the Potato War, recalling the French Flour War of 1775.

As in the eighteenth century, rioting was directed, not simply at the price of produce, but at the "big men" who controlled the market. In many parts of rural France and Germany, the vision of the moral economy was still very much alive, and in those places where the railway had not yet connected localities to the national market, traditional types of protest still prevailed. In regions where the economy was still much the same as it had been in the eighteenth century, fear of famine also played its part. In Ireland, the greatest famine of the century was under way, with one and one-half million people dying either from starvation or from disease stemming from it; the British government attempted to supply cheap grain and soup to the Irish, but its efforts were too little and too late.

Trade depression accompanied hunger and the numbers on relief shot up alarmingly in 1846–1847. Yet governments were sufficiently organized to be able to offer a combination of soup kitchens and public works projects, thus reducing the political consequences of hunger. The kinds of protests that did occur—bread riot, tax rebellion, sporadic machine breaking, occupation of common lands—were mainly of the traditional sort. But misery as such was not necessarily conducive to political action. As one Irish radical later noted:

Famine . . . effected a revolution very different from that which Mr.

O'Brien [leader of the Young Ireland movement] sought to accomplish. . . . The lower classes . . . are broken down both in body and
spirit. A ration of yellow meal is the highest object of their ambition,
and so they can procure this, they care for naught else. . . .

Against this background it is easy to understand why professional revolutionaries were quite unsuccessful in rousing the general population to
insurrection in 1846–1847.

As in the 1780s, when revolution did occur it happened almost by
accident—the result, as in 1789, of the collapse of government rather than
the premeditated action of radicals. Again, it was financial troubles that
forced governments to the fateful brink of reform. In 1847 the Prussian
king was ready to call his state's version of the Estates General, causing
Friedrich Engels to write: "At precisely the same moment in which
the week-kneed Prussian bourgeois classes find themselves virtually
forced by circumstances to change the system of government, the King's
many problems are forcing him to set that process of change in motion himself. . . ."

As in the past, it was Paris that lit the fuse of revolution, though in an
unintended manner. The liberal opposition to the government of Louis
Philippe had conducted a number of banquets during the winter of
1847–1848 aimed at increasing pressure for a moderate expansion of the
franchise and other civil-rights reforms. Most of the liberal agitators were
middle-class intellectuals whose major desire was to have the same rights
as the propertied bourgeoisie; they had no intention of offering the
lower classes equal shares, for they were aware of the inroads that radicalism and socialism had made among the urban workers. In 1847
Tocqueville warned the French Assembly that "before long the political
struggle will be restricted to those who have and those who have not;
property will form the great field of battle. . . ." Every effort was made,
therefore, to keep the reform campaign as moderate as possible, and the
liberals even acceded to a government ban on their largest banquet,
scheduled to be staged on the night of February 22, 1848.

The ban came too late, however, to call off the crowds of students,
journeymen, and other *menu peuple* who gathered at the site of the
banquet to voice their own particular frustrations. When the police
attempted to break up the crowd, rioting spread. The next morning, in
a manner reminiscent of the days preceding the fall of the Bastille, crowds
of students and workers gathered in the streets, fraternizing with elements
of the civil militia—the National Guard—and causing many soldiers to
defect. The government was still in control of the police and regular
army, however, and in clashes with street crowds the military used its
weapons, killing several rioters. As in 1789, the use of force was sufficient
to mobilize the full fury of the crowds; by the night of February 23,

barricades had been built in all parts of Paris, especially in those historic breeding grounds of insurrection like the Faubourg Saint Antoine.

The target of popular hatred was the government of Prime Minister François Guizot, and Louis Philippe wisely demanded its resignation. But the cry of compromise could not be heard over the roar of gunfire. As street fighting intensified on February 24, the king fled the city, abdicating in favor of his grandson, a boy of nine. In the wake of the hasty royal departure, crowds surged into the Tuileries Palace to pay their respects to the monarchy in the traditional custom of charivari. Flaubert fictionalized the scene in *Sentimental Education*:

> . . . the mob, less out of vengeance than from a desire to assert its supremacy, smashed or tore up mirrors, curtains, chandeliers, sconces, tables, chairs, stools. . . . They were the victors, so sure they were entitled to enjoy themselves. The rabble draped themselves mockingly in lace and cashmere. Gold fringes were twined around sleeves of smocks, hats with ostrich plumes adorned the heads of blacksmiths, and ribbons of the Legion of Honor served as sashes for prostitutes. . . . Jailbirds thrust their arms into the princesses' bed, and rolled on it as consolation for not being able to rape them. . . .
> In the entrance hall, standing on a pile of clothes, a prostitute was posing as a statue of Liberty, motionless and terrifying, with her eyes wide open.

It was as if the Parisian population was acting out the scenario of previous revolutions. Indeed, there was much that was theatrical in the February revolution. The gestures and symbols, as well as the stage settings, were those of 1789 and 1830. Delacroix's popular painting, *Liberty Leading the People*, provided the model not only for the poster art of the revolution but also for its first dramatic action. For middle-class liberals, the image of the people rallying behind the traditional bourgeois standard of liberty was a comforting thought, it symbolizing the deflection of the general population away from concrete economic demands in pursuit of an abstract notion of emancipation. The idealized female figure of Liberty offered spiritual fraternization without the threat of social leveling and appeared everywhere in February, on the mastheads of liberal journals, in plays, and in songs.

The radicals had their own imagery, though, much more in touch with the desires of the Parisian working classes. They had asked Delacroix to paint a sequel to his 1831 masterpiece to be entitled *Equality Leading the People*, but frightened of the radicals, he had refused. So they turned to radical painters like Honoré Daumier, who adapted the figure of Liberty to the aspirations of the laboring poor by transforming her into a maternal image, suckling the children of the republic. She nurtured rather than led, an appropriate symbol for those who were demanding something more than the freedom to starve, who wanted a "social republic" to deal with

their material as well as their spiritual well-being. Thus the arts joined in
the revolution from the very beginning, defining and sharpening existing
differences over what the insurrection was about.

The liberals were fortunate to have as their leader the poet-writer
Alphonse de Lamartine, who was adept in the dramatic arts of politics.
It was Lamartine who rehearsed the pattern of July 1830 and declared the
creation of a provisional government from the balcony of the city hall. He
promised the crowds the restoration of civil rights and access to the previously privileged National Guard. When the population shouted their
demands for a "social republic" and the "right to work," he went still
further by including the socialist reformer Louis Blanc in a government
otherwise dominated by middle-class liberals. Lamartine even managed to
persuade the crowd to adopt the Tricolor rather than the red flag as
symbol of the new republic, but his appeals to fraternity sounded hollow
to those who had learned since 1830 to distrust the Jacobin rhetoric of
the bourgeoisie. On the day after Lamartine had declared the republic, a
young worker interrupted a meeting of the provisional government to
proclaim: "Citizens, the revolution was achieved twenty-four hours ago
and the people are still waiting for results." Lamartine rose to reply, but
the worker shouted him down: "Enough of phrases, enough of poetry."

A prosaic atmosphere descended much more quickly in 1848 than
it had in 1789. Revolution is never the same the second or third time
around, and all those involved were aware of the lessons of history. The
pace of events was forced by the radical press and worker organizations
that sprang to life in February. Louis Blanc, as a member of the provisional government, was able to announce on February 26 that the provisional government had agreed to establish a series of public works
projects for the unemployed. These were to be known as the National
Workshops and, although they were not the cooperative "social workshops" that Blanc had advocated in his socialist writings before 1848, they
were a major concession to the workers by the liberal majority of the new
government. With more than one-half of the Parisian work force unemployed because of severe economic recession (made worse by the political
upheaval), it was a shrewd way of relieving popular discontent without
acceding to the more radical demands of the socialists and democrats. But
it was not without its cost. To pay for relief, the government levied a sur-
tax on the property-tax payers. Falling most heavily on the middle classes
and the peasantry, it was the most immediate cause of their growing
hostility toward the working classes.

The provisional government moved rapidly to legitimize itself through
popular elections as well. On March 2 Lamartine declared universal male
suffrage, with elections set for April 23. Radicals like Blanqui and Etienne
Cabet sensed that this early election would work to the advantage of the
bourgeoisie, who were much better organized to influence the outcome of
the voting, and this was demonstrated by the results, which saw the

election of an Assembly composed mainly of conservatives and moderate liberals. Twelve socialists were elected and radical democrats also gained a voice, but the laboring poor—particularly the peasantry—showed a strong tendency to vote for local notables. Paternalism proved stronger than fraternity, even in many urban working-class quarters. Blanqui, who had just been released from prison, failed to gain a seat. Election of officers for the National Guard had also gone against the proponents of the social republic; by the end of April 1848, the radicals were an isolated, impotent minority, though they were still feared by the liberal government, who imagined that the Left factions, once blocked in their attempt to gain power by legal means, now plotted a second revolution.

The government did all it could to undercut the radical position. In an effort to drain the concept of fraternity of its original social content, huge pageants of Concord and Fraternity were staged in April and May. Thousands were mobilized, but the ceremonies lacked the spontaneity and enthusiasm of their prototypes in the period 1792-1794. Instead of the people, it was the army and National Guard that marched, a clear sign that the strength of the state lay in its material and organizational assets, not in direct popular involvement. Unlike 1789 and 1830, the army had conducted itself in a thoroughly professional manner, obedient to the existing regime whether it be republican or monarchical. Lamartine skillfully diverted the crusading spirit of revolution into a conservative nationalism, and all efforts by the radicals to involve France in wars of liberation in neighboring countries failed. "We love Poland, we love Italy, we love all oppressed peoples," Lamartine declared, "but we love France above all else." The potential radicalizing effect of war was therefore avoided, and the armies of France were kept in readiness to maintain internal order.

The liberal republic wished to mobilize the people but only within the established institutions of the state: the parliament, army, and National Guard. The Parisian National Workshops, which by May had enrolled one hundred thousand unemployed, appeared as a threat to this objective. Thus, by the end of May the Assembly had voted to phase them out, sending the older poor back to their places of origin and enrolling the youth in the army. Radical leaders protested the decision but did not raise the barricades immediately; the delay allowed the government time to prepare its armed forces, and when on June 23 barricades did go up in several of the worker quarters of Paris it was the liberals, and not the radicals, who were ready. In fact, few of the radical leaders participated in the June uprising; the insurgents were mainly unemployed workers, most of them without clear political goals, and included only a tiny handful of convinced radicals or socialists. Members of the National Workshops were present, but it was mainly the indigenous *menu peuple*, including many of the same elements that had formed the crowds in 1789 and 1830, who were most involved in the fighting.

Regular troops, aided by the provincial National Guard brought to Paris by rail and steamship, were ordered to attack the barricaded quarters. The fighting lasted four days, leaving over four hundred of the insurgents dead, about the same number as had died in the February insurrection. This time, however, the fanatical spirit absent in February surfaced dramatically. Not only were the insurgents driven by desperate hatred, but the troops, in particular the provincial militia, broke discipline to indulge in atrocities. An estimated three thousand persons (including women and children) were massacred *after* the uprising had been declared defeated. Thousands more were shipped off to jail, later to be transferred to Algerian prison camps. Flaubert wrote in *Sentimental Education* that "the fanaticism of the rich counterbalanced the frenzy of the poor, the aristocracy shared the fury of the rabble, and the cotton night cap was just as savage as the red bonnet."

Marx later interpreted the June Days as the first example of class warfare and Tocqueville agreed with him that here was a struggle between the haves and the have-nots. Yet in reality, the social backgrounds of the insurgents and their oppressors were not that different; there were unemployed workers in the ranks of the militia as well as among the insurgents. Peasants reinforced the army while other small-property holders, the last of the *sans-culottes*, were among those who defended the Faubourg Saint Antoine. The small industrial working class of Paris was scarcely involved at all. Thus, class consciousness was still too weakly developed to call the June insurrection the first incident of class warfare, whatever legend may have made of it.

In many ways, the June Days marked the end rather than the beginning of an era, because in this moment of terror and counterterror the last spark of the traditional apocalyptic mentality revealed itself. For almost four months, politics had been conducted in a highly modern format of parties and parliaments. Even so, neither the government nor its radical opponents had created an adequate institutional channel for the hopes and fears of both the poor and those who looked upon the poor as the "dangerous classes." When liberal and radical leadership faltered in June, both groups resorted to the tradition of direct action, the result being the kind of fanatical struggle that everyone had sought to avoid since February.

Revolution in Other Parts of Europe

It is significant that the events in France did not provoke a revolutionary response from the most highly organized working-class movement of the period, namely, English Chartism. French radicals talked of joining hands with the Chartists, even of invading England, but the Chartists' only response to the events of 1848 was to organize one final petition campaign. When the petition campaign for universal suffrage failed in April 1848, the movement peacefully dissolved itself. However, unlike the defeat of the Parisian June Days, this did not disable the English workers' movement, which was by then far less dependent on millennial enthusiasm than on trade unions, cooperatives, and self-help institutions that had developed by the 1840s.

British labor showed a far greater institutional strength than any of its Continental counterparts. Its abhorrence of insurrectionary means was a sign of its maturity, because as Europe's only organized working class it had more to lose than did the more disorganized poor of other countries. Furthermore, as the product of Europe's first industrial revolution, it was swimming not against but *with* history. Freed from the *sans-culottes'* obsession with reviving old virtues, Chartists were able to move beyond insurrection to seek new ways of bettering the lot of the working classes. Whereas it took a decade for French labor to recover from 1848, English trade unionism flourished in the 1850s.

England was already beyond the stage in which the middle and working classes could be held together by revolutionary rhetoric; however, the classic Jacobin notion of revolution could still provoke a positive response in the much less developed countries of central and southern Europe. The French February revolution stimulated these countries' most politically aware elements—lawyers, doctors, officials, students, and occasionally business people—to petition for the end of absolutism and feudalism. In many of these states, social and political conditions were scarcely different from those of France in 1789, except that the liberal bourgeoisie knew the lessons of the French Revolution and wished to avoid its popular upheavals. Thus, they aimed at reform without revolution, trying to mobilize the support of the general population for liberal programs by appeals to fraternity in the sense of abstract nationalism rather than in the sense of concrete social equality.

Unfortunately for the liberals, events got out of hand when the lower ranks of society, the artisans and peasants, added their more specific social and economic kind of protest. In southwestern Germany the winds of revolution swept through Baden, Württemberg, and Bavaria in early March of 1848, causing the monarchs there to promise constitutionalism and the end to feudal and manorial rights. In Bavaria revolution was triggered by the relationship of King Ludwig to Lola Montez, a woman whose advanced views on such subjects as free love scandalized the *sans-culotte* elements. In several other German states, popular revolution showed signs of following the pattern of 1789, with the concern for communal revitalization absorbing the energies of the lower classes. In small towns revolution meant not only the abolition of feudal dues but also the expulsion of prostitutes and attacks on merchants and money-lenders, many of whom were Jews. There were demands that local self-government be restored, that the guild system be refurbished, and that the authority of the patriarchal household be strengthened. For the peasants and artisans, liberty still meant freedom from the forces of the capitalist market economy and the central state; equality and fraternity also took on a local, concrete meaning, contradicting the broader national interpretation favored by both the liberals and democrats.

By mid-March the revolutionary tidal wave had reached the two most important German states, Prussia and Austria. The Viennese Revolution of March 13, 1848, was largely the work of university students, who forced the hand of the king and installed themselves as a civil guard. For the next seven months their Academic Legion controlled the capital, and had the result of driving Prime Minister Metternich into exile and forcing the Hapsburgs to grant universal suffrage. Radicals in Budapest and Prague followed their example so that by late spring the entire Austrian Empire was in upheaval.

Once Vienna had fallen, Berlin could not be too far behind, and although the Prussian king Frederick William IV was willing to grant concessions in early March, he could not reconcile an unfortunate clash between the army and civilian crowds that caused the Prussian capital to explode on March 18. The army withdrew to the suburbs in preparation for attack, and although this highly professional force probably could have subdued the insurgents, the monarch refused to declare war on those he called his "dear Berliners," instead calling a liberal provisional government into being. As in Vienna, an alliance of radical intellectuals (with a large contingent of students) and *sans-culotte* elements was chiefly responsible for the insurrection. However, power was handed not to them, but to more moderate liberal elements, and thus it was not long before divisions in the revolutionary ranks—between moderate and radical intellectuals, but more importantly between the bourgeoisie and the *sans-culottes*—became evident.

A similar pattern of events overtook northern Italy in March. On March 18 the population of Milan armed itself with guns taken from the armories and pikes borrowed from the La Scala Opera House and threw out the hated Austrian occupiers, even managing to defeat the Austrian commander Radetzky, who acknowledged this event to be "one of those sorry masterpieces of the art of war." Italian recruits had simply deserted the Austrians, who were not able to rally sufficient morale to become an effective fighting force once again, until July. In the meantime, the Italian revolution had gained force under the leadership of the King of Piedmont, Charles Albert, who promised his followers that he would expel foreign rule and bring constitutionalism to Italy.

In both central and southern Europe, the first stages of revolution saw the rapid demise of the old absolutisms, which were overripe and ready for change. Much of liberalism's strength in both areas of Europe came not from an industrial middle class—because economic development was weak—but from the civil and military services whose outlook had been distinctly forward looking since the Napoleonic era. In many of the provisional governments, those who only a few weeks before had been occupying positions in the old administration were now wielding even greater power in the cabinet or as elected representatives. Their background enabled them to move quickly to provide the basic elements of political modernization: civil equality, centralization, and specialization of functions. Strengthening the nation-state and, where it did not exist, creating one was their obsession. Although they favored the abolition of feudalism because it was an obstacle to citizenship, their ideas on social and economic reform were much less clearly developed than their legal and constitutional proposals.

The fixation of German artisans and peasants on a more specific local definition of "liberty" and "fraternity" left the problem of nation building almost entirely in the hands of the educated elites. The collapse of individual states opened the way for the calling of a German National Assembly at Frankfurt in May 1848, a body that became known as the Professors' Parliament because of the large numbers of university graduates and officials who were elected as deputies. The commercial and industrial bourgeoisie were not nearly so well represented and the lower classes had no voice at all.

The general population had neither the political consciousness nor the organization to be involved in either the state or national parliaments of 1848. The gap between them and the intellectuals who claimed to speak for them was considerably greater than in France and England, though few recognized this at the beginning; Karl Marx and Friedrich Engels returned to the Rhineland from exile hoping to create the classic popular front they had prophesied in the *Communist Manifesto* a few months before. "When the February revolution broke out, we were under the spell of previous historical experience, particularly that of France," Engels remembered later. Neither the liberals nor the general population heeded Marx's call for unity, however. With the exception of a few cities like Vienna, Berlin, and Milan, there were no organized worker movements to speak of. And where they did exist, as in Berlin, it was members of the traditional crafts who were most active. The most easily mobilized workers in 1848 were those whose crafts were declining under the pressure of commercial and industrial modernization. For them, as for the peasantry, the revolution was the last opportunity to revive the lost world of the *menu peuple,* and many of them yearned for revitalization of guild traditions, something hardly compatible with a broader working-class movement.

What little political consciousness there was also tended to be more reminiscent of the *sans-culottes* than of modern working-class movements. Some journeymen had broken with the old paternalism to advocate full equality for women as well as men, but they were exceptional. As for the peasantry, their land hunger was perceived as a threat by almost everyone. Liberals feared their attacks on property and radicals distrusted their basically restorative impulses. To Marx's disappointment, it proved impossible to organize a popular front on the basis of an appeal to the symbols of liberty, equality, and fraternity. Those who used nationalism in a

similar attempt to rally the general population found that this, too, provoked very little support outside the intellectual elites. Moreover, nationalism had the additional effect of dividing the international revolutionary
movement by pitting Germans against Poles, French against Italians.

The Reaction Sets In

The defeat of the Paris uprising in June 1848 was an ominous sign for all
European revolutionaries. Yet the fact that the victorious liberal bourgeoisie did not immediately fall back on restoration of monarchy seemed to
offer a ray of hope. The French provisional government drew up a constitution that provided for popular election of a president of what was to
be called the Second Republic. Liberal governments in Austria and Prussia
also continued to think that they could rally popular support through
similar concessions. After June, however, they met increasing resistance
from both the left and the right, and when student radicals rose to take
over Vienna in October 1848, the students and their liberal allies were
crushed by the army. Shortly thereafter the conservative government of
Count Brandenburg replaced the Prussian liberals and immediately ad-
journed the parliament. The wave of the future was confirmed in December when Louis Napoleon, nephew of the original Bonaparte, won the
French presidential election. It seemed that under the "spell of historical
experience" France was repeating the Thermidore. Liberalism found
itself outmaneuvered in the struggle to mobilize the support of the general population.

Nevertheless, there was one more wave of upheaval in store for Europe.
In February 1849 the faltering Italian revolution got a second wind with
the declaration of a Roman Republic and the expulsion of the Pope from
the city. There were uprisings in the Rhineland, Baden and Dresden, as
well as a prolonged series of battles by the Hungarian rebels against
Hapsburg armies. The German National Assembly meeting at Frankfurt
chose the moment to offer the leadership of a united Germany to the
King of Prussia. When he refused what he called "a crown from the gutter"
in April 1849, the Assembly took the bold step of declaring a federal
republic. For this action, the Professors' Parliament was chased from
Frankfurt. Ultimately all the German rebellions were crushed with the help
of the Prussian army and thousands fled to exile through Switzerland.

By June of 1849 insurrection was failing everywhere. A brief uprising
in France aimed at preventing French troops from being used to put down
the Roman Republic was smashed. The Italian revolution was systematically defeated, as much by the clumsy politics of its leaders Mazzini and
Guiseppe Garibaldi as by the French and Austrian armies massed to crush
it. Hungary was reduced to dependence with Russian assistance and the
entire Austrian Empire was placed under tight central control. The possibility of some form of German national unity lingered until 1851, when

Prussian efforts at reforming the old German Confederation were shattered by stern Austrian resistance.

And if anyone thought that French example might again stir revolutionary movements in other parts of Europe, this hope was eliminated in December 1851 when Louis Napoleon executed a carefully planned coup to make himself undisputed dictator of France. Using a tactic that his uncle had employed so successfully fifty years before, he appealed over the heads of the parliamentary opposition to the people themselves. His coup against the Republic was followed by the announcement that the French people would vote on the action: "It becomes my duty to save the Republic and the country by appealing to the solemn judgment of the people, the sole sovereign I recognize in France." Resistance to the coup was crushed and almost ten thousand "enemies of the people" were sent to prison in Algeria. The subsequent plebiscite won 91 percent approval from the French people. Support of Napoleon was particularly strong in the rural areas, but he won majorities in the cities also, not only because his name was a symbol of order, but also because Bonapartism had managed to connect itself with elements of republican tradition, including nationalism, that gave it a genuine popular appeal.

Bonapartism cleverly combined elements of revolution with reaction to create a stable regime that lasted for another twenty years. The leaders of other major states—Austria's Prince Felix von Schwartzenberg, Prussia's Otto von Manteuffel, and Piedmont's Count Camillo di Cavour—all learned lessons from the Second Empire of Napoleon III. Like him, they were supreme realists, believing that politics was the art of the possible and nothing more. Although conservative by instinct, they indulged in none of the enthusiasm for revitalization of archaic institutions that had marked previous reactionary regimes, rather facing forward in the direction of political centralization and economic development.

In Prussia, Manteuffel struggled against the king's wish to restore the estates system and won; Prussia retained the form of constitutional government, though its franchise was weighted in such a way as to preserve the power of the propertied classes, and the monarch retained most of the real power. Both Manteuffel and Austria's Schwartzenberg talked about revitalizing the old guild system, but their basic economic policies favored industrial capitalism. No efforts were made to reimpose feudalism. Instead, the larger landowners were encouraged to improve their lands (at the expense of the peasantry) as a further incentive to economic development. These masters of what political theorist Constantine Franz was to call *Realpolitik* (the politics of reality) aimed at reinforcing the legitimacy of the state by ensuring economic prosperity. Power, military and industrial, replaced divine right as the legitimating principle of conservative regimes in the aftermath of 1848.

What was to be Europe's last great wave of revolution differed from 1789 and 1830 not only in demonstrating the enhanced repressive power of the state, but also by redefining the terms of future political debate. In 1848 the major issue was no longer whether Europe's future should lie with industrialization, but what form that industrialization should take. Similarly, the centralized nation-state showed itself to be an accepted norm. Now it was the question of how German and Italian unity were to be achieved, no longer whether that unity was desirable. Of course, there were still those ultraconservatives and utopian radicals who dreamed of transcending the limits of the industrialized nation-state, but after 1848 they were quite isolated. As the options narrowed, Europeans became increasingly concerned with means rather than ends, a sign that the long uncertain transition to modernity was nearing an end. In 1858 a German summed up his country's experience:

> Our nation of forty million dreamers and idealists has learned a good deal from the hard school of reality and it has fortunately forgotten some things. Above all it has become more practical. Romanticism, sentimentalism, transcendental philosophy and supranaturalism have now withdrawn from public life of our people into their private lives. For realism and steam, machines and industrial exhibitions, the natural sciences and practical interest now fill the great market place of life.

Not only Germany was obsessed with this new material vision of progress; one London newspaper rejoiced at the news of the 1851 Napoleonic coup because "the French begin to love their business much better than they love their theories of government." The enormous success of the London industrial exhibition of the same year seemed to reinforce the impression that people were interested in a less heroic vision of progress. Although no one could have known it at the time, Europe was on the eve of three decades of unprecedented economic growth, a period when real income began to rise significantly in the industrial nations, and the threat of famine was all but eliminated in the backward areas as well. But material progress was not the only cause of political stability; equally important was the fact that the institutions of the centralized state had gained universal assent. State and society had finally arrived at a workable relationship within the framework of the nation-state; the details were to be worked out in subsequent decades, but in general, Europe's transition from traditional to modern politics was over and the corresponding era of revolutions ended.

PART THREE

TRANSFORMATION OF EVERYDAY LIFE

Earlier chapters have dealt with the nature of the economic and demographic crisis that absorbed the attention of Europeans from the 1770s through the 1840s. Western society had faced similar challenge before, but the response never had been as socially or technologically radical as in this period. Europe's Industrial Revolution, the subject of Chapter 7, was the product of intense conflict over human and material resources, the outcome of which was in doubt until at least the third decade of the nineteenth century. So, too, was the future of the city, whose stormy history is detailed in Chapter 8. By the 1830s, however, industrial capitalism, the peculiarly Western form of economic development, was gradually establishing its hegemony, and when that happened the old society, with its vertical hierarchies, dissolved into new class divisions. Chapter 9 deals with what lay behind this change—not only shifts in wealth and power but also the revolutionary transformation of family structures and of individual and group mentalities.

7

The First
Industrial Society

The most easily measured dimension of Europe's Industrial Revolution is
the enormous quantitative increase in productivity per work hour that
took place in the first two-thirds of the nineteenth century. Only one prior
economic development, the invention of agriculture seven thousand years
earlier, compares with it in terms of the enormous increase in energy made
available to human beings. Up to 1800, 90 percent of the world's energy
was still derived from human and animal sources, a fact that tied the vast
majority of people to the land.

The agricultural revolution of the eighteenth century and the subsequent
use of chemical fertilizers increased the efficiency of plant and animal
energy converters to a considerable degree, but this gain in productivity
did not compare with that which was achieved by exploiting inanimate
sources of energy. In 1800 the total world production of coal was 15
million tons, most of it in England; by 1860 production rose to 132 million tons, and then in 1900 to 701 million tons. In the 1850s oil refining
was invented, and by 1860 the first gas engine was patented in France.
Michael Faraday generated electricity for the first time in 1831, and in the
1870s Edison invented the lamp. The year 1895 saw the great Niagara Falls
power station opened. Taken together, the inanimate energy available had
increased no less than *fifty times* in the course of the nineteenth century,
most of it after 1840.

The substitution of inanimate for animal and human sources of energy
is a convenient way of viewing the Industrial Revolution, but the substitution of machine-intensive for labor-intensive methods was much more
than mechanical mastery of nature's resources. Also involved was the
mastery and transformation of *human nature* by the revolutionary seizure

Chart 2   World Production of Inanimate Energy, 1800–1900[1].
(Figures after 1860 taken from Carlo M. Cipolla, *The Economic History of World Population,* 6th ed., Penguin Books, Baltimore, 1974, p. 59.)

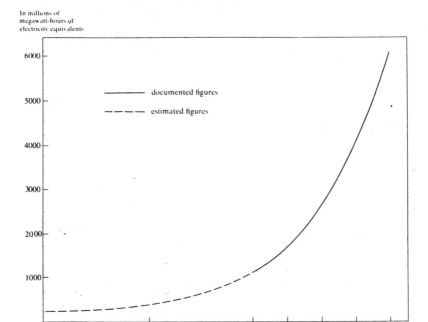

In millions of
megawatt-hours of
electricity equivalents

——— documented figures
– – – – estimated figures

1. Sources of inanimate energy are coal, petroleum, natural gas, water power

of control over the human being's time, over his emotional as well as physical energy. Seeking models for the kind of unprecedented activity in which they were engaged, the first captains of industry looked to the only other human endeavor besides slavery that could compare in scope with the task of discipline and organization they had set for themselves— namely, the military operations. When England's Josiah Wedgwood spoke of organizing his potteries he called it "hard, but then it is glorious to conquer so great an Empire with raw, undisciplined recruits. What merit must the General have who achieves such wonders under such disadvantageous circumstances. . . ." On the Continent, where the role of government was most direct, Prussian miners wore uniforms and saluted their supervisors. At royal factories in France, the workers "lived entirely in their place of work, like soldiers in barracks, and left them only on festival days." It is not surprising that Andrew Ure, the advocate of industrialization, compared early English factory owners to Napoleon.

Everywhere, both employers and workers knew that they were experiencing something unprecedented in the annals of human history. Conversion to inanimate sources to power required much more than the purchase of a few efficient machines; investment in fixed plants had revolutionary consequences not only for the entrepreneur's attitude toward the machinery but also for his concept of the workers who tended it. The relationship could no longer be that of the traditional craft workshop, where even the lowly apprentice had shared with the master artisan a certain dignity. Now that the ownership of the means of production was concentrated in the possession of a few employers, who no longer worked alongside their employees, the workers were of another species of being, "hands" whose worth was measured only by their labor. They were part of the specialized production process, instruments of organizations geared to a concept of time, work, and discipline very different from the past.

A goodly part of the early entrepreneur's sense of pride derived from a heroic effort to exert dominance over humans' minds as well as their bodies. In the figure of the industrial Napoleon marching his recruits to the tune of industrial progress is an image as powerful and prophetic as any of the military portraits of the period, yet the uniform of the captain of industry remained more that of the Puritan divine than of the proud princeling. He disciplined himself as he did his workers; visionary yet austere, he saw himself conquering moral as well as economic territory, improving the world in a dual sense by transforming human as well as physical nature. As Andrew Ure put it in *The Philosophy of Manufacturers* in 1835:

> The main difficulty did not . . . lie so much in the invention of a proper self-acting mechanism for drawing and twisting cotton as in the distribution of the different members of the apparatus into one cooperative body, in impelling each organ with its appropriate delicacy and speed, and above all, in training human beings to renounce their desultory habits of work, to identify themselves with the unvarying regularity of work of the complex automaton. It requires in fact a man of Napoleonic nerve and ambition to subdue the refractory tempers of work people accustomed to irregular spasms of diligence, and to urge on his multifarious and intricate constructions in the face of prejudice, passion, and envy.

The true character of Europe's Industrial Revolution lay here, in the transformation of human as well as physical nature.

Problems of Economic Growth

> It was not more than seventy or eighty years since, that a few humble mechanics in Lanarkshire, distinguished by scarcely anything more than mechanical ingenuity and perseverance of character, succeeded in forming a few, but important mechanical combinations, the effect

of which has been to revolutionize the whole of British society, and
to influence, in a marked degree, the process of civilization in every
quarter of the globe.

A member of the Manchester Antheneum, 1844

The Industrial Revolution had scarcely begun before its legend was created, complete with a set of heroes, the "humble mechanics," to match
those of the period's other great revolution, the conquerers of the Bastille.
The prophets of industrialization cannot be accused of underestimating the
impact of the factory system, but they did obscure the nature of the social
and political struggles that surrounded the triumph of mechanized manufacturing. Their apocalyptic expectation of new beginnings caused them to
ignore the human costs of change, in a period when the battle between
population and economic growth was extremely intense. It was not until
the 1840s that England was safely through that stage of uncertainty in
which many of today's new states find themselves; France and Germany
cannot be said to have converted to inanimate sources of energy until the
following decades. Italy and most parts of eastern Europe did not revolutionize their economies until the end of the nineteenth century, while
Spain and Portugal lagged still further behind. Ireland failed to industrialize at all, losing the battle of population in the 1840s and remaining a
strictly agrarian economy for the rest of the nineteenth century.

As we have seen, problems of economic development similar to those
that plague today's new states existed even in the most advanced European
nations up through the 1830s (see Chapter 2). Gains in agriculture and
manufacturing were constantly threatened by population growth, and
there was no incentive for capitalist entrepreneurs to convert to labor-
saving mechanical production as long as there was cheap labor to be hired.
The traditional modes of production were labor intensive, and the putting-
out system remained most profitable until the second quarter of the
nineteenth century. Efforts to introduce power-driven machinery frequently encountered popular opposition, not only from workers whose
labor was being displaced, but also from lesser entrepreneurs who saw
themselves threatened by the cost-cutting potential of factories larger than
their own small workshops. Until the 1830s, wage earners and masters of
small workshops formed a relatively solid front against large-scale enterprise.

The *sans-culottes* had demonstrated just how potent this combination
could be during the Revolution of 1789. Although their political power
was broken by 1794, the revitalization of the ideal of an economy of small,
independent owner-operators undoubtedly influenced the form and probably the pace of French economic development for decades thereafter.
There were many reasons that England outdistanced France on the path to
industrialization, but the fact that the latter's peasant and artisan economy
was sustained, even revitalized, had much to do with it. In England, where
the power of the native *sans-culotte* movement was repressed for most of
the period 1795–1820, there was less chance of successful resistance to
new modes of production, though there was struggle, which peaked in the

1830s and 1840s. The overthrow of the old systems of production was not just a simple matter of inventing a "few, but very important mechanical combinations"; it involved changing an entire cultural and social order, a radical, sometimes brutal transformation of habits and values by a combination of economic incentives and outright political coercion.

The Preconditions of Industrialization

There is no question that the potential for industrialization existed in England and, to a lesser degree, in France and western Germany from the 1770s onwards. The gradual inflation in the eighteenth century, driven in part by population increase, had spurred economic growth, and Europe's total trade doubled in the years 1780–1850. The fastest growing sector was trade with the non-Western world, but the internal market was also expanding. Per capita wealth in England had reached £70 by the end of the eighteenth century, a figure considerably higher than average wealth in India and Mexico today. This was being gradually translated into demands for consumer goods, particularly in those urban areas where the process of rising expectations (itself partially the product of the concurrent democratic revolution) was causing an increased demand for clothes, housing, and other symbols of status. An Englishman remarked in 1800 that the "frugality which once characterized the middling and lower classes of society amongst us is no more: the little tradesman and mechanic of the present day, fatally though impotently, ape the luxuries and fashionable vices of their superiors."

Unaccustomed to mass consumption and not a little uneasy about its social implications, the well-to-do denounced the "sin" of luxury among their social inferiors. They were joined in this by various revitalization movements, among them, the *sans-culottes* and student reform fraternities, who desired return to a simpler and more austere existence. This kind of puritanism lingered longer among the *sans-culottes* than it did among liberals or conservatives, however, for by the early nineteenth century the well-to-do were beginning to see the value of developing the consumption habit among the general population.

Control of markets in Asia and South America placed England in a particularly favorable position to capture the growing world demand. This country was well equipped not only with a shipping and trading tradition but also with the kind of liquid capital needed to increase productivity. England's immense wealth was still concentrated in land, but the English aristocracy was more willing than many of its Continental counterparts to invest in urban and overseas enterprise. The flow of capital from one sector of the economy to another was facilitated by a well-established system of banks that were lending at the incredibly low rates of 3–5 percent at the end of the eighteenth century. In contrast to France, where the state was a heavy borrower of capital, the needs of the British monarchy were relatively modest. After the end of the Napoleonic Wars, state borrowing declined considerably, so that even more capital was available to entrepreneurs.

English official policy favored economic growth in innumerable ways. For almost two hundred years it had been geared to profit, formerly in the areas of shipping and foreign trade, but now increasingly to the benefit of domestic production. Woolen manufacturers had managed to ban the import of competing cloth in the early eighteenth century, and after 1815 the English colonial administration in India entered into a Machiavellian program of destroying the Indian cloth industry in order to open the way for English cotton manufacturers. The connection between economic prosperity and political power was obvious to the French and Germans, as well as to the English.

England was favored by natural resources—coal and iron—that were to be the basis for heavy industry, but the profitability of their exploitation depended on cheap transportation from the mining areas to the production centers. Coal had been mined in the north of England and shipped inexpensively by sea to London for centuries. Extensive canal building from 1761 onward, often funded by aristocrats who wished to exploit mineral deposits on their lands, further decreased the costs of transportation. England was ahead of France and Germany in road building as well, thanks to improvements made by the Scottish engineer John Loudon McAdam and the emergence of many private turnpike companies. In Germany the rich Ruhr coal fields were not opened up until 1837, and there the transportation situation remained abysmal until railway nets were extended in the 1840s and 1850s. The first steam-powered railway was English, founded in 1825 as a link between the coal fields and the coast. Other countries quickly imitated the British example (the United States in 1827, France in 1828, Germany and Belgium in 1835), but there were only fourteen thousand miles of track on the Continent by 1850 because the cost of rail transport remained relatively high.

Poor transportation was not the only cost factor in economic growth, however. Internal tolls were not eliminated in France until the 1790s and in Germany until 1834 (the year of the founding of the German Customs Union); but they had disappeared in England long before the beginning of the nineteenth century. In this respect the link between economic development and the formation of the nation-state was clear, for the early advent of national unity both reduced the cost of shipping and expanded the potential market of regional products. Not until the Revolution of 1789 did France have a uniform currency or system of measurement; the introduction of the metric system was also a consequence of the universalizing, equalizing tendency that spread quickly to other countries in the course of the next century. That Britain and America remained loyal to the older system of pounds and inches (except in science) merely reflected the fact that these had already been standardized and there was no need for change.

Finally, the elements of talent and labor supply must be added to those of demand, capital, and material resources in assessing economic growth.

There is no question that the quality of inventiveness was abundant in the eighteenth century. We need not go through a complete list of mechanical inventions (Watt's rotary steam engine in 1784, Arkwright's spinning jenny in 1765, Whitney's cotton gin in 1796, to name only a few) to know that technical facility was available, even abundant. The great French *Encyclopedia* was filled with drawings of machines and manufacturing processes, many of which did not come into use until much later. In most cases, the mechanical capacity was available considerably before it became economically or socially feasible to use it. This was true not only of the steam engine, where crude versions had been used in mining since the seventeenth century, but also of weaving machines that only began to be used extensively when hand-loom weaving profits began declining.

Eighteenth-century entrepreneurs were no less inventive in the organization of industry. The first real factory in England can be dated to a silk-throwing mill built in 1719, though it was not until Richard Arkwright built a cotton-spinning plant at Cromford in 1771 that factories powered by inanimate sources of energy—first water and then steam—began to exist in any numbers, and then only in textiles. Breweries and grain mills provided models for efficient use of labor, but despite these forerunners, very few capitalists took up the idea of the mechanized factory in the eighteenth century. It seems ironic that, at a time when the young Robert Owen started his spinning mill in 1789 with a loan of a mere £100, more people were not willing to invest in a fixed plant. Yet as long as the traditional domestic system of manufacturing, organized around the putting-out system, continued to make heady profits of as much as 1,000 percent, it is understandable that most capitalists continued in their old ways, for it is always easier to follow tradition, particularly when a break with it means overturning established social and cultural as well as economic institutions. Labor-intensive industry was more than just a way of earning a living in 1800; it represented a whole way of life, whether it be the craft guilds or the family economy of the domestic system.

Industrial Discipline

If all the preconditions for industrialization existed, what then inhibited the widespread adoption of the factory system with its inanimate sources of energy? The chief inhibition was the very success of traditional methods of manufacturing (as measured in profits). As long as abundant labor existed, there was no reason that the capitalist entrepreneur should turn away from the old putting-out system. The temptation to use labor-saving devices arose only in times of "energy crisis," periods when the traditional form of energy, namely, human labor, became scarce or too highly priced.

This had happened in England during the 1760s and 1770s: because of an earlier ebb in the marriage rate, the supply of young persons diminished temporarily, the cost of labor went up, and business people found it difficult to keep up with demand at prices that were competitive. Finding themselves in a favorable bargaining position *vis-à-vis* their employers, many domestic workers were able to get higher wages and thus reduce the hours of work needed to make ends meet. Attempts to force them to work longer hours met with resistance because workers cherished their free time and, it was said, claimed "so many Holy-days that few of our Manu-facturing Work-folks are closely and regularly employed above two-thirds Parts of their Time." To the writer William Temple, who tended to take the employers' point of view in such matters, it seemed that "great wages and certainty of employment render the inhabitants of cities insolent and debauched." Dr. Johnson, among others, was convinced that "raising the wages of day labourers is wrong for it does not make them live better, but only makes them idler."

Not only the unwillingness of workers to labor long hours but also the traditional notion that labor-saving devices deprived human beings of both work and dignity restrained entrepreneurs in their attempts to increase productivity. The Holy Roman Empire banned ribbon machines from the German states as late as 1719, and where the machines were introduced, crowds of irate artisans, often supported by local property owners, attacked them and destroyed factories. In London in 1763 journeymen in the silk trade demanded an improvement in their wages; when the masters refused they masked themselves as sailors and "armed with Cutlasses and other Dangerous Weapons" cut up the silk in the workshops and destroyed several looms.

Machine breaking was not a blind protest against mechanization per se but rather a bargaining means that workers adopted as a last resort, risking severe penalties under the law. They were determined that the price of their own labor not be devalued by the machine. Cried silk weavers in 1773 when they demanded and got a guaranteed minimum price for their work:

> Suffer yourselfs no longer to be prevented by a set of Miscreants whose way to Riches and Power lays through your Families, by every attempt to Starve and enslave you, in a Land where Freedom and Plenty is the native Product; exert yourselves like Britons, nor let the latent spark be quench'd that glows in every manly Breast.

It is against this background that the hardening attitude of employers toward their workers, expressed in a willingness to experiment with new labor-saving machines, must be understood. The Dr. Johnsons of Europe were becoming more puritanical and less tolerant of idleness, more willing to blame the condition of the poor on the poor and thus to seek basic reform of their character. Daniel Defoe wrote:

> when I have wanted a man for labouring work and offer'd 9 shillings per week to strolling fellows at my door, they frequently told me to my face, they could get more abegging, and I once set a lusty fellow in the stocks for making the experiment.

Laws against begging and vagrancy became increasingly strict by the end of the eighteenth century. There began in England a systematic attack on traditional forms of leisure—feasts, games, the custom of the long weekend (Saint Monday). In Prussia the king limited the length of weddings and funerals in the name of national productivity. Preachers emphasized the sin of idleness, and schoolmasters taught this moral jingle:

> In works of Labour or of Skill
>   I would be busy too:
> For Satan finds some Mischief still
>   for idle Hands to do.

Joseph Tucker noted that "the Rules of Religion and the Rules of social industry do perfectly harmonize," a concept that children in the newly established Sunday and charity schools were drilled in. Sarah Trimmer, in *Economy of Charity* published in 1801, established the following industrial catechism:

> Question: What will God do to thieves of all kinds?
> Answer: Punish them.
> Question: What do masters and mistresses pay their servants for?
> Answer: Their time and labor.
> Question: Suppose a man, a woman, a boy, a girl, loiters away any
> of the hours they have agreed to work in, what do they do?
> Answer: They rob their master and mistress.

Poor houses and prisons were increasingly devoted to the task of reforming their inmates through the inculcation of the work ethic. William Temple noted that "the only way to make them [the poor] temperate and industrious is to lay them under a necessity of labouring all the time they can spare from meals and sleep, in order to procure the common necessities of life." Groups like the English Quakers and the German Pietists stressed not only the spiritual uplift of labor but its therapeutic functions. Disciplined work was thought of as the "cure" not only for crime and social deviance, but also for insanity. The idle mind was as dangerous as the idle hand.

The Factory System

It was a short step from this idea to the concept of the factory as a form of discipline. The reorganization of the work place sometimes preceded the application of inanimate energy, while sometimes the two processes occurred simultaneously. Either way, the *factory system*, the central institution of the coming Industrial Revolution, was much more than an economic innovation. It was a social, even a political institution designed with the model of the barracks and the reformatory very much in mind. The invention of the spinning jenny in 1765 offered the opportunity, through mechanization, of reducing the cost of making cotton yarn, while at the same time it encouraged the concentration of labor under one roof, where it could be controlled and disciplined. It is not insignificant that in France and Germany the first factories were state prisons, whose purpose was both to make money and to discipline the inmate population.

Labor-saving techniques were not only mechanical but also social in character. Long before most industries began substituting inanimate for human energy, they were rationalizing and specializing labor as a way of reducing costs. In America, where labor was very scarce, business people were quick to adopt crude assembly-line methods in which the manufacturing process was divided into a number of separate operations done by cheap "hands" rather than by highly paid skilled artisans. This nonmechanized form of industrialization was also going on as early as the 1760s in the Staffordshire potteries, spurred by Josiah Wedgwood's notion that the "infallible consequences of lowering the cost of workmanship will be proportional to the increase in the quantity got up." He proposed to speed the process of production by training workers for specialized tasks, or, as he put it, to "make such *machines* of the *Men* as cannot err."

The older artisans resisted the division of labor, informing Wedgwood that as artisans, "they shall never learn this new business." However, they were dismissed and replaced by young trainees, many of them women, who, having no commitment to the old craft notion of the masterpiece, more readily accepted the principle of division of labor. Similar training of unskilled women and children was subsequently employed in the mining, textile, and metal industries, where employers wished to overcome the resistance of artisans that could, on occasion, abort the reorganization process. Another employer noted

> the utmost distaste on the part of the men, to any regular hours or regular habits. . . . The men themselves were considerably dissatisfied, because they could not go in and out as they pleased, and have what holidays they pleased, and go on just as they had been used to do; and were subject, during after-hours, to the ill-natured observations of other workmen, to such an extent as completely to disgust them the whole system, and I [the employer] was obliged to break it up.

However, population growth after 1780 undermined the artisans' position. A labor seller's market had become a labor buyer's market in which skilled men found it difficult to compete with the cheap labor of women and children, the pauperized, and the unskilled. Naturally, the abundance of labor also slackened temporarily the necessity for mechanization, for it was still cheaper to farm out production than to build factories. Thus, the growth of factories lagged except in cotton spinning, which produced enough yarn to spur a further growth of the cottage weaving industry that lasted through the 1820s. As late as the 1830s, many employers continued to find domestic industry more profitable, and even then most continued to prefer the small shop to the larger enterprise in all but textiles.

Older artisans stubbornly refused to enter the new factories, both because these contradicted their sense of craft and because the subordination of human beings to machines was an affront to their social dignity. As Robert Owen noted:

> The most respectable part of the surrounding inhabitants were at first adverse to seek employment in the works, as they considered it disreputable to be employed in what they called a "public work." Such was the general dislike of that occupation at that time, that, with a few exceptions, only persons destitute of friends, employment and character were found willing to try the experiment.

The comparison between factory and workhouse did not escape employers either, only adding to the factory's attractiveness as far as they were concerned.

Although employers were often forced to pay premium wages to induce workers to enter their factories, they did so grudgingly because they believed these encouraged profligate spending on leisure, making for less work rather than more. They were more apt to use the stick rather than the carrot to encourage high productivity, and many early managers welcomed the machine not only for its economic advantages but also for the social control it provided. Machines were viewed as engines of moral and social improvement, as a Berlin report of 1819 put it:

> Factory owners are convinced that the weal and woe of the whole state depends on the success of their factories. . . . They have become accustomed to consider the productive workers and their subordinates and children to be incidental appendages to the machines, and that it is sufficient for them, if they have not necessary energy, that their bodies do not rot and that their hands go through the appropriate motions.

Wedgwood conditioned the surrounding countryside to the sound of his pottery's bell, fining persons late to work and ultimately expelling those with irregular habits. French employers levied fines for early marriage and excessive childbearing. Of particular nuisance to the early factory masters were the traditional holidays and the Saint Mondays—the habit of workers of missing the first days of the week and then working "desperately, night and day, to clear off their tavern score, and get more money to spend in dissipation." Wedgwood raged that "our men have been at play 4 days this week. . . . I have rough'd and smoothed them over, and promised them a long Christmas, but I know it is all in vain."

Masters believed themselves morally as well as economically justified in physically punishing workers, though as factories grew in size they found it difficult to attend to discipline personally. As a substitute, strict work codes were introduced that regulated every aspect of the factory day and afterhours as well. The factory became a walled world of its own, with gatekeepers closing out intruders and keeping the temptations of food and drink from the shop floor. Managers, trained to repress the "evils" of reading, singing, or conversing, established a social and moral distance between themselves and the workers, whom they viewed as a species different from themselves. Saint-Marc Girardin could not resist a comparison between employers and slave owners:

> Every manufacturer lives in his factory like the colonial planters in the midst of their slaves, one against a hundred, and subversion of Lyon is a sort of insurrection of San Domingo. . . . The barbarians who menace society are neither in the Caucasus nor in the steppes of Barbary; they are in the suburbs of our industrial cities. . . . The middle class must clearly recognize the nature of the situation; it must know where it stands.

Making a moral virtue of what had begun as an economic advantage, many early factory managers became, as Wordsworth described them in *The Prelude*:

> The Guides, the Wardens of our faculties
> And stewards of our labour, watchful men
> And skillful in the usury of time.
> Sages, who in their prescience would control
> all accidents, and to the very road
> Which they have fashion'd would
> confine us down, Like engines.

Despite worker resistance, control by the masters became in time almost complete; the life of the community, cultural and religious, was organized by the employer. He occupied the first pew in the church and presided over the charities and the schools. A French business person argued that "by teaching the worker to accept his condition religion gives him the most certain path to a calm spirit. . . . Religion is a good thing for all but especially for those who suffer." Manchester Sunday schools were "called in a sense of religious obligation to the aid of industry," utilizing strict discipline and rote learning to condition as well as instruct the young in the necessity of disciplined labor. Reading and writing were subordinated to the goal that children should "become reconciled to confinement, and are habituated to behave with silence and respect in the presence of their superiors."

"Industry is the great principle of duty that ought to be inculcated on the lowest class of people," wrote the English *Gentlemen's Magazine* in 1797, and English mill owners recognized in religion an essential aid to discipline. Methodism was particularly approved of because of the fanatical devotion to orderliness from which its name derived. Its founder's insistence on total subordination provided justification for harsh factory discipline, particularly of children. "Do not 'spare the rod and spoil the child,' " wrote John Wesley. "Do not give your child up to his own will, that is, to the devil. . . . Make them submit, that they may not perish. Break their wills that you may save their soul."

Consumption was sometimes controlled through the company store and leisure dictated by a restricted calendar of festivals and entertainment. In many of the new factory towns the employer also owned the housing; cottages built initially to attract labor later became instruments of control. Despite their upstart origins and new economic conceptions, manufacturers retained much of preindustrial patriarchalism. Without the support of the authoritarian attitudes and laws of the Old Regime, the degree of discipline involved in early industrialization would hardly have been conceivable. Yet, the new nation-states were hardly less severe. The Napoleonic regime reinforced the *livret* system that required workers to obtain a good conduct discharge from one employer before moving on to the next. Even those progressive industrialists like Robert Owen, who believed that the fruits of industry should be shared by labor and capital, were not adverse to regulating the lives of the workers. In degree of organization, Owen's New Lanark mills were scarcely different from Wedgwood's Etruria, Matthew Boulton's Soho, or the paternalistic enterprises in France and Germany.

There was something visionary, even a little fanatical, in the way the early factory owners pursued the mastery of the human being and nature. Their experiments reflected the same longing for revitalization that penetrated other groups in society; Robert Owen preached a millennium in which a new industrial type would emerge to build a new, more moral society. As a group, the owners were compulsive in character, prone to describing their enterprise in both military and moral language as conquest as well as salvation. The image of Wedgwood striding through his factories, smashing inferior products, venting rage on workers and shouting "this won't do for Josiah Wedgwood" is not exceptional. The masters were products of a society that was just beginning to democratize and that was still accustomed to authoritarian leadership. Also, these industrial leaders were attempting something novel that ran against the feelings of the community.

They were perceived as presumptuous, not only by the laboring poor but also by the aristocracy, who had nothing but contempt for the industrialists' attacks on traditional culture. That so many of the early commercial and industrial leaders belonged to dissenting religious sects or were members of minority groups (Huguenots and Jews, for example) explains in part why they were immune to pressures for conformity. Protestants in France, Quakers in England, Pietists in Germany were strongly represented among the first generation of the industrial revolutionaries. Only a century before, the Quakers had been among the "ranting" sects that had preached the apocalyptic spiritual transformation of the world. By the early eighteenth century they had become far more socially conservative but still retained something of their millennialist outlook. If, by then, Quakers tended to expel members for financial rather than moral bankruptcy, this meant only that they had secularized their original perfectionism.

The Struggle over Industrialization

Given its unpopularity among both the traditional laborers and certain segments of the old merchant and landowning classes, it is easy to understand why factory forms of production remained exceptional, being confined to textiles—largely to spinning—as late as the 1820s. It is quite possible that the traditionally profitable putting-out system might have persisted even longer had not another human "energy crisis" in the 1830s spelled its doom. Prices had remained ahead of wages throughout the Napoleonic Wars, producing tremendous profits. But this situation collapsed after 1815 when the European states replaced inflationary wartime spending with deflationary reductions in their military and civil services.

In England the money supply was further reduced by the artificially high price of grain, kept up by food tariffs (the Corn Laws) that powerful landowning elites had legislated through parliament in 1815. The big landowners were protected, but the tariffs on grain imports meant that English manufacturers would have much more trouble selling their goods to those nations that depended on the grain trade for ready cash. High food prices also hurt the domestic market by increasing the amount the average family spent on food (as much as 50 percent even in good times) and thus reducing the amount they could spend on manufactured goods. Furthermore, high food prices kept wage costs up, thus cutting into profits at a time of stagnating demand.

In 1830 it appeared that growth in real income had come to an end. For the first time since 1700 the extension of well-being in England seemed in real danger of being permanently reversed. Economic downturn was immediately translated into popular protest—the Revolutions of 1830 on the Continent, the Swing riots, machine breaking, and strikes in England. The fury of the *menu peuple* was turned against the "big men." There was a renewal of *sans-culotte* as well as trade union activity as the fears of the 1780s returned and people struggled over shrinking resources.

This crisis was to last through the 1840s, the economic depressions from 1826 to 1829 followed by those of 1839 to 1842 and 1846 to 1848. Bad harvests and production cutbacks resulted in high prices and unemployment. For two decades the entrepreneurial middle classes were involved in a two-front struggle, against the landed aristocracy on one side and elements of the pauperized laboring classes on the other. At times it seemed that the thrust of industrial development might be reversed. Yet, it was precisely when their backs were to the wall that the middle classes pressed forward the industrial revolution that had been only partially accomplished in previous, more prosperous decades.

Like its political counterpart, industrial revolution was a child of crisis, born from the capitalist desire to reverse rising costs of labor and falling profits. The response to declining demand was to manufacture more at a cheaper price and merchandise the products in a more aggressive way, even when this meant the ruin of better-made craft goods. This amounted to a final revolutionary assault on traditional manufacturing and commercial practices. Earlier skirmishes had shown that any such attack was sure to provoke resistance from large segments of the population, but this time the enterpreneurial middle class made sure of victory by simultaneously capturing the commanding heights of political as well as economic power. Fortified with victories in the Revolutions of 1830 and, in a less direct way through the English Reform of 1832, they accomplished their industrial conquest in the course of the next two decades.

Short of factory mechanization, the favored method to bring prices into line with competition was layoffs and severe wage cutting. The prices paid to English hand-loom weavers dropped eight times in the course of the 1830s, and workers in other trades were made to bear the burden of price reduction in a similar manner. This was usually accompanied by sterner discipline and longer hours. Employers in France as well as in England turned the screws on their work force, demanding longer workdays and heavier workloads, whether these were set by the pace of machines in factories or in a domestic setting. This meant a further round of attacks on the traditions of leisure, with stricter enforcement of factory rules and societal blue laws. By the 1840s the old games and festivals were discouraged to such an extent that the English reformer Joseph Kay lamented that "the poor have no relaxation but the alehouse or the gin palace."

Everywhere the independent artisan was undercut by competition with cheap mass-produced goods of inferior quality. Aggressive salespeople invaded local markets previously reserved for the artisans of the neighborhood and undersold them. Tailors, cabinet makers, artisans of all sorts were forced to leave their shops to sell in a wider market, something they had not done before. A Paris Chamber of Commerce Report made the following observation:

> Often they wandered around until evening without selling anything;
> then, fatigued from carrying a considerable load since morning,
> forced now to head for home and to pay for the primary material
> purchased on credit, they were forced to let the piece go at a very
> low price.

The crafts of weaving and tailoring collapsed with shocking suddenness after 1830. Finding they could not get cheap credit, artisans pawned or sold their tools, thereby losing all claim to the status of independent *menu peuple.* Though pride kept them from going into the new factories, they were forced to send their children there. As a song of the period went:

> If you go into a loom shop, where there's three or
>   four pairs of looms,
> They are all standing empty, encumbrances of the rooms:
> And if you ask the reason why, the old mother will
>   tell you plain,
> My daughters have forsaken them, and gone to weave by steam.

The Triumph of Capitalism

The world of the *sans-culottes* was dying, lending an additional note of desperation to the last surge of resistance to capitalist industrialization that erupted between 1830 and 1848. This time, however, the *menu peuple* had neither the internal strength nor the political allies to sustain the kind of resistance that had been evident in the 1790s; the old Jacobin–*sans-culottes* alliance had come undone. There had always been some tension between the larger bourgeoisie who identified with radical republicanism and those small owner-operators who were the grassroots *sans-culottes*, but earlier Jacobinism had been able to patch over these contradictions. After 1830, however, the alliance fragmented into nonegalitarian liberalism, henceforth the banner of the middle classes, and democratic or socialist radicalism, whose major constituency was the body of urban artisans and the newly emerging industrial working class.

Liberalism had emerged as an aggressive, forward-looking ideology that defended the absolute right of property against all claims of community. Liberty transcended fraternity, and equality was translated into a laissez-faire notion of competition that sorted human beings out according to economic success. Being poor was the individual's own fault. To try through a mistaken sense of fraternity or paternalism to help the poor only made their condition more dangerous. Only the sting of poverty could be counted on to make a person work and, therefore, as the French Minister of Commerce wrote in 1833, "whatever the lot of the worker is, it is not the manufacturer's responsibility to improve it." Middle-class women learned that it was wrong to give charity, for alms corrupted the poor and made them shun honest work.

In the eyes of the bourgeoisie, the boundary between the honest "deserving" poor and the "dangerous classes" of professional beggars and criminals had become blurred. Many unemployed working people were indeed forced to steal just to survive, and crimes against property rose in each of the economic crises of the 1830s and 1840s; the crime wave that swept Paris in the 1840s gave authorities there the excuse to treat honest workers in the same way they did the criminal classes. As Vicomte de Launay, a resident of Paris, noted:

> For the past month the sole topic of conversation has been the
> nightly assaults, hold-ups, daring robberies. . . . A concern for self-
> defense greatly troubled [bourgeois] family gatherings. . . . Friends
> and relatives are not allowed to go home without a regular arms
> inspection.

As in our own time, fears of crime were used to justify social distance and
political repression.

The abandonment of fraternity was evident in politics as well. In the
aftermath of their rise to power by the French Revolution of 1830 and the
English Reform Bill of 1832 respectively, the middle classes turned on the
sans-culotte movement that had been their ally only a few months before.
The attitude of the July Monarchy toward the worker's movement was
particularly harsh, while in England the industrialists showed themselves
ready to reject all fraternal and paternalistic appeals in their effort to
create a new industrial being. There the new Poor Law of 1834 eliminated
(in theory at least) all state support for the able-bodied poor; those who
could not or would not work were henceforth condemned to the workhouse, where conditions were so bad that self-respecting persons preferred
to starve rather than enter. French and German liberals were less willing to
push the attack on paternalism quite as far, but there was general agreement that the only way to "improve" the poor was to keep wages so low
that men, women, and children would be forced to work long hours to
survive. This legitimated wage cutting, the substitution of child for adult
labor, and mass unemployment. Should people be paid more than the
minimum wage, they would only waste it on idle pleasures. "Poverty is
unfortunately one of the conditions inseparable from the state of society,"
observed a French liberal. As William Temple expressed it, "Low wages
and uncertainty of employment near at hand . . . make the husbandman
temperate and humble."

In rejecting the traditional notions of fraternity and paternalism, liberals
aroused the bitter antagonism of both the *sans-culottes* and the new wage-
earning class without property. The former reacted with their old moral
fury, but the latter, having less attachment to the traditional concept of
community, were less likely to think possible a revival of fraternity between rich and poor. Instead, they accepted as irreversible the tendency of
industrial society to divide into separate classes as owners and workers.
When they spoke of "fraternity" they meant the solidarity of the working
class against the middle class, or, as journalist and Chartist James Bronterre
O'Brien put it in 1836:

> It is the workman's interest to do as little work, and to get as much
> for it as possible. It is the middleman's interest to get as much work
> as he can out of a man, and to give it as little for it. Here then are
> their respective interests, as directly opposed to each other as fight-
> ing bulls.

The landed aristocracy was also bitterly resentful of the middle class. Their conflict with the industrial bourgeoisie centered on the latter's effort to reform Parliament, and the attempt by groups like the English Anti-Corn Law League, founded in 1838, to lower the artifically high price of grain. In France, Germany, and Italy, political conflicts were similarly sharp, with industrialists contending that agrarian control of political power hindered economic progress and the landowners responding with a defense of the "moral economy" that often sounded much like the *sans-culottes* critique of the market economy. In subsequent decades, conservatives' antiliberal advocacy of traditional institutions would be able to attract certain elements of the disillusioned artisan group to its banner. However, aristocratic paternalism had little appeal for most of the new industrial work force, a major reason that the aristocracy ultimately lost its political struggles with the industrial bourgeoisie.

It is difficult to say just when the battle of industrialization was won by the middle classes, but certainly the abolition of the English grain tariffs in 1846 marked something of a turning point. Another indicator was the emergence of that body of people who regarded themselves as professional factory managers. By 1840 50 percent of English workers employed outside the agricultural and service sectors worked in factories. At first this was mainly in textiles, but by the 1870s metal working, machine manufacture, and chemicals also were operating by inanimate power. It may be estimated that the size of the average English workshop had increased seventeen times since the late eighteenth century.

As for the rest of Europe, change came more slowly. The Krupps' first steam engine was installed as late as 1835. Yet the advent of railroads in the 1840s did much to institutionalize the changes already evident in the textile industry. Demand for rails and boilers spurred the iron and coal industries, caused investment institutions to develop, and created a momentum for capital goods production generally. The production of iron in England rose 400 percent between 1830 and 1850, and the production of coal rose from fifteen million tons to forty-nine million in the same period. The Ruhr mines were opened; the Czech metal industry was born; and in the next two decades industrialization ceased to be a one-industry phenomenon and became a diversified affair with its own self-sustaining momentum. However, the Industrial Revolution could only be said to be complete when people accepted the factory form of organization as inevitable. From that point onward, the issue was no longer industrialization per se, but whether industry should continue to be organized on a capitalist basis or be replaced by socialist forms of production. In the 1840s this issue was at the center of debate, a sign that western Europe had passed an epochal turning point and was entering the modern industrial age.

8

The Birth
of the Modern City

Europe's medieval cities were neatly defined by their fortified walls. Most of these perimeters disappeared by the end of the eighteenth century only to be replaced by boundaries more appropriate to a mercantile age: the toll barriers. These constituted Paris's limits until 1850, but by that time the tollgate, like the parapet, was more a quaint relic of past history than a functioning part of Parisian city life. The boundaries of the great cities of the nineteenth century were not clearly marked, and travelers, particularly those who now traveled by rail, had great difficulty distinguishing at what point the country ended and the city began. The clearly defined city limits of the eighteenth century had disappeared, and it was no longer possible from ground level to capture the extent of any of Europe's larger metropolises. In 1861 Henry Mayhew found it necessary to take to the air, via balloon, to examine the city of London. Below him he saw the

> Leviathan Metropolis, with a dense canopy of smoke hanging over it, and reminding one of the fog of vapour that is so often seen steaming from the fields at early morning. It was impossible to tell where the monster city began or ended, for the buildings stretched not only to the horizon on either side, but far away into the distance, where, owing to the coming shades of evening and the dense fumes from the million chimneys, the town seemed to blend into the sky, so that there was no distinguishing earth from heaven.

Mayhew might well have been describing any of the great sprawling metropolitan areas of the twentieth century. The air traveler of today is inevitably impressed with the same physical characteristics and the same looming problems: unwieldy size, overcrowded conditions, foul pollution.

Contemporary European cities are, nevertheless, different in a number of important respects. Center areas have ceased to be cluttered with five- or six-story buildings and have sprouted skyscrapers; automobile highways have replaced railraods as the great arteries of the urban body; the worst slums have been cleared and their inhabitants relocated to less conspicuous areas. The poor no longer collect so visibly at the city's center, and poverty is concentrated among the aged, out of sight and mind.

Street life is less colorful today, if only because so much of commercial life is now indoors. The huge populations of hawkers—as many as thirty thousand in London in the 1850s—have all but disappeared, as have the dancing bears and puppet shows. Street begging still occurs, but rarely is it the occupation of children as it was a hundred years ago. The poor line up today, not at workhouse or prison gate, but in employment offices. There are places in London and Paris where nomadic men and women still gather to sleep the night unsheltered near steam vents, but it is as rare today as it was common in the nineteenth century to see whole families making do in this manner.

To capture what it was like to live in Europe's great cities at the beginning of their modern growth period, we must turn instead to urban areas of developing countries, to the *bustees* of Delhi, the *bidonvilles* of Tunis, or the *villas miserarias* of Buenos Aires. There the parallels to the late eighteenth and early nineteenth century urban environment are most striking, because it is there that a growth spurt similar to that Europe experienced in the period 1770–1850 is presently taking place. The urbanization of parts of Asia, Africa, and Latin America is taking place at an even more rapid rate, and the accompanying tensions are exacerbated by the higher levels of competition and aspiration now prevalent world wide. Nevertheless, the overall sequence of change, particularly the crisis generated in the first stages of urbanization, is strikingly similar to that experienced by Europe during the period 1770–1850.

City Growth from 1770 to 1870

Europe was the first major world area to urbanize. Previous examples of city growth, such as ancient Rome or Renaissance Florence, had encountered checks imposed by the economy and the political system, but beginning in the late eighteenth century an erratic pattern of expansion and contraction was transformed into a pattern of steady growth whose limits are not yet clear today. In 1800 only 2.9 percent of the European population was living in large cities of one hundred thousand population or over. By 1850 this proportion had risen to 4.9 percent, by 1900 it had jumped to 11.9 percent, and by 1950 the proportion had reached almost 20 percent. If we look at the growth of smaller-sized cities, the increase is even more striking. In both England and France in 1800 there was only one city of more than one hundred thousand population. In England by 1900 there were 24 cities of that number. In 1800 there were only 15 English cities of over twenty thousand inhabitants, but in 1900 there were 161. France, which had 34 cities over the twenty thousand size in 1801, had increased that number to 105 by 1891.

The proportion of the English population resident in the countryside dropped steadily during the nineteenth century, though absolute depopulation of the rural regions did not begin until the 1850s. In 1850 the population of urban districts surpassed that of rural districts for the first time, and so rapid was subsequent city growth that, by 1891, 72 percent of the English were urban residents. French urban growth was much slower than English, but the pattern was much the same. In terms of those actually employed in agriculture, the changes were even more dramatic. Again England led the way, with France and the eastern European countries maintaining their agricultural base somewhat longer.

Urban growth on such a scale was bound to have extraordinary repercussions, but the fact that increase of this size was also unprecedented in world experience added a significant dimension to the results. Europe's economic and political systems were unprepared for these changes; although economic growth and political modernization were themselves a cause of the growth of great cities, they were not necessarily adjusted to the demands of urbanization. The result was a condition common in most developing countries today, namely, *overurbanization*—an increase in the number of city dwellers beyond the capacity of existing urban economies and political systems to meet the basic needs of the new inhabitants.

Europeans began to sense the strain on their urban centers in the early eighteenth century. Economists of that time were writing of the inability of cities to expand beyond a few hundred thousand inhabitants. One contributor to the *Encyclopedia* of the 1760s stressed the tendency of cities to attract more talent than they could use, thus causing a "brain drain" in the countryside and intellectual unrest in the town. Contemporaries were particularly concerned about the giants of the eighteenth century, London and Paris, deploring their tendency to swallow people and investments without enriching the provincial population. Their domination of culture, high rates of consumption, and enormous political power were to be objects of anxiety well into the nineteenth century. Mayhew called London a leviathan; and another English citizen warned: "let them take care how they make the fate of the country depend on the will of the Metropolis." Thinking of the role of Paris in the French Revolution, the conservative Lord Liverpool asked, "What can be stable in these enormous cities? One insurrection in London and all is lost."

It was with similar anxiety that French peasants viewed Paris, East Prussian Junkers Berlin, and Hungarian nobles Vienna, but not all the fears were rural in origin. Paris had been locked in a struggle against Marseille and Lyon during the French Revolution. There was no affection between Berlin and provincial cities like Cologne and Königsberg and as

English industrial centers like Manchester and Leeds grew in the second and third decades of the nineteenth century, their business elites were as hostile to the hegemonic tendencies of London as any reactionary landowner, perhaps even more so. The fact is that in the first period of city growth from the mid-eighteenth century through the 1840s, Europe suffered not only from general *overurbanization* but also from an imbalance of growth among the cities themselves. The dominance of a single city, usually the capital, complicating and sometimes inhibiting the growth of other urban areas was the second prominent element in the crisis of urban growth. These political and economic problems persisted until midcentury when a more balanced pattern began to emerge.

Strains in Urban Life

For centuries cities had been subject to moderate increases in size, probably more because of the immigration of country people than to a natural increase caused by the surplus of births over deaths. Because vital statistics are notoriously unreliable before the nineteenth century, it is only by educated guesswork that we can determine the size of individual cities in the eighteenth century. We can be reasonably sure, for instance, that the fastest-growing center in the Western world was London, which increased in population from five hundred seventy-five thousand in 1750 to almost nine hundred thousand in 1801. Despite certain improvements in health and housing toward the end of the eighteenth century, London's death rates still exceeded the birth rates, meaning that most of this increase was due to immigration. So dependent was London on influx that only one-third of that city's residents were native-born. Paris's population had stagnated at about six hundred thousand for most of the eighteenth century, but almost one hundred thousand of this number were classified as "floating migrants" who had no permanent residence in the city. Only four of every ten residents were native-born.

Smaller cities were almost certainly less fluid in composition than the larger cities. In Germany, towns of two thousand to twenty thousand population appear to have had a generational continuity greater than both the larger cities and the countryside; but they acquired stability only by maintaining the privileges of residents and discouraging newcomers, something that larger cities like Berlin, Paris, and London could not do. Migration was the lifeblood of the larger cities, and even in periods of relative stagnation they depended on influx from the outside. It has been estimated that during the seventeenth century one in every six English inhabitants lived in London for some time during his or her life, usually when young. Some stayed, but many returned to their places of birth to claim inheritance and settle down. Some visits to London were of relatively long duration—seven years for apprenticeship, several years of study at the Inns of Court—but most were probably of much shorter duration, lasting only a few weeks or perhaps a season. Many of this temporary population were essentially rural laborers who left the city in the spring to work at ploughing and planting, returning only after the fall harvests. Cities swelled in late summer just before the harvest, because it was then that stocks of food were usually larger and cheaper in the cities than in the countryside. Diminished in size during the fall, the cities grew again during the winter months, providing employment or (if that failed) charity to seasonal migrants—men, women, and large numbers of children who crowded into cramped lodgings until the next spring.

These migrants were *in* but not necessarily *of* the cities, and yet it cannot be said that they were atypical of the eighteenth-century urbanite, who was probably more accustomed to geographical mobility than his counterpart today. There was a certain ease of movement across town-country boundaries, with cities like London and Paris so dominating the countryside around them, monopolizing their agricultural produce and controlling their commerce, that there was a constant coming and going of people as well as of things. Until well into the nineteenth century, milk was delivered by hand to the center of Paris, while in Berlin pigs and sheep being herded to market frequently stopped carriages. As late as 1861 there were thirty-two shepherds listed among the London population.

The kind of fluidity described here was not necessarily disruptive, for traditional European cities were fitted out with a range of institutions that met the needs of the huge transient population. Foremost was the traditional household structure that accommodated kin, apprentices, and even strangers in an orderly, authoritative fashion. The patriarchal household found a parallel in the urban guilds, which offered room and board to wandering artisans; of particular importance in France and Germany were the journeymen's hostels, where youths could obtain lodging, advice, and a job. Furthermore, there were the less formal institutions of accommodation found in the various quarters of the city, places where persons of particular regions or nationality gathered.

In London there was the Irish "Little Dublin"; while in Paris Savoyards, Limousins, and Auvergats had their distinctive locales demarcated by regional accent and costume. There were also craft quarters, identifiable by the colorful signs of the various trades. In a time before street numbers, it was by such symbols, together with the familiar smells and noises of the crafts, that the stranger oriented himself; when William Lovett arrived in London from Cornwall in the early nineteenth century, he sought out those who shared his place of origin. "They were, however, strangers to me, but coming from the same county, we soon became acquainted." In an age before commercial hotels and restaurants, it was by such traditions of fraternity that migrants survived and prospered.

However, with the beginnings of rapid population growth in the second half of the eighteenth century, traditional institutions were put to a severe test. We cannot be sure whether it was the push of the countryside or the pull of the city that caused the rapid population increase in London in the mid-eighteenth century or in Paris in the early ninteenth, but whatever the reason, traditional urban accommodations were unable to meet the challenge. *Overurbanization* reflected the countryside's inability to employ and retain its growing populations. In some places domestic industry helped the villages maintain high levels of population, but as the eighteenth century wore on, it became clear that many such areas were dangerously near the ceiling of subsistence. Under these circumstances, the cities looked more attractive to the poor and powerless, particularly in times of famine when privileged city markets had bread and the countryside did not. In France in 1775 rioting peasants actually invaded the Paris outskirts in search of flour and when bad harvests recurred in 1788, Paris swelled to almost seven hundred thousand because of panic migration from the countryside. As in the case of developing countries today, rural disorder and civil war intensified the drift to the cities from an already overpopulated countryside.

The increased numbers of urbanites rapidly outstripped urban employment opportunities, although the effects of underemployment were cushioned somewhat by the traditional welfare institutions of the towns. The patriarchal household, the journeymen's hostel, and the almshouse were sufficiently elastic to absorb some increase, but in time the strain on their facilities became too great. Then, instead of absorbing more migrants, they began to exclude newcomers. Also, in eighteenth century London, masters flooded with apprentices were beginning to see the value of treating them as cheap wage labor rather than as students of the trade.

The trend of most eighteenth-century cities was toward a laissez-faire economy. Guild restrictions were being abolished and workers, once sheltered by their institutions, were exposed to the free labor market. Similarly, the practice of boarding workers was breaking down and in its place cheap, unsupervised lodging houses were springing up. The commercialization of room and board had a dual effect, both disastrous for the newcomer: the price of urban subsistence rose and the social benefits declined. The migrant was directly exposed to the exploitation of fluctuating wages and prices, losing at the same time the social and psychological security of the patriarchal household or fraternal hostel.

No less troubling was the breakdown of cultural services within the growing cities. Contact with religion was broken as church building failed to keep up with urban sprawl. When England took a census of churchgoing one Sunday in 1851, it was found that only a quarter of the London population was present. Similarly, schools were in short supply, with the result that truancy was more common than attendance. Even the pleasures of the traditional city—religious processions, fairs, communal games—were diminishing. Revolutionary Paris had attempted to replace the old calen-

dar customs with a new set of patriotic festivals, but when these were repressed by more conservative regimes the old holidays proved beyond
restoration. Berlin retained its traditional Fishermen's Procession, London
its St. Bartholomew's Fair, Munich its harvest festival, but these were left
to the lower orders to attend, being too vulgar for the rich who now enjoyed themselves in private salons and clubs.

Even the court life restored in Paris after 1815 attracted neither devotion
nor interest. "A dog falling into the Seine would attract more curiosity
than the royal family taking a drive through Paris," noted one wit. Only
the military retained the splendor of the old spectacles, but popular participation was lost in the substitution of parades for processions. In an age
before the development of uniquely urban entertainments such as the
music hall and spectator sport, the uses of leisure had been made dangerously individualized and fragmented, symptoms of the general loss of
social cohesion that Wordsworth wrote about in *The Prelude:*

> endless stream of men and moving things!
> . . . the quick dance,
> Of colours, lights and forms; the deafening din;
> The comers and the goers face to face
> Face after face.

Life at the Top and the Bottom

Overurbanization encouraged other kinds of exploitation by creating a
desperate surplus labor supply. The story might have been different had
industrialization been synchronized with urbanization, but as is so often
the case in developing countries today, employment lagged behind city
growth. In Europe much of the first phase of industrial growth occurred
in the countryside or in lesser cities like Manchester, Lille, or Barmen.
The lack of resources in or around the great cities was one reason for this,
but also at fault were the restrictive practices of most established urban
trades. Guilds and privileged companies typical of eighteenth-century
cities left entrepreneurs no alternative but to turn elsewhere, and they
turned first to the overpopulated countryside. Not until the 1820s and
1830s, when provincial industrial towns began to grow, were urbanization
and industrialization aligned in a constructive manner. In the meantime,
the competition of provincial industry had caused the decline of the traditional urban crafts, forcing much of big-city labor into the service sector
of the economy.

In the mid-nineteenth century fully 60 percent of London's labor force
was occupied in unskilled or service jobs, almost one-third of that proportion—mainly women—in domestic service. In Paris in the 1830s only 22
percent of the work force was in the manufacturing sector and even there
many of the skilled workers were becoming technologically unemployed.

Many were turning to casual labor, which was seasonal and hardly something one could build a career upon. It was difficult for unions to organize service professions and casual labor lacking a fixed place of work; thus, for much of the nineteenth century the labor movement was weak inside London and other large cities.

Urban social life, always somewhat unstable, became even more so during the late eighteenth and early nineteenth centuries. Traditional social institutions were breaking down and had not yet been replaced by new ones. Nowhere was this more evident than in housing, one of the great disgraces of the period. As the well-to-do redefined their living pattern, first by excluding all boarders (except servants) from their households and ultimately by moving from the center of the city to the privacy of the suburbs, growing numbers of the young and the poor were thrown on their own devices. Efforts to provide public housing were nonexistent, and in many cases even the traditional refuge of the poor, shanty towns in the suburbs, was denied them by the development of middle-class housing on the edges of the city.

The drift of the well-to-do to the western suburbs had been going on in both Paris and London since at least 1800, with the result that land prices there rose and squatters were forced inward toward the center of the cities. Unlike twentieth-century cities such as Tunis and Calcutta, where the slums grow around the cities, the universal trend in Europe was for wealthy suburbs to spin out like ribbons along the transportation arteries leading to the old business districts. By the 1820s building was more rapid at the edges than in the center of cities. Cartoons decried the desecration of the countryside and it was written that:

> The richest crop for any field
> Is a crop of bricks for it to yield
> The richest crop that it can grow
> Is a crop of houses in a row.

The center was where the poor collected, not only because rents were cheapest there, but also because it was closest to the places of employment. Unskilled labor was forced to endure the noise of dockyard areas and the stench of the tanneries in order to be first on the early morning hiring line. Even when horse-drawn omnibus transportation became available in the 1820s, most city labor could not take advantage of it to commute to healthier, less crowded areas. These workers were trapped by the nature of their low-paid casual labor in dilapidated neighborhoods described by Eugene Sue in *The Mysteries of Paris* as consisting of "mud colored houses, broken by a few worm-eaten windows. Black, filthy alleys led to steps even blacker and more filthy and so steep that one could climb them only with the help of a rope attached to the damp wall by iron brackets."

The traditional social separation of rich and poor had been vertical. That is, the well-to-do occupied the desirable first floors of buildings, the poor their cellars and upper stories. Just as the classes mixed, so did work and leisure, with work carried on in or near the living quarters. However, this type of sociability was gradually disappearing in the older cities as the rich moved to the suburbs. In the newer industrial cities rich and poor had never had the chance to share one another's problems because their social segregation was apparent from the beginning.

Among the problems the well-to-do wished to avoid was the mortality of the old center of the city. In Paris the death rates of the crowded quarters were four times that of the affluent Faubourg Saint-Germaine. The causes included poor nutrition and overwork, but chief among the killing conditions were sheer density and lack of proper sanitation. Until midcentury, no major city properly disposed of its sewage. Paris still dumped its garbage and excrement in the streets to be flushed away at intervals into the Seine. London relied heavily on cesspools, which were reasonably effective until the invention of the modern water closet caused them to overload with the additional waste water and contaminate wells and other sources of water supply.

To make matters worse, much of the London water supply was taken from the Thames, itself so badly contaminated that in the summer of 1858 Londoners were driven out of town by what newspapers called the Great Stench. Zola described the Seine as a great sewer, "the surface . . . . covered with greasy matter, old corks and vegetable parings, heaps of filth. . . . " As late as 1850 Paris still had only 82 miles of underground sewers for its 250 miles of streets. Only one in every five houses had its own water supply and only on the first floor because of low water pressure. Most Berliners still drew their water from public fountains until the 1850s.

The burning of cheap coal added another threat to health, namely, sulfurous air pollution. The environment was particularly deadly for young children, who are very susceptible to congestive and digestive diseases, but in the periods 1831–1832, 1848–1849, and again in 1866, adults, too, were swept away in cholera epidemics that killed nineteen thousand in Paris and seven thousand in London in each of the first two visitations. Local health authorities were not prepared to deal with the disease. Only four days before the 1832 cholera visited London, the populace had been asked to join in a national day of fasting and penance by the clergy. Doctors objected, suggesting feasting would have been a more effective preventative, but not yet armed with a convincing germ theory they offered no really effective alternative.

Sanitary reformers like Edwin Chadwick had to struggle against both ignorance and vested interest to create a unified sewer and water system in London. In most cities, power over such things was still vested in a multitude of local authorities who feared raising tax rates. A multitude of private water and light companies also resisted centralized authority and the clergy refused to close festering graveyards because this meant loss of interment fees. Not until the regime of Napoleon III in the 1850s was there a government anywhere in Europe willing to force through a major centralization of city health agencies and invest the astronomical funds necessary to accomplish the modernization of urban services we now take for granted.

Varieties of Urban Disorder

Given the conditions of the center of the cities, it is a wonder that cities did not produce more social and political disorder than they did. Demographically their populations were volatile. Because so many of their immigrants were in the 20–40 age range, there were proportionately fewer young children or elderly in the city than in the countryside. To add to the cities' problem of social control, there were more unmarried persons, many of them living apart from their families, than married persons. There were also more women than men in many cities, explaining, perhaps, the rise in prostitution noted by many observers. An estimated thirty-four thousand women were employed in this way in Paris in 1850. In 1859 the London police listed 2,828 brothels, but these employed only a small percentage of all prostitutes, who may have numbered as many as fifty thousand. "Every hundred steps one jostles twenty harlots; some ask for a glass of gin; others say, 'Sir, it is to pay my lodging,' " noted one visitor. Equally serious was the massive part-time prostitution by otherwise respectable working girls who needed the money to get by in hard times.

Crime and prostitution rose during periods of economic deprivation, because both were closely linked to the problem of poverty. Although there are no accurate crime statistics for the eighteenth and much of the early nineteenth century, it is likely that crimes against property increased steadily until midcentury. Of particular concern in every large city were the numbers of juvenile offenders who, although they accounted for less crime than older age groups, seemed to many observers to constitute the beginnings of a semihereditary criminal class. Parents were suspected of sending their own children out to beg or steal and there was evidence of real-life Fagins who trained boys to careers in crime. A police official testified to the English Parliament:

Upon a vacant spot of ground I observed a collection of boys and a man in the midst of them, with a basket in his hand doling out provisions. . . . Here is an old thief, who keeps all these boys in pay, and comes out regularly in the middle of the day, and brings them their food, and receives the produce of their plunder.

Police were not able to check crime. London did not get a professional force until 1829, while Berlin had to wait until the 1850s before its inefficient tangle of jurisdictions was streamlined. Just as in the developing cities of today, street gangs recruited disoriented newcomers. Orphans, deserted children, and runaways found these a substitute for the paternity and fraternity denied them by the breakdown of their own families and other traditional institutions of social control. In the early nineteenth century these groups were perceived as forming a distinct "dangerous class" to which were attributed all types of urban disorder.

The floating population of cities was large—in Paris perhaps an eighth of the population in the 1830s—but it generated fears disproportional even to its great size. Because this population was packed into slums where death rates were appallingly high, it had less chance of reproducing itself than did the more respectable elements of the population. Furthermore, because it was rootless, the floating population had no real place in the political life of the cities. Vagrants and thieves had very little role in the major political disorders of the period, their expectations being too low and their life too anarchic to become a part of any of the collective movements that were formed by more stable elements of the urban population.

Politics was left to the more respectable strata of the laboring poor—artisans and shopkeepers who had been residents in the cities for some time and had a long-standing interest in this area. Studies of crowds show that it was not the urban nomads but those people with fixed residence and settled occupation who took the lead in urban protest through 1848. The so-called dangerous classes played a part only in so far as their fate caused the *sans-culottes* to become even more conscious of how vulnerable they were to a similar plunge into poverty.

Urban protest movements were typically defensive in character, efforts by respectable *menu peuple* to save themselves from joining those at the bottom of the urban barrel. In so far as decaying neighborhoods and the rise of crime can be said to have contributed to political disorder, they did so by causing the more settled part of the working population to struggle against those forces, political and economic, that seemed to threaten them with loss of rights and status. The thieving urchin and streetwalker were largely absent from riot, strike, and political demonstration, but their existence was part of the dynamic that made the period 1770–1850 one of the most explosive in Western urban history.

Governing the Cities

Discontents among the established working classes varied according to occupation. Among the artisans, whose traditional crafts were decaying under the pressures of industrial competition, the cause was structural and irreversible. Until the 1820s London's silk weavers had enjoyed protected, prosperous conditions that had allowed them to develop an extraordinary level of cultural and community activity. Faced with competition, however, their craft declined rapidly, and they lost first their jobs, then their homes, finally their community. "The whole race of them is rapidly descending to the size of Lilliputians," lamented a contemporary. Such was the situation in French and German cities as well, where the artisan class was undergoing similar disintegration.

Newer types of industrial work presented different problems, connected not with structural decline but with uneven growth. The concentration of factory production in towns began in England during the 1820s, in France in the 1850s, and in Germany in the 1860s. At first wages were relatively good, but in the 1830s declining profits began to press down on them. Workers in England and France were squeezed below the subsistence level, and in 1839 came the first modern industrial depression, throwing thousands out of work. In the new factory cities like Manchester and Lille, where there was little alternative employment, the situation was desperate. Older towns had charitable institutions to fall back on, but many of the new industrial towns and cities were not even legally incorporated and therefore could do nothing for their inhabitants administratively. As a result, thousands were forced to leave home and tramp until employment was restored, thereby increasing the already large nomadic population.

Recurring urban crises were as much a cultural and political as an economic and demographic product, however. A monarchical tradition of urban planning and state welfare was available but it was ill suited to the needs of the great cities. Earlier planners, such as those who had laid out Versailles or Karlsruhe, had been moved by administrative and military considerations; thus, city planning carried too much of the stigma of absolutism to be of use in a new democratic age. Except in America, where the nation's capital was laid out in a grand rational design, city planning remained mainly ornamental. Before 1850 European efforts were small scale, focused on either short-lived utopian communities or small provincial factory towns, but scarcely touching the problems of the great cities.

Even had there been a willingness on the part of the state to intervene, until the mid-nineteenth century engineering and surveying skills were too limited to undertake grand projects. Only then did technical education begin to catch up with basic needs like sewer design and road construction. As in many of today's developing countries, Europe's long urban crisis was partially the product of misallocation of educational resources. For the first two or three decades of the nineteenth century, Europe produced more generalists than it could absorb. In the 1820s Paris acquired its eternal reputation as the city of poets and writers, but what it really needed was engineers.

English universities trained virtually no scientists until utilitarian minded dissenters set up London University in 1828. A huge gap developed between the classically educated minority and the great mass of urban people, whose schooling was more neglected that that of their rural counterparts. The establishment of self-help institutions, such as George Birkbeck's London Mechanics Institute founded in 1824 was an attempt to meet urban needs; however, the results, together with the reform of urban education generally, were too little and too late.

Ultimately, however, the search for the causes of urban crisis returns to the politics of the cities that, during the period 1770–1850, combined radicalism and reaction in contradictory ways. The initial thrust of modern nation building put a great deal of strain on the capacities of a few key cities. They were made to bear the brunt of political activity, far more than had been the case during the old regimes. The French Revolution, for example, eliminated the old dualism between Versailles and Paris. As Balzac noted, "France in the nineteenth century was divided into two zones: Paris and the provinces. . . . Formerly Paris was the first among provincial cities, and the total court stood above the city. Now Paris and the royal court are one. . . ." The English and the Germans suspected that parliamentary reform would result in the same kind of centralization for their capitals, and the revolutionary periods of the nineteenth century seemed to bear this out. Until 1848 the politics of the capital seemed to dominate both the hinterlands and the provincial cities. Then, in that year the French countryside took the lead, with the aid of the regional National Guard, in suppressing the Parisian insurrection, thereby redressing the imbalance between capital and country that had existed since 1789.

The great cities appeared more politically radical than the rest of society; while this was not necessarily so, the image made for difficulties. After the peak of *sans-culotte* radicalism in the years 1793–1794, conservatives attempted to reduce the revolutionary potential of Paris by cutting its population. Ironically, radicals were often no less ambivalent about urban growth; for example, the *sans-culotte* emphasis on community had a strong antiurban flavor, and until the mid-nineteenth century "return to the land" was a powerful theme among both populist democrats and utopian socialists. From Babeuf's "Conspiracy of Equals" in 1795 to the Chartist land schemes of the 1840s, radicalism had a tendency to turn its back on the city. With both ends of the political spectrum hostile or, at the very least, ambivalent toward urban growth, it is little wonder that support for urban renovation was lacking prior to the 1850s.

In addition, Paris and London both hosted landowner-dominated parliaments reluctant to invest public monies in the city. Not until Napoleon III taught Europe in the 1850s that city planning could serve conservative purposes were parliaments willing to spend anything for slum clearance. By building wide boulevards through the thicket of inner Paris, Napoleon III eliminated the narrow streets and oblique angles that had been so helpful to revolutionary barricade builders. His renovation was a skillful fusion of conservative politics and urban planning that attracted the admiration of the rest of Europe and began a new era of city-country relations. This new era coincided with the emergence of the mature nation-state, whose integrative capacity overcame the rivalries between capitals and provinces. Thus ended the political stalemate that together with uneven demographic and economic growth, had caused so many complications in the birth of the modern European city.

9

The Making of the Middle and Working Classes

Benjamin Disraeli wrote the novel *Sybil* in 1845, in it describing England as:

> *two nations* between whom there is no intercourse and no sympathy; who are ignorant of each other's habits, thoughts and feelings, as if they were dwellers in different zones, or inhabitants of different planets, who are formed by a different breeding, are fed by a different food, are ordered by different manners, and are not governed by the same laws. [italics added]

Disraeli could just as well have been writing about Paris or the urban areas of western Germany or northern Italy, for there, too, the unmistakable signs of new social divisions were evident. Much more disturbing than the distance between rich and poor, which had always existed, was the fact that the "two nations" seemed to be locked in bitter antagonism, the newly emerged middle and working classes threatening one another on the political as well as social level.

The turbulent 1830s and Hungry Forties presented Europe with its first and perhaps most intense experience of class conflict, an era of social division that, despite its essentially secular origins, rivaled the religious strife of the sixteenth and seventeenth centuries in its violent, emotional character. Both the middle and working classes claimed for themselves the role of chosen people in what both now perceived as a new industrial millennium. Out of the intense economic and political struggles of the 1830s and 1840s emerged two diametrically opposed designs for the future of European society, one embodying the individualistic ideals of the middle classes, the other reflecting the collectivist sentiments of the urban working class. Two groups whose experience of industrialization had been so radically different were bound to present conflicting structures of thought and feeling, reflected not only in their respective ideologies of liberalism and socialism, but also in every aspect of their daily lives, in their families, and in their personal and social relations.

The formation of social identity on the basis of class—that is, position in the economic system—is typical of societies undergoing the transition from tradition to modernity. Something like the broad lines of class stratification that emerged in Europe during the early nineteenth century are characteristic of every industrializing country, whatever claims it may make to having no class distinctions. The kind of centralization and specialization of function that accompany economic and political modernization impose horizontal divisions based on function; therefore, even socialist countries, where social inequality is supposedly abolished, find class divisions a persistent problem.

Yet many of today's new states have managed to avoid the kind of deep divisions Europe experienced because they began industrialization with at least a nominal commitment to social justice and political equality, something that was lacking when Europe began to industrialize in the early nineteenth century. At that time the institutions of the nation-state, including the commitment to universal citizenship, were not in place. Thus, inequalities in wealth and economic function were greatly exacerbated by civil and political inequalities as well as the lack of adequate social welfare institutions. Without the powerful cohesion of the nation-state, Disraeli's "two nations" were bound to make their own irreconcilable claims to sovereignty, producing conflict that up to today leaves its mark on European social relations.

Breakdown of the Old Social Order

The notion of society divided into two or more classes was sufficiently novel for John Stuart Mill to remark with surprise in the 1830s that "'classes' revolved in their eternal circle of landlords, capitalists and labourers, until they seem to think of the distinction into those three classes as if it were one of God's ordinances and not man's. . . ." The terminology of "class" was new to the nineteenth century and had only begun to replace an older language of ranks, orders, and estates. Previously, people had thought of the social order as a pyramid, with an infinite series of gradations leading from the princes at the top to the paupers at the bottom. Certain broad horizontal distinctions were recognized (such as that between the person of gentle birth and the commoner), and it was usual for states to legislate the number of estates, thus fixing castelike distinctions between the aristocracy, burghers, and peasantry. But the various social orders were not thought of as being in conflict with one another in the way classes were later. The traditional social hierarchy linked its members in a series of reciprocal relationships of authority and dependence. The poor could not exist apart from the charity and patronage of the rich and, in turn, contemporaries had difficulty imagining how the rich could do without the deference and obedience provided by the poor. The notion of classes of people, divided from one another in the way Disraeli described, frightened both prince and pauper, though each for different reasons.

The reciprocal relationships on which traditional society was based were learned from childhood. Contacts between different ranks were frequent in the marketplace or workshop, in the fields, at rest and play. As mentioned previously, the rich took the children of the poor into their households as live-in labor; thus they were nurtured by the same food, ordered by the same manners, governed by the same laws as their betters. The patriarchal household ensured that the relationship between individuals was more than just an economic one. Familiarity was the very basis of authority, something that we, accustomed to more impersonal means of social order, find hard to comprehend. Henry Bourne, writing in 1725, noted that in moments of relaxation such as a harvest feast, "the Servant and His Master are alike, and every Thing is done with an equal Freedom. They sit at the same Table, converse freely together, and spend the remaining Part of the Night in dancing and singing, etc, without any difference or Distinction."

However, doing things together did not imply equality any more than family activities today mean that parents and children are equals. Periodic fraternity helped release the tensions built up in an otherwise authoritarian, hierarchical society. The wise landowner knew that the social barriers needed to come down now and then, if only to remind the poor just how great the social distance really was. This was one of the reasons that the aristocracy continued to sponsor popular amusements well into the nineteenth century, because, as one of them said, dancing and singing encouraged the servants to "return to their Labour with a Light Heart, and grateful Obedience to their Superiors."

There were an almost infinite number of gradations within the ranks of the elites themselves; the aristocracy was divided into greater and lesser nobles, the clergy stratified in a similar manner. Conflicts over precedence were common and sensitivity to social status was so highly developed that gentlemen fought duels over every real or imagined insult to their honor. Even among the laboring poor there were deep divisions. Apprentices brawled with one another and members of the guilds from one town inevitably scorned artisans from another. As an article in *Blackwood Magazine* suggested in 1825, status boundaries conformed to occupation:

> The ploughmen hold the mechanics in contempt as an inferior race of beings . . . ; the journeymen cabinet-makers cannot degrade themselves by associating with the journeymen tailors: the journeymen

shoemakers cannot so far forget their dignity as to make companions of the labourers: the gentleman's lackey cannot, on any account, lower himself to the level of the carman.

Servants were notorious for their snobbishness, a habit they learned from their masters, and even thieves had their pecking order, which they guarded jealously.

Servants were the last of nineteenth-century working people to give up the notion of rank and dependence, because they were the ones who remained in closest contact with the well-to-do at a time when other working people were being systematically excluded from the neighborhoods and houses of the rich. The breakdown of the old sense of hierarchy began in the late eighteenth century when the custom of living-in ceased to be attractive to the employers. Large landowners and master artisans ceased to board child labor in their own households and thus old patriarchal relationships fell into disuse.

Labourers now seldom live under their employer's roofs for these reasons: the number of unemployed labourers is such, that a Farmer is always sure of hands when he wants them. It is cheaper to hire day labourers . . . than to maintain Servants in the house, especially as they are always sent home on a rainy day.

Domestic architecture institutionalized this change; no longer were there the big kitchens and halls where the entire household could gather. In most of the houses built for the new capitalist landowning class, the rooms for family use were strictly delineated from those inhabited by maids, cooks, and permanent serving staff. As one observer put it, "Since Farmers lived in parlours, labourers are no more found in kitchens." In the cities, too, there was increasing social segregation of the kind that was happening in the countryside. Beginning in the late eighteenth century, the rich began to move away from the business areas in the center of the city to settle in purely residential suburbs. This trend accelerated in the early nineteenth century, with workers also on the move into their own segregated quarters. The result in Paris was described in a Report of the Paris Chamber of Commerce, 1855:

In the old days they [the poor] used to live on the upper floors of buildings whose lower floors were occupied by businessmen and other fairly well-to-do persons. A species of solidarity grew up among the tenants of a single building. Neighbors helped each other in small ways. When sick or unemployed, the workers might find a great deal of help, while, on the other hand, a sort of human respect imbued working class habits with a certain regularity. Having moved north of the St. Martin canal or even beyond the [customs] barriers, the workers now live where there are no bourgeois families and are thus deprived of this assistance at the same time they are emancipated from the curb on them previously exercised by neighbors of this kind.

The kind of communication—language, ritual, festival—that had characterized the old society was disrupted, without anything new being put in its place. An English commentator wrote in 1820:

> Everywhere, in every walk of life, it is too evident that the upper orders of Society have been tending, more and more, to a separation of themselves from those whom nature, providence, and law have placed beneath them. . . . Men have come to deride and despise a thousand of those means of communication that in former days knit all orders of people together.

Some attributed this to the special character of the city, and Adam Smith wrote of the rural laborer that

> while he remains in a country village his conduct may be attended to, and he may be obliged to attend to himself. . . . But as soon as he comes into a great city, he is sunk in obscurity and darkness. His conduct is observed and attended to by nobody, and he is therefore very likely to abandon it himself to every sort of low profligacy and vice.

But the same breakdown of communication was observed in the countryside as well, where the gentry were abandoning common pleasures for the exclusively aristocratic fashion of the hunt. Land reform had excluded the poor from their former playing fields, the common lands, and in many places even periodic fraternity had disappeared, as an observer from Lincolnshire noted. "Rude jollity and merriment of country feasts and fairs is much less frequent now, than formerly, . . . the refinement of manners, and the greater separation between different ranks of masters and servants, together with the extending influences of sectarian preachers have repressed much of this old hospitality."

Social distance was increasing, not only in leisure but also at work. The early factory and shop owners were familiar figures to their workers but by the 1830s professional managers and salespeople were replacing them. Visitors to industrial Manchester were struck by the social segragation that the Frenchman Leon Faucher noticed:

> The town, strictly speaking, is only inhabited by shopkeepers and operatives; the merchants and manufacturers have detached villas situated in the midst of gardens and parks in the country. This mode of existence . . . excludes social intercourse, and leads to local absenteeism. . . . The rich man spreads his couch amidst the beauties of the surrounding countryside and abandons the town to the operatives, publicans, mendicants, thieves, and prostitutes, merely taking

the precaution to leave behind him a police force, whose duty it is to preserve some little of material order in this pellmell society.

When rich and poor encountered one another, it was often in the worst circumstances. It was said that "the rich lose sight of the poor, or only recognize them when attention is forced to their existence by their appearance as vagrants, mendicants, or delinquents." Stigmatizing all poor people as dirty and unruly was a convenient way of reinforcing and justifying social distance. During the 1830s and 1840s it was not uncommon for the French bourgeoisie to talk of the "dangerous classes" as if all the poor were criminal by nature. In England, in the Parliamentary Register of 1800, workers complained that they were spoken of "by everyone posessing the power to oppress them in any degree in just the same manner in which we speak of animals which composed the stock upon a farm. This is not the manner in which our forefathers, the common people, were treated."

The poor were not insensitive to these changes; conditioned by the old patriarchal system to view their betters as figures of security and respect, they reacted initially with fear and resentment to breakup of the paternalistic order and attempted to find substitutes for the lost authority figures before they came to accept as desirable the independence imposed by the division of classes. Remember that in the eighteenth century the *sansculottes* rebelled against one kind of paternalism, royal and aristocratic, but held fanatically to a patriarchalism of their own, emphasizing the importance of "good fathers" and the subordinate role of women and children.

However, workers of the 1830s who owned no property were more likely to accept, and even rejoice at, the decline of paternalism. Unlike the small owner-operators who made up the *sans-culottes*, they had no patriarchal household to idealize and their break with tradition was therefore much more complete. "Orphans are we, and bastards of society," wrote one English worker. His French counterparts had begun to speak of themselves as brothers, emphasizing horizontal loyalties along class lines rather than the vertical ties associated with the an older kind of division by crafts. The break with hierarchy had gone so far that John Stuart Mill could write in 1848, in *Principles of Political Economy:*

> Of the working men, at least in the more advanced countries of Europe, it may be pronounced that the patriarchal or paternal system of government is one to which they will not again be subject. That question was decided when they were taught to read . . . ; when they were brought together in numbers, to work socially under the same roof; when railways enabled them to shift from place to place, and change their patrons and employers as easily as their coats; when they are encouraged to seek a share in the government, by means of the electoral franchise. The working classes have taken their interests

into their own hands, and are perpetually showing that they think the interests of their employers not identical to their own, but opposite to them.

Emergence of a Distinctive Middle Class

A similar self-consciousness had developed among the middle classes somewhat earlier, arising primarily out of their conflicts with the aristocracy. This was true not only of France, where that struggle was overtly political, but also in other countries where social, economic, and moral interests were at odds. Everywhere the middle classes were developing a sense of being the most productive members of the community. Following Carlyle, they saw society as divided into three groups: "Workers, Master Workers, and Unworkers," and their greatest contempt was reserved for the Unworkers, comprised of both the nobility and the idle poor. Patrick Colquhoun, a writer on economics, lumped together

> those who pass their lives in vice and idleness, or who dissipate the surplus labour acquired by inheritance or otherwise in gaming and debauchery, and the idle class of paupers, prostitutes, rogues, vagabonds, vagrants, and persons engaged in criminal pursuits who are the real nuisances to society. . . .

Antagonism toward aristocracy was not lacking among the eighteenth-century middle ranks, but the old merchant elites had often intermarried with the nobility or invested their money in land and office in an attempt to emulate the aristocratic life-style. The eighteenth-century professions—the clergy, physicians, and lawyers—also had close ties with nobility. They were a privileged elite, fond of their leisured status and hostile to the utilitarian standards of practice that might associate them with the ordinary trades. So antagonism to aristocracy came not so much from these traditional bourgeoisie, but from the new industrial entrepreneurs and members of lesser professions. They were very much outsiders to the social system and cultural values of aristocracy and, therefore, less likely to succumb to the enticements of patronage and favoritism. Often members of minority religious or ethnic groups—English Quakers, German Jews, French Protestants—they were unacceptable to established society and therefore keenly aware of their separate identity.

Separate ethnic or religious identity was not sufficient to create class consciousness, however, and the sense of solidarity that developed in the early nineteenth century was based on economic position. Not until the bourgeoisie became aware of themselves as the chief *producers* of wealth and ideas did their consciousness of superiority begin to emerge. This began in France during the French Revolution, dissipated somewhat during the Napoleonic period, and then burst forth again under the so-called

Bourgeois Monarchy of the 1830s. It was then that Balzac remarked that "the three orders have been replaced by what we nowadays call classes. We have lettered classes, industrial classes, upper classes, middle classes, etc."

A similar language of class appeared in England at the end of the Napoleonic Wars, when it became apparent that England's victories were due as much to its superior productive capacity as to its military establishment. "The middle classes, the wealth and intelligence of the country, the glory of the British name," became the political rallying cry of the 1830s. A similar consciousness appeared in Germany somewhat later, in Italy later still, but by the 1840s there existed in all Europe well-defined groups, conscious of themselves as being at the forefront of historical progress.

Friction between the bourgeoisie and the aristocracy was not new; struggles between these two groups had punctuated European history since the twelfth century. What was new was the fact that at this time the bourgeoisie had developed its own distinctive secular historical consciousness. In the past, religion had served the middle ranks as a source of personal worth. Now it was concrete political and economic achievements that sustained their newfound sense of superiority. Not only were there now more business people and professionals than ever before, but they were also developing their own distinctive secular ideology, liberalism, together with a unique life-style that, whether it was called Victorianism in England or Biedermeier in Germany, was recognized as distinctively bourgeois. Here was a new class, with its own distinctive culture and personality.

Central to understanding the peculiar mentality of the nineteenth-century middle class is the unique family life and upbringing that distinguished the bourgeoisie from both the aristocracy and the working classes. If only because they were wealthier and healthier than the vast mass of the population it is easy to see how their lives were different from those of the workers. Together with the aristocracy, they experienced the first significant fall in infant mortality. Thus, during the early nineteenth century when most middle-class parents (outside France) did not yet use birth control, their families were large. The numerous children that peer out at us from Victorian family portraits project an image of domesticated bliss. Yet the situation of the bourgeois family was very different from that of the similarly large aristocratic family with its intricate networks of kinship and patronage. As long as their children were small, middle-class fathers felt no apprehension. However, when these boys and girls began to approach maturity, the problems became considerable, as J.C. Hudson's *Parents' Handbook* of the 1840s noted:

> The pride and satisfaction with which a father regards his first, and as yet only son, in the days of cockades, white frocks, and naked knees, are exchanged for anxiety and apprehension, when, some eighteen years afterwards, he sees himself surrounded by a half a

dozen full-grown and fast-growing candidates for frock coats, Wellington boots, walking-canes, watch guards, and cigars.

Seriously problematic were the futures of the numerous sons and daughters. The middle classes were committed to treating their children equally, according to their sex. If the girls were to marry respectably, a good dowry was an absolute necessity. For the boys, an apprenticeship in trade was not good enough, yet placement in a military or bureaucratic position was often out of the question. The typical nouveau riche simply did not have access to the "old boy" networks that dominated those professions. Nor was education always considered, because among this first generation of industrial bourgeoisie there were very few who were formally educated. They had done without fancy education and their sons would do without it also.

Therefore, if there were not enough places in the family firm, a young man was sent into the world to make his own career. What began as a necessity was quickly transformed into a virtue and the middle classes applied to their own children the same principles they adopted toward the poor—namely, that no one had the right to expect charity. The middle-class hero was self-made, the autonomous individual who owed nothing to favoritism or birth, the "self-raised and self-sustained . . . a splendid example of the power of merit. . . ." Not every industrialist started from the bottom (in fact, few were without property to begin with), but even those who began life with certain advantages liked to think of themselves as "new men." They accepted rugged individualism as morally superior and therefore made a virtue of self-denial, hard work, and ceaseless struggle in their lives and the lives of their children.

This fanatic commitment to autonomy had a direct effect on the way the early nineteenth-century bourgeoisie brought up their children. They were among the first to believe in Wordsworth's dictum that "the child is father of the man," and they prepared their offspring from a very early age for personal autonomy. The aristocracy, with its vast kinship and patronage, had not had to worry much about the early inculcation of habits. Middle-class families, on the other hand, paid very special attention to infant care and training. They were particularly receptive to Rousseau's advocacy of maternal breast-feeding, domestic education, and the careful supervision of children through adolescence. Rousseau spoke with contempt of the aristocratic tradition of boarding out children at the age of seven or eight, saying "they are always looking for the man in the children without thinking about what he is before he is a man."

The late eighteenth century saw a torrent of educational literature aimed at the middle-class child. The work of the German J.B. Brasedow and the Swiss John Heinrich Pestalozzi distinguished the world of the child from that of the adult. To the literature about children was added literature for children, with the publications of John Newbery in the 1740s followed by the Grimm brothers' fairy tales in 1812 and the works of Hans Christian Andersen in the 1830s. Much of this writing was highly moralistic and, in the case of the Grimms, somewhat oppressive. It was not until the 1860s, when Lewis Carroll published the first fantasy for children, *Alice in Wonderland*, that children's books were freed from their original didactic purposes.

The preceding is not to say that the middle classes were any more harsh to children than earlier generations; in fact, mothers preferred to breast-feed their babies rather than send them out to an uncertain future with wet nurses. The middle classes were also pioneers in abandoning the ancient practice of swaddling, a custom they regarded as a barbaric restraint on the child's sense of movement and autonomy. At the same time, they were careful to replace external restrictions with internal controls. They placed heavy emphasis on early toilet training and demanded from children self-mastery, the hardening of emotions, and the development of intellectual control over all physical functions, including sexuality. Although opposed to arbitrary punishment, most middle-class parents followed John Wesley's strong condemnation of willfulness on the part of the child. "To humour children is . . . to make their disease incurable. A wise parent, on the other hand, should begin to break their will, the first moment it appears."

What seems to us a cruel commandment was seen by its advocates as an enormous humanization of child care. Was not control of the child's will preferable to the external restraints and brutal punishments still customary among the aristocracy and the working classes? Breaking the will was meant to make the child submissive, not to external authority, but to his or her own self-discipline. This seemed to middle-class writers to be the very basis of individual autonomy, the greatest gift a parent could give to a child. Indeed, this mode of child rearing appeared to have achieved its objective in so far as middle-class children often showed an extraordinary capacity for hard work, deferring personal and sexual pleasures in the pursuit of success in their chosen careers. Middle-class men and women were often heroic in their rejection of all emotional and social dependencies. This was one of the traits that allowed them to challenge convention and defy the powerful social pressures that had traditionally inhibited originality, but at the same time, it produced a tendency toward compulsive, uncompromising behavior.

Early repression of emotions helps explain the insensitivity of many bourgeoisie not only to the problems of the poor but also to their own social and sexual dilemmas. So intense was the fear of physical functions, that many, and particularly women, were never comfortable with their own bodies. This accounts in part for the notorious prudery of the Victorian age, and also for the great attack on all traditional forms of pleasure that reached its peak in the Sabbatarian and temperance movements of the mid-nineteenth century. Another symptom was the widespread attack on masturbation, which middle-class people referred to as self-abuse because, while socially harmless, it implied the absence of the cardinal bourgeois virtue: that of self-control.

Alienation from the senses was accompanied by alienation from social pleasures generally. John Stuart Mill summed up the torment of his generation when he said: "In our age and country every person with any mental power at all, who both thinks for himself and has a conscience, must feel himself, to a very great degree, alone." For many, this loneliness was overcome by youthful religious or political conversion. It was Rousseau who pointed out that children raised in the narrow confines of the nuclear family needed a "second birth" in order to be able to cope with the wider world:

> We are born twice over; the first time for existence, the second
> for life; once as human beings and later as men or as women....At a
> time prescribed by nature he passes out of his childhood, and this
> moment of crisis, brief though it is, has a prolonged influence.

The middle-class passion for millennialistic causes can perhaps be explained by the intense identity crisis experienced by many young men beginning their lonely conquest of a difficult world. This was less a problem for women, for whom the role of motherhood was fixed and immutable.

Middle-Class Culture and Personality

New patterns of family and child rearing had a powerful impact not only on individual psychology, but also on the definition of sex roles, yet another way in which the nineteenth-century bourgeoisie left its unique imprint on modern life. Fathers loomed large in the middle-class household, taking an active part in the education of their children. Their authority was an extension of the old patriarchal concept, only more sharply focused. Because apprentices and laborers were no longer included in the average middle-class household, it was the children who felt the full weight of paternal influence. James Mill taught Greek and Latin to his son at age five; other fathers were equally active in domestic education. At the same time, the role of mother was even more dramatically altered because middle-class family life centered almost exclusively on the single function of child rearing.

Among the bourgeoisie the wife ceased to be the helpmate she had once been in the smaller artisan or shopkeeping operation. Her role was now confined to childbearing (an absorbing occupation because she bore large numbers of children) and household management. As economic functions shifted outside the home and became the sole preserve of the male, the distinction between breadwinner and wife became starkly accentuated. Women were told to think of their husbands "labouring with busy hand, with anxious eye and thoughtful brow, for your support and comfort, and say 'Does he not deserve a happy home?'" In short, the wife ceased to be a producer and assumed the role of consumer, homemaker, and child bearer. Lacking public autonomy, she was urged to accept domestic subordination. A Mrs. Sewell wrote:

> It is the man's place to rule, and a woman's to yield. He must be held up as the head of the house, and it is her duty to bend so unmurmuringly to his wishes, that the rest of the household will follow her example, and treat him with the due respect his sex demands.

The fate of working-class women was entirely different. As young girls they went to work; as wives they supplemented their husbands' wages as best as possible; as widows they often returned to full-time employment in order to survive. In the early phases of industrialization, these women and their children often formed the core of the factory work force, their life of labor forming a sharp contrast to the middle-class cult of domesticity. Confined to the world of *Kirche, Küche, und Kinder* (church, kitchen, and children), the middle-class woman became identified with childlike qualities of innocence, emotionality, and intellectual immaturity. Rousseau believed women to be intellectually inferior, and later, Darwinists would place the female on a lower evolutionary step than males. Women who insisted on an active, public life—Anita Garibaldi, Flora Tristan, Mary Wollstonecraft, Lola Montez—were stigmatized as "hyenas in skirts." As deviates from the norms of their class, women authors were forced to adopt male names (George Eliot and George Sand) and even accept male dress in order to legitimize their activity.

At the same time that it refused women equal economic and political rights, bourgeois culture attributed greater moral sensitivity to women than to men. Despite this virtue, and perhaps because of it, they were thought of as weak and vulnerable. "True feminine genius is very timid, doubtful, and clingingly dependent; a perpetual childhood," wrote one American woman, contrasting true womanhood with the aggressive autonomy of the ideal middle-class male. "Her intellect is not for invention or creation, but for sweet ordering, arrangement, and decision." The proper middle-class wife did not work outside the home; her daughters were educated domestically and chaperoned publicly. Their role was both ornamental and sacramental, for as keepers of the "temple of the hearth" women were to be helpmates able, in the words of Mrs. Sara Ellis, "to raise the tone of *his* mind from low anxieties and vulgar cares." [italics added]

Most middle-class women took their dual role as wife and mother as sacred and dedicated themselves with religious devotion to running their suburban villas. However, there were those like Mary Wollstonecraft and George Sand who found home too much like a secular cloister. They resented the double standard of male-female conduct and agreed with early socialist William Thompson that "home . . . is the eternal prison of the wife; the husband paints it as the abode of calm bliss, but takes care to find outside of doors, for his own use, a species of bliss which is not so calm, but of a more varied and stimulating description." However, this was a minority view.

Female virtues were supposed to be private and domestic; by the 1830s the concept of "Home, Sweet Home" was widely accepted in middle-class circles. The concept of home as sacred, the true source of spiritual strength, was reflected in Samuel Smiles's observation that "home is the first and most important source of character. . . . From that source, be it pure or impure, issue the principles and manners which govern society." This domestic utopianism was reflected in the thousands of single dwellings that sprang up in the western suburbs of all the great European cities. In abandoning the crowded city centers and separating their place of work from family life, the middle classes abandoned the tradition of the household economy. Home as "man's castle," moated socially against the chaos of the outside world and drawbridges lifted against the invasion of the problems of the poor and the unfortunate, became their ideal. Homesickness, a malady new to the time, was middle class in origin. As Ruskin put it in *Sesame and Lilies* in 1865, the home replaced even the Church as "the place of Peace; the shelter, not only from all injury, but from all terror, doubt, and division."

> In so far as it is not this, it is not home; so far as the anxieties of the outer life penetrate into it; and the inconsistently minded, unknown, unloved, or hostile society of the outside world is allowed by either husband or wife to cross the threshold, it ceases to be home; But so far as it is a sacred place, a vestal temple, a temple of the hearth watched over by Household Gods . . . —so far it vindicates the name, and fulfills the praise, of Home.

Such a sacred place required new domestic rituals. The fetishes of cleanliness, not only of the home but also of the reputation of its inhabitants, and the sacrosanct nature of family life—all these can still be detected in middle-class life today but without the moral fervor that was present at their origins. Home and family were to the bourgeoisie central sources of personal and social revitalization. "Our God is a household God, as well as a heavenly one," observed Ruskin, reflecting the cult of domesticity that extended to men as well as to women. Bourgeois men might practice a double standard of morality, however, for they spent much of their lives outside the home. While their wives and children were chaste and protected, this did not prevent them from exploiting prostitution and the child labor of the poor. Middle-class men deserved their reputation for hypocrisy, though it should be noted that they were far more "domesticated" than the aristocracy had ever been.

There is no denying that there was a strong element of idealism, even utopianism, in middlè-class notions of marriage and family. Marriages of convenience, arranged for economic reasons between two families, continued, but to a much lesser extent than among the aristocracy. The middle classes were the first to associate marriage with the now familiar romantic concept of love. Partners must be "right" for one another, emotionally as well as socially, a harmonic concept that made marriage a substitute for the broader spiritual fellowship that had been previously associated with church and community. Sentimentalized love was supposed to make the home "a bright, serene, restful, joyful nook of heaven in an unheavenly world."

Ironically, the idea of marriage as a secularized form of salvation led logically not only to much stricter domestic morality but also to the modern concept of divorce. The French Revolution experimented with divorce reform, laying it aside during the Napoleonic era, while the English carried through an important liberalization of divorce in 1857. Shelley was only carrying the idealism of middle-class marriage to its logical conclusion when he argued that "husband and wife ought to continue so long united as they love each other." Love became a substitute for divine grace, which sanctified marriage but also, in its absence, justified divorce. In the same vein, middle-class utopian thinkers like Robert Owen and Charles Fourier could even argue that any relationship between the sexes was justified as long as it was accompanied by affection. Throughout the nineteenth century, various experiments in free love, communal living, and marriage reform were predominantly middle class in origin. The aristocracy refused to take such things seriously and the laboring poor were so pressed by necessity that among them sex, marriage, and child rearing never became the subject of high spiritual expectations.

Of course, most middle-class people were quite content to develop their version of spiritual perfection within the restricted boundaries of conventional marriage. Taught to fear their own sexual impulses, middle-class males wished to cloister their own wives and daughters. Among the aristocracy extramarital affairs were accepted as normal, and illegitimate offspring were supported, sometimes even given legal recognition. The new middle classes viewed paternity more narrowly, however, and were particularly fearful of adultery on the part of their wives and loss of virginity of their daughters. For the respectable woman, sex was confined to one purpose only, namely, procreation. Had not the medical literature declared she was incapable of any other desire? Dr. William Acton stated:

> The best mothers, wives; and managers of households, know little or nothing of sexual indulgences. Love of home, children, and domestic duties are the only passions they feel. As a general rule, a modest woman seldom desires any sexual gratification for herself. She submits to her husband, but only to please him; and, but for the desire of maternity, would far rather be relieved of his attentions.

The sexual attentions of middle-class men tended to turn elsewhere; mistresses and prostitutes fulfilled their desire for pleasure. They therefore came to associate pleasure seeking strictly with these women and the lower classes generally, a fact that helps account for the middle-class belief that all poor people tended, if not sufficiently controlled, to become lewd and licentious. In the class-conscious society of the nineteenth century, the image of woman split into two apparently contradictory versions: on one hand was the idealized image of the respectable middle-class woman—passive, domesticated, desexualized; on the other hand was the distorted picture of the degraded, aggressive virago of the streets. In reality, both images were projections of middle-class male fantasy. As Dr. Action pointed out, "Many men, and particularly young men, form their ideas of women's feelings from what they notice early in life among loose, or, at least, low and vulgar women. . . ." Taught as children to feel guilty about their own sexual urges, bourgeois males naturally tended to displace unacceptable feelings on those women who, because of their poverty, were forced to sell their bodies in the massive market of nineteenth-century prostitution. For their wives and daughters, on the other hand, they reserved a properly desexualized version of sentimentalized love.

Life Among the Laboring Poor

It is not difficult to understand why Disraeli believed the gulf between the middle and working class to be unbridgeable by the 1840s. This was not a case of the traditional difference between rich and poor in a society where, despite differences in wealth, all persons shared the same basic values. In this case, differences went beyond wealth and involved mutually exclusive patterns of thought and feeling that were the products of very different mentalities. Like the middle class, urban workers were developing a collective sense of their own worth. They, too, were becoming aware of themselves as *producers,* though in a manner radically different from that of the bourgeoisie. Both felt themselves superior to the idle aristocracy, but while the bourgeoisie emphasized the productive contribution of capital and intellect, the working classes stressed the value of labor and skill. Consciousness of the value of labor dawned first in those areas where capitalist industrialization, with its separation of employer (capital) and employee (labor), had proceeded furthest. Thus the English radical John Knight wrote in 1834:

It is high time for all the English workmen to be aware and no longer be driven in the road to ruin by their blind employers. . . . We must . . . learn to look beyond the improvement of our own particular branch of business and improve the conditions of the whole body of English labourers. . . . With this in view we ought to ascertain the intrinsic value of labour; for until we have learned that it is impossible to ascertain to what extent we are robbed of the fruit of our labour.

On the Continent, class consciousness was slower in emerging, though the French in many trades were becoming aware of themselves as the "industrious classes" in the 1830s, and the value of labor (as opposed to capital) was an issue in the German Revolutions of 1848. But even where the conflict was not sharply focused, the laboring poor could not help but be aware of the differences between themselves and the bourgeoisie on matters social, cultural, and even psychological. One major difference lay in the family life and upbringing of the laboring poor. They continued to be subject to horrendous child mortality, even higher than it had been in the countryside. In Manchester the life expectancy of workers was only twenty-four years, as compared with the English average of forty years. The child mortality rate among Glasgow's poor was two and a half times that of the city's suburban middle class. Birth rates were correspondingly great, with large families remaining the norm for the rest of the nineteenth century in most industrial cities. Children were a necessity to help make ends meet, and at a time when child labor was as prized as that of adults, parents were often forced to rely on the earnings of their little ones for maintenance.

The decline of domestic industry and the crafts caused "husbands to take over the duties of the household, and wife and children were the bread-winners at the factory." Mines took boys as young as six, and it was reported that in one exceptional case a child of two did manual labor in a cotton factory. Not until effective child labor laws began to be passed, in England in 1833, in Prussia in 1839, and in France in 1841, did the worst abuses come to an end. By that time mechanization had made much child labor outmoded, so many children simply switched to jobs such as street selling that were not covered by regulations. As late as 1851, less than 50 percent of London's children were attending school on a regular basis, and when compulsory attendance came twenty years later, the poorest families continued to encourage truancy because they needed their children's wages to stay alive.

The changes in child rearing going on among the middle classes were simply out of the question among the poor. They viewed children as a god-sent gift (or, alternatively, as a divine curse) and continued the customs of earlier generations of swaddling and external restraint. The poor taught a self-reliance of a different kind—not so much self-discipline as group-disci-pline—by which the individual learned that his or her survival depended on the survival of others. As in preindustrial society, the poor had to find ways of maintaining older children outside the home. They could not adhere to Mrs. Beeton's advice that "it ought to enter into the domestic policy of every parent to make her child see that the home is the happiest place in the world. . . ." Girls in rural Oxfordshire were sent away to be servants at the age of twelve or fourteen. The youth of Silesia and the

Tyrol were still sent off to the city because there was no place for them at home.

Indeed, the population explosion of the nineteenth century made most parents even more dependent than before on extrafamilial institutions to support their children. Migration, the traditional recourse of the surplus young, expanded enormously in the late eighteenth century; first it was the English seeking their fortunes in the New World, then beginning in the 1840s, the Irish and Germans. Later, as population expansion spread south and east, the Italians and the Balkan peoples began to move in vast numbers. Only France, where the rate of population growth was already beginning to slow by the end of the eighteenth century, did not contribute to what amounted to one of the greatest population movements in recorded history.

Between 1821 and 1932 Europe lost an estimated 60 million persons to migration, and within its boundaries ethnic divisions were substantially redrawn as great numbers of Irish crossed into England, and Germans, Poles, and Italians flocked to Paris. It is estimated that there were at least thirty thousand Germans living in Paris in the 1840s, with another twenty thousand in London. Some were political exiles, but most of them were young journeymen seeking the work they could not find at home. English mechanics, much in demand for their skills, crossed over to the Continent, but it was the Italian peasants who ranged the farthest, making long seasonal journeys that found them harvesting in Latin America in the spring, working the North American fields in summer and fall, and then returning to their families during the winter before renewing the long journey once again.

The middle-class malady of homesickness did not exist among the poor; division of families had been their lot for centuries and the concept of "Home, Sweet Home" remained a luxury for much of the nineteenth century. However, despite the conditions prevailing in the 1830s and 1840s, new sources of cohesion were appearing; ironically, it was the new industrial cities (as opposed to older cities) that, despite their horrors, gave workers' families a new form. In the first phases of industrialization, migration to the cities divided families and disrupted communities. An overwhelming number of the early migrants were young, many of them women, detached from home and family. The second generation of migrants arriving from the 1840s onward were also young and unattached, but they did not face the same problems as the first because they now had contacts in the cities who could provide jobs, housing, and companionship. Migration tended to follow regular patterns, between particular rural districts and particular neighborhoods in the cities. It was not uncommon for job seekers to "claim kin," residing for a time with uncles or cousins until accustomed to city ways, and then marrying and establishing an independent household.

Thus, for those with such contacts the new cities were not as socially inhospitable as their physical appearance might indicate. Indeed, the advantages seemed clear enough to many of the young persons who made the move: marriage opportunities were greater than in the countryside and factory wages, though still very low, were nevertheless better than those of the declining rural crafts or farm labor. Furthermore, the availability of work allowed for the stabilization of family life. While rural youth were forced to migrate because of the lack of opportunity, sons and daughters of industrial workers, employed in the factories, lived with their parents for longer periods of time.

Often young marrieds would live with their parents until able to find a place of their own, and the old folks would go to live with their children once they were no longer able to earn a living, making themselves useful cooking or tending children while the young mothers worked. Cooperation among kin was a necessity of survival under conditions of high death and birth rates. "An orphan is kin to everyone," the saying went; since one of every three children by age fifteen had lost at least one parent, the number of children for whom aunts and uncles were substitute parents was naturally enormous in a period when the apparatus of the modern welfare state was nonexistent and the workhouse still the object of loathing by the respectable poor.

However, the stabilization of family life did not mean that the new working classes adopted either bourgeois child-rearing methods or the individualistic orientation associated with them. They remained much less concerned about inner control. Brought up by a variety of people—grandparents, siblings, peer groups, and so on—working-class children tended to be more sensitive to the social and emotional needs of the group. Gaining respect in middle-class culture meant demonstrating rugged individualism. Among the poor, ambition was likely to produce distrust, even outright hostility. They spoke of "hating to see folk try to get on," not because they were envious by nature, but because they learned that one person's good fortune was often another's disaster. Working-class upbringing also put less emphasis on intellectual command of emotions and physical functions; there was less fear of sexuality as such and virginity had less value. Instead, it was the unwanted consequences of sex—illegitimate children, disease, poverty—that were feared. Working girls were a good deal less anxious about pregnancy, one reason being that in stable neighborhoods, as in the traditional village, social pressure usually obligated the man involved to marry the mother.

Working-class children experienced no adolescent identity crisis. They grew up too fast and their choices in life were too limited to be subject to that kind of anxiety. Dickens aptly described London street urchins as looking like little, stunted men. The street was their school, where the facts of life, learned from pals or by watching animals, were an open book and seemed as natural as eating and drinking. Although most tried to uphold the standard of monogamous marriage, the poor were much less likely to idealize human relationships with the notions of romantic love that were popular among the middle class. Marriage was a thing of necessity and the parent-child relationship a matter of survival. If workers in Paris and Berlin rarely bothered to have their marriages solemnized by the church or their newborns baptized, it was not because they were immoral or promiscuous, but because death intervened in their world so frequently that there seemed less reason to sentimentalize or formalize relationships that might soon be destroyed by disease or accident.

The kind of emotional sanctification that the bourgeoisie gave to private relationships—husband and wife, parents and children—was neither possible nor even desirable. On the contrary, where survival depended on maintaining ties with large numbers of kin and fellow workers, too great an emphasis on privacy and domesticity could be disastrous. It was collective, not individual, identity that was the source of personal strength and communal revitalization. The poor reacted with repugnance to the highly individualized life-style of the rich in the same way the rich poured scorn on the communal rites of the poor. "In my mind community is the finest thing that could exist," wrote one young French woodworker in 1841, "with it, pride, ambition, avarice, tyranny will fall; without community the people will always be cast into the abyss . . . without community no happiness for the people. . . ."

If the advent of industrial society narrowed the meaning of family among the middle class, it did just the opposite among the poor. They did not hold the sentimentalized notion of nuclear family that the bourgeoisie cherished. Necessity pressed too hard, overcrowding was too great, and the smell of sweating bodies was too strong to make this a cloistered "Home, Sweet Home." Kin ties were spread out over whole neighborhoods, and much of the sociability remained where it had always been, in the streets. A man from Salford remembered:

> A man's work, of course, usually fixed the place where his family dwelt; but lesser factors were involved too: his links, for instance, with local kith and kin. Then again, he commonly held a certain social position at the near-by pub, modest perhaps, but recognized, and a credit connection with the corner shop. Such relationships, once relinquished, might not easily be reestablished. All these things, together with fear of change, combined to keep poor families, if not in the same street, at least in the same neighborhood for generations. . . . Whatever newcomers we got were never the "country gorbies" whom my grandfather remembers as the "butt of the workshops" in his youth, but families on the way up or down from other slums in the city: yet new neighbors or old, all shared a common poverty.*

Even within the forbidding factories, a sense of community could be

*Robert Roberts, *The Classic Slum*, Penguin Books, London, 1971, p. 29.

kept alive by the observance of births, deaths, and traditional holidays. Swiss factory owners found that the only way to prevent time-wasting conviviality was to organize it. So they, like some employers in England and Germany, sponsored annual feasts, financed self-improvement groups, even built playing fields. But most of the conviviality was of the workers' own making, shaped by age-old traditions of the craft shop or invented new out of the conditions of the factory. Paradoxically, the colorful rituals of the guilds appeared to take on new life in the early nineteenth century, serving the need of desperate people for mutual support. Handshakes, toasts, initiations, and oaths—all these flourished in what seemed to be a totally hostile atmosphere.

The earliest of modern working-class organizations, the mutual benefit societies, revived traditional feast days by giving them a new social function. The rules of one English Friendly Society read: "There shall be a feast, annually, on Whit Monday, and each member residing within ten miles shall appear decent and clean, in order to go to church, and answer his name by ten o'clock in the forenoon or forfeit one shilling." Individual propriety was insisted on, but as a means to collective ends, not as a thing valued for itself. Improvement was a collective rather than an individual enterprise, and when working people came together in Lyon in the 1840s, it was not just the men who were present at the meetings of the socialist Icarian movement but women and children as well. According to one of those present, the evenings passed agreeably:

> We recited fables, we sang politico-socialist songs that were, for the most part, written by young Icarians. We discussed all sorts of political and social questions. It was an excellent way for men to get used to speaking. To please women and children the evening usually ended playing games.

The necessities and pleasures of life were woven together during the crisis years of the 1830s and 1840s. For the workers, leisure took on a meaning different from that assumed by their social superiors; working days of fourteen to sixteen hours permitted little free time and new towns had none of the diversions that older cultural or administrative cities had to offer. They were barren of even the traditional fairs and religious festivals, and it would not be until the second half of the century that commercial substitutes—music halls and, ultimately, the cinema—became available.

Culture, therefore, developed in close association with the place of work. It was there that the working classes spent most of their waking hours and where they exchanged gossip, read newspapers aloud so that illiterates could share the news, and developed their sense of social identity. Little wonder that, in the first phase of industrialization, workers' consciousness of themselves as a class was so strongly conditioned by their place in the productive process. The conditions of work, together with the absence of opportunity for developing other kinds of identities, meant that religious, regional, even ethnic and national differences were submerged in a growing consciousness of the value of labor as such, without distinction as to trade or background. The experience of industrialization, so deeply exploitative and divisive, caused workers to reject the competitive individualism of their social betters in favor of a broad notion of brotherhood. As Tyneside workers in the 1830s put it, "Man is formed a social being . . . in continual need of mutual assistance and support. . . ."

Growth of Working-Class Consciousness

The awareness of shared interests gradually evolved out of the struggles and experiences that can be traced back at least as far as the 1790s, though, throughout the French Revolution, the poor had shown themselves to be more aware of their role as consumers than their role as producers. High bread prices and unfair market practices that threatened the traditional standard of living provoked popular protest. Issues such as wages and conditions of work were secondary, and although there was a prehistory of strike activity, during the eighteenth century this was largely defensive in nature. Workers did combine to protect the price of their products, but they did so sporadically and without permanent union organization. The eighteenth-century state was active in suppressing worker associations of all kinds, and the National Assembly merely was observing this practice when in 1791 it banned all trade associations. In England, too, the government seized upon the radicalism of the 1790s to pass a ban on worker unions, and in Germany controls on journeymen's associations were stiffened and strikes repressed.

The experience of factory industrialization did not immediately stimulate new attitudes on the part of workers and unionization was inhibited by the fact that so many women and children were employed in the new mills. Although factory women were active in early strike activity, the main thrust of labor agitation in the first decades of the nineteenth century followed from a more traditional artisan consciousness. For at least two centuries, craft workers had been accustomed to dealing with employers by threatening the use of violence. Eighteenth-century English weavers had destroyed the stock and machines of those masters who threatened their livelihood, and in the years 1811–1816, a particularly strong wave of machine breaking took place in England. Threatening notes, signed by the mythical Ned Ludd, were sometimes enough to frighten masters into concessions, but when warnings were not effective, offenders were visited and their property damaged or destroyed. In France the situation was much the same, although the outbreak was not as strong. In the twentieth century, the historian H. Sée wrote about one situation:

> When, in 1819 two manufacturers in Vienne (Isère) were about to introduce a mechanical device for shearing cloth, the shearing masters

raised an objection and addressed a petition to the mayor, in which they pointed out that the machines needed only four men to work them. They would shear and finish a thousand ells of cloth in twelve hours, thereby putting numerous workers out a job. When the machines arrived from Lyon under police guard, the workers prepared to break open the packing cases in order to smash up the machinery. The military was forced to attack, the ringleaders were arrested, but twice acquitted by a Grenoble jury: public opinion was on their side.

Similar attacks on machinery occurred in Silesia and Bohemia in 1844, and during 1848 another wave of Luddism followed.

On the surface, Luddism appeared to reflect worker hostility to the machine itself, but in reality the pattern of machine breaking was always highly selective. Only those machines were destroyed that were thought to be causing unemployment. Thus, Luddism reflected the old conception of the limited good: there was only so much work to go around and the machine was taking more than its share. There was no belief in an infinitely expanding future as yet—but then, many workers were still peasants psychologically, even sociologically. The miners of the Carmaux in France still tilled the soil when not working underground. In many places, domestic industry encouraged the survival of the *sans-culotte* mentality by providing income that supplemented shopkeeping or farming.

Alongside these traditional forms of protest, sometimes drawing strength from them, grew newer forms of worker organization. Although illegal until 1824, English worker associations were growing rapidly during the first decades of the nineteenth century. By necessity, they disguised themselves as benefit clubs (called Friendly Societies), associations for leisure activities, Mechanics Institutes, religious groups, and fraternal orders. It is estimated that there were already over nine thousand Friendly Societies with seven hundred thousand members in Britain by 1803, a remarkable form of voluntary association that was a forerunner of the kinds of producer and consumer cooperatives that would flourish in the 1830s and 1840s. When the restrictions on unionization were lifted in 1824, the ground had been well prepared for organization among both the traditional crafts and the new factory industries. The General Union of Carpenters and Joiners was founded in 1827, the Grand General Union of Cotton Spinners in 1829, the Operative Builders Union in 1833, and the Miners Association in 1841. The beginnings were relatively small, with only about one hundred thousand active members in 1842, but the dream of unionizing all working people was already apparent in the abortive attempt to establish a Grand National Consolidated Union in 1834.

In France the Napoleonic Code was much more tolerant of employer than of employee associations. Workers' unions did not become fully legal until 1864, though mutual benefit societies provided cover for worker organizations in the 1830s. It was during this period that Parisian printers began to organize as a friendly society, one that went beyond the usual widows' funds and funeral benefits to advocate uniform wages and the general improvement of working conditions. But the scale of French industry remained small and it was difficult to organize a multitude of small workshops. The tradition of employer paternalism remained stronger in France than in England and strikers were treated as rebellious children rather than responsible bargaining agents. Declared one factory owner, "In my factory, I tell my workers if they have any complaints they may send the two oldest employees and I will talk with them, because I am sure they would be reasonable." Strikes remained illegal in France and Germany until the 1860s.

Older workers were accepting of this, but younger ones were not. Wrote one young worker: "Our elders had grown up under the gloved hand of the nobles and priests. . . . The lower class had been kept in utter ignorance, and all they had been taught well was their catechism." The level of literacy and political awareness appears to have increased around 1830. Many workers had joined conspiratorial societies during the 1820s and 1830s because there seemed to be no other way to deal with their plight and were active in the French Revolution of 1830 and the English reform agitation of 1830–1832.

There were armed revolts of the laboring population in Paris in 1832, 1834, and 1839; Lyon rose twice, in 1831 and 1834; and there were serious disturbances in Lille, Toulouse, Clermont, and Saint Étienne. In almost all cases a confused mixture of political and economic motives were involved. Some of the revolts were largely worker inspired, but there were also insurrections such as that in Paris in 1839 in which radical students led by August Blanqui were the prime instigators. The Jacobin tradition of revolution was very much alive in secret societies such as Blanqui's *Friends of the People, Society of Families,* and *Society of Seasons,* but it was not until the late 1830s and early 1840s that workers took an interest in public as opposed to conspiratorial organization, a change that coincided with the birth of class consciousness in places like Paris, Berlin, Lyon, Birmingham.

An important sign of the dawning of this new awareness was the tendency of the natural leaders of the working class, the skilled artisans, to abandon their craft snobbery. Younger artisans tended to take the lead in this for they had less to lose. French journeymen's associations opened their ranks to those engaged in other trades and the banner of the British Boilermakers Union carried the slogan "Nothing human is alien." During the 1840s German workers poured into Paris and there joined ranks with workers of other nations in a series of colorful, if short-lived, democratic movements. In England fraternization went so far as to create for a few months in 1834 the Grand National Consolidated Trades Union of all the crafts. For years thereafter, English workers still talked of the possibility of the entire work force putting down their tools for a Sacred Month, the original model for the general strike, and in 1836 English radicals and workers came together to discuss a petition campaign for reform of Parliament that would include universal male suffrage. Out of this came the Chartist movement in 1838, the single most impressive political organization of its time and largely, though not entirely, the work of the laboring class.

The experience of industrialization had cut workers off from their earlier allies among middle-class radicals. But by their well-disciplined marches and agitation, workers proved they were capable of producing by themselves a highly organized, forward-looking movement. Mill was right when he said that "the poor will not much longer accept morals and religion of another people's making." During the 1840s Chartists staged "sit-ins" at parish churches, demanding the end of tithes and singing hymns of their own creation. Of Manchester W. Cooke Taylor said that workers "have very speedily laid aside their old habits and associations, to assume those of the mass in which they are mingled. The manufacturing population is not new in its formation alone; it is new in its habits of thoughts and actions. . . . "

The consciousness of large segments of the urban poor was evolving from that of passive acceptance to dynamic pursuit of collective improvement. Workers' movements in France, England, and Germany during the 1840s were the first to emancipate themselves fully from the myth of the golden age of the past. Much more than the *sans-culottes,* who were politically radical but socially and economically conservative, they were able to transcend earlier concerns with revitalization and come to grips with the realities of the new industrial age. As a popular song of the 1840s, "The State of Great Britain," suggests, they were determined to master the industrial tide:

> Now some can live in luxury while others weep in toil;
> There's very pretty difference now and a century ago.
> The world will shortly move by steam, it may appear so strange.
> So you must all acknowledge that England wants a change.

Here was a significant departure from the *sans-culotte* ideal of a society of propertied *menu peuple,* a concept that tended to become a part of the conservative ideology once it had been discarded by the radical left in the 1840s; here, too, was a rejection of the individualistic competitive ethos of bourgeois capitalism. The new working class accepted its status as wage earners without property and justified its alternative version of industrialization on the basis of its labor power alone. Ultimately this consciousness would transform itself into a strong socialist movement, though that process was only beginning at midcentury (see Chapter 11). The new working class had thrown off paternalism and had heeded the call for an expanded notion of fraternity that would join all working people, regardless of trade, regardless even of sex, into one movement. Flora Tristan was telling French workingmen that "in 1791 your fathers proclaimed the immortal Declaration of the Rights of Man. . . . In turn, free the last slaves remaining in France; proclaim the Rights of Women." During the 1840s French feminist and workers' causes merged, while in England working women joined working men in supporting Chartism.

During this period sex distinctions meant less to working people than they did to the middle class. The bourgeoisie continued to worship patriarchy privately in their cult of domesticity, and among them the symbols of paternal authority were further expanded into an almost religious attachment to "fatherland." But among the most advanced segments of the working class neither form of patriarchalism had much appeal. The working-class movements of the mid-nineteenth century developed the symbols of fraternity to the point that they transcended even national boundaries. Later, the European working classes would also come to accept the nation-state, but not until it offered them some measure of democracy, beginning in the 1860s and 1870s. As long as the propertied classes, who rejected the notion of universal suffrage, dominated the nation-state, the "two nations" of which Disraeli spoke would be locked in a conflict that transcended immediate material interests to involve questions about the ultimate future of European society. However, in time the harsh inequalities of the 1830s and 1840s would soften, and class antagonism would become less intense; nevertheless, the class lines etched in this, the formative period of European society, were too deep ever to be entirely erased.

PART FOUR

CULTURAL TRANSITION

For much of the period 1770–1850, the direction of cultural change remained uncertain. The French Revolution triggered a radical rethinking of the meaning of culture, a process that continued for the next sixty years. This was an epoch of unprecedented creativity in the arts, science, music, and literature, and has been a source of inspiration to Europeans and non-Europeans ever since. However, its importance lies as much in the institutions it created. The epoch began in the 1790s with the attempt to create a broad new definition of culture appropriate to the democratic age. Frustrated in this effort, intellectuals experimented with a series of other cultural forms before adopting eventually the highly specialized and stratified concept of culture that exists in Europe today. Chapter 10 traces the first radical stages of this process (leaving the discussion of the conservative effects of professionalization to Chapter 12). Chapter 11 assesses the origins of modern liberal, conservative, and socialist ideologies by placing these in the context of a society grappling with the dilemmas of epochal transition, a period in which intellectuals took up the role of prophets of the new age.

on the throne if he would agree to recognize the Rhine as the natural frontier of France. The emperor would have none of this, however, and by his resistance almost managed to split the coalition. Only the work of the English minister Castlereagh kept the allies together long enough to sign a Quadruple Alliance in March 1814, in which they pledged to support one another until a final settlement could be arrived at. With unity restored, the allied armies marched on Paris; in April Napoleon was forced to abdicate, leaving the way open for the only solution Russia, Austria, Prussia, and England could agree on, namely, the restoration of the Bourbon pretender, Louis XVIII.

The decision to restore the pretender was arrived at, not out of royalist fanaticism, but in the knowledge that this was the regime least likely to factionalize a France exhausted after more than twenty years of almost continuous warfare. Alexander demanded that the restoration have a constitutional basis and Louis XVIII agreed. The so-called Charter of 1814 recognized the legal and administrative transformation brought about by the revolutionary and imperial regimes, adopted the Napoleonic Code in its entirety, recognized the Concordat of 1801, and accepted as final the transfers of property that had occurred during the previous twenty-five years.

Though the king was to have the trappings of absolute power, there was to be a legislature elected by a limited number of propertied citizens. This was certainly not a democratic constitution, but then political equality had been a dead letter since at least 1799. To many of the French the restoration appeared considerably more liberal than the Napoleonic regime and, for a population seeking stability and peace, this was sufficient to produce acceptance, if not actual enthusiasm. If it was a restoration, it was a restoration of the monarchy of 1791, not of 1789. The peacemakers had no wish to set off new upheavals by turning back the clock. Indeed, there could be no reversal of the social and political development that, even if it had been tenuous in 1804, had been strongly institutionalized through years of war. The social mobilization that war required had confirmed a modern consciousness of citizenship. There could be no reversion to a decentralized system of Estates once this new identity had been baptized by years of sacrifice and struggle.

Peacemaking, 1814-1815

The political leaders of Europe were wise to see that almost twenty years of war fought on new principles required a peace that was equally revolutionary. Peacemaking began in Vienna in September 1814. Prince Metternich wished the conference to be a social as well as diplomatic success and for several months the Austrian capital did its best to revive the sociability of the Old Regime in an endless round of balls and entertainments. If, however, the princes and bishops deposed by twenty-five years

10

Europe's Cultural Revolution

In every period of rapid social change the problem of culture emerges. At no time does it become more critical, however, than in the first stages of modernization. As in the Chinese Cultural Revolution of the late 1960s, the purpose as well as the organization of culture is called into question. If the traditional forms have been religious in character, then secularization immediately becomes an issue. And where the old priesthood has been replaced, there is inevitably a debate between those who believe culture should continue to serve moral purposes and those who would subordinate it to the utilitarian objectives of economic or political development. This debate often centers on the question of elite versus mass culture. Should it be a general culture, accessible to all, or a specialized system of knowledge in which various professional groups monopolize the responsibility of creating, communicating, and preserving ideas?

Debates over purposes soon become conflicts over the means of implementation. There arises the question of organization of culture, for while every traditional society has its educational institutions (often centering around the family and household), the introduction of formal learning is bound to cause disruption. Then, too, there is the question of how the media of communication, the press and, more recently, radio and television, will be organized. Here the balance between oral and written culture is at issue. Societies in transition are inevitably faced also with the question of how the cultural activities associated with leisure will be transformed. And last but not least, there is the question of the role of the intellectual in society. Should it be as leader or servant of the people? Should it be that of generalist or expert? The answers to all these questions will be determined to some degree by the way other political and social decisions are made, for cultural revolution is an integral part of a much broader spectrum of changes. In turn, decisions made about the purpose and organization of culture will have profound effects on all other areas of life.

Today's new states often begin with a model of culture provided them by some more modernized society. Europe had no such prior experience to work from and, therefore, confrontation with the problem of modernizing culture was experimental and—in the period 1770–1870—highly creative. The debate over the nature of culture had begun long before the eighteenth century, however, with the Renaissance struggle between the defenders of classical learning and the advocates of vernacular literature. But this remained a debate within a tiny elite group and hardly involved the mass of the people, who remained illiterate. The Reformation of the sixteenth century raised the question of mass literacy for the first time. Simultaneously, the invention of printing caused people to debate the value of a written versus an oral culture; yet, it cannot be said that any consensus had been reached by 1770. The intense cultural conflicts that accompanied the English Civil War of the seventeenth century did much to challenge traditional conceptions, but the violent repression of the Puritan vision of a community of literate believers retarded debate for almost a hundred years.

The questions of what literacy was for, how it should be organized, and what the role of the intellectual should be were revived only in the last half of the eighteenth century. Thus began a long debate that was not settled until a century later, when culture, like economics and politics, began to acquire a permanent set of new institutions. Until that time culture was in constant crisis, with the future shape of the school, the press (newspapers, magazines, and printed books), libraries, galleries, and museums remaining quite uncertain. The organization of the arts was equally open to question, and the role of the creative intellect remained socially and politically as well as culturally unsettled for most of the same period. Only after 1848 did the modern pattern of schooling and professionalization take firm hold, and only then was it possible to institutionalize the role of the intellectual within—or, as in the case of Bohemians, outside—society. Significantly, both the cultures and countercultures that we call modern emerged simultaneously with breakthroughs in the areas of economic and political development.

The Debate over Literacy

To understand the period of turmoil from 1770 to 1850, as well as the cultural institutions that came out of it, we must start with the most fundamental of the changes involved, namely, literacy. It has been estimated that the rate of functional literacy (meaning the ability to read and to write at least one's signature) was about 30 percent for English males and somewhat less for English females in 1650. The literacy of the French and German populations was probably somewhat lower than that of the English. Generally, literacy was lower in the countryside than in the towns, though there were exceptions in places where the aristocracy or the clergy, the chief sponsors of formal education prior to 1789, had invested unusually large amounts in schools. Available figures show that literacy had made remarkable strides in the early seventeenth century, but that the pace fell off during the early eighteenth. In England really rapid advance in literacy was not resumed until the middle of the nineteenth century, whereas in France the rise from about 50 percent to almost 100 percent literacy began as early as 1789.

Despite the general upward trend, it is clear that there were long periods when the progress of mass literacy was in doubt. One of these periods was the earlier part of the eighteenth century. Popular revolts in the previous century had made the elites think twice about offering literacy to the people. The effect of subsequent upheavals, particularly that in 1789, was the repression not only of popular learning but also of all forms of popular culture. "Ignorance is the Mother of Devotion and Obedience," it was said, and an Englishman named Soame Jenyns remarked in 1757 that ignorance was surely "the appointed lot of all born to poverty and the drudgeries of life... the only opiate capable of infusing that sensibility, which can enable them to endure the miseries of the one and the fatigues of the other...."

The leaders of the French Enlightenment were also guided by the impression that prosperity depended on keeping the poor ignorant. One of the *philosophes* wrote that nothing could be more destructive to France than "giving an education to the children of the lower classes of her people that will make them condemn those drudgeries for which they were born." During the French Revolution the English upper classes panicked at the though of the poor reading Thomas Paine, and one bishop condemned even Sunday schools as being "schools of Jacobinical rebellion." When the ardent conservative Hannah More went about the task of instilling in children patriotic principles in the 1790s, she made sure that when they learned to read they did not learn to write. Even so, her schools were attacked by local landowners, who raved that "of all the foolish inventions and new fangled devices to ruin this country, that of teaching the poor to read is the very worst."

This was not just an attack on learning as such, but also on the culture of the poor in general. Landowners were just as active in repressing the laborers' traditional means of communication and recreation: games, fairs, and festivals. "The labouring people should never think themselves independent of their superiors; for, if a proper subordination is not kept, riot and confusion will take (the) place of sobriety and order." The easiest way to control the culture of the poor was to eliminate those places where they congregated. Landlords closed common lands that had once been

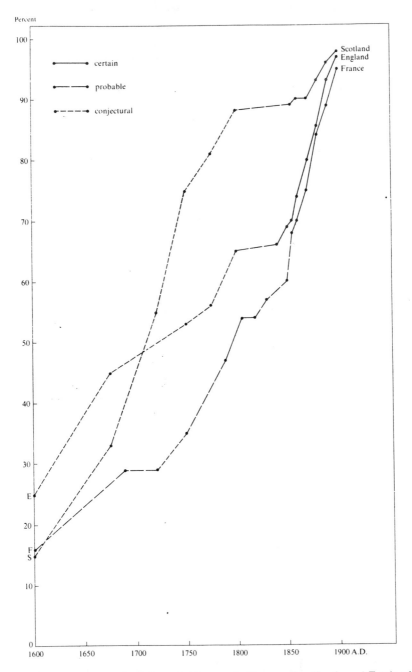

Chart 3   Estimated adult male literacy in France, Scotland, and England
with Wales, 1600–1900.

playing fields, and in the towns no attempt was made to create places of recreation. By 1833 Sir John Herschel could say of England that "the pleasant field-walk and village-green are becoming rarer and rarer every year. Music and dancing . . . have become so closely associated with ideas of riot and debauchery, among the less cultivated classes, that a taste for them for their own sakes can hardly be said to exist. . . ." In France the same purpose was served by converting traditional holy days into a new work calendar that allowed far less time for fairs and other diversions. In Berlin the authorities did their best to repress those ancient carnival rites like the Fishermen's Parade that had become associated in the official mind with insurrection.

However, radical intellectuals and their allies among the *sans-culottes* joined the struggle from the 1790s onward. They called for a new set of popular cultural institutions, for if knowledge were power, then it must be made available to very citizen. Culture, said Rousseau and his follower Jacques Louis David, must serve "not the utility of a particular caste, but the general utility of the nation, of the masses." David proposed to create a truly popular culture of revolutionary processions and rituals. The *sans-culottes* shared his fierce hatred of lawyers and other experts who, they felt, hoarded culture in the same way immoral merchants hoarded grain. They spoke harshly of "metaphysical education" and wished to keep things simple, personal, and practical.

Following the educational theories of Rousseau and the Swiss reformer Pestalozzi, the *sans-culottes* conceived of education as a process of "inspiration," bringing out the best in a person's social/moral character rather than implanting abstract knowledge. Education should be free and equal (at least for males), a source of spiritual community to replace that of traditional religion. Essentially the *sans-culotte* culture was a secularized version of the earlier idea of a community of literate believers. "We will never have good generals, good magistrates until a sound education has transformed men," declared Jacques-René Hébert.

This radical notion inspired experiments in every country in Europe. The Germans were particularly attracted by the concept of cultural revolution, especially in the absence of political revolution in their country. Their leading educational reformers, including Fries and Fichte, were of Pietist background and believed in the internal reformation of the human being. In *Addresses to the German Nation* in 1807, Fichte spoke of a German revolution being first and foremost a revolution of consciousness, a notion that Hegel was later to elaborate and one that attracted all German radicals, including Marx, through the 1840s.

In England the circle around William Blake had similar visions of an altered state of human consciousness. Blake located authority within the individual and rejected all other laws, natural or divine, that might inhibit this vital power. He even went so far as to reject abstract science, for Newton's mechanical laws of the universe reminded him too much both of tyranny of the state and that of the factory. Because the technological demands of the Industrial Revolution had not yet fully imposed themselves, questions of the superiority of specialized knowledge did not trouble either Blake or the Germans. Indeed, until the 1830s the intellectuals' vision of progress tended to place greater emphasis on the spiritual rather than on the material improvement of humankind.

But the cultural radicalism of the 1790s came to naught in France after the defeat of the *sans-culotte* movement. Under Napoleon, education was shaped to serve the goals of the state rather than those of the community, and the reorganization of the school system established a hierarchy of institutions based on division of intellectual labor. By 1815 France had the world's most advanced scientific establishment, together with a secondary and university system (built around the famed *École Polytechnique*) that was the envy of the world. But the primary education system remained backward, with mass literacy distrusted by the Church and conservatives generally.

The Struggle for Freedom of the Press

Political repression was not the only reason for the dimming of the bright dawn of democratic education. Population explosion outdistanced the ability of both formal and informal education to cope with the swollen child population. The patriarchal household was breaking up at the end of the eighteenth century, and its educational functions were not immediately replaced; much of the transmission of practical and general knowledge had taken place outside the school in preindustrial Europe, but with the disruption of the apprenticeship system the supply of schools was much too small to meet demand. Artisan masters viewed youngsters as cheap labor, not as pupils. Factory managers made no pretense of education and the workday in the mills was so long (up to twelve hours) and so exhausting that children had no time for learning. Even after the factory legislation of the 1830s made schooling of child labor mandatory, there were rarely enough facilities to meet demand. The new cities had grown so fast that one-third of the children in English factory towns were without school places. In Prussia things were better, but even there the first stages of urbanization may have produced a drop in literacy among the very poor. Whereas the town had previously had higher literacy than the countryside, now it often lagged behind.

The slow, sometimes faltering progress of literacy among the poor did not necessarily mean a rupture of working people's cultural traditions, however. While they may not have been able to read and write, they were not culturally deprived in a Europe where the written word had long been less important than the oral. Learning was transmitted by telling and listening, two skills that were highly developed. In the eighteenth century, newspapers had been heard more often than read. As an editor named Charles Leslie observed, "The greatest part of the people do not read books; most of them cannot read at all, but they will gather about one that can read, and listen to an *Observator* or *Review* [names of newspapers]." Although factory owners specifically forbade reading on the job, the old tradition of one worker reading aloud while the others labored survived in many trades until the end of the nineteenth century.

This tradition of collective learning was further reinforced by the very high price of books and newspapers. In the eighteenth century an edition of *Tom Jones* cost as much as a month's supply of tea and sugar for a family of six. The price of an English newspaper rose from one pence in 1700 to six pence in 1806 as a result of stamp and paper taxes designed to destroy the cheap radical press. But instead of inhibiting reading, the stamp taxes merely made it a collective enterprise. It is estimated that each copy of a newspaper passed through at least thirty hands. Working people clubbing together for subscriptions and collective reading formed the very basis of the new working-class culture in places like Lyon, Berlin, and Birmingham.

Reading, singing, dancing, and political and economic discourse all blended together; culture remained for the working class something more than abstract book learning. The kind of disciplined and specialized studies that the middle classes offered working people through evening schools like the London Mechanics Institute, founded in 1824, did not sit well with them. "You must remember," said one worker, "we have machines all day long, and we don't want 'em at night." William Lovett put it another way when he rejected the notion that learning must be distinguished from life and work. Education should be "the equal and judicious development of all . . . faculties, and not the mere cultivation of the intellect." Culture was inseparable from the daily cares of life, and it was therefore natural that working people should define it not as something for individual advantage, but for the benefit of all. Like the *sans-culottes* before them, the new working class of the 1840s defined "culture" as that which makes people "wiser, better, and happier members *of the community*" [italics added].

Working people viewed literacy and the printing press as a heaven-sent weapon of social progress. During the 1820s, when the struggle for freedom of the press was at its height in both France and England, radical reformer Richard Carlile wrote:

> The art of Printing is a multiplication of the Mind, and since the art is discovered, the next important thing is to make it applicable to the means of acquirement possessed by the humblest individual among mankind . . . a compression of sound moral truths within pamphlets, as the smallest and cheapest forms of giving effect to this multiplication of mind, is the most conducive to the general good, and to the future welfare of mankind.

Thus, learning must not be allowed to establish distinctions among people, but must bind them together.

The Distribution of Schooling

This association of learning with progress was akin to that which the middle classes had come to cherish, though the bourgeois definition of culture diverged significantly from that of the working class. Unlike the old aristocracy, the middle class could not view mass education as an absolute evil. The professional middle class had risen by virtue of education and thus was committed to it not only as a ladder of mobility, but also as a means of building a new industrial order. The right kind of education could just as well instill obedience as subvert it, as long as it was accompanied by the proper discipline. Thus, factory owners became the moving force behind the creation of schools for the poor, either through state aid or charity. In these schools children were taught to sit straight in their places, to obey the rules of silence, and to work by the bell—all proper habits for future industrial workers. All other pursuits apart from dry, rote learning were eliminated.

Games were associated with idleness and were therefore not acceptable; "recreation" consisted of wood chopping and making rope. Visitors were struck by the order and quiet of the schools, for above all else it was the old oral culture that was to be exorcised. Blake was appalled by what he called the "silency" of the classroom, and Wordsworth refused to become headmaster of a school planned by Josiah Wedgwood's son when he learned of its mechanical means of discipline. Neither could accept the notion of the mind as a passive receptacle to be crammed with that "useful" knowledge that factory owners like Dickens's fictional Mr. Gradgrind found so attractive. "Teach these boys and girls nothing but Facts," Gradgrind tells the teacher, Mr. Choakumchild in *Hard Times*. "Facts alone are wanted in life. Plant nothing else, and root out everything else."

Despite persistent fears of popular upheaval, the industrial middle classes had developed a commitment to mass education and freedom of the press. Henry Brougham was one of the first to grasp the possibility of the steam-driven rotary press and began the Society for the Diffusion of Useful Knowledge in 1829 for the purpose of using it to uplift the general population. The *Edinburgh Review* wrote in 1839 that "we must build more schools or more prisons," though Dickens was quick to point out that many of the new schools were too much like prisons. The poor learned to refer to them as "bastilles" and one frustrated schoolmaster reported that next to the desire to have their children's wages, the things that most turned parents against the school was "the dislike of having their children anyways in subjection to the children of other people and to any kind of punishment."

Despite conservative objections. France in 1835 had followed Prussia's example in providing state funding for primary education. The Jacobin projects of universal education were revived under the bourgeois monarchy of Louis Philippe, although free education had to wait until the 1880s.

The English took similar faltering steps that would ultimately lead them to the Compulsory Education Act of 1870. Yet the system of education the middle-class liberals had in mind was very different from the free and equal education that the *sans-culottes* had talked about forty years earlier. François Guizot wrote in 1835 that "far from education being a means of social change, it should rather reflect social distinctions and should accept to be limited by the divisions of society." As soon as the French bourgeoisie achieved political power in the 1830s, they dropped the old Jacobin notion of equal education and endorsed a three-tiered system of primary schools, secondary schools, and universities. The first would take care of the needs of working children up to the age of ten or eleven. Higher levels of education, all of which remained very expensive, were thereby reserved for the middle and upper classes.

Thus, while literacy was no longer at issue and rose rapidly from the 1840s onward (in England the rate was 67.3 percent for males in 1841, 75.4 percent in 1861, 86.4 percent in 1881, 97.2 percent in 1900), the educational system that had developed clearly reflected the emerging class structures and the purposes of industrial capitalism. Culture was not to be an inherent right, but a *thing* to be acquired at a price. Furthermore, it was to be subject to the same division of labor as any other commodity; produced by specialists, it was subject to economic forces like any other mass-produced product. The creation of the modern press and book trade coincided precisely with the victory of the industrial middle classes in the 1830s, and publishing underwent the same process of industrialization as all the other trades.

The first steam press had appeared in England in 1814, but its full potential was not exploited until almost two decades later when the freedom of the press (and the profits of publishing) were assured. The first modern newspaper, *La Presse,* appeared in France in 1833, guided by the remarkable entrepreneur Emile de Girardin, who was the first to finance the press through the sale of advertisements. Once the press has been put on a firm capitalist industrial basis, its production outstripped anything that had gone before. "Until printing was very generally spread," noted Charles Babbage, mathematician and mechanical wizard, "civilization scarcely advanced by slow and languid steps; since the art has become cheap, its advances have become unparalleled, and its rate of progress vastly accelerated."

In July 1830 the owners of large Parisian print shops had ordered their employees into the streets to join the crowds calling for the overthrow of Charles X. Once the revolution was won, they dispensed with the pretense of democracy and began an industrialization of the press that put many artisan printers out of work. As in other forms of production, the modernization of publishing proceeded at the expense of the skilled craft. The price of books was reduced by as much as half in the period 1830–1850, driving the less efficient presses out of the market. A flood of books and magazines poured forth, revolutionizing retailing as well as production. Although the price of Dickens and Balzac was still far too high for the ordinary person, there were now "penny dreadfuls" with titles like *Varney the Vampire, or the Feast of Blood* and *Fatherless Fanny, or the Mysterious Orphans* on sale in the new railway stations. Along with cheap imitations of prominent novels (*Oliver Twiss* was one example), the reader could find a vast array of new pornographic works with enticing titles such as *Star of Venus* and *Peeping Tom*.

The *sans-culotte* dream of a democratic culture was aborted. Commercialization moved far more swiftly than the radicals had anticipated and their effort to harness the printing press to moral or social progress was quickly disappointed. Democrats had hoped to give the steam press a social purpose, but instead it made itself the commercial arbiter of cultural values. "Not the external and physical alone is now managed by machinery, but the internal and spiritual," declared Thomas Carlyle, who had come to despair of cultural apocalypse. By the 1840s it was clear that the so-called March of Intellect could no longer be equated with the improvement of the common people. The press ceased to bind society together and instead served to widen class divisions. Karl Marx, who began his political career in the early 1840s writing articles for the liberal *Rhine Gazette,* found when he returned to Germany in 1848 to resume his political journalism, that the bourgeois owners of the paper would no longer tolerate socialist views opposed to their own liberalism. He was forced to set up his own newspaper because the press as a commercial enterprise could not tolerate attacks on the capitalist system of which it was an important part. Once this division had begun, intellectuals had to choose between commercial success and the shoestring existence of radical journalism.

The Changing Role of Intellectuals

The changing definition of culture was bound to affect the role of secular intellectuals. At a time when culture was at the center of the struggles over societal regeneration, they were inevitably drawn into politics; nor was there anything new about this involvement. Although the clergy had played a central role in traditional Europe, the state bureaucracy had undermined its position by 1789. In most European states (with the exception of England) the clergy had been edged out of its monopoly on education in the period just before 1789. In Austria the reforming Emperor Joseph II actively pursued a policy of secularization, and when the Jesuits were expelled from France in 1764 it was a sign that the role of religion would henceforth be confined more and more to the private sphere. However, the question of the decline of the influence of the clergy among the general population is more complicated. There is little doubt that the higher echelons of the churches had become increasingly alienated from the faithful in the eighteenth century, but a distinction must be made between popular anticlericalsim and secularization as such.

As institutionalized religious observance declined, new highly personalized faiths arose to take its place. Pietism in Germany and Methodism in England are two prime examples. These established deep roots among the emerging industrial middle classes, also attracting artisans and peasants. Forms of religious revivalism continued well into the nineteenth century, even during the time when the established churches were losing members. The English Wesleyan membership increased ten times in the period 1790–1850, indicating the degree to which sectarian forms of religion grew in almost inverse proportion to the decline of the established churches. In Catholic countries where sectariansim was repressed, the desire for spiritual fellowship was more likely to take a much more secular antiChristian form. form.

Long before the eighteenth century, culture had ceased to be identified solely with institutionalized religion. Now, however, it was even ceasing to be identified with social privilege, its ancient patron and main economic support during the Enlightenment. At the beginning of the eighteenth century the monarchy and aristocracy were still the prime support of artistic production. This included not only painting, music, and sculpture, but also those crafts of book printing, furniture making, and public building that together with what we today would call the "fine arts," were still grouped together under the category of artisan trades. The term "masterpiece" came directly from the craft tradition and it was still common to class the musician and painter with the printer or mason. The term "artist" had not yet emerged, except perhaps in painting, and "art" still meant skill.

For most of the eighteenth century artists occupied the same general social status as craftsmen, though there were exceptions to this rule. Sometimes the roles were interchangeable as in the case of Samuel Richardson or Benjamin Franklin, both of whom were printers at the same time they were writers. The modern distinction between the creative artist and the skilled artisan had not yet emerged, for both groups viewed the function of their craft to be that of faithful reproduction of truth or beauty. Even those men and women we would describe as most original still preferred to see themselves as mirrors of the beautiful and the good, not as the orginial source of creation. Art was, like all other human endeavor, still inferior to divine creation and the artist was therefore subject to rules at least as strict as those of the craft guilds.

French artists and men of letters continued to be organized in the traditional manner of the crafts until 1789, and even then the concept of an artists' or writers' guild lingered on well into the nineteenth century, when it had one of its last revivals under the National Workshop plan of 1848. Most artists and writers still felt comfortable with the old notion of production for a selected market at high prices. They remained skeptical of a mass market, which they regarded as lowering the quality and honor of their trade. Voltaire argued that "taste is like philosophy. It belongs to a very small number of privileged souls. It is unknown in bourgeois families, where one is constantly occupied with one's fortune."

Before 1830 the bourgeoisie were indeed more interested in investing in business than in art, but there were sufficient signs of a growing market for Wedgwood to expand his production of vases by industrial methods and for book publishers to hire more writers to turn out novels for a fixed fee per page. In England this labor-intensive expansion of culture was under way in the early eighteenth century, causing considerable distress among those like Defoe who saw it as a threat to the standing of the writer as independent craftsman:

> Writing . . . is becoming a very considerable Branch of the English Commerce. The Booksellers are the Master Manufacturers or Employers. The several Writers, Authors, Copyers, Sub-writers, and other Operators with Pen and Ink are the workmen employed by the said Master Manufacturers.

Alexander Pope, a defender of aristocratic patronage, denounced the hack writers who lodged in Grub Street, London, a place that lent its name to commercial journalism from the 1720s onward.

Fielding also condemned Grub Street as "a democracy, or rather a downright anarchy." Those who made their living turning out political pamphlets or semipornographic tracts were very marginal people, despised by those who hired them and unwelcome in the resepctable world of the salons. Attempts by the state to suppress "low literature" often had the backing of established intellectuals like Voltaire who had forgotten their own humble origins in the scramble for patronage and respectability. Thus the hacks in France were kept alive mainly by the clandestine presses operating in places like Switzerland. Smugglers managed to evade both the censor and the customs inspector to bring their cheap books to villages of France, while writers like the future revolutionary Marat lived hand-to-mouth, always just one step ahead of their persecutors. Marat's police record read:

> Marat: bold charlatan. M. d'Azir asks, in the name of the Society of Medicine, that he be run out of Paris. Many sick persons have died in his hands, but he has a medical degree, which was bought by him.

In Germany the abundance of Grub Street hacks at the end of the eighteenth century was a product of population growth. Young writers identified with the fate of Goethe's tragic hero, Werther, and Schiller's play *The Robbers*, written in 1781, had the effect of associating the misunderstood intellectual with the image of the outlaw. This generation was now ready for the new concept of culture that Rousseau had introduced in 1750 in the *Discourse on the Sciences and Arts*, a shattering attack on culture's previous association with luxury and privilege. Wrote

Rousseau: "The beautiful is that which pleases the most people," and the judge of beauty and goodness should not be a limited patron class but the hearts of common people. On the other hand, the notion of an aesthetic "general will" was bound to displease the older generation of entrenched *philosophes*. Of the major figures of the French Enlightenment, only Diderot was willing to place the intellect at the service of society.

Generational tensions among intellectuals were apparent on the eve of the French Revolution. Wrote the reformer Pierre Gerbier in June 1789: "Where does so much agitation come from? From a crowd of minor clerks and lawyers, from unknown writers, starving scribblers, who go about rabble-rousing in clubs and cafes. These are the hot heads that have forged the weapons with which the masses are armed today." In reality the young intellectuals were as little prepared for revolution as were the general population, yet they responded with the same enthusiasm. As we have seen, art for revolution's sake could be a lucrative business for the unemployed craftsman, but for those like David and Marat, culture had a much nobler mission to perform in arousing genuine feelings of liberty, equality, and above all, fraternity.

According to David, intellect would serve the entire community. He was an enemy of monopoly and saw to it that its symbol, the Royal Academy, was destroyed in 1793, to be replaced by voluntary associations of artists who could demonstrate in their life and work the fraternal ideal. It was this shared sense of purpose that inspired the young English poet William Wordsworth to write of 1789: "Bliss it was to be alive; But to be young was very Heaven." Because spiritual revitalization was at the heart of the Jacobin-*sans-culotte* notion of revolution, it was natural that the intellectuals should be attracted to it. Blake's vision of social apocalypse involved casting off intellectual as well as political chains, while Southey proclaimed that "Earth shall once again be Paradise, whilst wisdom shall secure the state of bliss which ignorance betrayed," a direct reference to battle for popular culture that was being fought not just in France, but in Germany and England as well.

There was a strong temptation for intellectuals to take on the role of the old priesthood, especially in the cultural vacuum that the collapse of Church institutions left. But while Blake called himself a "priest of an unapprehended inspiration," he and his fellow radicals did not mean by this that they possessed superior creative ability. On the contrary, they adapted the notion of the priesthood of all believers to the revolutionary setting, believing the creative impulse would flow from below rather than above. An artist like Blake was still close enough to the status of artisan to identify with the *sans-culotte* desire for a simple fraternal culture in which there would be no hierarchy of specialized knowledge. Poetry and art should become a part of people's lives because they were inherent in human nature itself. Wordsworth wrote at this time (in 1800) that "the Poet is distinguished from other men by the greater promptness to think and feel with immediate external excitement. . . . But these passions and thoughts and feelings are the general passions, thoughts and feelings of men." Culture was therefore conceived of as a fraternal process by which the good and the beautiful in all humanity were to be brought out and nurtured.

The vision of a democratic culture disappeared rapidly after 1794, however. Born on the wave of apocalyptic expectations, it evaporated when the promise of new beginnings failed. In France itself the utilitarian notion of art was swiftly diverted into the propagandistic efforts of the Napoleonic Empire. David himself became one of its glorifiers, and other intellectuals quickly learned to despise democracy once they had been installed in the bureaucratic hierarchy of the French academic system. Among the foreign friends of revolution, most also became disillusioned. Wordsworth, Coleridge, and Southey became staunch Tories, while in Germany, Fichte and Hegel abandoned politics in favor of a more individualistic kind of emancipation. In many places intellectuals reinterpreted revolution as personal/internal rather than political/external change. Although they did not cease to think of themselves as progressive, German intellectuals talked of a revolution of consciousness as opposed to a revolution of society. As one of them put it: "Germany, of all the European countries, is the most inclined to revolutions of the spirit, least inclined to political revolutions." A parody of Wordsworth's turnabout, contained in W. H. Auden's *New Year Letter,* written in 1940, tells the story of many of the former friends of revolution:

Thus Wordsworth fell into temptation
In France during a long vacation
Saw in the fall of the Bastille
The Parousia of liberty
A liberal fellow traveller ran
With Sans-culotte and Jacobin,
Nor guessed what circles he was in
But ended as the Devil knows
An earnest Englishman would do,
Left by Napoleon in the lurch
Supporting the Established Church.

Romantics of the 1820s and 1830s

When Shelley wrote the *Defence of Poetry* in 1821 he contended that the poet "ought personally to be the happiest, best, and wisest and most illustrious of men," even though he could no longer hold out similar prospects to the rest of humanity. Like many an old Jacobin, Shelley did not think political revolution any longer possible or, for that matter, advisable. However, while many intellectuals became conservative in their political and social views they did not give up their faith in spiritual apocalypse. In the wake of the 1790s they tended to focus their enormous energies on a more narrowly defined cultural revolution that came to be called romanticism and that Victor Hugo defined as "liberalism in literature."

Certainly creative freedom became much more important than either equality or fraternity to the romantics. They placed genius on a plane above ordinary mortals and saw themselves as standing outside the social order as prophets or victims or both. Keats wrote, "I have not the slightest feeling of humility toward the Public." By 1820 the term "artist" was self-consciously separated from the lowly status of artisan. For the generation that grew up after 1789, nothing could be more degrading than to suggest that their work was a skill rather than personal inspiration. The test of greatness now lay in the originality and willingness of the artist to transcend all those things that bind down the ordinary human being, to break all rules, and, in short, to be original.

The romanticism of the post–1815 period reflects the gradual separation of the artist and writer from the traditional crafts through the growth of a free-market economy of art and publishing. In this period of transition, it was still sometimes possible, however, for intellectuals to identify their cause with that of the general population, despite the growing social distance. Romantics could still respond to the call of revolution as long as revolution stood for liberty and did not place real limits on their individuality. Byron, romantic poet and English Lord, died for the cause of Greek independence, and his example inspired Victor Hugo and his circle of young followers, which included Gérard de Nerval, Joesph Borel, Théophile Gautier, Delacroix, and Théodore Géricault, to struggle against restoration monarchy in the 1820s. They went out of their way to shock the social order with outlandish dress and eccentric behavior, declaring war on all previous social and artistic standards.

In 1830 Hugo announced that he would smash once and for all the classical canons of drama with the play *Hernani*. Its preface read like a political manifesto: "Tear down theory, poetic systems. . . . No more rules, no more models. . . . Genius conjures up rather than learns. . . . For talent to surrender would be for God to be a lackey." On the night of February 25, 1830, the theatre resembled a riot, with Hugo's clique, led by Gautier in a flaming red vest, hurling insults at the bourgeois gallery as if they were firing guns from a barricade. As it turned out, the performance of *Hernani* was indeed rehearsal for the July Revolution some months later, for many of those that had defied convention on the stage were on the barricades. In Brussels the connection between romanticism and revolution was even more clearly demonstrated when crowds attending Daniel Auber's opera, *The Revolt of the Portici*, streamed out of the theatre to declare Belgium's independence from Holland in August 1830.

Of all the works of the period, none illustrates so well the romantic notion of the relation of art and politics as does Delacroix's famous painting, *Liberty Leading the People*, completed in 1831 as a direct tribute to the Revolution of 1830. At its center is the wholly idealized female figure of

Liberty carrying the Tricolor and inspiring armed students and street people to valor on the barricades. It is the idea of liberty that moves the crowd, just as it was the idea of liberty that moved Delacroix to paint the picture, but as for concrete political organization or real social equality, neither he nor his fellow romantics had much interest or sympathy. The spirit of 1830 evaporated quickly, and after a brief showing Delacroix's painting was put away where it would not disturb the peace and prosperity of the bourgeois monarchy.

Most romantics also put away their thoughts of revolution after 1830. Many were absorbed in the industrial revolution of the publishing trades; some, like Balzac and Dumas, became immensely rich, though most others were confirmed in their role as hack journalists, aware of the growing distance between the writer and the audience. As Elias Regnault pointed out, cultural products "have their market price, like asphalt or Marseille soap. Spiritual rates shift in the same fashion as industrial rates." Faced with the full implications of industrial capitalism, intellectuals (particularly the less successful ones) could no longer pretend to occupy an ivory tower. Some began to refer to themselves as an "intellectual proletariat" and all were forced to define themselves in terms of the emerging class differences that were apparent from the 1830s onward.

Emergence of the Avant-Garde

To those who could not identify with the middle class, there was still the option of placing themselves on the side of progress by proclaiming themselves *avant-garde*. The notion had been invented by Henri de Saint-Simon, who just before his death in 1825 prophesied a new industrial Europe in which the artists, along with scientists and entrepreneurs, would bring forth a new age of social harmony. The artists were to guide the new industrial society to a moral order. In *Opinions littéraires, philosophiques et industrielles* that Saint-Simon wrote in 1825, there appears a fictional discussion between an artist and a scientist:

> It is we, artists, who will serve you as avant-garde; the power of the arts is in fact most immediate and most rapid: when we wish to spread new ideas among men, we inscribe them on marble or on canvas. . . . We address ourselves to the imagination and to the sentiments of mankind; we should therefore always exercise the liveliest and most decisive action; and if today our role appears nil or at least very secondary, what is lacking to the arts is that which is essential to their energy and to their success, namely, a common drive and a general idea.

Until the French Revolution, intellectuals still viewed themselves as standing apart from the historical process, stressing spiritual perfection but having little to do with the more mundane aspects of economic development.

The followers of Saint-Simon began to move toward a more active definition of themselves, however, taking the important step of attempting to reconcile spiritual with industrial progress. Saint-Simon talked of "a most beautiful destiny for the arts, that of exercising over society a positive power, a true priestly function, and of marching in the van of all intellectual faculties in the epoch of their greatest development!"

His follower Emile Barrault predicted that "henceforth the fine arts are the religion and the artist is the priest," making a cult of intellect that was particularly attractive to those who wished to put their talent to practical use but who were hostile to the direction that capitalist industrialization was taking. The composer Franz Liszt was inspired by the Saint-Simonian ideal to write his Revolution Symphony in 1830 and he in turn influenced George Sand, who already in the 1820s was developing what she called the "art for the people" movement, in which workers were encouraged not only to read but to write. Some of these proletarian poets were published and the revival of the craft traditions was similarly encouraged.

But perhaps the boldest application of the idea of the avant-garde came after 1830 when the Saint-Simonians set up their experiment in social harmony at Ménilmontant (see Chapter 11). There their leader, Barthélemy Enfantin, attempted to bring about the reintegration of art and life, making choral music a central feature of communal life. Architecture was equally important and plans were made to build a Temple of the Future that would put to use the latest industrial materials of iron and glass in a beautiful and socially useful way. Many of the Saint-Simonians were young graduates of the École Polytechnique, eager to apply engineering to social problems. Other early socialists, including Charles Fourier and Etienne Cabet, were equally concerned to place culture at the service of society. Fourier so valued the arts that he dictated that "a good ear for music, politeness, and an aptitude for the fine arts" be the requirements for entry into his utopian society.

Most of the socialist communities of the 1830s and 1840s were, in fact, applications of the concept of the avant-garde. Intellectuals took the lead in most of them, and while they showed less enthusiasm for cultural democracy than had been evident in the 1790s, it was clear that they did not want to give up their commitment to social progress. Even when the communal experiments failed, complete disillusionment was rare. Many of the Saint-Simonians, including Ferdinand de Lesseps, turned their interests to public projects. Lesseps became famous building the Suez Canal, while Enfantin became an important railway developer. Much of the social idealism of the 1830s was absorbed into the creation of a modern ethics of professional engineering and architecture.

The attempt to bring together cultural and social progress had reached its high point in the 1830s and 1840s, and even then the concept of the avant-garde was encountering considerable criticism from both left and right. After the failure of the Revolution of 1830 and again after 1848, many of the former avant-garde turned away from politics completely. Paris developed what was called *la vie Bohème,* a modern counterculture of young persons that bears striking resemblance to the Bohemianism of today in its fascination with drugs, the occult, and magic. Balzac described the Bohemians of the 1830s as "some rich, others poor, all equally idle . . . who, with no outlet for their energies, threw themselves not only into journalism and conspiracies, literature and art, but into the most extravagant excesses and dissipations." They were almost entirely middle class, mainly young, and most of them waiting to go on to other things. Victims of overcrowding in the professions, they had nothing to do but make of life a kind of art.

The real artists and writers among them, like Gautier, were so disaffected with political action after 1830 that they turned their attention entirely to art, preaching that it must be an end in itself, serving no purpose either commercial or social. This was the beginning of the art for art's sake movement, which created a vision of culture separate from the commercialized one offered by the industrial bourgeoisie, but also at variance with the emerging working-class notions. In 1848, when he was asked to paint a sequel to the great *Liberty Leading the People* to be entitled *Equality Leading the People,* Delacroix refused, saying, "I have buried the man of yore with his hopes and his dreams of the future." The most famous advocate of art for art's sake in the 1850s, Charles Baudelaire, had wielded a rifle in 1848 when he still believed that "art is inseparable from morality and utility," but in the wake of the 1851 Napoleonic coup he, too, withdrew from politics, becoming something like the dandy he described with the following lines:

A great man and a saint, for his own sake.
Lives and sleeps in front of a mirror
Is a man of leisure and general education
Is rich and loves work
Works in a disinterested manner
Does nothing useful
Is either a poet, a priest, or a soldier
Is solitary
Is unhappy
Never speaks to the masses except to insult them
Never touches a newspaper.

The last time educated persons would be conspicuous on the barricades was in 1848, and even then they approached revolution with a hesitancy that had been missing in earlier upheavals. One reason for this was the process of professionalization, which had upgraded their lives materially (see Chapter 12). Also involved was the industrialization of culture, which subdivided its various functions and made it difficult for the individual to connect his concerns with those of other intellectuals or with the larger problems of society in general. For a time during the early nineteenth century, it seemed as if intellectuals might identify themselves with other trades or perhaps constitute themselves as a separate social class.

After 1850 the threat of proletarization passed away and the status of most professionals rapidly became middle class. While they might not identify entirely with the industrial bourgeoisie, intellectuals nevertheless came to consider culture their special kind of property. When during the 1840s property in general was called into question, they, too, were forced to choose between the wage-earning proletariat and the middle class. While there were exceptions, just as there had been exceptions to the pattern of intellectual radicalism before 1848, most intellectuals took a conservative position at this juncture. Unlike their predecessors of the 1790s, they saw no reason culture should be either democratized or redistributed.

11

Intellectuals
and Ideologies

It is fashionable today to speak of the "end of ideology" in Western
Europe and America.* Politics in these places tends to revolve around
established parties that pursue their goals pragmatically, without apparent
reference to broad systems of ideas. Sectarian groups on both the left and
the right adopt a prophetic role, offering their programs as universal
solutions to the problems of humanity, but the population remains suspicious of their pronouncements. This situation stands in sharp contrast to
that in much of the rest of the world, where ideologies compete with one
another for hegemony, both between and within new states.

In contrast to the interest-group politics of Europe, parties in developing countries take on a resemblance to religious movements, offering moral
beliefs and even a whole way of life to their adherents. This is true not only
of those states that are the inheritors of the Marxist tradition, but also of
those that reject this in favor of, for example, a unique Arab or African
socialism. Even conservative regimes appear compelled to claim a special
mission in history, leading humanity to salvation through their particular
idea systems. Leaders such as Mao, Nkrumah, Nasser, Perón, and Sukarno
have all at one time or another adopted the role of prophet, pronouncing
the universal validity and historical predestination of their particular social
and political programs.

The prevalence of ideology appears to be related to the stage of social
and cultural transition, as well as to the necessity of rapid nation building.

---

*Ideology is defined here as a system of ideas that is critical and prescriptive
at the same time and that offers both an explanation of history and a program for
reaching a set of universalistic goals.

Peoples suddenly cut loose from traditional value systems find in ideology a way of regaining stability through a belief system that sustains them both socially and psychologically in a swirling world of change. Often ideological symbols and rituals are borrowed from religion, but unlike religion, ideology is temporally oriented, offering answers that refer to this world rather than the next. Most importantly, ideology offers an explanation of change itself, thus providing the believer with reasons for abandoning the past and making commitment to a new future; however eccentric or irrational an ideology may seem to an outsider, it is usually viewed as highly rational by those who adhere to it. It serves their need for moral and social support as they traverse the uneven path from the particularistic values of traditional society to the universal norms of more modern social and political society. Only when this is accomplished does the emotional content diminish, replaced by more tangible material concerns.

Conditions very similar to those that exist in new states today existed in Europe's age of ideology, roughly from 1789 to 1848. Historian James Froude, looking back on the turmoil of these years, described in his biography of Thomas Carlyle the spirit of the time:

> All around us, the intellectual lightships had broken from their moorings, and it was then a new and trying experience. The present generation which has grown up in an open spiritual ocean, which has got used to it and has learned to swim for itself, will never know what it was to find the lights all drifting, the compasses all awry, and nothing left to steer by except the stars.

This was a period extremely fertile in the realm of political and social ideas. Modern liberalism, conservatism, socialism, and nationalism all have their origins in it, and the great theorists of the era—Mill, Marx, Tocqueville, Mazzini, Proudhon, Hegel, to name only a few—still provide the major reference points for both Western and non-Western ideologies. It is not simply the quality of their thought that accounts for this impact, for although this was indeed an era of genius, it was as much the form in which genius chose to cast its thoughts as the ideas themselves that made this a recurring source of almost religious inspiration.

The Birth of Ideology

This is particularly true of the first generation of theorists, those like Chateaubriand, Claude Henri de Saint-Simon, Charles Fourier, Hegel, and Robert Owen, all of whom were old enough to have experienced the French Revolution, for they were acutely aware of a personal historical mission. Some, like Saint-Simon, presumed themselves divinely inspired, and even those who disassociated themselves completely from religion still adopted the stance of prophecy. From the 1780s to the 1840s, Europe was filled with prophets ready and willing to guide a civilization that had "nothing left to steer by except the stars." Their pronouncements were indeed cosmic in scope and apocalyptic in form, and the fanatical style of genius led often enough to a diagnosis of madness. "The constitution of many men of genius is really the same as that of idiots," concluded one French doctor. But madness had long been associated with divine inspiration, and thus prophetic statements and bizarre behavior produced more believers than skeptics during the first four decades of the nineteenth century.

The subsequent generation of genius, which included Karl Marx, John Stuart Mill, and Pierre-Joseph Proudhon, was much less eccentric. These theorists attempted to put ideology on a firmer scientific foundation, relying less on personal charisma and emotional appeal. They differed, also, in their relationship to their followers. The first generation had assumed an avant-garde role, speaking *for* the inarticulate general population. However, by the 1840s this oracular, authoritarian tradition was being questioned by both the general population and the intellectual leaders themselves. By that time, also, genuine class consciousness had developed and working people were speaking for themselves; as popular movements evolved, charisma gave way to organizational skill, and ideology to expertise. The ideas of the early nineteenth-century theorists persisted, but no longer as belief systems organized in a cultlike manner. After 1850 ideology was gradually adapted to the needs of mass political movements, thereby losing many of its original features. As programs for parties competing for rather than against the power of a particular social and political system, liberalism, conservatism, socialism, and nationalism began to lose their original universal, apocalyptic form. Except where parties were still ostracized by the state (as in the case of Marxist socialism in Germany), political ideas ceased being belief systems that demanded total commitment to a particular way of looking at the world and became means of achieving power.

The history of ideology is as much psychological and social as it is intellectual; its origins lie in the period when Europe's educated elites were first experiencing social and cultural dislocation. As in today's new nations, intellectuals were the first to articulate alternatives to the old order, and they did this in a form consistent with the traditional role of the thinker, namely, that of the priesthood. As conscious competitors with the old clergy, it was natural that the new prophets should adopt a religious style in appealing to the people. In the end, however, neither the old religions nor their secular competitors were very successful in reaching the general population. The peasantry proved largely impenetrable to ideology and the new urban working classes developed a culture of their own quite independent of the intellectuals.

In today's new states even those who are illiterate can be reached through modern means of communications and mobilized through efficient military or political organizations; therefore, the ideologist's relationship to his followers is quite different. There is less room for eccentricity where leaders claim to be *of* as well as *for* the people; however, in Europe prophets were not operating within the context of the modern nation-state and therefore rarely made a pretense of being one of the common folk. They were consciously avant-garde, showing the way for the whole world without much regard to a particular constituency or even a particular nation. Up to 1840 the history of ideology and that of popular movements were largely independent of one another; once they came together ideology itself was radically transformed. The next section traces this evolution.

The First Ideologists

Although the Enlightenment may have been the source of many nine-teenth-century ideas, the broad ideological formulation of those ideas and the almost religious fervor with which they were held is attributable largely to the special conditions present during subsequent stages of Europe's eco-nomic and political development. The eighteenth century presented its ideas dispassionately. Eighteenth-century *philosophes* were critical to the point of skepticism. Themselves victims of religious censorship, they were cynical about enthusiasm generally and wary about committing themselves to any grand system of ideas; they were cautious, present-minded reformers and not apocalyptic prophets of the future. For the most part, they be-lieved the role of the intellectual to be circumscribed and the best they hoped for was monarchical reform through appeal to enlightened opinion. Wrote Voltaire, "If opinion is queen of the world, the philosophes govern that queen." They intended no appeal to the population at large, whom they believed beyond the reach of reasoned argument.

With a few exceptions, the advanced thought of the eighteenth century reflected the isolation of the intellectuals from state and society. The *philosophes* viewed society as a collection of individuals, each operating according to self-interest and viewed the bond of society—religion, com-munity, and especially birth—as encumbrances. The best society was the one that allowed the greatest freedom of activity compatible with the so-called laws of human and physical nature. It was consistent with the sociological position of the *philosophes* that they should attempt to stand outside both society and history, passing judgment by an abstract and essentially static conception of natural law. They judged institutions by whether they were "natural" or "unnatural," the definition of which the *philosophes* declared "self-evident to any rational man." They did not attempt to implement these judgments by political means and confined their influence to an advisory role, making little attempt to organize support in the broader society. Nor did they attempt to organize them-selves apart from the salon and coffee house. As individuals who viewed themselves as standing outside history, they regarded personal commit-ment to causes not only politically dangerous but socially unacceptable.

Before 1789 the only movement that involved educated persons emo-tionally was Freemasonry, which had begun in the early eighteenth century as a middle-class movement of moral reform, cultivating an austere, "natural" life-style. By the 1770s, however, Freemasonry had begun to take on the features of a cult, complete with mystical beliefs and rituals of commitment that made it a secular rival to the more conventional type of faith. Freemasonry's belief in the natural goodness and equality of the human being had a strong influence on the Revolution of 1789, not only through its ideas (strongly influenced by Rousseau), but also in the way those ideas were formulated. Both the Jacobin and the *sans-culotte* movements readily adopted the kind of emotional commitment that characterized Freemasonry, and suited the ritual and rhetoric previously associated with religion to their political purposes. The elaborate ceremonies of dedication during the years 1793-1794, the civil sermonizing, and the cults of Marat and the Supreme Being led the historian Jules Michelet to comment: "The Revolution did not adopt a church. Why? Because it was a church itself."

Jacobin leadership was drawn from the educated elites, but was entirely different from the earlier *philosophes* in style and orientation. Instead of standing apart from society and history, intellectuals now immersed themselves in both, replacing the cultivated skepticism of the eighteenth century by emotional commitment. "Atheism is aristocratic," declared Robespierre, whose conception of an egalitarian Republic of Virtue demanded faith in the existence of God, immortality of the soul, and the Ten Commandments. Believing themselves the chosen prophets of a new age, the Jacobins adopted an oracular stance that was reminiscent of the traditional priesthood. But the peasantry proved largely unreachable, and the urban *sans-culottes* developed their own secular religion that was often in competition with that of the Jacobins. They had their own saints, rituals, and hymns of revolution. We have seen that the *sans-culotte* was a true believer, highly susceptible to rumor, and committed to collective action.

"Sans-cullotisme was a species of morality," notes one historian; its reliance on moral revitalization was its strength as well as its weakness. Like Jacobinism generally, commitment to an ideal rather than developed organizations largely held it together. Furthermore, its ideology did not evolve much beyond the natural law moralism of the eighteenth century. Its chief mentors—Rousseau, Gabriel Bonnet de Mably, and Abbé Morelly—had taught the natural equality of humanity. Because this was supposedly self-evident, society need only be persuaded of the truth in order for the actual conditions of equality to come into being.

Even Gracchus Babeuf, who in the *Manifesto of the Conspiracy of the Equals* carried Rousseau's ideas to their logical conclusion by advocating a redistribution of property, developed no historical or sociological theory that would have justified his agrarian communism in other than moral terms. Although he spoke vaguely of a new age of equality, he produced no historical argument for the inevitability of change; nor did he identify any particular social group as the carrier of social change. Generalizations about "mankind" were not refined beyond a loose distinction between the rich and the poor, groups assumed to have the same abstract human nature despite their obvious differences in education and background. True to the tradition of the *philosophes*, revolutionaries like Babeuf and his disciple Buonarroti continued to believe that people needed only to be convinced of the virtue of equality in order for the good society to be actualized. They departed from them only in so far as they advocated a religious mode of conversion as opposed to rational persuasion and predicted a sudden, apocalyptic change in the human condition rather than its gradual reform through enlightenment.

The embryonic ideological movements of the 1790s did not manage to produce secular theories of historical change mainly because their constituencies were drawn from social groups that were attempting to revitalize old values rather than forge new ones. In both France and England the popular democratic movements of this period comprised artisans, peasants, and other small urban-property holders intent on using democracy as a way of holding back the power of the state and the encroachment of the market economy of capitalism. Their feelings toward history were therefore ambivalent and their thinking insufficiently future oriented to create new ideologies by themselves.

From the 1790s through the 1820s the popular democratic movement went underground in France, England, Italy, and Germany, and during this long period of political repression, the development of ideology passed largely into the hands of the educated. Among both the bourgeoisie and aristocracy the experience of the French Revolution and the Napoleonic period overcame their earlier distaste for ideology and the enthusiasm associated with it. It was during this time that the upper classes learned the dangers of their earlier skepticism, and by the time of the Restoration in 1815, the atheism fashionable in the eighteenth century had been almost entirely abandoned. Both middle-class and aristocratic theorists were arguing that some kind of religion was necessary for the maintenance of social and political order. Not only the conservatives Joseph de Maistre and Louis Vicomte de Bonald, but also their archenemy Napoleon viewed the Church as the pillar of the state. The liberal Czar Alexander made the same case in advocating the Holy Alliance, while the Bourbons found it useful to readmit their old enemies, the Jesuits, to France.

Liberalism and Nationalism

Among the emerging middle class it was not so much religion but the secular ideology of liberalism that provided certainty. In England, where the middle classes had long been associated with religious dissent, a certain moral self-righteousness had long buttressed the quest for greater economic and political freedom. In France and Germany justifications for liberty were couched in equally moralistic terms. The word "liberalism," defining such a set of beliefs, came into the English language shortly after 1815; the term had been used earlier in Spain by opponents of Napoleon, and its usage became general on the Continent in the 1820s. Liberals could claim as predecessors intellectuals of the eighteenth century—Adam Smith, Voltaire, and Immanuel Kant among them—but while the ideas of laissez-faire economists and natural law philosophers may have predated nineteenth-century liberalism, its format was quite new.

The liberals of the early nineteenth century transformed the ideas of economic competition, religious tolerance, and equality of opportunity from an essentially abstract critique of existing society into a systematic advocacy of a new order. Thinkers such as Jeremy Bentham, J.B. Say, and Friedrich List not only justified the creation of a laissez-faire economy on rational grounds, but set forth as well a theory of historical development that made this not only right but also inevitable. Adam Smith had fashioned an abstract liberal economics before the outlines of a new industrial society were really visible. Writing in the 1770s, he did not have to deal with the historical consequences of freedom of trade as James Mill and François Guizot were later forced to do. There is little wonder that the early nineteenth-century defense of the free-market economy, with its advocacy of the total emancipation of property from collective control, was much more moralistic in tone and buttressed by example from history as well as philosophy, for by then there was an identifiable industrial and commercial capitalism, together with a self-confident bourgeoisie, whose achievements were now their own justification. Wrote James Mill in 1826:

> The value of the middle classes of this country, their growing numbers and importance, are acknowledged by all. These classes have long been spoken of, and not grudgingly, by their superiors, themselves, as the glory of England; as that which alone has given us our eminence among nations; as that portion of our people to whom every thing that is good among us may with certainty be traced.

Liberalism was based on the interests of a particular class but claimed a universal appeal. It did not pretend to be democratic; instead, it argued that the entrepreneurial and professional elites, self-made persons who kept open the door of opportunity to new talent from below, were destined to lead the world to greater material and intellectual progress. The greater the freedom given to the individual to pursue his interests, the greater would be the future benefit.

The basic support for liberalism was, of course, middle class, but those attracted by its justification for liberation from feudal and state control were of sufficiently varied background to make its claim to universality creditable. Numbered among its early advocates were members of the old aristocracy, including Lafayette, Saint-Simon, Lord Byron, and Freiherr vom Stein. In western Germany several lesser princes eager to gain back their sovereignity from Napoleon supported liberalism. In Italy large land-owners were in its ranks, and in Hungary and Poland, the lesser gentry. In France a tactical alliance existed between liberals and the nobles of Brittany, including Chateaubriand, who were opposed to any Bourbon restoration of absolute monarchy. Prussia's aristocracy of service, the bureaucracy, was also identified with liberalism.

However, liberalism could also appeal to the peasantry, at least up to the point that feudal obligations were overthrown. From then on the market orientation of bourgeois landowners and merchants threatened the peasants and they turned away from liberalism. It was mainly in the towns that liberalism gained support among the lower social orders. Until the 1830s, democratic radicalism continued to be closely associated with liberal movements, for they shared a broad range of goals: acquisition of civil equality, desire for freedom of speech and press, and restriction of absolutism. The core of *sans-culotte* radicalism was still mainly the smaller-property owners, and that which separated them from the bour-geoisie seemed less significant than that which separated both from the idle rich and the parasitic poor.

Even those who strongly sympathized with the poor did not perceive before 1830 the interests of the liberal elites as opposed to those of the general population. Saint-Simon and Etienne Cabet, who can be claimed to be founders of socialism, both identified themselves with the liberal opposition in the 1820s. Saint-Simon, who was among the first to perceive industrialism as the wave of the future, found no contradiction between his desire to bring peace and prosperity to all humankind and his advocacy of technocratic rule by bankers and industrialists. Another of the early socialists, Charles Fourier, believed that industrialists would find his utopian communities an ideal investment. Owen also believed that the "industrious classes," middle and working class, would unite against their common enemy, the privileged, unproductive aristocracy.

The universal appeal of early liberalism can also be attributed to its close association with nationalism, another of the new ideologies and a term coined in the 1840s. Nationalism also was a creation of intellectuals, notably those military and bureaucratic elites who were deeply involved in state building from the French Revolution onward. From the moment in 1789 when the Abbé Sieyès identified the interests of the French nation with those of the Third Estate, nationalism became a liberal cause, particularly in those countries like Italy and Germany where feudalism and absolutism were linked to the interests of particularism and privilege. However, the nation was also the rallying cry for the *sans-culotte* move-ments of the 1790s, and thus nationalism remained a bridge between liberalism and democratic radicalism until the 1840s. Nationalism was even associated with early socialism. Fichte's nation-state promised social welfare to all inhabitants; the nationalism of Guiseppe Mazzini also carried strong social content. Like most nationalists of this period, Mazzini saw no contradiction between the objective of unifying a particular people and the cause of all humanity. His Young Europe movement declared that "every people has its special mission, which will cooperate towards the fulfillment of the general mission of humanity. That mission constitutes its nationality."

In the period before national unity became a reality, nationalism was more like a religious cult than a secular political movement. Its leaders— Mazzini, Adam Mickiewicz, and Friedrich Jahn—assumed the role of prophets. Their followers, mainly intellectuals like themselves, behaved like members of a millenarian sect awaiting the day of redemption. During the Napoleonic period, they had been forced to form underground brotherhoods such as the Italian Carbonari and the German *Tugendbund* (League of Virtue), each with its pantheon of secular saints, mysticism, and colorful rituals. Also involved, however, was a quest for certainty in a world of swirling change.

In many of the liberal and nationalist secret societies of the 1810s and 1820s, ideological commitment was a solution to problems of personal identity, and many youths found it a way to individual as well as societal salvation. French citizens were converted to Polish nationalism, Germans to the Italian movement, and so on; they experienced the kind of total emotional absorption typical of ideological movements in new states today, allowing them to forget their diverse social and regional origins. As an ideology, nationalism was indeed capable of producing the feeling of selfless communion usually associated with mystical religions. Mazzini himself spoke of this, describing:

> a kind of compulsion, inexplicable to myself, that directs all my actions and that—being in the nature of religious stimulus to which, when I feel it, it seems a crime not to give way—will always remain a secret from everyone else, since I know not how to explain it, and others would not understand it.

Varieties of Conservatism

The English conservative Edmund Burke was convinced that ideology itself had been a chief cause of the French Revolution. Had liberals and radicals not seduced the public by their abstractions, the problems of the old regimes would have been resolved pragmatically and peacefully. But, despite their distrust of ideology, it was not long before conservatives had developed one of their own. It is often said that conservatism (the word dates from the 1830s) was a response to liberalism, but in fact it developed stimultaneously and not at all as merely a defense of the status quo.

Like both liberalism and nationalism, the conservative ideologies that developed during and after the Napoleonic period were forward looking, based on the interests of the old elites but universal in their appeal. They were not a blind defense of the past, but rather visions of the future based on principles of political authority and social order adapted to changing conditions. Conservatives were not, as John Stuart Mill described them, "the stupid party." Among their number were some of the most brilliant intellects of the time—François René de Chateaubriand, Samuel Taylor Coleridge, Alexis de Tocqueville, Benjamin Disraeli, Joseph de Maistre, and Thomas Carlyle, to name only a few—individuals who could hardly be accused of turning their backs on the present. The emergence of a positive ideology was possible only because conservatives recognized the irreversibility of the changes that were occurring and the need to formulate a program for the future. Chateaubriand wrote that he felt separated by "whole centuries" from the Old Regime, while de Maistre explicitly rejected return to the past as a way of countering revolution: "The counter-revolution will not be a revolution in reverse but the opposite of revolution."

Although they proclaimed the ideal of legitimacy, conservatives showed themselves to be selective in the kind of monarchy they would support. Chateaubriand fought both the Jacobins and Napoleon, but when the Bourbons were restored he found himself again in opposition because they, too, continued the thrust of centralization and thus were enemies of liberty. Decentralization of authority was a key concept of conservatism. Its major constituency was of course the aristocracy, but this did not mean that conservative ideologists were blindly loyal to the old aristocracy. English conservatives of the 1820s were convinced that by adopting agrarian capitalism the nobility had done as much as the middle class in bringing about social disorder. They spoke of the "abdication of the aristocracy" and talked of the need to create new elites that would be noble in spirit as well as title. In Prussia, the Gerlach brothers led a circle of religious conservatives (in which Bismarck was a member) who were no less critical of the service nobility, whom they accused of selling out to the state in exchange for honors and offices.

Although conservatism was identified with the restoration of religion, it did not necessarily advocate established religion or commit itself to the existing priesthood. On the contrary, many of its ideologists believed that religion could only be saved by emancipating it from the old relationship of crown and altar. The Oxford Movement was dedicated to purifying the Church of England by cutting its ties with the state, and it was Coleridge who suggested a National Church with a new priesthood, or as he called it, a "clerisy," that would serve to guide the nation to a new age:

> The object of the National Church . . . was to secure and improve civilization without which the nation could be neither permanent nor progressive . . . National Education . . . the shaping and informing spirit, which eliciting the latent in men, trains them up to be citizens of the country, free subjects of the realm.

Long before Disraeli used the term "Tory Democracy," conservatives were proclaiming themselves the true friends of the common people. In Europe, conservatism preceded socialism in developing a systematic critique of liberalism's laissez-faire economy. The concept of a society operating on the principle of individual self-interest was not only unworkable but immoral; it was the cause of the misery of the poor and the corruption of the rich. By the 1820s English conservatives were developing an alternative to liberal economics that in many ways foreshadowed the Keynesian formula of government spending to maintain full employment. At times, the editors of the conservative *Blackwood's Magazine* seemed outright utopian in their proposals for increased credit and resettlement of the landless poor. Tories were severe critics of the liberal New Poor Law of 1834 and among the earliest advocates of factory legislation designed for the protection of the worker.

Although French and German conservatives reserved their strongest responsibility for the peasantry (which they idealized almost beyond recognition), they were also concerned with ways to restore social harmony to an urban society in which, as Chateaubriand put it, "all is transitory: religion and morals are no longer admitted, or else each interprets them after his own fashion." Their answer was the restoration of a sense of responsibility to the rich and a sense of loyalty to the poor. At times, ideological conservatism could border on radical populism, as in the case of the English radical writer Thomas Cobbett. During the violent English agrarian unrest of 1830, small landholders were often found siding with the landless laborers against the encroachments of capitalist agriculture. According to Cobbett, in the ideal conservative society, the property owner would recognize in ownership an obligation higher than that of profit; he would recognize the organic nature of society in which no man is an island. "The landowners, farmers and working classes, husbandry manufacturers, and trading, must thus prosper and suffer together; their interests cannot be separated."

As for the lower orders, they must accept authority and reject the myth of equality, because the latter is the handmaiden of tyranny. This was the argument of Alexis de Tocqueville, who traced the connection between the leveling of social hierarchy and the rise of despotism. Juxtaposed to mass society was an ideal of a hierarchy of talent and virtue. Chateaubriand argued that what was wrong with the liberal notion of competitive individualism was that "the authority of expertise and age, of birth and genius, talent or virtue—all is rejected: a few individuals clamber to the top of the ruin, proclaiming themselves giants and roll down like pygmies."

Above all else the new society demanded leaders. Carlyle praised hero-worship, Hegel lauded the aristocracy of capacity, and Disraeli, himself an eccentric personality, developed a cult of genius. It is not surprising that the core of conservative support should come from the old elites, particularly the clergy and the landowning aristocracy, but there were many nobles who found paternalism to be unprofitable and so advocated liberalism, just as there were some middle-class industrialists who found the concept of hierarchy compatible and became conservatives. Many of the early

conservative ideologues—Adam Muller, Coleridge, Friedrich Stahl, Disraeli—
were themselves of nonnoble, even non-Christian origin. They were attracted
to conservatism for intellectual, social, even psychological reasons.

Like nationalism and liberalism, early conservatism had something of
the character of a cult, especially where it was associated with sectarian
religious conviction. The members of Gerlach circle were a tightly knit
group of Pietists, related to one another by birth, and strongly distrustful
of the outside world. It is significant that conservatism was so strongly
appealing to Jewish converts to Christianity like Stahl and Disraeli;
conservatism served to confirm their spiritual rebirth as well as their newfound social status. In its early stages, ideological conservatism did not
develop a mass following, but then neither did nationalism or liberalism.
Like them, it remained a sectarian phenomenon, offering spiritual salvation
and a way of life to its true believers.

Early Socialism

We have noted already that *sans-culotte* radicalism could not produce a
coherent, forward-looking ideology because it represented groups that had
little stake in the future of the new industrial world. Having relied previously on its alliance with liberalism, it found itself abandoned when
liberalism unabashedly took up the cause of industrial capitalism. For the
menu peuple there was only one place to turn: namely, to the newest
entry in Europe's ideological competition, socialism. Naturally, small-
property holders were reluctant to accept any theory that attacked private
property as such, and contacts between democratic (or *sans-culotte*)
radicalism and socialism remained sporadic. The earliest attempt to spread
socialist ideas among the *sans-culottes*, Babeuf's "Conspiracy of the
Equals" movement, was a very minor episode in Paris during the years
1795–1796, leaving no result apart from legend. Babeuf had advocated the
redistribution of property rather than its abolition, and his ideal society
was a rural republic of small landholders, consistent with the *sans-culotte*
dream of political equality and social fraternity, but scarcely addressing
the problems of industrial capitalism. It could not have been otherwise,
for neither industry nor capitalism was sufficiently advanced in the 1790s
to call forth modern socialism. Nor had the wage-earning working class
sufficiently emancipated itself from the *sans-culotte* concern with revitalization to provide a solid constituency for such movements.

By the 1830s, however, all this was changing. With the birth of a new
proletarian consciousness, vague ideas of social justice embodied in radical
rhetoric began to crystallize into mature socialist ideologies. It was then
that the veteran revolutionary Auguste Blanqui was converted to the
notion of the dictatorship of the proletariat, while Etienne Cabet and
Louis Blanc began to put the "social question" before that of political
democracy. In the utopian novel *Voyage to Icaria*, Cabet addressed himself in 1840 to the plight of the wage-earning working class as such. The

novel received wide circulation, and in workers' districts of Paris and Lyon Cabet became something of a prophet. His was an appeal for moral revitalization, but within the context of an industrial society. In Icaria:

> You would see here neither cabarets, nor roadhouses, nor cafes, nor smoking joints, not the stock-exchange, nor gaming or lottery houses, nor establishments for shameful or culpable pleasures, nor barracks and guardrooms, nor gendarmes and stool-pigeons, just as there are no prostitutes or pickpockets, no drunkards nor medicants; but instead you would find everywhere PRIVIES as elegant as they are clean and convenient, some for women, others for men, where modesty may enter for a moment without fear for itself or for public decency.

Blanc's book *Organization of Work*, with its concept of the "right to work," came in 1839. It advocated the establishment of state financed "social workshops," producer cooperatives that would ultimately drive private enterprise out of business and thus create the basis for a social as well as political democracy.

The shift from *sans-culotte* radicalism to working-class socialism was gradual and not always direct. Most of the early socialist thinkers, including Robert Owen, Charles Fourier, Etienne Cabet, and Louis Blanc, were middle class by origin and most saw themselves as for but not of the general population. The heritage of early socialism was, in fact, often paternalistic, sometimes quite out of touch with the realities of proletarian existence in the great industrial cities. Marx lumped all the early socialists of the 1830s and 1840s under the label "utopians," but if by this is meant sentimental dreamers, then the term obscures almost as much as it reveals. Although the early socialists were largely out of touch with the workers' movement—trade unionism and democratic radicalism—they were by no means unrealistic about the options open to European society during the first phases of economic and political development. Their ranks included a number of eminently practical, even highly successful individuals. Robert Owen was one of the most respected industrialists of his time; the Saint-Simonian movement attracted engineers, and the manager of the Crueset iron works left his post to join it. In America, wealthy persons like Horace Greeley were keenly interested.

Earlier utopian writers such as Tommaso Campanella and Sir Thomas More had been largely speculative, holding up the design of an ideal society as a didactic mirror rather than a real option. But to nineteenth century utopians, the possibility of perfection was very real. "It is no more a theory of Utopia as in days of Plato and More, but a real, tangible verity, a plan for prudent, practical development . . . ," wrote one Englishman. By the 1830s and 1840s utopian socialism constituted a major movement on both sides of the Atlantic. The large-scale ideas were European, the small-scale experiments mainly American. It has been estimated that there were over one thousand communities founded in the United States alone, with others scattered throughout Russia and South America. To Cabet, who set out for Texas after the failure of the Revolution of 1848 to found the utopian community called Icaria, their success seemed an established fact:

> We have the words dream and utopia continually thrown in our face. Let us, in answer, establish and realize Icaria. There will not be any obstacle to our communizing everything on the most perfect systems which modern science can offer us; the plans and positions of our roads, towns, and manufactures will be laid out from the beginning in the most advantageous manner; we shall aim at perfection, in our work-shops, our dwellings, our furniture, our clothing—in fact everything.

To the early prophets of socialism, everything seemed possible, including human perfection. They were heirs to an eighteenth-century notion of natural law, believing that people need only be shown the truth in order to be acted upon. On the other hand, they had abandoned the reserved skepticism of the *philosophes* for an active emotional involvement with history. "To do great things, it is necessary to be passionate," said Saint-Simon. Change could be expected to come rapidly, even apocalyptically, as long as the faith was strong. Though he was no friend of Christianity, Robert Owen adopted its language in preaching the perfectability of humankind:

> Whatever ideas individuals may attach to the term Millenium, I know not, but I know that society may be found so as to exist without crime, without poverty, with health greatly improved, with little, if any, mis-ery, and with intelligence and happiness increased a hundredfold.

In contrast to the liberals and conservatives, the early socialists believed rule by self-interest, whether middle class or aristocratic, immoral and outmoded. Although they differed among themselves as to the degree of liberty and equality that was compatible with human perfection (Owen was authoritarian, Fourier distrusted equality, Cabet differed with both), they agreed that a competitive system could only lead to social chaos and moral degeneration. They could not agree among themselves as to whether private property should be abolished, but they were all certain that what-ever form of wealth existed needed to be organized for the general good. Whatever the relationship of liberty and equality to early socialism, frater-nity was its ultimate standard. What all the early socialists found most repug-nant was the loss of community, reciprocity, and social harmony. The terms they invented to describe their solutions—communism, socialism, perfectionism, harmonism—reflected their priorities. A follower of Saint-Simon, Victor Considerant, wrote:

> We live in an age when wars, political commotions, senseless and cruel party conflicts, the misery and the atrocious suffering common to mankind of all ages of development have been condensed into a

very brief hour and with fearful intensity. Moreover, the sense of social injustice is today more highly developed than it ever has been: pain is more acutely felt, evil speaks louder, and on all sides there is a realization for the urgent need for reform.

If they were united on the need for fraternity, the early socialists were divided on the origins of social discord and the means of redress. Saint-Simon introduced the idea (later developed by Marx) that the cause was the emergence of a new industrial age that had introduced new forms of class conflict. But his followers, led by Barthélemy Enfantin, appeared to ignore their master on this point and found the chief cause of dissension to be spiritual, a lack of love. Charles Fourier, who as a traveling salesperson had direct experience with the system of commercial capitalism, blamed disharmony more on this than on industry, while others found fault in the family arrangements, age relations, child rearing, male/female roles, and all manner of social relationships indirectly related to the economic system. Fourier was particularly critical of big cities, which he associated with crime and social decay, but not all early socialists were hostile to the urban environment. Cabet derived much inspiration from London and Paris. Most agreed with Robert Owen that poverty was the chief cause of violence and disorder, yet none of the prophets was very rigorous in social or psychological investigations. Although some knew the effects of industrialization firsthand, most were armchair critics in the tradition of the eighteenth-century intellectuals.

As vague as they were about cause, the early socialists were extraordinarily precise about their solutions. Owen, who had worked out elaborate systems of worker welfare at his mills in Scotland in 1815, proceeded to draw up very precise plans when he turned his attention to the building of New Harmony in Indiana in 1824–1825. Nothing was neglected in planning arrangements that would eliminate destructive competition and introduce social harmony. Architecture, communal sleeping quarters and eating arrangements, education, work, leisure—all were brought into productive harmonic arrangements. Saint-Simon left only rather vague proposals for the realization of social community when he died in 1827, but his followers built their community at Ménilmontant outside Paris in 1831 according to their own very detailed blueprint. The Saint–Simonians developed a series of daily rituals that emphasized their master's dictum: "Love one another and help one another." Choral music, embodying the concept of harmony, was central to their leisure activities. Special dress that buttoned in the back was designed to remind members of their interdependence.

Cabet described Icaria in great detail, while J. A. Etzler introduced fascinating details of lighting, air conditioning (with perfume), and even elevators into his literature. At John Humphrey Noyes's Oneida Perfectionist community even the sex life of the members was regulated to produce the greatest possible social harmony. In order to prevent antisocial pairing off of couples, no two people were allowed to have intercourse on a regular basis. Furthermore, so that sex would not divide the young from the old, relations between different ages—older women with young men, older men with young women—were specifically provided for. "Father" Noyes even prescribed the type of intercourse—namely, nonejaculation for males, so as to protect women against pregnancy and to encourage female orgasm. In his later years, Noyes advocated what he called "complex marriage," a system of selective mating aimed at perfecting the Oneida community biologically as well as spiritually.

But perhaps Charles Fourier, the son of a Besançon shopkeeper, worked out the most detailed plan of all. He spent years propagating the concept of phalansteries, model communities that he hoped to finance by private subscription. Unlike his fellow socialists Noyes and Cabet, Fourier saw no need to abolish private property in order to achieve social harmony; instead, he wished to attract the well-to-do to his communities so that their wealth and talent might contribute to the general good. The phalansteries were designed so as to accommodate rather than modify individual differences. Fourier was content to accept not only differences in wealth but also differences in interests, talents, and personality. He believed he had identified 405 kinds of motivations (he called them "passions") and he calculated that a phalanstery numbering exactly 1,602 persons could be arranged so as to create a functioning community without psychological or social tension.

Like all of the early socialists, Fourier was a provincial. He detested the Paris of the early nineteenth century and dreamed of sowing the countryside with ideal communities. His ideal was essentially agricultural, and the domestic and productive tasks needed to operate it were quite simple. No person would be assigned a specific job; instead, each individual would do what pleased him or her, changing jobs as frequently as desire dicated. In this way everything would get done without the pain of boredom or overexertion. Each family would have its separate living quarters, but the children would be educated in peer groups, thus relieving that burden from the parents. As a believer in the equality of women, Fourier provided day-care facilities so that mothers could also follow their interests. In sexual matters, too, individual choice prevailed. Every variation, including homosexuality, was provided for, and divorce was readily available. Like most other early socialists, Fourier was particularly concerned with generational relations. He generously provided for the two groups that in traditional society had been most subject to exploitation, namely, the young and elderly.

Fourier believed that once one phalanstery had established its obvious superiority to existing forms of social organization it would produce a chain reaction of further change. Like Owen, Blanc, and Cabet, he expected that cooperation would drive competition out of business, thereby opening a new moral age. Fourier advertised his ideas in the Paris press and waited in a café for investors; even when a benefactor failed to appear, he refused to turn to the state or to politics to support his conceptions. As someone who had lost a fortune during the Revolution of 1789, Fourier had a deep distrust of both monarchy and popular democracy. He hated revolutionaries and was fearful of the lower classes generally. Like so many of the early socialists he was quite apolitical, believing that education rather than legislation would bring about the new society.

Of the major figures of the period, only Owen, Cabet, and Blanc looked to mass movements or the state as a means of redress. Even so, Owen's role in politics was very sporadic, and Blanc's concept of state financed social workshops did not emerge until the 1840s, when the early, apolitical stage of socialist ideology was already in eclipse. Ambivalence toward politics reflected the instability and weakness of the state at the point before political modernization was complete. Religious traditions also reinforced the tendency to seek salvation in nonpolitical ways. Early socialism drew strength from Christianity both spiritually and organizationally. Of those who called themselves socialists, only Blanqui was a dedicated atheist. Saint-Simon's book *New Christianity* of 1825 was pure social gospel. Owenism drew converts from Quaker and Mormon communities, and Cabet's socialism mixed easily with popular religion in Lyon.

In most cases religious chiliasm reinforced secular notions of millennium. During periods of intense political activity such as occurred in the years 1830–1832, both popular religion and socialism lost strength to political organizations, but when revolution and reform failed to fulfill the promise of social relief, all sectarian movements experienced an enormous revival. In England, the failure of the rural Swing Rebellion of 1830 was followed by a resurgence of Primitive Methodism with its intense belief in personal salvation. In France, the Saint-Simonians abandoned politics to concentrate on building a new spiritual order at Ménilmontant. Frustration with the Reform Act of 1832 turned the English working-class movement in the direction of Owen's millennialistic dream of massive, sudden change. Apocalyptic visions such as the Labour Exchange, the Grand National Consolidated Trades Union, and the Sacred Month (the general strike during which workers would refuse to produce) all rose and fell in rapid succession as people sought salvation outside the political system. The 1830s and 1840s were a time when people sought in ideological community a substitute for the sense of belonging previously associated with traditional social and religious groups. However, once new class cultures began to institutionalize themselves in the 1840s and 1850s, the need for ideology was less strongly felt.

The Beginnings of Working-Class Socialism

Saint-Simonianism began to break up after its leader, *"Père"* Barthélemy Enfantin, was found guilty in 1834 of disturbing public morality by advocating divorce. Fourier died in 1837, and only Cabet continued to preach social redemption in a prophetic manner. The first generation of socialists had envisioned large-scale social experiments taking place on European soil, but with the failure of revolution in 1830 and again in 1848, their successors redefined their goals, often emigrating to North or South America, where they contented themselves with small-scale experiments.

This change reflected not only the disappearance of a particular generation of prophets, but also the end of an age of social transition that had inspired a certain kind of social experimentalism. By the 1840s the thrust of capitalist industrialization was so strong that economic options narrowed considerably. Although Saint-Simon had been one of the first to grasp that the rise of industry was the key feature of the new age, other socialists had remained ambivalent. Fourier's phalansteries took as their economic model the farm rather than the factory, and most of the communal experiments in the United States preferred a mixed economy of agriculture and craft production. By this time urbanization also was too far advanced to encourage a return to the land. The hegemony of the great cities was no longer contested, and thus the early Owenite and Fourier models of less than two thousand inhabitants appeared outdated.

The first generation of prophets had all had small-town or rural origins. Those who flocked to the American communes of the 1830s and 1840s were of the same general type: shopkeepers, small artisans, provincial intellectuals, but rarely big-city types. Those communal traditions that had inspired their concepts of fraternity were becoming increasingly obsolete; they were not part of the experience of the new factory proletariat of new cities like Manchester, Barmen, or Mulhouse. It must also be noted that nation building had reached the point at which the realities of centralized power could no longer be ignored. Decentralization, the dream that many early socialists shared with conservatives, was dated by the 1840s, not only because state power had increased, but also because popular movements were now focusing on capturing rather than combating central power. While hostility to the state would linger on in the form of anarchism in more backward places like Spain and Italy, communalism of the old type was forced to retreat to those frontier regions of America where the state power was still weak.

The fact is that the constituency of utopian socialism was disappearing. The displaced artisan or small farmer, the unemployed intellectuals and déclassé aristocrats were all social types doomed to extinction. The communal movements did not generally attract people of big-city backgrounds; nor did they touch the lives of the new factory proletariat. The latter showed interest in the cooperative ideas of Owen and Cabet but generally turned these to their own specific needs without committing themselves to the entire system. There is no question that unions and consumer cooperatives owed much to the early socialists, but the kind of millennialism so attractive to the followers of prophets like Owen and Enfantin had little appeal for the new proletariat. The utopians were attempting to recover something of a lost ideal through a secular form of religion. The proletariat was so thoroughly de-Christianized as to be immune to the appeal of millennialist ritual and symbol, and the charisma of prophecy.

The constituency of utopian socialism had been strongly attracted by the paternalistic character of its leaders, who liked to call themselves "*Père*" or "Father" and who spoke of their followers as their "children," reflecting a patriarchal order that was being disrupted but that was not yet completely replaced by either the narrowly private bourgeois nation of domestic patriarchy or the broad working-class concept of fraternity. The familylike models that early socialists worked from were particularly appealing both to rootless middle-class youth (as is still the case today) and to members of the *sans-culotte* strata desperate for revitalization of their old moral order. But utopia could scarcely be expected to appeal to the new industrial proletariat, whose experience with family was so radically different from that of either of these groups.

Finally, the early socialists were too ambivalent toward property to be able to attract a following among the wage-earning population that owned no property. The utopians' ideological emphasis was on fraternity, not equality, and while they all made provision for the poor in their schemes of human development, their schemes were intended either for the purposes of reconciliation of the interests of the rich and the poor (Saint-Simon and Fourier) or for the conversion of the poor to the habits of the rich (Owen and Noyes). Early socialist ideologists spoke of "humanity" or "the people," as if there were no fundamental class differences that could not be overcome in short order. They preferred to see themselves standing above class division, raising the mass of the people to their level. In this respect, they were little different from those liberal and conservative ideologists who believed in the universality of their particular missions. Almost all early nineteenth-century ideologists, whether they were liberals, conservatives, or socialists, were educated persons with little firsthand experience of the life of the laboring poor, particularly of the wage earners of the great cities and new industrial centers.

Early socialism enjoyed one last, brief revival in 1848 when several of the major followers of early prophets, including Pierre Leroux, Victor Considerant, and Pierre Buchez, were elected to the Assembly of the French Second Republic. Louis Blanc became a member of the February provisional government and was instrumental in setting up relief projects (the National Workshops). Paris crowds proclaimed his slogan "Right to Work." Cabetist and Fourierist clubs sprang into being, and for a moment it seemed that substantial social reform might be achieved. But the utopians failed to unite, and Blanc remained isolated within a government that consisted almost entirely of moderately liberal bourgeoisie. Although a beneficiary of the February revolution, Blanc abhorred violence and could not bring himself to support the insurrection of the June Days, thereby losing support among the workers even before being forced into exile at the end of 1848.

The year 1848 showed how far socialism and the workers' movement had come since 1830. On the one hand, disciples of Saint-Simon and Fourier, such as Pierre Leroux and Victor Considerant, had become much more politically conscious and less contemptuous of the general population. Utopian socialism was gradually blending in with the mainstream of the workers' movement and adapting itself to the institutions of the modern nation-state. Its leaders were giving up their position of standing above political and social strife and were siding openly with the workers against the bourgeoisie, thereby abandoning their old reconciliatory position. They were adjusting to changes among the workers themselves, who were becoming more conscious of the fundamental differences between themselves and the propertied classes. Industrial workers were abandoning the *sans-culotte* myth of "the people" and adopting class terms to describe themselves. Daniel Stern wrote of "a large section of the popular classes which had come to form a separate class, as it were, a nation within the nation, . . . People are beginning to use a new term for them, the industrial proletariat."

Karl Marx, the son of a liberal Jewish convert to Christianity and veteran of the ideological wars of the 1840s, was among the first to sense the importance of these changes. Born in 1817, he was one of a new generation of socialists who were too much the product of the new industrial age to yearn for the disappearing verities of the past. In his youth, Marx had been a philosophical idealist and an advocate of democratic radicalism and as late as 1848 could still be seduced by the old Jacobin formula of revolutionary alliance of the bourgeoisie and the working class. In the *Communist Manifesto* of 1847–1848, he predicted a revolution leading directly to socialism, a prophecy which proved entirely mistaken. Chased from Germany as a result of the failure of the Revolution of 1848, Marx and his close collaborator Friedrich Engels had time to reflect on the irreconcilable differences between the middle and working classes.

Their conclusion was that henceforth no ideology, whatever its moral or rational appeal, could expect to erase economic and social reality. On the contrary, the kind of class conflict that the early socialists had wished to extinguish was now accepted by Marx and Engels as the driving force of history. Those attributes of modernity that early socialists had feared, industrialization, urbanization, and proletarization, Marx's "scientific socialism" incorporated into a conception of dynamic class conflict that would ultimately result in the overthrow of tyranny and the abolition of inequality. It was not ideas or even politics that would produce socialism, but rather the combination of social-economic evolution and determined working-class organization. For Marx there were no shortcuts in history. Apocalyptic change, including old style Jacobin insurrection, was foolhardy against the forces of the modern nation-state. Capitalism should be allowed to work itself out, producing the very proletariat that would ultimately destroy it. The role of the socialist-intellectual was not to struggle against history, but to illuminate and guide it, because the real

moving force was not genius standing above history, but the general
population toiling in it.

Ideology after 1848

After 1848 all factions seemed to accept the constraints imposed by history and therefore to be less eager for immediate, total solutions to
pressing social problems. The public was well prepared for the evolutionary theories of Charles Darwin when he published the *Origin of the
Species* in 1859. Science now seemed to refute all apocalyptic notions of
change and to suggest a more gradual kind of human progress. Liberalism
tended to abandon the notion that capitalist industrialization would bring
about freedom and prosperity overnight. The great advocate of self-
improvement, Samuel Smiles, told his readers in the 1880s that "so long
as our present social arrangements exist . . . the vast mass of men will
necessarily remain workers to the last . . . men cannot be raised in masses,
as mountains were in the early geological states of the world." Another
liberal, Heinrich von Trietschke, wondered whether freedom was really
compatible with national development: "I hold freedom, etc., to be mere
phrases so long as no nation exists, for it is the only basis for any development of the state. The path that leads most quickly to this national unification is the one most cherished by men, even if it should be despotism."

Liberalism was abandoning its earlier claims to universality and becoming explicitly linked to the interests of the propertied classes and the
nation state. A similar change was affecting conservatism, which was also
putting aside its earlier idealism and cosmopolitanism. In France, ideological conservatism gradually succumbed to opportunism, while in England,
practical politics increasingly obscured the ideological differences between
liberals and conservatives. After 1848, ideology was everywhere in decline.
The age of prophets was over, and a new kind of leadership was installed.
It was less intellectual and more expert. The composition of the liberal
and conservative movements was changing in the second half of the
century; there were fewer intellectuals and more business people, these being
closer to the culture and interests of their constituency. Party organization, which was becoming increasingly bureaucratic, pushed eccentricity
out of public into private life; it was now less permissible for politicians to
hold controversial views. Even among those socialists who had earlier
advocated free love and female emancipation there was a tendency to play
down these ideas. Fourier's leading disciple, Victor Considerant, abandoned many of the master's more controversial ideas, and there can be no
sharper contrast between the early prophets and their successors than Karl
Marx himself, who blended bourgeois respectability with radical politics.

The more that socialists identified with the workers' movement the
less eccentric and sectarian they became. Of the early socialists, the one
with the largest popular following—Cabet—was the most conventional in

life-style. Pierre-Joseph Proudhon, whose anarchist ideas were influential in France throughout the second half of the nineteenth century, was the only socialist theorist to actually be of working-class origins and he was very conservative in his views on the family and marriage. Although a fanatical believer in liberty and equality, he was staunchly antifeminist; a national as well as a male chauvinist, he was proslavery during the American Civil War and a lifelong anti-Semite. As a person who had once been an enthusiast of Fourier and who wrote that during his youth "there was no system, no heresy in which, as I discovered it, I did not believe," Proudhon in later life accurately reflected the turning away from social experimentalism that followed 1848.

Working-class leaders tended to be far more pragmatic in their approach to social problems than the utopian intellectuals had been. Workers did not abandon the idea of human progress, but rejected quick solutions in favor of step-by-step organization. Whereas in the 1830s Owen had envisioned revolutionary apocalypse as leading to establishment of individual producer and consumer cooperatives, English workers reversed the sequence. They founded the Rochdale Society of Equitable Pioneers in 1844, as the first of a series of very successful cooperatives that started in a small, unpretentious way but that, by the 1860s and 1870s, were proclaimed as potential replacements for capitalist institutions because of the very high rate of profit they returned to the shareholders. One of Fourier's followers, Justin Godin, showed just how practical profit sharing could be when he turned his stove-making plant into what he called the *Familistère* in 1859.

Without abandoning the ultimate hope for a just society, workers all over Europe began to organize themselves through unions, parties, and cooperatives for what they now saw as a long struggle. Traces of the earlier utopianism remained, but generally socialist groups like Ferdinand Lassalle's General German Workingmen's Society, founded in 1863, preferred to organize *within* the existing political system. "We were not initiated in the profoundest mysteries of capital formation," recalled one of Lassalle's followers, "but we knew very well that capital and the capitalists were our enemies, and we also knew that we could overcome them only through the development of power, that is, through organization." The abandonment of millennialism, together with the acceptance of the inevitability of class divisions, made it easier for socialists to rationalize their participation in institutions to which they were theoretically opposed. The tension between theory and practice, one of the contradictions that early ideologists had attempted to transcend both morally and psychologically, now seemed tolerable.

The intellectual leaders of socialism abandoned their earlier attempts to measure society against an absolute moral standard. In the newspaper of the London cooperative movement in 1867 it was stated: "We have seen the new moral world, and we don't like it. . . ." The new guide was history itself, which pointed the way toward the day when the proletariat would be strong enough to bring about social equality. The leaders of working-class movements were no longer primarily middle-class intellectuals forced to transcend the social distance between themselves and the workers by substituting an ideological bond for concrete social solidarity.

The ideologists of the early nineteenth century had been dogmatic and authoritarian. As in today's developing areas, they were ahead of the general population in their ability to recognize and articulate the problems of economic and political modernization and they mistook this advantage for genius. As a result they tended to be rigid and quarrelsome. Owen could not get along with Owenites; Cabet was sued by his supporters for misappropriation of funds; Noyes ended his days in exile from Oneida. The next generation of leaders tended to be drawn more directly from their respective constituencies, and those intellectuals like Marx and Engels who were able to exert an influence on socialism in the second half of the century did so by adjusting the role of prophet to that of scientific observer, leading while appearing to follow, a skill that their predecessors had never managed to acquire.

This reversal reflected not only the changing role of the intellectual but also the transformation of society generally. The gap between the educated elite and the general population was narrowing with respect to education and political awareness. After 1848 the workers' movement and socialism merged effectively for the first time. Socialism became unequivocably equalitarian and democratic, while the working classes moved beyond trade union consciousness to political awareness. Nonpolitical solutions to large-scale social problems became less attractive, and millennialism lost its appeal.

Whereas early nineteenth-century social movements took on the characteristics of religious cults, their successors were far more secular. The visionary spirit of early socialism could live on within the unions and cooperative movements without inhibiting practical political action; liberalism and conservatism also lost their apocalyptic flavor and ceased to resemble revitalization movements. Their advocates no longer felt the need for ideological cohesion when a well-established class system gave them the sense of social solidarity they desired. After 1850 neither employers nor workers really needed a belief system around which to shape their lives. Once the old paternalistic hierarchy had been replaced by the new class cultures, highly articulated and ritualized ideologies seemed superfluous.

PART FIVE

FINAL RESULTS

Europeans born after 1830 belong more to the present age than they do to that of their parents. The gap between them and previous generations was more than a matter of years; it was a matter of two ages of humankind. For those who could remember the 1820s this sense of epochal transition was particularly strong; William Thackeray wrote in "De Juventate" in 1860:

> It was only yesterday; but what a gulf between now and then! Then was the old world. Stage-coaches, more or less swift, riding horses, pack-horses, highway-men, knights in armour, Norman invaders, Roman legions, Druids, Ancient Britons painted blue and so forth — all these belong to the old period. . . . But your railroad starts the new era, and we of a certain age belong to the new time and the old one. . . . We are of the age of steam.

Already in 1848 a new mentality was evident. History ceased to be a series of disastrous stops and starts and became a clearly defined evolutionary process, guided by powerful modern institutions like the factory, *the school, and the parliamentary party. The revolutions of that year were Europe's last internally generated upheavals, for the initial challenge of modernization had now been met, and European life was set in a pattern that seemed remarkably like that of the present. Chapter 12 deals with this process through the year 1870, when, with the unification of Italy and Germany, Europe assumed a recognizably contemporary political and social form.*

12

End of the Revolutionary Era, 1848–1870

The pattern of upheaval that had characterized European history from the 1780s altered dramatically in the 1850s. After the great peaks of domestic violence in 1848–1849 came the peaceful valleys of the next two decades; when violence did intrude it was in the form of war—first in the Crimea in 1854–1856, then during Italian unification in 1859, and finally in the three wars of German unification in 1864, 1866, and 1870–1871. Not only did the levels of internal violence drop, but the form of protest changed as well. Violence against the central state was much less frequent in France from 1851 onward; the same trend was noticeable in England before that time and in Germany somewhat after that date. Tax strikes and anticonscription riots were slower to pass away in parts of southern and eastern Europe, but there, too, old patterns were disappearing. Consumer protest was giving way to producer grievances, with wage strikes displacing the traditional grain riot. Nationwide movements now overshadowed local demonstrations, as trade unions and political parties became the recognized channels of popular discontent. This transition took considerable time because, until the 1850s, unionization was illegal in many parts of Europe. By 1870, however, it was clear that the ancient struggle against the state had been replaced by a contest for its power.

This remarkable shift in the goals and forms of popular agitation was the result of several converging forces, and appeared to be associated with the massive urbanization of the post-1850 decades, as well as with the advance of industrialization. An even more important factor was the transformation of the political system itself, involving both the opening of new channels to power through the recognition of mass based political parties and the legalization of trade unions, and the strengthening of the repressive power of the state. Most of all, this shift reflected the nationalization of economic and political processes that had occurred relatively early in England and France, but that was not accomplished in Germany and Italy until 1871.

The Acceleration of Economic Development

The nationalization of politics was both a cause and effect of economic and demographic integration. Beginning in the 1840s, the great impelling force of both was the railroad, a form of transport whose full commercial uses began with the Liverpool-Manchester line in 1830. So successful was the railway that by 1850 there were already fourteen thousand miles of track spread across the face of western and central Europe. The rapid growth reflected heavy investment from both private and public sources; the state was interested in rail partly for its obvious military possibilities, first demonstrated by a Prussian mobilization exercise in 1846. By 1870 there were sixty-five thousand miles of track, with trains reaching fifty miles per hour and carrying freight and passengers for much less cost than horse-drawn traffic.

The early railway frightened animals and people, as well as outraging noble landlords and city slum dwellers, both of whom were displaced by its right of way; yet, at the same time it created a lasting sense of wonderment. Thomas Macaulay wrote that

> every improvement of the means of locomotion benefits mankind morally and intellectually as well as materially . . . facilitates the interchange of the various productions of nature and art, but tends to remove national and provincial antipathies, and to bind together all the branches of the great human family. . . .

Also in England, William Greg wrote that the "most salient characteristic of life in this latter portion of the nineteenth century is its SPEED," and went on to observe how the obsession with getting places displaced the earlier concern with where the world was going, because in "a life of *haste* . . . we have no time to reflect where we have been and whither we intend to go . . . still less what is the value, and the purpose, and *the price* of what we have seen, and done, and visited."

More tangibly, the railway boom pushed the Industrial Revolution beyond textiles into a second phase of capital goods production that centered on the metal-producing and metal-working industries. Iron and steel were needed for rails and rolling stock, this need, in turn, accelerating the mining and chemical industries. Furthermore, the huge amounts of capital required by railway builders encouraged new capitalist institutions.

The creation of investment banks like the Crédit Mobilier of France
in 1852 and the Kredit Anstalt of Austria in 1856 made capital
formation easier. In England, the legalization in 1862 of limited-liability
stock companies made it possible to widen the circle of investors, because
now the individual was liable to creditors only for the amount he or
she invested.

Family firms lost importance in those new industries where huge funds
were needed, and subsequent capitalist development, centering on the metal,
chemical, and electrical sectors, would be on a vast national scale. Latecomers to industrialization, like Germany, were to rely less on individual
initiative and more on state intervention. Everywhere there was a shift in
management, with trained managers taking over from the old style owner-
operator. In mode of operation as well as in scale, big business left behind
the more personal world of the early nineteenth century. The prominent
bourgeoisie of the later nineteenth century may have retained a certain
ideological attachment to the ideal of the self-made entrepreneur, but in
practice they rapidly departed from the business practices and life-styles
of the previous generation.

The political impact of the railways was equally vast; communications
were greatly improved, and rail links were reinforced by the telegraph,
first used in 1843, and the reformed postal services. In England alone, the
number of letters posted increased six times during the period 1840–1860.
It is highly significant that Germany's first railroads, developed in the
1830s and 1840s, ran mainly east-west, thus linking Prussia with the
western German states. North-south routes were much slower to develop,
a fact that put Prussia's great rival, Austria, at a disadvantage in their long
struggle for economic hegemony over the other German states. In addition, the extensive rail nets strengthened Prussia militarily; that its armies
were able to defeat Austria in 1866 can be attributed to their superior
use of rail in mobilization and maneuver.

Railroads also smoothed the process of urbanization by breaking down
barriers between large cities and provincial centers, between city and
country, and, ultimately, within various sectors of the city itself. The
process of urbanization, a major cause of conflict between city and country before 1850, had reached the point where further, even more rapid
city growth was accepted as inevitable, even desirable. England passed the
point in 1851 where more than half its population was urban (as the
English census defined "urban districts"). Germany crossed a similar line
within the next fifty years, France only by 1930. But while there were
still large differences in urban density between western and central or
southern Europe, it now mattered less where people lived than how they
lived, because the habits and expectations we associate with urban life
were spreading even to smaller communities. After 1850 the homogeniz-
ation of consumer tastes quickened considerably. National markets replaced regional onces; mass literacy ironed out dialect differences; uniformly

produced clothing replaced folk costume. Differences in life-style tended to be more those of class than of region.

Turning to the cities themselves, we can see that by 1850 the problem of overurbanization had begun to resolve itself. Cities were growing at an even greater rate, but this growth was absorbed without disruptive results because new urban institutions developed to replace the faltering, inelastic forms of the old city. Urban expansion was becoming more a function of cities' own natural increase than of immigration. This was due to improving urban health conditions and to the disappearance of overpopulation in the countryside. In the second half of the nineteenth century, the rural population declined in absolute terms for the first time. People were now leaving the farms with no thought of returning to the soil; thus the ancient circular movement between town and country was coming to an end and the phenomenon of the "comers and the goers," the floating population, was gradually disappearing. A more permanent, settled kind of urban population was coming into being, a population better adjusted and more committed to the rhythms of modern city life.

The disappearance of the seasonal migrant, who left the city in the spring and returned when harvest was finished, was due in large part to changes in agriculture itself. A labor-intensive phase ended with the great agricultural depression of the 1870s and 1880s. Improved transportation allowed Europe to import grain and meat from Russia, the Americas, and Australia, cutting rural production and encouraging existing farms to shift to more efficient means of mechanical production. From East Elbian estates, Po valley farms, and English gardens, rural wage laborers turned to the city, never to return to the countryside.

These newcomers did not have to pioneer a new urban frontier as earlier generations had done. While old city ways of accommodating newcomers (the patriarchal household and the journeymen's hostel) had almost totally disappeared, a newer set of social and employment agencies better adjusted to class society in an industrial age now replaced them. Especially in the industrial towns, the post-1850 generation of immigrants benefited from the fact that members of family and community had preceded them. Instead of wandering the streets in search of cheap lodging, they ordinarily went directly to someone they knew who was expecting them. In working-class communities, young people "claiming kin" were welcomed, given a place to stay, and, when times were good, opportunity for employment. In towns like Preston and Saint Etienne, factory owners encouraged workers to recommend relatives because this guaranteed a steady, loyal work force. Similarly, family and friends acted as informal employment agencies for domestic servants, the largest category of female employment in large cities. Remembered one middle-class matron: "Many a younger sister has come to our house, to find a place and remained till she could hear of a promising one."

The laboring poor solved problems of housing in the same way. They

were not adverse to taking in boarders because these additional contrib-
utors allowed families to rent better accommodations than they would
have been able to afford as a small nuclear unit. Large kin groups were
found to be an asset in the big city. Children, who in the rural areas had
been forced out of the home at a very early age, were staying with their
parents until their late teens. Old people, for whom there had been no
useful role in peasant society, were now invited into households as cooks
and babysitters, substituting for mothers out at work. Instead of dis-
integrating, the family was adapting to the urban environment, redefining
itself but managing to bring order out of disorder in the face of great odds.
By the second half of the nineteenth century, even the lowly London
Irish had achieved a semblance of settled existence despite crowded conditions. Wordsworth's "endless stream of men and moving things" had
settled into a connected pattern of life; and in the slum districts of the
cotton towns R. Parkinson saw a strong sense of neighborhood emerge:

> There is an acquaintance with each other arising from having been
> born or brought up in the same street; having worked for the same
> master; attended the same place of worship; or even from having
> seen the same face, now grown "old and familiar," though the name
> and even the occupation of the individual might be unknown alto-
> gether, passing one's door at wonted hours, from work to meal, from
> meal to work, with a punctuality which implied regular and steady
> habits, and was itself a sufficient testimony of character.

Neighborhoods were now almost completely segregated by class, but
this, too, added to their stability. By the 1850s it was very rare for persons of different means to inhabit the same building. The middle-class
drift to the suburbs had been occurring for more than fifty years, but
what finally put an end to old residence patterns were the changes within
the center of the city itself, the result of both economic and political
development. The final decay of the old urban craft structure meant that
connection between residence and place of work was effectively severed.
Some small-scale artisans still lived above their shops, but as larger retail
outlets took over the marketing of goods most no longer sold directly to
the consumer. Tailors, for example, found themselves working for those
who sold their work for them to the new ready-made clothing stores that
were a prominent retailing innovation of the second half of the nineteenth
century. Itinerant hawkers gave way to department stores that were becoming part of the new shopping districts of major cities.

The Stabilization of Urban Life

The "retail revolution" had much to do with the transformation of the
center of the city, but railroads were an equally powerful force in several
ways. First of all, the intrusion of railways into the great cities, beginning

with London in the 1830s and extending to the Continent in the 1840s, caused massive relocation of people, mainly the poor. Lines were cut through the crowded low-rent districts, where fewer legal and economic obstacles were encountered. Dickens described the wide railway cuts in London in geological terms:

> The first shock of a great earthquake had, just at the period, rent the whole neighborhood to its centre. Traces of its course were visible on everyside. Houses were knocked down; streets broken through and stopped . . . mounds of ashes blocked up rights of way, and wholly changed the law and customs of the neighborhood. In short, the yet unfinished and unopened railroad was in progress, and, from the very core of this dire disorder, trailed smoothly away upon its mighty course for civilization and improvement.

At first evicted renters clung close to their old jobs and lodgings, making the overcrowding of the center of the cities even greater than before. Ultimately, however, the finished railways had the effect of draining away population, because they made it possible for workers to commute to their jobs and thus to move away from the center of the city. This movement of population from the center to new working-class districts at the edges proceeded slowly. Railway fares were at first too expensive for most workers. Not until 1864 did the London railways introduce a workers' fare, and even then it was not until the 1880s that cheaper rates became universal. For a long time it was only the better-paid skilled workers who could afford to separate home and work. The unskilled, casual labor force continued to live close to the docks, warehouses, and factories in overcrowded, unhealthy conditions.

However, the centralization of city populations had now been checked and even reversed. Birmingham's city center lost population in the 1850s and the rebuilding of Paris, which involved cutting great boulevards through the slums, had effects similar to railroad construction on many of that city's older, denser quarters. From our perspective, the resulting urban sprawl seems hardly more desirable, but we tend to forget the terrible effects in terms of health, underemployment, and tension that social compression had created. Perhaps most important of all, the second half of the century saw industrialization finally synchronize with urbanization, so that cities like Barmen in Germany could finally drop their restrictions on immigration and welcome workers from the surrounding countryside. As employment opportunities caught up with population, Europe's struggle with overurbanization was at an end. Henceforth, cities seemed to be able to expand infinitely without undue stress or strain.

Industrialization also helped solve the other major problem of the pre-1850 period, namely, the disturbing hegemony of capital cities over the provinces. Although their remarkable growth began in the 1820s, England's provincial industrial centers were not sufficiently developed to challenge London until at least two decades later. By that time, the large numbers of provincial cities with population over one hundred thousand, plus their economic vitality and civic pride, had redressed the balance. "France, Germany, and the Netherlands do not exhibit provincial towns to be compared to Manchester, Glasgow, Birmingham, Sheffield or Leeds," boasted one person from England. While it was true that other nations were slower to develop so strong a city system, each extension of the Continental railway system from the 1840s onward tended to diminish the hegemony of the capitals, lessening the drain of intellectuals from the provinces and thus encouraging first provincial and then national culture.

Railroads made it possible, for example, for students to return home more regularly, thereby reducing the impact of the "intellectual proletariat" that had earlier plagued both Berlin and Paris. Exchanges of services and goods between capital and province became easier, with the result that old barriers were broken down. Railroads also made the great cities more accessible to the countryside, as was demonstrated in 1848 when rural elements brought in by train helped crush the June Days uprisings. In the short run, modern communications may have heightened fear of the great cities, but their long-term effect, politically as well as militarily, was to build national unity and repeal the old capital-provincial division. For England, the Great Exhibition of 1851 in London marked a turning point in this respect, for it became a truly national event when an estimated 17 percent of the English population visited its exhibits.

In the early nineteenth century, the provinces feared the hegemony of the capitals. Now more confident of their own strength, they were ready to encourage the capitals in a different kind of conquest, namely, external imperialism. It was not by accident that it was the second Napoleonic emperor who convinced the French to rebuild Paris as a symbol of national power. The redesign of Berlin and Vienna followed the same formula: appeal to national pride in an age of growing international competition. Even conservative landowner Otto von Bismarck, who in 1848 had spoken of Berlin as if it were a cancer, viewed the capital as the keystone of political order once he had established himself as Imperial Germany's master in the 1870s.

Cities were less likely to be described in pathological terms after 1850. Indicators of the urban population's physical health were more favorable, though sanitary reform proceeded very slowly. A rising standard of living in the second half of the century probably did more than anything else to diminish the mortality rate. Urbanites ate better because improved transportation restored fresh meats and vegetables to their markets. Housing improved only gradually, and although most of the poor still lived in inadequate dwellings, at least the skilled workers were able to obtain better housing in the suburbs. In addition, the provision of schools finally began to catch up with need, although as late as 1871 London was over one hundred thousand places short. There remained pockets of appalling poverty in all European cities, and as late as 1900 it was found that as much as 30 percent of the population of York was living below the subsistence level.

Despite persistent poverty, however, the cities were no longer viewed as the breeders of social disorder. While preindustrial insititutions of social control had almost entirely disappeared by 1870, they no longer left a vacuum. We have seen how the working-class family, once it adjusted to new urban conditions, fulfilled its role toward newcomers. The work of Adolf Kolping among Catholic working men in Cologne led to a network of church sponsored hostels. Protestants followed suit, and in England George Williams started in 1844 an association for bachelors that he called the Young Men's Christian Association. The revival of the French *compagnonnages* (journeymen's associations) had run its course by the 1840s, but efforts at providing for the unattached men and women were carried forward by the Society of St. Vincent de Paul, founded in 1835.

The working classes proved adept at providing for themselves through their trade unions, cooperative societies, and self-education endeavors. The 1860s and 1870s saw the emergence of a rich mixture of voluntary associations concerned with every aspect of life from cradle to grave. The kind of associational structures that grew up in the cities were undoubtedly a cause of the decline of drunkenness and violence that took place after 1850. More efficient policing of the cities also had something to do with this, but a much larger share of the credit must go to the remarkable voluntary efforts, particularly among the working classes themselves.

During the 1840s Manchester was the "shock city" of the Western world, visited and reviled by almost every major social critic of the age, from the conservative Alexis de Tocqueville to the young radical Friedrich Engels. Yet little more than a decade later, attitudes had shifted significantly. In *Chambers' Edinburgh Journal*, of 1858, Manchester's virtues were almost as visible as its blemishes:

> Manchester streets may be irregular, and its trading inscriptions pretentious, its smoke may be dense, and its mud ultra-muddy, but not any or all of these things can prevent the image of a great city rising before us as the very symbol of civilization, foremost in the march of improvement, a grand incarnation of progress.

Symbols of degradation and disorder associated with the early nineteenth-century city were still the stock and trade of urban imagery, yet they had lost their previous apocalyptic associations. Crime and poverty had become problems to be solved rather than omens of future disaster. When Queen Victoria visited Manchester in 1851, she dutifully observed "a painfully unhealthy-looking population" but one that was surprisingly respectful:

> The streets were immensely full, and the cheering and enthusiasm most gratifying. The order and good behavior of the people, who

were not placed behind any barriers, were the most complete we have seen in our many progressions through capitals and cities— London, Glasgow, Dublin, Edinburgh, etc. . . .

The notion of the "dangerous classes" was losing currency, not so much because the professional criminal and prostitute were disappearing, but because the ordinary laboring poor were less involved. The respectable working class was less likely to rub shoulders with the thief. The new industrial centers, which offered an abundance of female employment, had lower levels of prostitution than the older cities, where the surplus of young women, casually and poorly employed, had been forced on the streets. Respectable folk deliberately removed themselves from the rough sports and low life of taverns and flophouses to organize a variety of team sports and evening entertainments of their own. This was how the English music halls began in the 1850s, with customers providing the music themselves. In a similar manner, sports developed as a means of self-improvement. In the 1860s regulations were imposed on football and it was in 1867 that the famous Queensberry Rules of boxing were instituted. From that time, both sport and entertainment became increasingly commercialized, but for the moment, both represented a lively, spontaneous urban culture that met the needs of the working classes.

It was also at midcentury that public executions were finally abandoned, creating a vacuum in the excitement of urban life that was conveniently filled by the advent of the popular newspaper. In 1854 the *Times* of London was circulating about fifty-five thousand copies daily; in 1867 the city's popular *Daily Telegraph* had surpassed two hundred thousand daily.The public face of the city was also changing. During the 1840s, the Prussian king had sponsored the restoration of the Cathedral of Cologne as a symbol of his feudal allegiances. By contrast, the new conservatives, beginning with Napoleon III, showed no reluctance to tear down the old in order to build a stable new order. The reconstruction of Paris carried out in the 1850s was aimed at clearing away narrow streets that had been used by insurrectionaries in 1848. At the same time, the new wide arteries of the city advanced its economic development. City boosters finally found a substitute for court pageantry in the series of exhibitions begun in London in 1851. Not to be outdone, Paris staged its own Universal Exhibition in 1855, beginning a competition that reached its peak with the Paris Exhibition of 1889, for which Gustave Eiffel built the famous tower. Thus, this great city became a symbol of both national political and economic power.

The Consolidation of the Upper Classes

The growth of cities reflected the achievement of a worldwide agricultural revolution. European agriculture remained strong during the period 1850-1870 but it was then thrown into disastrous depression. Its farmers could not compete with the cheaper food imported from Russia and the Americas, a cause of rural depopulation though not the only one. Competition forced larger landowners to become more efficient, to use fertilizers and machines that cut into employment. This time there was little popular resistance to mechanization, for people had begun to leave the land in increasing numbers in the 1850s. The age of rural resistance—of rick burning and land occupation—was clearly over as millions turned their backs both on agricultural employment and rural craft industries.

Despite the massive move to the cities, factory employment did not automatically swallow up the entire population. In England, the factories' share of the work force remained about the same during the period 1850–1870 as it had in the preceding period. Related fields like mining, transport, and building grew much faster. Domestic service and shop-keeping also registered significant gains, mainly at the expense of agriculture. Artisan and domestic manufacturing did not disappear overnight, and in Germany and France the small workshop remained dominant, even as late as 1900. As in earlier phases of industrialization, the growth of factories tended to spur a parallel growth of domestic work, particularly the low-wage "sweated" trades, such as tailoring and shoemaking. In cities like London and Vienna, the putting-out system still accounted for a large share of women's labor.

Yet the artisans and small owner-operators of the 1850s and 1860s were not in the same position as their *sans-culotte* forerunners. Their communal and corporate identity had all but disappeared. With the final abolition of guild structures in Germany, the artisans there had to choose between becoming self-employed small business people or joining the wage-earning proletariat. Many English and French as well as German artisans managed to accomplish the formei, becoming the core of what we call the modern lower-middle class. Others found business competition too stiff and opted for the relatively greater security of a clerk's job or simply sank into the proletariat. One German master baker put it this way: "What good is it to a poor shoemaker or tailor that he has the right to become a banker or cloth manufacturer or to establish a factory, to climb to the moon, when I cannot do it?"

The old lower-middle strata were rapidly being expanded by a new lower-middle class, composed of clerks, schoolteachers, and lesser officials of all sorts. They were like the traditional *sans-culottes* in that they aligned themselves socially with neither the rich nor the poor, but they lacked the former's concrete fraternal associations, largely because they no longer shared a common corporate or communal tradition. If Parisians, they were more likely to live in the new suburbs than in the traditional insurrectionary locales like the Faubourg Saint Antoine. The skilled elements of the new working class tended to perpetuate some of the old sense of fraternity within the trade union movement, but they had little in common with the clerks and schoolteachers.

Until the twentieth century, the lower-middle class possessed nothing like the cohesion that characterized the wealthier industrial and professional middle class. The landowning elites would face economic disaster during the agricultural depression of the 1870s, but the urban bourgeoisie were thriving. Their numbers grew faster than the population as a whole. If the solid middle class can be defined as the servant-keeping class, then the growth of the number of domestic servants after 1850 can be a measure of its expansion. In England, the number of servants rose 28 percent, more than double the pace of the population at large. Servant keeping was only one aspect of the conspicuous consumption that set off the prosperous bourgeoisie from the less fortunate. The self-made individuals of the early nineteenth century were giving way to a new, status-conscious generation who, while they still stressed the ethic of hard work, were beginning to invest at least some of their resources in their own pleasures.

Leisure pursuits such as dance and sport, which had once been confined to the aristocracy, were now shared by the wealthy regardless of title. Children of the middle class were flooding the traditional enclaves of the aristocracy—the elite schools, universities, and the military—and the fraternity of schoolmates was carried over into careers, club life, and military service. In Germany the reserve officer corps, an institution that had previously divided the Junkers from the middle classes, now united them. Everywhere the wealthier middle class (referred to henceforth as the upper-middle class) was giving up its effort to replace the old aristocracy and began to join them in their favorite occupations. Because the landowning elites were falling on hard times due to the problems of agriculture, they were now more willing to admit the nouveau riche. Through marriage and career, a new upper class came into being.

The aggressive, moralistic stage of middle-class culture was beginning to wane at mid-century. By then the middle classes had ceased to be "new men" socially or politically. Once they began to establish their power, to develop kin ties and patronage connections, they could relax the emphasis on personal and class self-reliance. First the French and then the British and Germans began to restrict their family size, in part because large numbers of children were beginning to conflict with the more luxurious life-style popular among the wealthier bourgeoisie. Also, as they began to adopt the grander style previously associated with the aristocracy, children became a more expensive item. Keeping up with the Joneses meant larger dowries for daughters and expensive schooling for sons. Even among the wealthy, the individual child's chances were diminished if there were too many siblings. Thus the middle class began to cut its birth rate, thereby easing the problem of surplus sons and daughters. Child-rearing practices became less strenuous, women were liberated from prolonged childbearing, and men ceased to be so tyrannical at home. By the 1850s there were signs that the bourgeoisie were turning over to the schools more of the socialization process. Childhood and adolescent experience therefore became less repressed and lonely. While self-reliance was still upheld, there was a tendency for middle-class norms to merge with those of the aristocracy, especially when the interests of these two groups were challenged by an increasingly militant working class.

The Institutions of the Working Class

Together the upper-middle class and the aristocracy constituted no more than 5 percent of European society in 1870. The growing lower-middle class may have accounted for as much as 20 percent; thus the laboring classes constituted the remaining 75 percent. Of these, perhaps 15 percent can be counted as skilled workers, the rest having no particular training. As the top of society began to close ranks, the identity of the working class became more sharply outlined. It is important to note, however, that only a minority of all workers were employed in factories, and of these only a minority were in the skilled category that could command regular, well-paid employment. Most workers would hold a number of different jobs over their lifetime. For the vast majority, income fluctuated wildly according to age, sex, season, and just plain luck. For them, as for the poor before them, life itself remained very uncertain. Death rates were oppressively high, particularly among infants, and consequently, birth rates remained high at a time when other groups, first the middle classes and then the skilled workers, were lowering their fertility rate.

However, even the poor had benefited from the general lowering of adolescent and adult death rates, from the disappearance of certain types of epidemic diseases, and from the leveling off of food prices. Up to 1850 food prices fluctuated wildly, increasing 400 and 500 percent in times of bad harvest. Although cereal prices rose gradually during the period 1850–1870, surpluses and improved transportation prevented a repetition of violent increases in prices. At a time when Prussian workers were still spending about two-thirds of their income on food alone (depending on size of family), the stabilization of food prices constituted a very real gain; so, too, did the improved quality of diet available. Meat consumption in Germany rose from 13.7 kilograms per person per year in the early nineteenth century to more than twice that amount by 1871. The Crimean War spurred canning techniques, and the discoveries by Louis Pasteur in the 1850s led to expanded production of all dairy products. Instead of competing with foreign grain, European farming was able to shift to animal husbandry and thereby maintain some of its former prosperity while at the same time increasing the amount of protein in the ordinary diet.

It has been estimated that in England during the 1860s real wages rose by as much as 35 percent for skilled workers and somewhat less for unskilled and agrarian labor. In France and Germany, the late 1860s and early 1870s brought similar improvement as wages steadily pushed ahead of prices, though, of course, this improvement was not evenly distributed. The income gap between the middle and working classes widened enormously at this time and there is no reason to think that the grip of poverty was greatly loosened for the vast majority. Unskilled males, females, and the elderly of both sexes suffered structural unemployment. Steady jobs were still exceptional and the notion of a "career" was confined to the middle classes.

Surveys of poverty in London made in the 1880s indicated that no less than 30 percent of the population was living below the poverty line at any given moment in time. An even larger proportion of Londoners (an estimated six out of seven workers) experienced destitution at some time in their lives, especially when young or very old. Families with large numbers of children were most likely to find themselves impoverished because of the low income of the father. Elderly people had no social security apart from their children, who were often too burdened themselves to provide much support; thus, families and individuals went through cycles of poverty quite independent of the recurrent trade depressions that affected society at large.

Only the top 15 percent of the working class could expect, barring accident, illness, or depression, to ride above the poverty line, for they were the only ones able to save, to afford decent housing and the new commercial forms of leisure. Significantly, they were also the first among the laboring classes to limit fertility, and they were more likely to send their children to school beyond the elementary grades. The fact that they could afford some middle-class amenities did not mean they identified with the bourgeoisie, however; in fact, it was from this same group of skilled workers that the new trade union leadership of the 1860s was recruited. Unions had been legal in England since 1824 and by 1850 they already had 1.5 million members. Expansion in the next two decades was even more impressive, but it took place almost entirely within the skilled trades, mining, and to a lesser extent, transportation. Much the same was true in France, where unionization was tolerated in 1864, and in Germany where clandestine organizing among skilled workers increased during the same period.

Before 1850 strike activity outside England had been almost entirely defensive in nature. Workers united in hard times to defend themselves against wage cutting, and because they could easily be replaced, they often lost these battles. However, after 1850 the strike became an offensive weapon for the improvement of wages and working conditions. Skilled workers were learning to wait for times of high employment to make their demands. They no longer thought in terms of maintaining a customary standard of living, but of improving things for themselves. They were adapting to the realities of the market mechanism of supply and demand, wisely using periods when workers were scarce to strike for greater benefits. Similar sophistication was evident in the revival of workers' political movements that had been dormant since the 1848 period. In 1864 English trade unionists invited their Continental colleagues to London to discuss coordination of tactics. There the First International was formed.

This shift to national and even international organization by the skilled working class was all the more significant, because prior to 1850 it had often been those same groups that had led movements protesting the intrusion of national markets and central government. This remarkable reorientation reflected not only the displacement of the old artisan communal and corporate identities, but also the growth of a mature class consciousness within the framework of national politics. *Sans-culotte*-type radicalism—spontaneous, intensely localized, defensive—was passing, and among the first to grasp this change were Karl Marx and Friedrich Engels. They came to realize that the *sans-culotte* struggle against a national market and the central state was futile and that the workers' movement had to adopt a program of working with history rather than against it. Engels later wrote:

> The time is past for revolutions carried through by small minorities at the head of unconscious masses. When it gets to be a matter of the complete transformation of social organizations, the masses themselves must participate, must understand what is at stake. . . .

During the 1850s and 1860s, Marx and his followers fought to impose their view of history on the utopians and anarchists who had previously dominated socialism and on those radicals who stood in the Jacobin or *sans-culotte* tradition of revolution. It was a measure of their success that at the meetings of the First International Marx was able to exclude the millennialistic followers of Owen and Mazzini. The Proudhonist and Bakuninist factions, the direct descendents of the *sans-culotte* tradition of direct democracy and local independence, proved more difficult to defeat, because they represented those areas of Europe, notably Spain and Italy, but also France, where industrialism and nationalization were making slower progress. Nevertheless, the International did adopt Marx's view that the working classes must not fight against the state but turn it to their own purposes. They voted for legislating factory acts and other ameliorative measures, convinced by Marx: "In putting through such laws the working class does not strengthen the ruling classes. On the contrary, it transforms them from operating against the workers into becoming their agents."

By 1870 there was a momentous change in the way Europeans regarded history. The ideologists of the early nineteenth century tried to transcend it through apocalyptic visions of a golden age. The effort to escape history was natural enough to those groups like the déclassé intellectuals and *sans-culottes* who were a part of a dying social order, but both the industrial bourgeoisie and the urban working classes of the 1860s evaluated history from an entirely different position. They embraced change, even became obsessed with it to the point that they no longer struggled violently against the existing order of things. Even the radical socialists came to accept the idea that industrial capitalism had to run its course before a social republic could be accomplished. Once the idea of history as progress had been implanted, the concept of revolutionary apocalypse ceased to appeal. Earlier revolutions had so accustomed Europeans to the idea of rapid change that the necessity of insurrection was no longer so apparent. Thinking history on their side, even the most impatient were now willing to wait out the long-term millennium.

The Professionalization of Culture

The intellectual ferment that had characterized earlier decades was dissipating. Writing in the 1830s, Balzac observed that "the new barbarians are the intellectuals." By the 1860s, however, Matthew Arnold had the intellectuals on the other side of the barricades; in *Culture and Anarchy*, which he wrote in 1869, he portrayed them as the defenders of the social order. This turnabout reflected the effort after 1848 by all professions to reform themselves and thus deprive "democrats and socialists . . . of a special grievance." The English civil service reformer Sir Charles Trevelyan remembered that "the revolutionary period of 1848 gave us a shake and created a disposition to put our house in order."

The three learned professions—law, medicine, and the clergy—had finally reacted to attacks on their privileged position by reforming themselves. The bar reconciled the ancient conflict between the genteel barristers and the lower-status attorneys and solicitors by improving the pay and standards of the latter. In other professions the level of education also improved and uniform standards of licensing were introduced. Radical agitation by young German lawyers in 1848 forced governments there to improve employment prospects in the civil service. In England, too, there was a move afoot to substitute examinations for patronage, in this case to satisfy Queen Victoria's fear that a new generation of democratic politicians would use the old system to "fill the public offices with low people without breeding or feelings of gentlemen." The examinations favored the wealthy university trained, thus serving to maintain the elite composition of the civil service.

Reacting to similar pressures, medicine also was changing. Since 1770 the existing group of privileged physicians had been besieged by surgeons, apothecaries, and midwives, all demanding equal status; the latter were "trades" in the preindustrial sense. English surgeons had separated themselves from barbers only in 1745, but by 1800 they had their own Royal

College of Surgeons. Like all the lesser professions, they were eager to protect themselves from being reduced to the status of trades. During the period 1770–1850, there was severe competition between them and the practitioners of folk medicine, "worm and water doctors, bone setters, and others, whose name is Legion." By 1850 the medical profession had won out by legislating national licensing standards, and with the exception of the female midwives, who were reduced to the status of wage labor by the male medical professions, the lesser branches of medicine had made themselves respectably middle class.

The new British Medical Association and the French Academy of Medicine, founded in 1832 and 1820 respectively, served as models for the other learned "trades" wishing to gain the status of professionals. Engineers, architects, accountants, and teachers found they, too, could attain financial and social security by forming professional associations, excluding the less qualified, and setting standards of ethics to guard against commercial quacks and charlatans. In France, engineering became a profession as early as the 1850s; in England, where engineering was closer to the craft tradition, the process took longer. But the British census did list engineers as professionals in 1861 and architects in 1881. Accountants, notaries, teachers, even the lowly journalists followed soon after. As they were elevated to this new status, all social indentification with the trades dissolved and they became fully identified with the middle class.

Chief among the ways used by the professions to raise their status was the substitution of formal secondary education for the traditional apprenticeship. The period 1840–1870 saw an enormous increase in secondary schools all over Europe; in France the annual number of secondary diplomas rose from thirty-two hundred to seventy-two hundred in this period. In England this was the era of the rebirth of the boarding schools (called public schools); headmaster Edward Thring could report that "hundreds now go to schools who thirty years ago would not have thought of doing so. This learning to be responsible, and independent, to bear pain, to play games, to drop ranks, and wealth and home luxury, is a priceless boon."

Elite secondary schools served to create a new upper class by bridging the previous division between the aristocracy and the industrial middle class, and the middle classes were now willing to tolerate aristocracy as long as it was an aristocracy of merit. "Let them govern," said one liberal, "but let them be fit to govern." Students were becoming aware of their elite status and so less likely to be rebellious. The schools, with their separation of the sexes and cloistered atmosphere, created a new definition of adolescence that was passive and apolitical. After 1848 students everywhere ceased to play an active part in politics; school and university were to be preparation for the world, not a part of it. Games and competitive examinations channeled youth's energies; within the confines of middle-class cultural institutions, intellectual achievement became highly

individualized and the connection between learning and social commitment was thereby broken.

With the decline of apprenticeship and the elevation of many of the
subprofessions from the status of trades to that of learned enterprises, the
barriers between intellectuals and the working classes became increasingly
insurmountable. The era of the self-educated person was over, because
with the industrialization of culture knowledge became so specialized and
abstract that formal education was a necessity. Until free secondary
education became the right of every child in the mid-twentieth century,
access to academic culture and the professions was effectively restricted
to middle- and upper-class people who could afford to pay for culture as
a commodity. Even the few working people who did manage to rise
through education's competitive process found they were forced to abandon their native culture, sometimes even their native tongue. As education
became a primary mode of individual mobility after 1850, it also became
increasingly detached from the older concept of cultivation and more a
way of inculcating certain ideas and habits. The moral and communal
functions of learning, as stressed by both the *sans-culottes* and the utopians, took second place to the development of highly specialized scientific disciplines.

The gap between the cultures of different social classes had become so
pronounced that by 1870 many people talked as if "culture," identified
now with elite education and the upper classes, was rapidly disassociating
itself from "civilization," the term used to describe the practical concerns
of the general population. As for the intellectuals, they were increasingly
contemptuous of civilization, which they described as materialistic and
demeaning. In turn, the leaders of the working class viewed intellectuals
with increasing suspicion. There were still those like John Ruskin, Richard
Wagner, Matthew Arnold, and Gottfried Semper who hoped through the
arts to introduce beauty and goodness to industrial society, but unlike the
avant-garde of earlier generations they preferred to experiment on a small
scale rather than carry their artistic radicalism into the political sphere.

The English Pre-Raphaelite Brotherhood was a direct product of the
Revolution of 1848, but while it dedicated its artistic endeavors to a social
purpose, its members remained fearful of socialism as such. Ruskin's Saint
George's Guild (1871–1881) was another example of the attempt to place
art at the service of humanity, but it, too, was an entirely elite venture.
Except for a few rare spirits like Gustave Courbet and William Morris,
most artists and writers were unwilling to grapple with the realities of the
new industrial order and were completely out of touch with the working
classes. Morris, who became one of the leading English converts to Marxism, was especially critical of the elitist avant-garde notion of the intellectual leading the masses:

> The world is everywhere growing uglier and more commonplace, in
> spite of the conscious and very strenuous efforts of a small group of

people toward the revival of art, which are so obviously out of joint with the tendency of the age, that while the uncultivated have not even heard of them, the mass of the cultivated look upon them as a joke. . . .

Among intellectuals the role of prophet gave way to that of expert. After 1850 the separation of art and politics became especially pronounced through the art for art's sake movement. The avant-garde lost its political meaning and became involved in what it has been concerned with almost ever since, that is, a desperate race to keep ahead of change rather than an effort to guide history in socially useful directions. Henceforth, intellectuals would talk about a "revolution in painting" or a "revolution in medicine," while in reality culture and revolution went their separate ways, to be reunited only much later at the time of the Russian Revolution.

The Unification of Italy

The leadership of the radical left was changing after 1850 and so, too, was the nature of European conservatism; resistance to change was giving way to the desire to control and shape events for conservative purposes. In England, reform had become part of the Tory platform. Pressure for extension of the franchise had been building during the 1860s and when rioting broke out in 1866, in London, the conservative government of Benjamin Disraeli took the leadership of reform. The Voting Act of 1867 broadened the suffrage to include not only most of the urban middle classes but also large numbers of tax-paying skilled workers. Passage was, as Disraeli himself put it:

a leap in the dark, but I have the greatest confidence in the sound sense of my fellow-countrymen, and I entertain a strong hope that the extended franchise which we are now conferring upon them will be the means of placing the institutions of this country on a firmer basis . . . will tend to increase the loyalty and contentment of a great portion of her Majesty's subjects.

Conservatives were now willing to advocate radical changes, even nationalism, when it suited their purposes. The unification of Germany and of Italy had seemed an unfulfillable dream prior to 1848, with the nationalists a distinct minority—mainly radical intellectuals who found themselves confronted with the unyielding power of the established states. Yet by 1870 the governments of these same states had become the allies of nationalism. What words had not been able to accomplish was done by the sword, and conservatives, who had previously been the strongest defenders of localism, picked up and carried the banner of nationalism, once the banner of the radical left.

It was no accident that Napoleon III, France's second emperor in less than fifty years, was the model for this new brand of conservatism. Louis Napoleon rose to power in a manner reminiscent of his uncle's career, first in alliance with the left when he was elected president of the Second Republic in December 1848 as much for his vague socialist reputation as for his program of law and order. Initially his most dangerous enemies were the monarchists; when they blocked his re-election to the presidency in 1851, he prepared a coup to confirm his power. This coup, on December 2, 1851, provoked widespread resistance, particularly in the southeastern provinces of France, where dedicated republicans capitalized on the traditional peasant distrust of centralized power to raise the flag of insurrection. This was brutally put down and ten thousand persons were exiled to Algeria. At the same time, however, Napoleon conciliated his enemies by promising universal suffrage and progressive reforms.

Over 90 percent of the French population ratified his coup in the plebiscite that followed, and a year later he felt strong enough to exchange the title of president for that of emperor, becoming officially Napoleon III. Again his move was ratified by plebiscite, and for the next eighteen years he ruled what amounted to a form of constitutional monarchy, encouraging economic growth, sponsoring urban renewal, and by the 1860s, granting rights of free press, assembly, and unionization. In 1868 he was even prepared to grant the legislature considerable influence over the executive, a concession that even the most liberal regimes of the early nineteenth century had been reluctant to consider.

This blend of conservatism and social reform was perhaps congenial to a descendent of the first Napoleon, who had taught Europe how to buttress an authoritarian regime with concessions to political and economic modernization. Yet even strongly legitimist regimes were beginning to follow a similar strategy during the 1850s and 1860s; in Prussia, the Revolution of 1848 was not followed by the usual sort of reaction. The conservative Manteuffel ministry retained the liberal constitution of 1850 and made no effort to return to the old estates system, even though the Hohenzollern king yearned for its restoration.

When Count Camillo Cavour became prime minister of the Kingdom of Piedmont in 1852, he, too, moved ahead with modernization, steps that soon made that state the magnet for liberal and nationalist hopes in Italy. Even the Austrian Empire did not lapse back into feudalism after 1848, and conservatives, who in the pre-1850 period had been reluctant to recognize centralized government as necessary, were now embracing its powers. This undoubtedly reflected economic and social changes working to break down particularism, but it also demonstrated an instinct for political survival under the pressure of international modernization. Prussia's Catholic Rhine province ceased to talk of separatism after 1850, mainly because that area was becoming so firmly linked by rail and trade to the eastern parts of the kingdom. The Revolutions of 1848 saw the last great outburst of resistance to central authority in both western and central Europe. Thereafter, tax and conscription riots, centrifugal movements of all kinds, rapidly disappeared. The expansion of communication had much to do with this, but it was also the result of changing political strategies on the part of groups previously opposed to national integration.

It is indicative of the enormous changes occurring at midcentury that nationalism became respectable even among conservatives. As a political instrument it changed hands from the radical left to moderate liberalism and, finally, to conservatism. Count Cavour, the Piedmontese liberal-conservative, was one of the first to grasp its possibilities. Upon assuming office in 1852, he outlined his program: "You will see, gentlemen, how reforms carried out in time, instead of weakening authority, reinforce it; instead of precipitating revolution, they prevent it." Cavour set out to transform Piedmont into a constitutional monarchy with an economic base favorable to industrialization, and the kingdom rapidly became the center for Italian nationalists on the run after the disasters of 1848.

Cavour tolerated the formation of the Italian National Society under the leadership of Daniele Manin because Manin's concept of nationalism differed fundamentally from Mazzini's variation of the pre-1848 period. The National Society had purged its program of the ideological elements of the old revolutionary nationalism; its members were willing to work through existing political institutions to achieve unification and, therefore, were not a threat to the Piedmontese state. Furthermore, their nationalism was purged of social content, those vague socialist yearnings of Mazzini that frightened away bourgeois support. Italian nationalism was thereby split roughly along class lines, with the industrial middle classes supporting the Manin version, while the original millennialistic nationalism of the aging Mazzini and his follower Giuseppe Garibaldi continued to be supported by a coalition of radical intellectuals and members of the lower classes.

Conservatives like Cavour could work with, even capitalize on the new, nonideological nationalism. It was used to build up the regime of Victor Emmanuel II in the eyes of Italians, while in return Piedmont committed itself to serve the purpose of unification. Cavour began not with radical rhetoric, but with careful military and diplomatic preparation, currying favor with France for the purpose of offsetting the traditional enemy of Italian unity, Austria. In June 1858 he met secretly with Napoleon III at Plombières to make a deal that would give Piedmont hegemony over northern Italy in return for giving the boundary states of Nice and Savoy to France. In any future war with Austria, France would aid Piedmont in establishing the unity of northern Italy, and its southern regions would be transformed into a confederation under the guidance of the Pope.

Now that the French alliance was confirmed, Cavour's only problem was how to provoke war with Austria; however, the Austrians solved this for him by invading in 1859. French help was forthcoming and the Austrians were pushed back, though Napoleon III was forced by international pressures to back out of the war, leaving Cavour and the Piedmontese short of their ultimate military and political objectives. Despite some territorial gains made by Piedmont in the subsequent Peace of Villafranca, Italian unification appeared to have been frustrated once again. This time, however, Italian nationalists did not have to wait long; war had shaken the existing northern Italian states and members of the National Society were able to seize control of them. Using the plebiscite technique to good advantage, they arranged pledges of allegiance to Piedmont. Northern and southern Italy remained divided, however, and it was not until the Mazzinian adventurer Garibaldi led the famous Expedition of the Thousand to Sicily in 1860 to liberate that area from foreign Bourbon rule that a southern solution was forthcoming. Cavour feared that the forces of Garibaldi, representing the old revolutionary nationalism, might sweep the country, endangering not only the reactionary states but his own moderate regime. Thus, Victor Emmanuel was forced to lead Piedmontese forces into the south to take command of the situation. He linked up with the Garibaldian movement near Rome in September 1860 and there the king and the popular hero shook hands in a symbolic demonstration of social and national unity.

In subsequent months a somewhat truncated version of Italian unification was hammered out. While the radical nationalists wished to claim Rome, Cavour excluded it for the time being, knowing that any move against the Pope would provoke French intervention. Venice was also excluded because of fear of Austria; thus, when the Kingdom of Italy was declared in March 1861, millennialistic hopes were bound to be disappointed. Yet the same military and diplomatic skill that had brought Cavour this far did not fail him. Venice was obtained when Italy sided with Prussia in the Austro-Prussian War of 1866, and Rome was "liberated" when Prussia defeated France in the Franco-Prussian War of 1870–1871, thus leaving the Pope at the mercy of his old enemies. (See the map of Europe in 1871 on page 280.)

The Italy that came into being was a faithful reproduction of the politics that had created it. Like Piedmont, it was a constitutional monarchy dominated by bourgeois and aristocratic interests; the vast majority of the poor were excluded from the franchise. Italians had gained their national liberty, but not the equality and fraternity that had been so much a part of nationalism's earlier vision. Yet most Italians seemed willing to pay this price as long as national unity brought tangible economic benefits. As the industrial progress promised by Cavour began to be achieved in the 1870s and 1880s, the coalition of liberal bureaucrats and capitalist interests that had been primarily responsible for unification could sweep aside those critics on the left who mourned the loss of nationalism's earlier social purpose. Mazzini, who died in 1872, summed up his personal disappointment when he remarked: "I had thought to evoke the soul of Italy, but all I find before me is its corpse."

The Making of the German Empire

Another convert to national unification as a social and political strategy was the arch conservative Otto von Bismarck, who accomplished for Prussia and Germany what Cavour had done for Piedmont and Italy. As a provincial Prussian landowner, the young Bismarck was infamous before 1848 for his fundamentalist religiosity and unbending antimodernism. Like most Prussian reactionaries he was not only antinational but antiparliamentary, anti-industrial, even—because it represented centralization—antibureaucratic. He was devoted to the divine right of kings and loyal to the Prussian military tradition, the only aspects of central government that harmonized with his aristocratic background; Bismarck detested the 1850 Constitution, which seemed to him a concession to "Bonapartism."

Nevertheless, by the mid-1850s even Bismarck had begun to divest himself of the more ideological elements of his conservatism, for he began to see that the strength of the state lay as much with the power of its technology as with the spirit of its army. He even began to appreciate the uses of a parliament in creating stable relationships between state and society. But Bismarck's real break with reaction came in 1857, when he wrote to a friend that it might be necessary to use revolutionary elements of modernity—political participation, centralization, even nationalism—to shore up the Prussian regime. He stated at this time, "I also recognize as my own the principle of struggle against revolution, but . . . in politics I do not believe it possible to follow principle in such a way that its most extreme implications always take precedent over every other consideration. . . ."

Fifty years earlier, Prussians had learned the necessity of "revolution from above" from the first Napoleon; now Bismarck was taught the lessons of government by plebiscite by Bonaparte's nephew, Napoleon III. Mass participation, even universal suffrage, were shown to be no threat to the state as long as social and economic development had reached such a point that centrifugal forces were no longer dominant. Furthermore, the unification of Italy under Cavour's leadership had demonstrated that monarchy had little to fear from nationalism when this was separated from its earlier association with radicalism. Bismarck began to apply these lessons when he was called by King William I to become Prussian prime minister in 1862. The appointment of a person with a reputation for political extremism was the desperate act of a regime that was facing stiff liberal parliamentary opposition over the issue of military reform. Bismarck made it clear in his opening speech to parliament that he was determined to break the deadlock by any means available: "The great questions of the day will not be settled by speeches and majority decision—that was the mistake of 1848 and 1849—but by blood and iron."

Liberalism's strength had grown enormously during the 1850s as the result of rapid industrial progress in northern Germany. At first Bismarck tried to defeat the opposition through a series of confrontations, but when this failed he opted for a different strategy designed to undercut liberalism's popular appeal. Instead of opposing the nationalist movement, Bismarck would lead it; even if this meant betraying the tradition of legitimism, the goal of preserving the Prussian state justified any means. Although Bismarck never claimed to be anything more than a Prussian nationalist, he broke almost every other tenet of his earlier conservatism in the years that followed.

Bismarck's first concession to German nationalism was to plunge Prussia into a war with Denmark over Schleswig-Holstein in 1864. An easy victory was achieved with the aid of other German states, including Austria; but in the peacemaking that followed, Prussia became entangled in controversy with the Austrians. Austria could lay moral claim to the leadership of Germany, but industrial backwardness, together with Catholic heritage, put it at a disadvantage in the eyes of the north German Protestant middle classes; Bismarck was able to exploit this by provoking a war with Austria in 1866. The Prussian armies used railway and telegraph communications to good advantage at the Battle of Königgrätz, defeating the Hapsburgs and thereby assuming leadership over what was to be called the North German Confederation. The defeated Hapsburgs were allowed to keep their territories, and most of the south German Catholic states that had allied with Austria were likewise allowed to continue their independence.

Bismarck might well have let things stand as they were in 1866, except that the unstable international situation provided one more golden opportunity to use war to Prussia's advantage. He therefore welcomed war with France in 1870 as an opportunity to bring southern Germany under Prussian hegemony. Once the Prussian military had demonstrated its enormous strength in victory over the French, even Bismarck's sternest liberal opponents were willing to proclaim him a national hero. At the Hall of Mirrors at Versailles in occupied France, Bismarck enacted in 1871 the crowning of William I as the head of a new German Empire that included the north and south German states, but not Austria. (See the map of Europe in 1871 on page 280.)

Like Cavour's 1861 version of Italy, German unification stopped well short of the goals of the earlier generation of nationalists. They had envisioned all German-speaking people united by democracy under one flag. Bismarck's Second Empire left out large numbers of ethnic Germans, particularly those who resided in the Austrian Empire. Furthermore, despite Bismarck's declaration of universal suffrage, the citizens of this new nation-state were denied real equality and fraternity, for the forces that had made the new Germany, namely, the aristocratic military elites and the wealthy industrial bourgeoisie, had no interest in democracy or social justice. Bismarck had rallied the middle classes to his "revolution from above" by exaggerating the threat of revolution from below. Remembering his declaration in 1862 that this time Germany's solution would be that of "blood and iron," few could have been surprised that the German nation-state, dominated by Prussia, took a distinctly authoritarian turn.

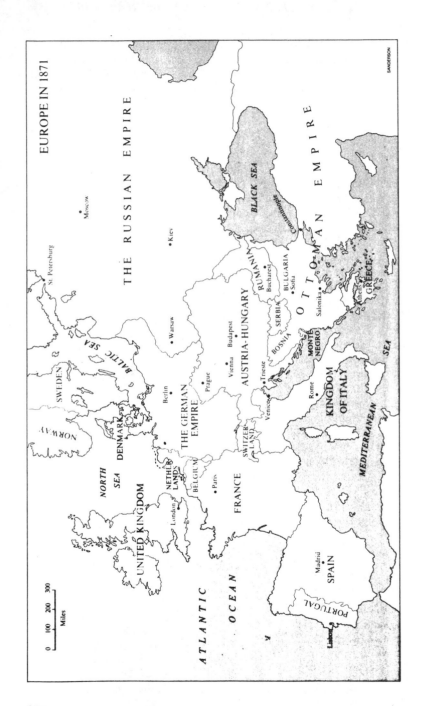

EUROPE IN 1871

THE RUSSIAN EMPIRE

St. Petersburg
Moscow
Kiev
Warsaw

SWEDEN
NORWAY

BALTIC SEA

DENMARK
Berlin
THE GERMAN EMPIRE

NORTH SEA

UNITED KINGDOM
London

NETHER-LANDS
BELGIUM

SWITZER-LAND

FRANCE
Paris

Prague
Vienna
AUSTRIA-HUNGARY
Budapest

RUMANIA
Bucharest
SERBIA
BULGARIA
Sofia
BOSNIA
MONTE NEGRO

BLACK SEA
Constantinople

OTTOMAN EMPIRE

GREECE
Athens
Salonika

Trieste
Venice
Rome
KINGDOM OF ITALY

MEDITERRANEAN SEA

SPAIN
Madrid

PORTUGAL
Lisbon

ATLANTIC OCEAN

0   100   200   300
Miles

SANDERSON

280

The Military, Bureaucracy, and the Nation-State

By 1871 the political face of Europe had been entirely transformed. Of course, Austria remained a multinational empire, Poland was still under Russian and Prussian control, and in eastern Europe there were still many national minorities just beginning to struggle for their independence. Nevertheless, the two "revolutions from above" in Italy and Germany had the effect of stabilizing the European international system until 1914, and in addition, of bringing a new era of domestic tranquillity. In both those countries, internal violence diminished dramatically as groups that had once fought against the state began to organize peacefully to compete for its power. Even where people remained in rigid opposition, as did the German socialists, they had to think twice before resorting to the old techniques of insurrection.

This was a reflection of the means by which unification had been achieved, namely, military power. In the early nineteenth century the army had been a source of instability, but now its effect was just the opposite. Increasingly, armies became the focus of national pride. This was evident as early as the Crimean War, and popular militarism grew enormously in the next fifteen years. Berliners, who in 1848 had chased a hated military force from their city, now showed a very different attitude toward the armies returning victorious from Austria or France. According to one observer, there was "no trace of the former animosity against the military which used to be noticeable among the lower classes. The commonest working man looked upon the troops with the feeling that he belonged or had belonged to them." In fact, as armies grew so did conscription, and by 1870 many Prussian working men had served in the regular army and spent time in the reserves. The fact that the army was used for a popular purpose helps explain the declining resistance to conscription. Popular militarism among the middle classes can also be explained by the fact that the officer corps was now open to them as never before.

Civil/military frictions were further reduced by the withdrawal of the military from police functions, a point reached in the 1850s with the growth of a professional civilian police. Armies were less in contact with civilian populations and were both more professional and more reliable. They could be called on as useful instruments to implement coups or put down insurrections. The French army served the former purpose in 1851; in 1871 it assisted in the latter role in reducing the resistance of the Paris Commune. Radicals like Friedrich Engels, who watched these developments carefully, realized that the modernization of the military after 1850 drastically reduced the chances of successful revolution. Political turmoil within the ranks had previously restricted the use of troops in insurrectionary situations, but now the armed forces were more reliable and possessed the tactical ability that made radicals think twice about street fighting.

The railway had greatly enhanced the mobility of the army, as was proved during the June Days of 1848. Furthermore, the fate of the Paris Commune of 1871 demonstrated the effect of the new firepower made available to armies by industrialization. Beginning first with the Prussian breechloading rifle in 1841 and culminating with the invention of the machine gun in the 1860s, the firepower available to the infantryman had increased sixty times in these two decades. The development of the breechloading, steel barreled artillery piece by 1870 also marked an epochal turning point in the history of warfare. Engels realized that the day of the barricade was over as early as 1848, because as he pointed out, "even during the classic period of street battles, the barricade had a moral rather than a material effect." Henceforth, insurrection would have to militarize if it were to have any chance of success. In the twentieth century, revolutionaries have learned to arm themselves with more than ideas, but this was out of the question for European radicals of the nineteenth century; the concept of the urban guerrilla belongs to the twentieth century, not the nineteenth.

In all the great revolutions from 1789 through 1848, it was the relatively peaceful collapse of government that had given the revolutionaries their initial advantage. In the second half of the nineteenth century, civil government became far more stable, largely because of the transformation of the civil as well as the military services. Even in the most backward states, bureaucracy was becoming more of a career, with fixed salary, rights of seniority and tenure, even pension plans. The self-image of officialdom was changing from that of a quasi-political elite to a specialized cadre of experts. The old political role of the bureaucracy was giving way to a much more reliable professionalism, and this, like the removal of the military from civilian affairs, had the effect of neutralizing the civil service and stabilizing the relations between state and society.

After 1850 many governments that previously had allowed officials to hold elected positions enacted restrictions on their political rights. The events of 1848 had radically altered the image of the bureaucracy as *the* representative of public interest. Too many officials had wavered politically, and conservatives wished to remove them from the public scene. Thereafter, even the most conservative governments began to recognize in the elected deputy a better measure of public interest than the unrepresentative bureaucrat. During the reign of Napoleon III and under Bismarck, the French and Prussian governments began cultivating (and organizing) public opinion and popular participation in an unprecedented manner. Napoleon used the plebiscite effectively, while Bismarck subverted the opposition of liberal officials by instituting universal suffrage in 1869, a move that benefited conservatives more than liberals. The existence of popularly elected legislatures also gave governments the excuse to argue that civil servants could no longer be allowed the freedom they had once enjoyed. Wrote German historian Gustav Schmoller:

The official of the years 1713 to 1848 acted in lieu of both public debate and popular representation. Today where the parties in public discussion and in parliamentary conflict question every state act we must have officials in many positions who obey more readily than was the case earlier; we can no longer tolerate independent bureaucrats in the lower and middle ranks as we did in the small absolutist states of the eighteenth century.

Rationalization and routinization of bureaucracy reduced the civil service to the politically neutral role it occupied in most modern states today. This was partly the result of the differentiation of legislative and executive functions, but it also reflected social developments that reduced the social prestige of the bureaucracy and made it more difficult for individual officials to command automatic authority as they had done earlier. Neither the industrial middle class nor the laboring poor were so willing after 1848 to vote on the basis of personality instead of program. Training in law was losing some of the advantage it had had in an earlier stage of nation building when debates were largely legal and constitutional. The basic issues were shifting, focusing increasingly on questions of economic and social policy for which those with a classical legal education had few answers. Most officials were probably happy to leave the difficult issues to party politicians.

The bureaucracy had once bridged the gap between state and society, but when society itself had become sufficiently organized to participate positively in the business of state, that role was outmoded. This was reflected in the growing reliance on legislative institutions, the acceptance of expanded suffrage, and the beginnings of organization of national parties on a mass basis. It is ironic that the extension of the franchise, as well as the regularization of relations between the legislative and executive branches, should have emerged under the conservative regimes of the 1860s. However, remember that liberals and radicals had tended to distrust popular representation as being too easily manipulated by reactionaries. Conservatives had shared this distrust, but now they were quicker to grasp the possibility of mass support that advocacy of mass suffrage would bring. Before 1850 the word "party" had been universally a term of contempt, standing for disorderly factionalism. Under these conditions, Tocqueville had despaired of representative institutions ever developing enough strength to counterbalance the executive. Yet gradually, everywhere in western Europe, the legislature began to develop insitutions that could compete for rather than against constituted authority, thus legitimating parliament for both conservatives and radicals who wanted a strongly integrated modern state. After 1850 parliaments began to develop standing committees and permanent staff that allowed them to take a constructive role in formulating state policy.

Often it was the executive itself that took the lead in organizing a

stable party system. Governments, beginning with the French Second
Empire and the Manteuffel regime in Prussia from 1849 to 1858 found
it useful to organize elections in order to gain stable majorities. In response, other groups adopted similar methods and, thus, grassroots organizations came into being. These were often slow in evolving, however, and
modern parties did not fully develop until 1900 in most countries.
Deputies continued to be unpaid and the idea of the professional politi-
cian was a novelty even in the 1890s. Yet the composition of deputies
gradually changed; there were fewer civil servants, doctors, and intellectuals of the old type, and more lawyers, trade unionists, and small business
people, representing a much broader cross section of society.

Expertise replaced oratory as the level of classical education declined
and that of practical experience rose. The gradual withdrawal of civil
servants from politics obviously benefited the autonomy of the legislative
branch, which became the sole representative of national opinion besides
the press and thus invaluable to even the most conservative regimes
concerned to keep their finger on the public pulse. They worked out a
division of functions in which parliament no longer represented a threat
to the state but served rather to integrate and insitutionalize the struggles
of national groups competing for power. Once this was established, the pre-
1848 pattern of instability—revolution and reaction—virtually disappeared.

By the 1870s and 1880s many European leaders were less concerned
with internal than external state building. Their attention turned toward
imperial expansion, to what were eventually to become the new states of
the twentieth century. This was a sure sign that the era of internal instability was over and that the important questions of economic and political
development were answered, at least for the time being. All the elements
of a modern polity, including national integration, mass participation, and
division of functions, were in place. So, too, was the industrial economy,
and now both economy and polity were ready for export to the African
and Asian territories controlled by Europeans. In the future, western
Europe would be troubled far more by revolts against its rule from without than by rebellion from within.

Suggestions for Further Reading

The books listed below by chapter represent only those works in English most accessible and readable. Students who wish to explore further in other languages will find extensive bibliographies in many of these volumes.

Introduction

Among the best general introductions to modernization theory is S. N. Eisenstadt, *Modernization: Protest and Change* (Prentice-Hall, Englewood Cliffs, New Jersey, 1966). Also good are Reinhard Bendix, *Nation-Building and Citizenship* (Wiley, New York, 1964); Reinhard Bendix, ed., *State and Society* (Little, Brown, Boston, 1968); and Samuel P. Huntington, *Political Order in Changing Societies* (Yale U Pr, New Haven, 1968). Useful correctives to the biases inherent in some of this literature are provided by Barrington Moore, Jr., *The Social Origins of Dictatorship and Democracy* (Beacon Pr., Boston, 1966) and by Eric J. Hobsbawm, *Age of Revolution, 1789–1848* (Mentor, NAL., New York, 1962).

Chapter 1   Population, Economy, and Society in 1770

For a sweeping account of preindustrial Europe, see Fernand Braudel, *Capitalism and Material Life, 1400–1800* (Harper & Row, New York, 1974). Of equal importance are B. H. Slicher van Bath, *Agrarian History of Western Europe, 500–1840* (St. Martins, London, 1963); Marc Bloch, *French Rural History* (U of California Pr, Berkeley and Los Angeles, 1966); and G. E. Mingay, *English Landed Society in the Eighteenth Century* (Routledge, London, 1963). On the history of the family see Philippe Ariès, *Centuries of Childhood* (Vintage, New York, 1962), Peter Laslett, *The World We Have Lost* (Scribner, New York, 1965), and David Hunt, *Parents and Children in History* (Basic Books, New York, 1970). Also see Eric J. Hobsbawm, *Primitive Rebels* (Norton, New York, 1959) and Mack Walker, *German Home Towns* (Cornell U Pr, Ithaca, 1971).

Chapter 2   Population Explosion and Economic Crisis, 1770-1850

The population crisis is described by E. A. Wrigley, *Population and History* (World University Library, London, 1969) and H. J. Habbakkuk, *Population Growth and Economic Development since 1750* (Leicester U Pr, Leicester, 1972). The best account of resulting pauperization is Olwen Hufton, *The Poor of Eighteenth Century France* (Oxford U Pr, Oxford, 1974). Also useful are M. Dorothy George, *London Life in the Eighteenth Century* (Harper & Row, New York, 1964) and Cecil Woodham-Smith, *The Great Hunger* (Harper & Row, New York, 1963). On specific aspects of the demographic crisis see Edward Shorter, *The Making of the Modern Family* (Basic Books, New York, 1975) and John R. Gillis, *Youth and History* (Academic Press, New York, 1974).

Chapter 3   Collapse of the Old Regime: State, Society, and Culture in the 1770s and 1780s

C. B. A. Behrens, *The Ancien Régime* (Harcourt, Brace & World, New York, 1967) and M. S. Anderson, *Europe in the Eighteenth Century* (Holt, Rinehart & Winston, New York, 1961) provide excellent background. On specific social groups see Hans Rosenberg, *Bureaucracy, Aristocracy and Autocracy: The Prussian Experience, 1660-1815* (Harvard U Pr, Cambridge, Mass., 1958); Franklin L. Ford, *Robe and Sword* (Harper & Row, New York, 1965); and Henri Brunschwig, *Enlightenment and Romanticism in Eighteenth Century Prussia* (U of Chicago Pr, Chicago, 1974). On prelude to revolution, read Robert R. Palmer, *The Age of the Democratic Revolution*, 2 vols.(Princeton U Pr, Princeton, 1959-1964).

Chapter 4   Revolution in France, 1789-1804

A useful essay on the theory of revolution is contained in Lawrence Stone, *The Causes of the English Revolution* (Harper & Row, New York, 1972). Of utmost importance are Georges Lefebvre's two great works *The Great Fear* (Vintage, New York, 1973) and *The Coming of the French Revolution* (Vintage, New York, 1957). For the urban revolutions, see Jacques Godechot, *The Fall of the Bastille* (Scribner, New York, 1970); George Rudé, *The Crowd in History* (Wiley, New York, 1964); and Albert Soboul, *The Sans-Culottes* (Doubleday, Garden City, New York, 1972). Also see Alexis de Tocqueville, *The Old Regime and the French Revolution* (Doubleday, Garden City, New York, 1955); Gwyn A. Williams, *Artisans and Sans-culottes* (Norton, New York, 1969); and John McManners, *The French Revolution and the Church* (Harper & Row, New York, 1969).

Chapter 5 War and Peace in the Napoleonic Era, 1804-1815

On Napoleon, read J. M. Thompson, *Napoleon Bonaparte* (Oxford U Pr,
Oxford, 1952) or Geoffrey Bruun, *Europe and the French Imperium*
(Harper & Row, New York, 1964). For the English response see Edward
P. Thompson, *The Making of the English Working Class* (Vintage, New
York, 1966). For Germany, see Walter M. Simon, *The Failure of the
Prussian Reform Movement, 1807-1819* (Cornell U Pr, Ithaca, 1955) and
Gordon A. Craig, *The Politics of the Prussian Army, 1640-1945* (Oxford
U Pr, Oxford, 1955). For the problem of war see Theodore Ropp, *War in the
Modern World* (Duke U Pr, Durham, North Carolina, 1969) and Alfred Vagts,
A History of Militarism (Free Press, New York, 1967). In addition, see
H. G. Schenk, *The Aftermath of the Napoleonic Wars* (Fertig, New York,
1967).

Chapter 6 The Search for Stability, 1815-1848

Particularly useful on the period of the Restoration is Guillame de Bertier
de Sauvigny, *The Bourbon Restoration* (U of Pa Pr, Philadelphia, 1966), as
are Raymond Carr, *Spain, 1808-1939* (Oxford U Pr, Oxford, 1966) and
Theodore Hamerow, *Restoration, Revolution, Reaction: Economics and
Politics in Germany, 1815-1871* (Princeton U Pr, Princeton 1958). The
patterns of upheaval in France, Germany, and Italy are dealt with in
Charles Tilly, Louise Tilly, and Richard Tilly, *The Rebellious Century*
(Harvard U Pr, Cambridge, Mass., 1974). On specific revolutions, see
David Pinkney, *The French Revolution of 1830* (Princeton U Pr, Prince-
ton, 1972); Peter Stearns, *1848: The Revolutionary Tide in Europe*
(Norton, New York, 1974); and Eric J. Hobsbawm and George Rudé,
Captain Swing (Pantheon, New York, 1968). William L. Langer, *Political
and Social Upheaval, 1832-1852* (Harper & Row, New York, 1969)
presents a detailed overview.

Chapter 7 The First Industrial Society

A detailed history of industrialization is provided by David S. Landes,
*The Unbound Prometheus: Technological Change and Economic Devel-
opment in Western Europe from 1750 to the Present* (Cambridge U Pr,
Cambridge, 1968). Equally useful are Eric J. Hobsbawm, *Industry and
Empire* (Penguin, Baltimore, 1969), Carlo Cipolla, *The Economic History
of World Population* (Penguin, Baltimore, 1962), and John H. Clapham,
The Economic Development of France and Germany, 1815-1914 (Cam-
bridge U Pr, Cambridge, 1936). The cultural bases of industry are dealt
with in Reinhard Bendix, *Work and Authority in Industry* (Harper & Row,
New York, 1956) and Karl Polanyi, *The Great Transformation* (Beacon

Pr, Boston, 1957). For ecological effects see W. G. Hoskins, *The Making of the English Landscape* (Penguin, Baltimore, 1971).

Chapter 8   The Birth of the Modern City

The statistical picture is provided by Adna Weber, *The Growth of Cities in the Nineteenth Century* (Cornell U Pr, Ithaca, 1967). For the quality of city life, see Louis Chevalier, *Working Classes and Dangerous Classes in Paris during the First Part of the Nineteenth Century* (Fertig, New York, 1973), Asa Briggs, *Victorian Cities* (Harper & Row, New York, 1963), and Stephen Thernstrom and Richard Sennett, eds., *Nineteenth Century Cities* (Yale U Pr, New Haven, 1969). Also see George Rudé, *Paris and London in the Eighteenth Century* (Viking, New York, 1973) and J. J. Tobias, *Urban Crime in Victorian England* (Schocken, New York, 1972). A photographic record of London life is provided by Gordon Winter, *A Cockney Camera* (Penguin, Harmonsworth, England, 1971).

Chapter 9   The Making of the Middle and Working Classes

Most useful is Edward P. Thompson, *The Making of the English Working Class* (Vintage, New York, 1966) and articles contained in Peter Stearns and Daniel Walkowitz, *Workers in the Industrial Revolution* (Transaction Books, New Brunswick, New Jersey, 1974). On the middle classes see Charles Moraze, *The Triumph of the Middle Classes* (Doubleday, Garden City, New York, 1968) and H. Perkin, *The Origins of Modern English Society, 1780–1880* (Routledge & Kegan, London, 1969). Victorian women are discussed in Martha Vicinus, ed., *Suffer and Be Still* (Indiana U Pr, Bloomington, 1972) and Walter Houghton, *The Victorian Frame of Mind* (Yale U Pr, New Haven, 1957). For changes in family life, see Michael Anderson, *Family Structure in Nineteenth Century Lancashire* (Cambridge U Pr, Cambridge, 1971).

Chapter 10   Europe's Cultural Revolution

The broad outlines of cultural change are discussed in Raymond Williams, *Culture and Society* (Harper & Row, New York, 1966). On the struggle over literacy, read Richard Altick, *The English Common Reader* (U of Chicago Pr, Chicago, 1957) and Brian Simon, *Studies in the History of Education, 1780–1870* (Lawrence and Wishart, London, 1960). On romanticism and the avant-garde see M. Abrams, *Natural Supernaturalism: Tradition and Revolution in Romantic Literature* Norton, New York, 1971); César Graña, *Bohemian and Bourgeois* (Basic Books, New York, 1964); Donald D. Egbert, *Social Radicalism and the Arts in Western Europe* (Knopf, New York, 1970); and Marcel Brion, *The Art of the*

Romantic Era (Praeger, New York, 1966). Also read Robert W. Malcolmson, *Popular Recreation in English Society, 1700-1850* (Cambridge U Pr, Cambridge, 1973) and W. J. Reader, *Professional Men* (Basic Books, New York, 1966).

Chapter 11   Intellectuals and Ideologies

For general background see John Bowle, *Politics and Opinion in the Nineteenth Century* (Oxford U Pr, New York, 1964) and J. L. Talmon, *Political Messianism* (Praeger, New York, 1960). For the major ideologies see Guido de Ruggiero, *The History of European Liberalism* (Beacon Press, Boston, 1959); Karl Mannheim, Chapter II, "Conservative Thought" in *Essays on Sociology and Psychology* (Routledge & Kegan, London, 1953); Carlton J. Hayes, *The Historical Evolution of Modern Nationalism* (Russell, New York, 1968); George Woodcock, *Anarchism* (Meridian World Pub., Cleveland, 1962); George Lichtheim, *The Origins of Socialism* (Praeger, New York, 1969); and Frank E. Manuel, *Utopias and Utopian Thought* (Houghton Mifflin, Boston, 1966). On religion read Alec R. Vidler's brief *The Church in an Age of Revolution* (Penguin, Baltimore, 1961).

Chapter 12   End of the Revolutionary Era, 1848-1870

Two excellent introductions to post-1848 France are provided by Theodore Zeldin, *France, 1848-1945*, vol. I (Clarendon, Oxford, 1973) and J. M. Thompson, *Louis Napoleon and the Second Empire* (Norton, New York, 1967). Equally comprehensive are Theodore S. Hamerow, *The Social Foundations of German Unification, 1858-1871*, 2 vols. (Princeton U Pr, Princeton, 1969-1972); Geoffrey Best, *Mid-Victorian Britain, 1851-1875* (Schocken, New York, 1972); W.L. Burn, *Age of Equipoise: A Study of the Mid-Victorian Generation* (Norton, New York, 1964); and Arthur J. Whyte, *The Evolution of Modern Italy* (Norton, New York, 1965). On the diplomacy of the period see A. J. P. Taylor, *The Struggle for Mastery in Europe, 1848-1914* (Oxford Pr, Oxford, 1954). Demographic changes are dealt with in Neil Tranter, *Population since the Industrial Revolution* (Croom Helm, London, 1973) and J. A. Banks, *Prosperity and Parenthood* (Routledge & Kegan, London, 1954). For changes in working-class life read Eric J. Hobsbawm, *Labouring Men* (Basic Books, New York, 1964); Guenther Roth, *The Social Democrats in Imperial Germany* (Bedminster Press, Totowa, New Jersey 1963); and George Lichtheim, *Marxism: An Historical and Critical Study* (Praeger, New York, 1961).

Index